THE GREATEST WORKS OF
KAHLIL GIBRAN

THE GREATEST WORKS OF KAHLIL GIBRAN

(Twelve books in one omnibus edition)

JAICO PUBLISHING HOUSE
MUMBAI • DELHI • CALCUTTA
BANGALORE • HYDERABAD • CHENNAI

© Jaico Publishing House

No part of this book may be reproduced or utilized in any form or by any means, electronic or mechanical including photocopying, recording or by any information storage and retrieval system, without permission in writing from the publishers.

THE GREATEST WORKS OF KAHLIL GIBRAN
ISBN 81-7224-134-8

First Jaico Impression : 1991
Fifth Jaico Impression : 1998
Sixth Jaico Impression : 1999
Seventh Jaico Impression :2000

Published by:
Ashwin J. Shah
Jaico Publishing House
121, M.G. Road,
Mumbai-400 023

Printed by:
Saurabh Print-O-Pack
A-16, Sector IV, Noida-201301 (U.P)

CONTENTS

THE ILLUSTRATIONS IN THIS
VOLUME ARE REPRODUCED FROM
ORIGINAL DRAWINGS BY THE AUTHOR

BOOK ONE

BOOK ONE

THE PROPHET

THE PROPHET

ALMUSTAFA, the chosen and the beloved, who was a dawn unto his own day, had waited twelve years in the city of Orphalese for his ship that was to return and bear him back to the isle of his birth.

And in the twelfth year, on the seventh day of Ielool, the month of reaping, he climbed the hill without the city walls and looked seaward; and he beheld his ship coming with the mist.

Then the gates of his heart were flung open, and his joy flew far over the sea. And he closed his eyes and prayed in the silences of his soul.

But as he descended the hill, a sadness came upon him, and he thought in his heart:

How shall I go in peace and without sorrow? Nay, not without a wound in the spirit shall I leave this city.

Long were the days of pain I have spent within its walls, and long were the nights of aloneness; and who can depart from his pain and his aloneness without regret?

Too many fragments of the spirit have I scattered in these streets, and too many are the children of my longing that walk naked among these hills, and I cannot withdraw from them without a burden and an ache.

It is not a garment I cast off this day, but a skin that I tear with my own hands.

Nor is it a thought I leave behind me, but a heart made sweet with hunger and with thirst.

Yet I cannot tarry longer.

The sea that calls all things unto her calls me, and I must embark.

For to stay, though the hours burn in the night, is to freeze and crystallize and be bound in a mould.

Fain would I take with me all that is here. But how shall I?

A voice cannot carry the tongue and the lips that gave it wings. Alone must it seek the ether.

And alone and without his nest shall the eagle fly across the sun.

Now when he reached the foot of the hill, he

turned again towards the sea, and he saw his ship approaching the harbour, and upon her prow the mariners, the men of his own land.

And his soul cried out to them, and he said:
Sons of my ancient mother, you riders of the tides,
How often have you sailed in my dreams. And now you come in my awakening, which is my deeper dream.
Ready am I to go, and my eagerness with sails full set awaits the wind.
Only another breath will I breathe in this still air, only another loving look cast backward,
And then I shall stand among you, a seafarer among seafarers.
And you, vast sea, sleeping mother,
Who alone are peace and freedom to the river and the stream,
Only another winding will this stream make, only another murmur in this glade,
And then I shall come to you, a boundless drop to a boundless ocean.

And as he walked he saw from afar men and women leaving their fields and their vineyards and hastening towards the city gates.

And he heard their voices calling his name, and shouting from field to field telling one another of the coming of his ship.

And he said to himself:

Shall the day of parting be the day of gathering?

And shall it be said that my eve was in truth my dawn?

And what shall I give unto him who has left his plough in midfurrow, or to him who has stopped the wheel of his winepress?

Shall my heart become a tree heavy-laden with fruit that I may gather and give unto them?

And shall my desires flow like a fountain that I may fill their cups?

Am I a harp that the hand of the mighty may touch me, or a flute that his breath may pass through me?

A seeker of silences am I, and what treasure have

The archer sees the mark upon the path of the infinite, and He bends you with His might that His arrows may go swift and far.

Let your bending in the Archer's hand be for gladness;

For even as He loves the arrow that flies, so He loves also the bow that is stable.

THEN said a rich man, Speak to us of Giving.
And he answered:

You give but little when you give of your possessions.

It is when you give of yourself that you truly give.

For what are your possessions but things you keep and guard for fear you may need them to-morrow?

And to-morrow, what shall to-morrow bring to the over-prudent dog burying bones in the track-less sand as he follows the pilgrims to the holy city?

And what is fear of need but need itself?

Is not dread of thirst when your well is full, the thirst that is unquenchable?

There are those who give little of the much which they have—and they give it for recognition and their hidden desire makes their gifts unwhole-some.

And there are those who have little and give it all.

These are the believers in life and the bounty of life, and their coffer is never empty.

There are those who give with joy, and that joy is their reward.

And there are those who give with pain, and that pain is their baptism.

And there are those who give and know not pain in giving, nor do they seek joy, nor give with mindfulness of virtue;

They give as in yonder valley the myrtle breathes its fragrance into space.

Through the hands of such as these God speaks, and from behind their eyes He smiles upon the earth.

It is well to give when asked, but it is better to give unasked, through understanding;

And to the open-handed the search for one who shall receive is joy greater than giving.

And is there aught you would withhold?

All you have shall some day be given;

Therefore give now, that the season of giving may be yours and not your inheritors'.

You often say, " I would give, but only to the deserving."

The trees in your orchard say not so, nor the flocks in your pasture.

They give that they may live, for to withhold is to perish.

Surely he who is worthy to receive his days and his nights is worthy of all else from you.

And he who has deserved to drink from the ocean of life deserves to fill his cup from your little stream.

And what desert greater shall there be, than that which lies in the courage and the confidence, nay the charity, of receiving?

And who are you that men should rend their bosom and unveil their pride, that you may see their worth naked and their pride unabashed?

See first that you yourself deserve to be a giver, and an instrument of giving.

For in truth it is life that gives unto life—while you, who deem yourself a giver, are but a witness.

· · · · ·

And you receivers—and you are all receivers—
assume no weight of gratitude, lest you lay a yoke
upon yourself and upon him who gives.

Rather rise together with the giver on his gifts
as on wings;

For to be overmindful of your debt is to doubt
his generosity who has the free-hearted earth for
mother, and God for father.

THEN an old man, a keeper of an inn, said, Speak to us of Eating and Drinking.

And he said:

Would that you could live on the fragrance of the earth, and like an air plant be sustained by the light.

But since you must kill to eat, and rob the newly born of its mother's milk to quench your thirst, let it then be an act of worship,

And let your board stand an altar on which the pure and the innocent of forest and plain are sacrificed for that which is purer and still more innocent in man.

When you kill a beast say to him in your heart:

" By the same power that slays you, I too am slain; and I too shall be consumed.

" For the law that delivered you into my hand shall deliver me into a mightier hand.

" Your blood and my blood is naught but the sap that feeds the tree of heaven."

And when you crush an apple with your teeth,
say to it in your heart:

" Your seeds shall live in my body,

" And the buds of your to-morrow shall blossom
in my heart,

" And your fragrance shall be my breath,

" And together we shall rejoice through all the
seasons."

And in the autumn, when you gather the grapes
of your vineyards for the winepress, say in your
heart:

" I too am a vineyard, and my fruit shall be
gathered for the winepress,

" And like new wine I shall be kept in eternal
vessels."

And in winter, when you draw the wine, let there
be in your heart a song for each cup;

And let there be in the song a remembrance for
the autumn days, and for the vineyard, and for the
winepress.

THEN a ploughman said, Speak to us of Work.
And he answered, saying:

You work that you may keep pace with the earth and the soul of the earth.

For to be idle is to become a stranger unto the seasons, and to step out of life's procession that marches in majesty and proud submission towards the infinite.

When you work you are a flute through whose heart the whispering of the hours turns to music.

Which of you would be a reed, dumb and silent, when all else sings together in unison?

Always you have been told that work is a curse and labour a misfortune.

But I say to you that when you work you fulfil a part of earth's furthest dream, assigned to you when that dream was born,

And in keeping yourself with labour you are in truth loving life,

32

And to love life through labour is to be intimate with life's inmost secret.

But if you in your pain call birth an affliction and the support of the flesh a curse written upon your brow, then I answer that naught but the sweat of your brow shall wash away that which is written.

You have been told also that life is darkness, and in your weariness you echo what was said by the weary.

And I say that life is indeed darkness save when there is urge,

And all urge is blind save when there is knowledge.

And all knowledge is vain save when there is work,

And all work is empty save when there is love;

And when you work with love you bind yourself to yourself, and to one another, and to God.

33

And what is it to work with love?

It is to weave the cloth with threads drawn from your heart, even as if your beloved were to wear that cloth.

It is to build a house with affection, even as if your beloved were to dwell in that house.

It is to sow seeds with tenderness and reap the harvest with joy, even as if your beloved were to eat the fruit.

It is to charge all things your fashion with a breath of your own spirit,

And to know that all the blessed dead are standing about you and watching.

Often have I heard you say, as if speaking in sleep, "He who works in marble, and finds the shape of his own soul in the stone, is nobler than he who ploughs the soil.

"And he who seizes the rainbow to lay it on a cloth in the likeness of man, is more than he who makes the sandals for our feet."

But I say, not in sleep, but in the overwakefulness of noontide, that the wind speaks not more sweetly to the giant oaks than to the least of all the blades of grass;

And he alone is great who turns the voice of the wind into a song made sweeter by his own loving.

Work is love made visible.

And if you cannot work with love but only with distaste, it is better that you should leave your work and sit at the gate of the temple and take alms of those who work with joy.

For if you bake bread with indifference, you bake a bitter bread that feeds but half man's hunger.

And if you grudge the crushing of the grapes, your grudge distils a poison in the wine.

And if you sing though as angels, and love not the singing, you muffle man's ears to the voices of the day and the voices of the night.

THEN a woman said, Speak to us of Joy and Sorrow.

And he answered:

Your joy is your sorrow unmasked.

And the selfsame well from which your laughter rises was oftentimes filled with your tears.

And how else can it be?

The deeper that sorrow carves into your being, the more joy you can contain.

Is not the cup that holds your wine the very cup that was burned in the potter's oven?

And is not the lute that soothes your spirit the very wood that was hollowed with knives?

When you are joyous, look deep into your heart and you shall find it is only that which has given you sorrow that is giving you joy.

When you are sorrowful, look again in your heart, and you shall see that in truth you are weeping for that which has been your delight.

Some of you say, " Joy is greater than sorrow," and others say, " Nay, sorrow is the greater."

But I say unto you, they are inseparable.

Together they come, and when one sits alone with you at your board, remember that the other is asleep upon your bed.

Verily you are suspended like scales between your sorrow and your joy.

Only when you are empty are you at standstill and balanced.

When the treasure-keeper lifts you to weigh his gold and his silver, needs must your joy or your sorrow rise or fall.

THEN a mason came forth and said, Speak to us of Houses.

And he answered and said:

Build of your imaginings a bower in the wilderness ere you build a house within the city walls.

For even as you have home-comings in your twilight, so has the wanderer in you, the ever-distant and alone.

Your house is your larger body.

It grows in the sun and sleeps in the stillness of the night; and it is not dreamless. Does not your house dream? and dreaming, leave the city for grove or hilltop?

Would that I could gather your houses into my hand, and like a sower scatter them in forest and meadow.

Would the valleys were your streets, and the green paths your alleys, that you might seek one another through vineyards, and come with the fragrance of the earth in your garments.

But these things are not yet to be.

In their fear your forefathers gathered you too near together. And that fear shall endure a little longer. A little longer shall your city walls separate your hearths from your fields.

And tell me, people of Orphalese, what have you in these houses? And what is it you guard with fastened doors?

Have you peace, the quiet urge that reveals your power?

Have you remembrances, the glimmering arches that span the summits of the mind?

Have you beauty, that leads the heart from things fashioned of wood and stone to the holy mountain?

Tell me, have you these in your houses?

Or have you only comfort, and the lust for comfort, that stealthy thing that enters the house a guest, and then becomes a host, and then a master?

Ay, and it becomes a tamer, and with hook and scourge makes puppets of your larger desires.

39

Though its hands are silken, its heart is of iron.

It lulls you to sleep only to stand by your bed and jeer at the dignity of the flesh.

It makes mock of your sound senses, and lays them in thistledown like fragile vessels.

Verily the lust for comfort murders the passion of the soul, and then walks grinning in the funeral.

But you, children of space, you restless in rest, you shall not be trapped nor tamed.

Your house shall be not an anchor but a mast.

It shall not be a glistening film that covers a wound, but an eyelid that guards the eye.

You shall not fold your wings that you may pass through doors, nor bend your heads that they strike not against a ceiling, nor fear to breathe lest walls should crack and fall down.

You shall not dwell in tombs made by the dead for the living.

And though of magnificence and splendour, your house shall not hold your secret nor shelter your longing.

For that which is boundless in you abides in the mansion of the sky, whose door is the morning mist, and whose windows are the songs and the silences of night.

ND the weaver said, Speak to us of Clothes.
And he answered:

Your clothes conceal much of your beauty, yet
they hide not the unbeautiful.

And though you seek in garments the freedom
of privacy you may find in them a harness and a
chain.

Would that you could meet the sun and the wind
with more of your skin and less of your raiment.

For the breath of life is in the sunlight and the
hand of life is in the wind.

Some of you say, " It is the north wind who has
woven the clothes we wear."

And I say, Ay, it was the north wind,

But shame was his loom, and the softening of the
sinews was his thread.

And when his work was done he laughed in the
forest.

Forget not that modesty is for a shield agains
the eye of the unclean.

And when the unclean shall be no more, wha

were modesty but a fetter and a fouling of the mind?

And forget not that the earth delights to feel your bare feet and the winds long to play with your hair.

AND a merchant said, Speak to us of Buying and Selling.

And he answered and said:

To you the earth yields her fruit, and you shall not want if you but know how to fill your hands.

It is in exchanging the gifts of the earth that you shall find abundance and be satisfied.

Yet unless the exchange be in love and kindly justice it will but lead some to greed and others to hunger.

When in the market-place you toilers of the sea and fields and vineyards meet the weavers and the potters and the gatherers of spices,—

Invoke then the master spirit of the earth, to come into your midst and sanctify the scales and the reckoning that weighs value against value.

And suffer not the barren-handed to take part in your transactions, who would sell their words for your labour.

To such men you should say:

" Come with us to the field, or go with our brothers to the sea and cast your net;

" For the land and the sea shall be bountiful to you even as to us."

And if there come the singers and the dancers and the flute-players,—buy of their gifts also.

For they too are gatherers of fruit and frankincense, and that which they bring, though fashioned of dreams, is raiment and food for your soul.

And before you leave the market-place, see that no one has gone his way with empty hands.

For the master spirit of the earth shall not sleep peacefully upon the wind till the needs of the least of you are satisfied.

THEN one of the judges of the city stood forth and said, Speak to us of Crime and Punishment.

And he answered, saying:

It is when your spirit goes wandering upon the wind,

That you, alone and unguarded, commit a wrong unto others and therefore unto yourself.

And for that wrong committed must you knock and wait a while unheeded at the gate of the blessed.

Like the ocean is your god-self;

It remains for ever undefiled.

And like the ether it lifts but the winged.

Even like the sun is your god-self;

It knows not the ways of the mole nor seeks it the holes of the serpent.

But your god-self dwells not alone in your being.

Much in you is still man, and much in you is not yet man,

But a shapeless pigmy that walks asleep in the mist searching for its own awakening.

And of the man in you would I now speak.

46

For it is he and not your god-self nor the pigmy in the mist that knows crime and the punishment of crime.

Oftentimes have I heard you speak of one who commits a wrong as though he were not one of you, but a stranger unto you and an intruder upon your world.

But I say that even as the holy and the righteous cannot rise beyond the highest which is in each one of you,

So the wicked and the weak cannot fall lower than the lowest which is in you also.

And as a single leaf turns not yellow but with the silent knowledge of the whole tree,

So the wrong-doer cannot do wrong without the hidden will of you all.

Like a procession you walk together towards your god-self.

You are the way and the wayfarers.

And when one of you falls down he falls for those behind him, a caution against the stumbling stone.

Ay, and he falls for those ahead of him, who, though faster and surer of foot, yet removed not the stumbling stone.

And this also, though the word lie heavy upon your hearts:

The murdered is not unaccountable for his own murder,

And the robbed is not blameless in being robbed.

The righteous is not innocent of the deeds of the wicked,

And the white-handed is not clean in the doings of the felon.

Yea, the guilty is oftentimes the victim of the injured.

And still more often the condemned is the burden bearer for the guiltless and unblamed.

You cannot separate the just from the unjust and the good from the wicked;

For they stand together before the face of the sun even as the black thread and the white are woven together.

And when the black thread breaks, the weaver shall look into the whole cloth, and he shall examine the loom also.

If any of you would bring to judgment the unfaithful wife,

Let him also weigh the heart of her husband in scales, and measure his soul with measurements.

And let him who would lash the offender look unto the spirit of the offended.

And if any of you would punish in the name of righteousness and lay the axe unto the evil tree, let him see to its roots;

And verily he will find the roots of the good and the bad, the fruitful and the fruitless, all entwined together in the silent heart of the earth.

And you judges who would be just.

What judgment pronounce you upon him who though honest in the flesh yet is a thief in spirit?

What penalty lay you upon him who slays in the flesh yet is himself slain in the spirit?

And how prosecute you him who in action is a deceiver and an oppressor,

Yet who also is aggrieved and outraged?

And how shall you punish those whose remorse is already greater than their misdeeds?

Is not remorse the justice which is administered by that very law which you would fain serve?

Yet you cannot lay remorse upon the innocent nor lift it from the heart of the guilty.

Unbidden shall it call in the night, that men may wake and gaze upon themselves.

And you who would understand justice, how shall you unless you look upon all deeds in the fullness of light?

Only then shall you know that the erect and the fallen are but one man standing in twilight between the night of his pigmy-self and the day of his god-self,

And that the corner-stone of the temple is not higher than the lowest stone in its foundation.

THEN a lawyer said, But what of our Laws, master?

And he answered:

You delight in laying down laws,

Yet you delight more in breaking them.

Like children playing by the ocean who build sand-towers with constancy and then destroy them with laughter.

But while you build your sand-towers the ocean brings more sand to the shore, And when you destroy them the ocean laughs with you.

Verily the ocean laughs always with the innocent.

But what of those to whom life is not an ocean, and man-made laws are not sand-towers,

But to whom life is a rock, and the law a chisel with which they would carve it in their own likeness?

What of the cripple who hates dancers?

What of the ox who loves his yoke and deems the elk and deer of the forest stray and vagrant things?

What of the old serpent who cannot shed his skin, and calls all others naked and shameless?

And of him who comes early to the wedding-feast, and when over-fed and tired goes his way saying that all feasts are violation and all feasters law-breakers?

What shall I say of these save that they too stand in the sunlight, but with their backs to the sun?

They see only their shadows, and their shadows are their laws.

And what is the sun to them but a caster of shadows?

And what is it to acknowledge the laws but to stoop down and trace their shadows upon the earth?

But you who walk facing the sun, what images drawn on the earth can hold you?

You who travel with the wind, what weather-vane shall direct your course?

What man's law shall bind you if you break your yoke but upon no man's prison door?

What laws shall you fear if you dance but stumble against no man's iron chains?

And who is he that shall bring you to judgment if you tear off your garment yet leave it in no man's path?

People of Orphalese, you can muffle the drum, and you can loosen the strings of the lyre, but who shall command the skylark not to sing?

AND an orator said, Speak to us of Freedom.
And he answered:

At the city gate and by your fireside I have seen
you prostrate yourself and worship your own
freedom,

Even as slaves humble themselves before a tyrant
and praise him though he slays them.

Ay, in the grove of the temple and in the shadow
of the citadel I have seen the freest among you wear
their freedom as a yoke and a handcuff.

And my heart bled within me; for you can only
be free when even the desire of seeking freedom
becomes a harness to you, and when you cease to
speak of freedom as a goal and a fulfilment.

You shall be free indeed when your days are not
without a care nor your nights without a want and
a grief,

But rather when these things girdle your life and
yet you rise above them naked and unbound.

And how shall you rise beyond your days and
nights unless you break the chains which you at

the dawn of your understanding have fastened around your noon hour?

In truth that which you call freedom is the strongest of these chains, though its links glitter in the sun and dazzle your eyes.

And what is it but fragments of your own self you would discard that you may become free?

If it is an unjust law you would abolish, that law was written with your own hand upon your own forehead.

You cannot erase it by burning your law books nor by washing the foreheads of your judges, though you pour the sea upon them.

And if it is a despot you would dethrone, see first that his throne erected within you is destroyed.

For how can a tyrant rule the free and the proud, but for a tyranny in their own freedom and a shame in their own pride?

And if it is a care you would cast off, that care has been chosen by you rather than imposed upon you.

And if it is a fear you would dispel, the seat of that fear is in your heart and not in the hand of the feared.

Verily all things move within your being in constant half embrace, the desired and the dreaded, the repugnant and the cherished, the pursued and that which you would escape.

These things move within you as lights and shadows in pairs that cling.

And when the shadow fades and is no more, the light that lingers becomes a shadow to another light.

And thus your freedom when it loses its fetters becomes itself the fetter of a greater freedom.

AND the priestess spoke again and said: Speak to us of Reason and Passion.

And he answered, saying:

Your soul is oftentimes a battlefield, upon which your reason and your judgment wage war against your passion and your appetite.

Would that I could be the peacemaker in your soul, that I might turn the discord and the rivalry of your elements into oneness and melody.

But how shall I, unless you yourselves be also the peacemakers, nay, the lovers of all your elements?

Your reason and your passion are the rudder and the sails of your seafaring soul.

If either your sails or your rudder be broken, you can but toss and drift, or else be held at a standstill in mid-seas.

For reason, ruling alone, is a force confining; and passion, unattended, is a flame that burns to its own destruction.

Therefore let your soul exalt your reason to the height of passion, that it may sing;

And let it direct your passion with reason, that your passion may live through its own daily resurrection, and like the phœnix rise above its own ashes.

I would have you consider your judgment and your appetite even as you would two loved guests in your house.

Surely you would not honour one guest above the other; for he who is more mindful of one loses the love and the faith of both.

Among the hills, when you sit in the cool shade of the white poplars, sharing the peace and serenity of distant fields and meadows—then let your heart say in silence, "God rests in reason."

And when the storm comes, and the mighty wind shakes the forest, and thunder and lightning proclaim the majesty of the sky,—then let your heart say in awe, "God moves in passion."

And since you are a breath in God's sphere, and a leaf in God's forest, you too should rest in reason and move in passion.

AND a woman spoke, saying, Tell us of Pain. And he said:

Your pain is the breaking of the shell that encloses your understanding.

Even as the stone of the fruit must break, that its heart may stand in the sun, so must you know pain.

And could you keep your heart in wonder at the daily miracles of your life, your pain would not seem less wondrous than your joy;

And you would accept the seasons of your heart, even as you have always accepted the seasons that pass over your fields.

And you would watch with serenity through the winters of your grief.

Much of your pain is self-chosen.

It is the bitter potion by which the physician within you heals your sick self.

Therefore trust the physician, and drink his remedy in silence and tranquillity:

For his hand, though heavy and hard, is guided by the tender hand of the Unseen,

And the cup he brings, though it burn your lips, has been fashioned of the clay which the Potter has moistened with His own sacred tears.

AND a man said, Speak to us of Self-Knowledge.
And he answered, saying:

Your hearts know in silence the secrets of the days and the nights.

But your ears thirst for the sound of your heart's knowledge.

You would know in words that which you have always known in thought.

You would touch with your fingers the naked body of your dreams.

And it is well you should.

The hidden well-spring of your soul must needs rise and run murmuring to the sea;

And the treasure of your infinite depths would be revealed to your eyes.

But let there be no scales to weigh your unknown treasure;

And seek not the depths of your knowledge with staff or sounding line.

For self is a sea boundless and measureless.

Say not, "I have found the truth," but rather, "I have found a truth."

Say not, "I have found the path of the soul." Say rather, "I have met the soul walking upon my path."

For the soul walks upon all paths.

The soul walks not upon a line, neither does it grow like a reed.

The soul unfolds itself, like a lotus of countless petals.

THEN said a teacher, Speak to us of Teaching. And he said:

No man can reveal to you aught but that which already lies half asleep in the dawning of your knowledge.

The teacher who walks in the shadow of the temple, among his followers, gives not of his wisdom but rather of his faith and his lovingness.

If he is indeed wise he does not bid you enter the house of his wisdom, but rather leads you to the threshold of your own mind.

The astronomer may speak to you of his understanding of space, but he cannot give you his understanding.

The musician may sing to you of the rhythm which is in all space, but he cannot give you the ear which arrests the rhythm, nor the voice that echoes it.

And he who is versed in the science of numbers can tell of the regions of weight and measure, but he cannot conduct you thither.

For the vision of one man lends not its wings to another man.

And even as each one of you stands alone in God's knowledge, so must each one of you be alone in his knowledge of God and in his understanding of the earth.

AND a youth said, Speak to us of Friendship.
And he answered, saying:

Your friend is your needs answered.

He is your field which you sow with love and reap with thanksgiving.

And he is your board and your fireside.

For you come to him with your hunger, and you seek him for peace.

When your friend speaks his mind you fear not the "nay" in your own mind, nor do you withhold the "ay."

And when he is silent your heart ceases not to listen to his heart;

For without words, in friendship, all thoughts, all desires, all expectations are born and shared, with joy that is unacclaimed.

When you part from your friend, you grieve not;

For that which you love most in him may be clearer in his absence, as the mountain to the climber is clearer from the plain.

And let there be no purpose in friendship save the deepening of the spirit.

For love that seeks aught but the disclosure of its own mystery is not love but a net cast forth: and only the unprofitable is caught.

And let your best be for your friend.

If he must know the ebb of your tide, let him know its flood also.

For what is your friend that you should seek him with hours to kill?

Seek him always with hours to live.

For it is his to fill your need, but not your emptiness.

And in the sweetness of friendship let there be laughter, and sharing of pleasures.

For in the dew of little things the heart finds its morning and is refreshed.

AND then a scholar said, Speak of Talking.
And he answered, saying:

You talk when you cease to be at peace with your thoughts;

And when you can no longer dwell in the solitude of your heart you live in your lips, and sound is a diversion and a pastime.

And in much of your talking, thinking is half murdered.

For thought is a bird of space, that in a cage of words may indeed unfold its wings but cannot fly.

There are those among you who seek the talkative through fear of being alone.

The silence of aloneness reveals to their eyes their naked selves and they would escape.

And there are those who talk, and without knowledge or forethought reveal a truth which they themselves do not understand.

And there are those who have the truth within them, but they tell it not in words.

In the bosom of such as these the spirit dwells in rhythmic silence.

When you meet your friend on the roadside or in the market-place, let the spirit in you move your lips and direct your tongue.

Let the voice within your voice speak to the ear of his ear;

For his soul will keep the truth of your heart as the taste of the wine is remembered.

When the colour is forgotten and the vessel is no more.

AND an astronomer said, Master, what of
Time?

And he answered:

You would measure time the measureless and
the immeasurable.

You would adjust your conduct and even direct
the course of your spirit according to hours and
seasons.

Of time you would make a stream upon whose
bank you would sit and watch its flowing.

Yet the timeless in you is aware of life's timelessness,

And knows that yesterday is but to-day's memory
and to-morrow is to-day's dream.

And that that which sings and contemplates in
you is still dwelling within the bounds of that first
moment which scattered the stars into space.

Who among you does not feel that his power
to love is boundless?

And yet who does not feel that very love,
though boundless, encompassed within the centre

73

of his being, and moving not from love thought to love thought, nor from love deeds to other love deeds?

And is not time even as love is, undivided and paceless?

But if in your thought you must measure time into seasons, let each season encircle all the other seasons,

And let to-day embrace the past with remembrance and the future with longing.

AND one of the elders of the city said, Speak to us of Good and Evil.

And he answered:

Of the good in you I can speak, but not of the evil.

For what is evil but good tortured by its own hunger and thirst?

Verily when good is hungry it seeks food even in dark caves, and when it thirsts it drinks even of dead waters.

You are good when you are one with yourself.

Yet when you are not one with yourself you are not evil.

For a divided house is not a den of thieves; it is only a divided house.

And a ship without rudder may wander aimlessly among perilous isles yet sink not to the bottom.

You are good when you strive to give of yourself.

Yet you are not evil when you seek gain for yourself.

For when you strive for gain you are but a root that clings to the earth and sucks at her breast.

Surely the fruit cannot say to the root, "Be like me, ripe and full and ever giving of your abundance."

For to the fruit giving is a need, as receiving is a need to the root.

You are good when you are fully awake in your speech.

Yet you are not evil when you sleep while your tongue staggers without purpose.

And even stumbling speech may strengthen a weak tongue.

You are good when you walk to your goal firmly and with bold steps.

Yet you are not evil when you go thither limping.

Even those who limp go not backward.

But you who are strong and swift, see that you do not limp before the lame, deeming it kindness.

You are good in countless ways, and you are not evil when you are not good,

You are only loitering and sluggard.

Pity that the stags cannot teach swiftness to the turtles.

In your longing for your giant self lies your goodness: and that longing is in all of you.

But in some of you that longing is a torrent rushing with might to the sea, carrying the secrets of the hillsides and the songs of the forest.

And in others it is a flat stream that loses itself in angles and bends and lingers before it reaches the shore.

But let not him who longs much say to him who longs little, "Wherefore are you slow and halting?"

For the truly good ask not the naked, "Where is your garment?" nor the houseless, "What has befallen your house?"

THEN a Priestess said, Speak to us of Prayer. And he answered, saying:

You pray in your distress and in your need; would that you might pray also in the fullness of your joy and in your days of abundance.

For what is prayer but the expansion of yourself into the living ether?

And if it is for your comfort to pour your darkness into space, it is also for your delight to pour forth the dawning of your heart.

And if you cannot but weep when your soul summons you to prayer, she should spur you again and yet again, though weeping, until you shall come laughing.

When you pray you rise to meet in the air those who are praying at that very hour, and whom save in prayer you may not meet.

Therefore let your visit to that temple invisible be for naught but ecstasy and sweet communion.

For if you should enter the temple for no other purpose than asking you shall not receive:

78

And if you should enter into it to humble yourself you shall not be lifted:

Or even if you should enter into it to beg for the good of others you shall not be heard.

It is enough that you enter the temple invisible.

I cannot teach you how to pray in words.

God listens not to your words save when He Himself utters them through your lips.

And I cannot teach you the prayer of the seas and the forests and the mountains.

But you who are born of the mountains and the forests and the seas can find their prayer in your heart,

And if you but listen in the stillness of the night you shall hear them saying in silence:

Our God, who art our winged self, it is thy will in us that willeth.

"It is thy desire in us that desireth.

"It is thy urge in us that would turn our nights, which are thine, into days, which are thine also.

"We cannot ask thee for aught, for thou knowest our needs before they are born in us:

"Thou art our need; and in giving us more of thyself thou givest us all."

THEN a hermit, who visited the city once a year, came forth and said, Speak to us of Pleasure.

And he answered, saying:

Pleasure is a freedom-song,

But it is not freedom.

It is the blossoming of your desires,

But it is not their fruit.

It is a depth calling unto a height,

But it is not the deep nor the high.

It is the caged taking wing,

But it is not space encompassed.

Ay, in very truth, pleasure is a freedom-song.

And I fain would have you sing it with fullness of heart; yet I would not have you lose your hearts in the singing.

Some of your youth seek pleasure as if it were all, and they are judged and rebuked.

I would not judge nor rebuke them. I would have them seek.

For they shall find pleasure, but not her alone;

83

Seven are her sisters, and the least of them is more beautiful than pleasure.

Have you not heard of the man who was digging in the earth for roots and found a treasure?

And some of your elders remember pleasures with regret like wrongs committed in drunkenness.

But regret is the beclouding of the mind and not its chastisement.

They should remember their pleasures with gratitude, as they would the harvest of a summer.

Yet if it comforts them to regret, let them be comforted.

And there are among you those who are neither young to seek nor old to remember;

And in their fear of seeking and remembering they shun all pleasures, lest they neglect the spirit or offend against it.

But even in their foregoing is their pleasure.

And thus they too find a treasure though they dig for roots with quivering hands.

But tell me, who is he that can offend the spirit?

Shall the nightingale offend the stillness of the night, or the firefly the stars?

And shall your flame or your smoke burden the wind?

Think you the spirit is a still pool which you can trouble with a staff?

Oftentimes in denying yourself pleasure you do but store the desire in the recesses of your being.

Who knows but that which seems omitted to-day, waits for to-morrow?

Even your body knows its heritage and its rightful need and will not be deceived.

And your body is the harp of your soul,

And it is yours to bring forth sweet music from it or confused sounds.

And now you ask in your heart, "How shall we distinguish that which is good in pleasure from that which is not good?"

Go to your fields and your gardens, and you

shall learn that it is the pleasure of the bee to gather honey of the flower,

But it is also the pleasure of the flower to yield its honey to the bee.

For to the bee a flower is a fountain of life,

And to the flower a bee is a messenger of love,

And to both, bee and flower, the giving and the receiving of pleasure is a need and an ecstasy.

People of Orphalese, be in your pleasures like the flowers and the bees.

AND a poet said, Speak to us of Beauty.

And he answered:

Where shall you seek beauty, and how shall you find her unless she herself be your way and your guide?

And how shall you speak of her except she be the weaver of your speech?

The aggrieved and the injured say, "Beauty is kind and gentle.

"Like a young mother half-shy of her own glory she walks among us."

And the passionate say, "Nay, beauty is a thing of might and dread.

"Like the tempest she shakes the earth beneath us and the sky above us."

The tired and the weary say, "Beauty is of soft whisperings. She speaks in our spirit.

"Her voice yields to our silences like a faint light that quivers in fear of the shadow."

But the restless say, "We have heard her shouting among the mountains,

"And with her cries came the sound of hoofs, and the beating of wings and the roaring of lions."

At night the watchmen of the city say, "Beauty shall rise with the dawn from the east."

And at noontide the toilers and the wayfarers say, "We have seen her leaning over the earth from the windows of the sunset."

In winter say the snow-bound, "She shall come with the spring leaping upon the hills."

And in the summer heat the reapers say, "We have seen her dancing with the autumn leaves, and we saw a drift of snow in her hair."

All these things have you said of beauty,

Yet in truth you spoke not of her but of needs unsatisfied,

And beauty is not a need but an ecstasy.

It is not a mouth thirsting nor an empty hand stretched forth,

But rather a heart inflamed and a soul enchanted.

88

It is not the image you would see nor the song you would hear,

But rather an image you see though you close your eyes and a song you hear though you shut your ears.

It is not the sap within the furrowed bark, nor a wing attached to a claw,

But rather a garden for ever in bloom and a flock of angels for ever in flight.

People of Orphalese, beauty is life when life unveils her holy face.

But you are life and you are the veil.

Beauty is eternity gazing at itself in a mirror.

But you are eternity and you are the mirror.

AND an old priest said, Speak to us of Religion. And he said:

Have I spoken this day of aught else?

Is not religion all deeds and all reflection,

And that which is neither deed nor reflection, but a wonder and a surprise ever springing in the soul, even while the hands hew the stone or tend the loom?

Who can separate his faith from his actions, or his belief from his occupations?

Who can spread his hours before him, saying, "This for God and this for myself; This for my soul and this other for my body"?

All your hours are wings that beat through space from self to self.

He who wears his morality but as his best garment were better naked.

The wind and the sun will tear no holes in his skin.

And he who defines his conduct by ethics imprisons his song-bird in a cage.

The freest song comes not through bars and wires.

And he to whom worshipping is a window, to open but also to shut, has not yet visited the house of his soul whose windows are from dawn to dawn.

Your daily life is your temple and your religion.

Whenever you enter into it take with you your all.

Take the plough and the forge and the mallet and the lute,

The things you have fashioned in necessity or for delight.

For in reverie you cannot rise above your achievements nor fall lower than your failures.

And take with you all men:

For in adoration you cannot fly higher than their hopes nor humble yourself lower than their despair.

And if you would know God, be not therefore a solver of riddles.

Rather look about you and you shall see Him playing with your children.

And look into space; you shall see Him walking in the cloud, outstretching His arms in the lightning and descending in rain.

You shall see Him smiling in flowers, then rising and waving His hands in trees.

THEN Almitra spoke, saying, We would ask now of Death.

And he said:

You would know the secret of death.

But how shall you find it unless you seek it in the heart of life?

The owl whose night-bound eyes are blind unto the day cannot unveil the mystery of light.

If you would indeed behold the spirit of death, open your heart wide unto the body of life.

For life and death are one, even as the river and the sea are one.

In the depth of your hopes and desires lies your silent knowledge of the beyond;

And like seeds dreaming beneath the snow your heart dreams of spring.

Trust the dreams, for in them is hidden the gate to eternity.

Your fear of death is but the trembling of the shepherd when he stands before the king whose hand is to be laid upon him in honour.

93

Is the shepherd not joyful beneath his trembling, that he shall wear the mark of the king?

Yet is he not more mindful of his trembling?

For what is it to die but to stand naked in the wind and to melt into the sun?

And what is it to cease breathing but to free the breath from its restless tides, that it may rise and expand and seek God unencumbered?

Only when you drink from the river of silence shall you indeed sing.

And when you have reached the mountain top, then you shall begin to climb.

And when the earth shall claim your limbs, then shall you truly dance.

AND now it was evening.

And Almitra the seeress said, Blessed be this day and this place and your spirit that has spoken.

And he answered, Was it I who spoke?

Was I not also a listener?

Then he descended the steps of the Temple and all the people followed him. And he reached his ship and stood upon the deck.

And facing the people again, he raised his voice and said:

People of Orphalese, the wind bids me leave you.

Less hasty am I than the wind, yet I must go.

We wanderers, ever seeking the lonelier way, begin no day where we have ended another day; and no sunrise finds us where sunset left us.

Even while the earth sleeps we travel.

We are the seeds of the tenacious plant, and it is in our ripeness and our fullness of heart that we are given to the wind and are scattered.

Brief were my days among you, and briefer still

97

the words I have spoken.

But should my voice fade in your ears, and my love vanish in your memory, then I will come again,

And with a richer heart and lips more yielding to the spirit will I speak.

Yea, I shall return with the tide,

And though death may hide me, and the greater silence enfold me, yet again will I seek your understanding.

And not in vain will I seek.

If aught I have said is truth, that truth shall reveal itself in a clearer voice, and in words more kin to your thoughts.

I go with the wind, people of Orphalese, but not down into emptiness;

And if this day is not a fulfilment of your need and my love, then let it be a promise till another day

Man's needs change, but not his love, nor his desire that his love should satisfy his needs.

Know, therefore, that from the greater silence I shall return.

The mist that drifts away at dawn, leaving but dew in the fields, shall rise and gather into a cloud and then fall down in rain.

And not unlike the mist have I been.

In the stillness of the night I have walked in your streets, and my spirit has entered your houses,

And your heart-beats were in my heart, and your breath was upon my face, and I knew you all.

Ay, I knew your joy and your pain, and in your sleep your dreams were my dreams.

And oftentimes I was among you a lake among the mountains.

I mirrored the summits in you and the bending slopes, and even the passing flocks of your thoughts and your desires.

And to my silence came the laughter of your children in streams, and the longing of your youths in rivers.

And when they reached my depth the streams and the rivers ceased not yet to sing.

But sweeter still than laughter and greater tha longing came to me.

It was the boundless in you;

The vast man in whom you are all but cells and sinews;

He in whose chant all your singing is but a soundless throbbing.

It is in the vast man that you are vast,

And in beholding him that I beheld you and loved you.

For what distances can love reach that are not in that vast sphere?

What visions, what expectations and what presumptions can outsoar that flight?

Like a giant oak tree covered with apple blossoms is the vast man in you.

His might binds you to the earth, his fragrance lifts you into space, and in his durability you are deathless.

You have been told that, even like a chain, you are as weak as your weakest link.

This is but half the truth. You are also as strong as your strongest link.

To measure you by your smallest deed is to reckon the power of ocean by the frailty of its foam.

102

To judge you by your failures is to cast blame upon the seasons for their inconstancy.

Ay, you are like an ocean,

And though heavy-grounded ships await the tide upon your shores, yet, even like an ocean, you cannot hasten your tides.

And like the seasons you are also,

And though in your winter you deny your spring,

Yet spring, reposing within you, smiles in her drowsiness and is not offended.

Think not I say these things in order that you may say the one to the other, "He praised us well. He saw but the good in us."

I only speak to you in words of that which you yourselves know in thought.

And what is word knowledge but a shadow of wordless knowledge?

Your thoughts and my words are waves from a sealed memory that keeps records of our yesterdays,

And of the ancient days when the earth knew not us nor herself,

And of nights when earth was upwrought with confusion.

Wise men have come to you to give you of their wisdom. I came to take of your wisdom:

And behold I have found that which is greater than wisdom.

It is a flame spirit in you ever gathering more of itself,

While you, heedless of its expansion, bewail the withering of your days.

It is life in quest of life in bodies that fear the grave.

There are no graves here.

These mountains and plains are a cradle and a stepping-stone.

Whenever you pass by the field where you have laid your ancestors look well thereupon, and you shall see yourselves and your children dancing hand in hand.

Verily you often make merry without knowing.

Others have come to you to whom for golden

promises made unto your faith you have given but riches and power and glory.

Less than a promise have I given, and yet more generous have you been to me.

You have given me my deeper thirsting after life.

Surely there is no greater gift to a man than that which turns all his aims into parching lips and all life into a fountain.

And in this lies my honour and my reward,—

That whenever I come to the fountain to drink I find the living water itself thirsty;

And it drinks me while I drink it.

Some of you have deemed me proud and over-shy to receive gifts.

Too proud indeed am I to receive wages, but not gifts.

And though I have eaten berries among the hills when you would have had me sit at your board,

And slept in the portico of the temple when you would gladly have sheltered me,

Yet it was not your loving mindfulness of my days and my nights that made food sweet to my mouth and girdled my sleep with visions?

For this I bless you most:

You give much and know not that you give at all.

Verily the kindness that gazes upon itself in a mirror turns to stone,

And a good deed that calls itself by tender names becomes the parent to a curse.

And some of you have called me aloof, and drunk with my own aloneness,

And you have said, "He holds council with the trees of the forest, but not with men.

"He sits alone on hill-tops and looks down upon our city."

True it is that I have climbed the hills and walked in remote places.

How could I have seen you save from a great height or a great distance?

How can one be indeed near unless he be far?

And others among you called unto me, not in words, and they said:

"Stranger, stranger, lover of unreachable heights, why dwell you among the summits where eagles build their nests?

"Why seek you the unattainable?

"What storms would you trap in your net,

"And what vaporous birds do you hunt in the sky?

"Come and be one of us.

"Descend and appease your hunger with our bread and quench your thirst with our wine."

In the solitude of their souls they said these things;

But were their solitude deeper they would have known that I sought but the secret of your joy and your pain,

And I hunted only your larger selves that walk the sky.

But the hunter was also the hunted;

For many of my arrows left my bow only to seek my own breast.

And the flier was also the creeper;

For when my wings were spread in the sun their shadow upon the earth was a turtle.

And I the believer was also the doubter;

For often have I put my finger in my own wound that I might have the greater belief in you and the greater knowledge of you.

And it is with this belief and this knowledge that I say,

You are not enclosed within your bodies, nor confined to houses or fields.

That which is you dwells above the mountain and roves with the wind.

It is not a thing that crawls into the sun for warmth or digs holes into darkness for safety,

But a thing free, a spirit that envelops the earth and moves in the ether.

If these be vague words, then seek not to clear them.

Vague and nebulous is the beginning of all things, but not their end,

And I fain would have you remember me as a beginning.

Life, and all that lives, is conceived in the mist and not in the crystal.

And who knows but a crystal is mist in decay?

This would I have you remember in remembering me:
That which seems most feeble and bewildered in you is the strongest and most determined.

Is it not your breath that has erected and hardened the structure of your bones?

And is it not a dream which none of you remember having dreamt, that builded your city and fashioned all there is in it?

Could you but see the tides of that breath you would cease to see all else,

And if you could hear the whispering of the dream you would hear no other sound.

But you do not see, nor do you hear, and it is well.

The veil that clouds your eyes shall be lifted by the hands that wove it,

And the clay that fills your ears shall be pierced by those fingers that kneaded it.

And you shall see

And you shall hear.

Yet you shall not deplore having known blindness, nor regret having been deaf.

For in that day you shall know the hidden purposes in all things,

And you shall bless darkness as you would bless
light.

After saying these things he looked about him,
and he saw the pilot of his ship standing by the
helm and gazing now at the full sails and now at
the distance.

And he said:

Patient, over patient, is the captain of my ship.

The wind blows, and restless are the sails;

Even the rudder begs direction;

Yet quietly my captain awaits my silence.

And these my mariners, who have heard the
choir of the greater sea, they too have heard me
patiently.

Now they shall wait no longer.

I am ready.

The stream has reached the sea, and once more the great mother holds her son against her breast.

Fare you well, people of Orphalese.

This day has ended.

It is closing upon us even as the water-lily upon its own to-morrow.

What was given us here we shall keep,

And if it suffices not, then again must we come together and together stretch our hands unto the giver.

Forget not that I shall come back to you.

A little while, and my longing shall gather dust and foam for another body.

A little while, a moment of rest upon the wind, and another woman shall bear me.

Farewell to you and the youth I have spent with you.

It was but yesterday we met in a dream.

You have sung to me in my aloneness, and I of your longings have built a tower in the sky.

But now our sleep has fled and our dream is over, and it is no longer dawn.

The noontide is upon us and our half waking has turned to fuller day, and we must part.

If in the twilight of memory we should meet once more, we shall speak again together and you shall sing to me a deeper song.

And if our hands should meet in another dream we shall build another tower in the sky.

So saying he made a signal to the seamen, and straightaway they weighed anchor and cast the ship loose from its moorings, and they moved eastward.

And a cry came from the people as from a single heart, and it rose into the dusk and was carried out over the sea like a great trumpeting.

Only Almitra was silent, gazing after the ship until it had vanished into the mist.

And when all the people were dispersed she still stood alone upon the sea-wall, remembering in her heart his saying:

"A little while, a moment of rest upon the wind, and another woman shall bear me."

BOOK TWO

THE WANDERER

His Parables and His Sayings

THE WANDERER

I met him at the crossroads, a man with but a cloak and a staff, and a veil of pain upon his face. And we greeted one another, and I said to him, " Come to my house and be my guest."

And he came.

My wife and my children met us at the threshold, and he smiled at them, and they loved his coming.

Then we all sat together at the board and we were happy with the man for there was a silence and a mystery in him.

And after supper we gathered to the fire and I asked him about his wanderings.

He told us many a tale that night and also the next day, but what I now record was born out of the bitterness of his days though he himself was kindly, and these tales are of the dust and patience of his road.

And when he left us after three days we did not feel that a guest had departed but rather that one of us was still out in the garden and had not yet come in.

GARMENTS

Upon a day Beauty and Ugliness met on the shore of a sea. And they said to one another, "Let us bathe in the sea."

Then they disrobed and swam in the waters. And after a while Ugliness came back to shore and garmented himself with the garments of Beauty and walked his way.

And Beauty too came out of the sea, and found not her raiment, and she was too shy to be naked, therefore she dressed herself with the raiment of Ugliness. And Beauty walked her way.

And to this very day men and women mistake the one for the other.

Yet some there are who have beheld the face of Beauty, and they know her notwithstanding her garments. And some there be who know the face of Ugliness, and the cloth conceals him not from their eyes.

THE EAGLE AND THE SKYLARK

A skylark and an eagle met on a rock upon a high hill. The skylark said, " Good morrow to you, Sir." And the eagle looked down upon him and said faintly, " Good morrow."

And the skylark said, " I hope all things are well with you, Sir."

" Aye," said the eagle, " all is well with us. But do you not know that we are the king of birds, and that you shall not address us before we ourselves have spoken? "

Said the skylark, " Methinks we are of the same family."

The eagle looked upon him with disdain and he said, " Who ever has said that you and I are of the same family? "

Then said the skylark, " But I would remind you of this, I can fly even as high as you, and I can sing and give delight to the other creatures of this earth. And you give neither pleasure nor delight."

Then the eagle was angered, and he said, " Pleasure and delight! You little presumptuous creature! With one thrust of my beak I could destroy you. You are but the size of my foot."

Then the skylark flew up and alighted upon the back of the eagle and began to pick at his feathers. The eagle was annoyed, and he flew swift and high that he might rid himself of the little bird. But he failed to do so. At last he dropped back to that very rock upon the high hill, more fretted than ever, with the little creature still upon his back, and cursing the fate of the hour.

Now at that moment a small turtle came by and laughed at the sight, and laughed so hard that she almost turned upon her back.

And the eagle looked down upon the turtle and he said, " You slow creeping thing, ever one with the earth, what are you laughing at? "

And the turtle said, " Why I see that you are

turned horse, and that you have a small bird riding you, but the small bird is the better bird."

And the eagle said to her, " Go you about your business. This is a family affair between my brother, the lark, and myself."

THE LOVE SONG

A poet once wrote a love song and it was beautiful. And he made many copies of it, and sent them to his friends and his acquaintances, both men and women, and even to a young woman whom he had met but once, who lived beyond the mountains.

And in a day or two a messenger came from the young woman bringing a letter. And in the letter she said, " Let me assure you, I am deeply touched by the love song that you have written to me. Come now, and see my father and my mother, and we shall make arrangements for the betrothal."

And the poet answered the letter, and he said to her, " My friend, it was but a song of love out of a poet's heart, sung by every man to every woman."

And she wrote again to him saying, " Hypocrite and liar in words! From this day unto my coffin-day I shall hate all poets for your sake."

TEARS AND LAUGHTER

Upon the bank of the Nile at eventide, a hyena met a crocodile and they stopped and greeted one another.

The hyena spoke and said, " How goes the day with you, Sir? "

And the crocodile answered saying, " It goes badly with me. Sometimes in my pain and sorrow I weep, and then the creatures always say, ' They are but crocodile tears.' And this wounds me beyond all telling."

Then the hyena said, " You speak of your pain and your sorrow, but think of me also, for a moment. I gaze at the beauty of the world, its wonders and its miracles, and out of sheer joy I laugh even as the day laughs. And then the people of the jungle say, ' It is but the laughter of a hyena.' "

AT THE FAIR

There came to the Fair a girl from the country-side, most comely. There was a lily and a rose in her face. There was sunset in her hair, and dawn smiled upon her lips.

No sooner did the lovely stranger appear in their sight than the young men sought her and surrounded her. One would dance with her, and another would cut a cake in her honor. And they all desired to kiss her cheek. For after all, was it not the Fair?

But the girl was shocked and startled, and she thought ill of the young men. She rebuked them, and she even struck one or two of them in the face. Then she ran away from them.

And on her way home that evening she was saying in her heart, " I am disgusted. How unmannerly and ill bred are these men. It is beyond all patience."

A year passed during which that very comely

girl thought much of Fairs and men. Then she came again to the Fair with the lily and the rose in her face, the sunset in her hair and the smile of dawn upon her lips.

But now the young men, seeing her, turned from her. And all the day long she was unsought and alone.

And at eventide as she walked the road toward her home she cried in her heart, " I am disgusted. How unmannerly and ill bred are these youths. It is beyond all patience."

THE TWO PRINCESSES

In the city of Shawakis lived a prince, and he was loved by everyone, men and women and children. Even the animals of the field came unto him in greeting.

But all the people said that his wife, the princess, loved him not; nay, that she even hated him.

And upon a day the princess of a neighboring city came to visit the princess of Shawakis. And they sat and talked together, and their words led to their husbands.

And the princess of Shawakis said with passion, " I envy you your happiness with the prince, your husband, though you have been married these many years. I hate my husband. He belongs not to me alone, and I am indeed a woman most unhappy."

Then the visiting princess gazed at her and said, " My friend, the truth is that you love your husband. Aye, and you still have for him a passion unspent, and that is life in woman like unto Spring in a garden. But pity me, and my husband, for we do but endure one another in silent patience. And yet you and others deem this happiness."

THE LIGHTNING FLASH

There was a Christian bishop in his cathedral on a stormy day, and an un-Christian woman came and stood before him, and she said, " I am not a Christian. Is there salvation for me from hell-fire? "

And the bishop looked upon the woman, and he answered her saying, " Nay, there is salvation for those only who are baptized of water and of the spirit."

And even as he spoke a bolt from the sky fell with thunder upon the cathedral and it was filled with fire.

And the men of the city came running, and they saved the woman, but the bishop was consumed, food of the fire.

THE HERMIT AND THE BEASTS

Once there lived among the green hills a hermit. He was pure of spirit and white of heart. And all the animals of the land and all the fowls of the air came to him in pairs and he spoke unto them. They heard him gladly, and they would gather near unto him, and would not go until nightfall, when he would send them away, entrusting them to the wind and the woods with his blessing.

Upon an evening as he was speaking of love, a leopard raised her head and said to the hermit, " You speak to us of loving. Tell us, Sir, where is your mate? "

And the hermit said, " I have no mate."

Then a great cry of surprise rose from the company of beasts and fowls, and they began to say among themselves, " How can he tell us of loving and mating when he himself knows naught thereof? " And quietly and in disdain they left him alone.

That night the hermit lay upon his mat with his face earthward, and he wept bitterly and beat his hands upon his breast.

THE PROPHET
AND THE CHILD

Once on a day the prophet Sharia met a child in a garden. The child ran to him and said, " Good morrow to you, Sir," and the prophet said, " Good morrow to you, Sir." And in a moment, " I see that you are alone."

Then the child said, in laughter and delight, " It took a long time to lose my nurse. She thinks I am behind those hedges; but can't you see that I am here? " Then he gazed at the prophet's face and spoke again. " You are alone, too. What did you do with your nurse? "

The prophet answered and said, " Ah, that is a different thing. In very truth I cannot lose her oftentimes. But now, when I came into this garden, she was seeking after me behind the hedges."

The child clapped his hands and cried out, " So you are lost like me! Isn't it good to be lost? " And then he said, " Who are you? "

And the man answered, " They call me the prophet Sharia. And tell me, who are you? "

" I am only myself," said the child, " and my nurse is seeking after me, and she does not know where I am."

Then the prophet gazed into space saying, " I too have escaped my nurse for awhile, but she will find me out."

And the child said, " I know mine will find me out too."

At that moment a woman's voice was heard calling the child's name. " See," said the child, " I told you she would be finding me."

And at the same moment another voice was heard, " Where art thou, Sharia? "

And the prophet said, " See, my child, they have found me also."

And turning his face upward, Sharia answered, " Here am I."

THE PEARL

Said one oyster to a neighboring oyster, " I have a very great pain within me. It is heavy and round and I am in distress."

And the other oyster replied with haughty complacence, " Praise be to the heavens and to the sea, I have no pain within me. I am well and whole both within and without."

At that moment a crab was passing by and heard the two oysters, and he said to the one who was well and whole both within and without, " Yes, you are well and whole; but the pain that your neighbor bears is a pearl of exceeding beauty."

BODY AND SOUL

A man and a woman sat by a window that opened upon Spring. They sat close one unto the other. And the woman said, " I love you. You are handsome, and you are rich, and you are always well-attired."

And the man said, " I love you. You are a beautiful thought, a thing too apart to hold in the hand, and a song in my dreaming."

But the woman turned from him in anger, and she said, " Sir, please leave me now. I am not a thought, and I am not a thing that passes in your dreams. I am a woman. I would have you desire me, a wife, and the mother of unborn children."

And they parted.

And the man was saying in his heart, " Behold another dream is even now turned into the mist."

And the woman was saying, " Well, what of a man who turns me into a mist and a dream? "

THE KING

The people of the Kingdom of Sadik surrounded the palace of their king shouting in rebellion against him. And he came down the steps
of the palace carrying his crown in one hand and
his sceptre in the other. The majesty of his appearance silenced the multitude, and he stood before them and said, " My friends, who are no
longer my subjects, here I yield my crown and
sceptre unto you. I would be one of you. I am
only one man, but as a man I would work together with you that our lot may be made better.
There is no need for a king. Let us go therefore
to the fields and the vineyards and labor hand
with hand. Only you must tell me to what field
or vineyard I should go. All of you now are
king."

And the people marveled, and stillness was
upon them, for the king whom they had deemed
the source of their discontent now yielded his

crown and sceptre to them and became as one of them.

Then each and every one of them went his way, and the king walked with one man to a field.

But the Kingdom of Sadik fared not better without a king, and the mist of discontent was still upon the land. The people cried out in the market places saying that they would be governed, and that they would have a king to rule them. And the elders and the youths said as if with one voice, " We will have our king."

And they sought the king and found him toiling in the field, and they brought him to his seat, and yielded unto him his crown and his sceptre. And they said, " Now rule us, with might and with justice."

And he said, " I will indeed rule you with might, and may the gods of the heaven and the earth help me that I may also rule with justice."

Now, there came to his presence men and women and spoke unto him of a baron who mistreated them, and to whom they were but serfs. And straightway the king brought the baron before him and said, " The life of one man is as weighty in the scales of God as the life of another. And because you know not how to weigh the lives of those who work in your fields and your vineyards, you are banished, and you shall leave this kingdom forever."

The following day came another company to the king and spoke of the cruelty of a countess beyond the hills, and how she brought them down to misery. Instantly the countess was brought to court, and the king sentenced her also to banishment, saying, " Those who till our fields and care for our vineyards are nobler than we who eat the bread they prepare and drink the wine of their wine-press. And because you know not this, you shall leave this land and be afar from this kingdom."

Then came men and women who said that the bishop made them bring stones and hew the stones for the cathedral, yet he gave them naught, though they knew the bishop's coffer was full of gold and silver while they themselves were empty with hunger.

24

And the king called for the bishop, and when the bishop came the king spoke and said unto him, "That cross you wear upon your bosom should mean giving life unto life. But you have taken life from life and you have given none. Therefore you shall leave this kingdom never to return."

Thus each day for a full moon men and women came to the king to tell him of the burdens laid upon them. And each and every day for a full moon some oppressor was exiled from the land.

And the people of Sadik were amazed, and there was cheer in their heart.

And upon a day the elders and the youths came and surrounded the tower of the king and called for him. And he came down holding his crown with one hand and his sceptre with the other.

And he spoke unto them and said, "Now, what would you of me? Behold, I yield back to you that which you desired me to hold."

But they cried, "Nay, nay, you are our rightful king. You have made clean the land of vipers, and you have brought the wolves to naught, and we come to sing our thanksgiving unto you. The crown is yours in majesty and the sceptre is yours in glory."

Then the king said, " Not I, not I. You yourselves are king. When you deemed me weak and a misruler, you yourselves were weak and misruling. And now the land fares well because it is in your will. I am but a thought in the mind of you all, and I exist not save in your actions. There is no such person as governor. Only the governed exist to govern themselves."

And the king re-entered his tower with his crown and his sceptre. And the elders and the youths went their various ways and they were content.

And each and every one thought of himself as king with a crown in one hand and a sceptre in the other.

UPON THE SAND

Said one man to another, " At the high tide of the sea, long ago, with the point of my staff I wrote a line upon the sand; and the people still pause to read it, and they are careful that naught shall erase it."

And the other man said, " And I too wrote a line upon the sand, but it was at low tide, and the waves of the vast sea washed it away. But tell me, what did you write? "

And the first man answered and said, " I wrote this: ' I am he who is.' But what did you write? "

And the other man said, " This I wrote: ' I am but a drop of this great ocean.' "

THE THREE GIFTS

Once in the city of Becharre there lived a gracious prince who was loved and honored by all his subjects.

But there was one exceedingly poor man who was bitter against the prince, and who wagged continually a pestilent tongue in his dispraise.

The prince knew this, yet he was patient.

But at last he bethought him; and upon a wintry night there came to the door of the man a servant of the prince, bearing a sack of flour, a bag of soap and a cone of sugar.

And the servant said, " The prince sends you these gifts in token of remembrance."

The man was elated, for he thought the gifts were an homage from the prince. And in his pride he went to the bishop and told him what the prince had done, saying, " Can you not see how the prince desires my goodwill? "

But the bishop said, " Oh, how wise a prince,

and how little you understand. He speaks in symbols. The flour is for your empty stomach; the soap is for your dirty hide; and the sugar is to sweeten your bitter tongue."

From that day forward the man became shy even of himself. His hatred of the prince was greater than ever, and even more he hated the bishop who had revealed the prince unto him.

But thereafter he kept silent.

PEACE AND WAR

Three dogs were basking in the sun and conversing.

The first dog said dreamily, " It is indeed wondrous to be living in this day of dogdom. Consider the ease with which we travel under the sea, upon the earth and even in the sky. And meditate for a moment upon the inventions brought forth for the comfort of dogs, even for our eyes and ears and noses."

And the second dog spoke and he said, " We are more heedful of the arts. We bark at the moon more rhythmically than did our forefathers. And when we gaze at ourselves in the water we see that our features are clearer than the features of yesterday."

Then the third dog spoke and said, " But what interests me most and beguiles my mind is the tranquil understanding existing between dog-doms."

30

At that very moment they looked, and lo, the dog-catcher was approaching.

The three dogs sprang up and scampered down the street; and as they ran the third dog said, " For God's sake, run for your lives. Civilization is after us."

THE DANCER

Once there came to the court of the Prince of Birkasha a dancer with her musicians. And she was admitted to the court, and she danced before the prince to the music of the lute and the flute and the zither.

She danced the dance of flames, and the dance of swords and spears; she danced the dance of stars and the dance of space. And then she danced the dance of flowers in the wind.

After this she stood before the throne of the prince and bowed her body before him. And the prince bade her to come nearer, and he said unto her, "Beautiful woman, daughter of grace and delight, whence comes your art? And how is it that you command all the elements in your rhythms and your rhymes?"

And the dancer bowed again before the prince, and she answered, "Mighty and gracious Majesty, I know not the answer to your questionings. Only

this I know: The philosopher's soul dwells in his head, the poet's soul is in his heart; the singer's soul lingers about his throat, but the soul of the dancer abides in all her body."

THE TWO GUARDIAN ANGELS

On an evening two angels met at the city gate, and they greeted one another, and they conversed.

The one angel said, " What are you doing these days, and what work is given you? "

And the other answered, " It has been assigned me to be the guardian of a fallen man who lives down in the valley, a great sinner, most degraded. Let me assure you it is an important task, and I work hard."

The first angel said, " That is an easy commission. I have often known sinners, and have been their guardian many a time. But it has now been assigned me to be the guardian of the good saint who lives in a bower out yonder. And I assure you that is an exceedingly difficult work, and most subtle."

Said the first angel, " This is but assumption. How can guarding a saint be harder than guarding a sinner? "

And the other answered, "What impertinence, to call me assumptious! I have stated but the truth. Methinks it is you who are assumptious!"

Then the angels wrangled and fought, first with words and then with fists and wings.

While they were fighting an archangel came by. And he stopped them, and said, "Why do you fight? And what is it all about? Know you not that it is most unbecoming for guardian angels to fight at the city gate? Tell me, what is your disagreement?"

Then both angels spoke at once, each claiming that the work given him was the harder, and that he deserved the greater recognition.

The archangel shook his head and bethought him.

Then he said, "My friends, I cannot say now which one of you has the greater claim upon honor and reward. But since the power is bestowed in me, therefore for peace' sake and for good guardianship, I give to each of you the other's occupation, since each of you insists that

35

the other's task is the easier one. Now go hence and be happy at your work."

The angels thus ordered went their ways. But each one looked backward with greater anger at the archangel. And in his heart each was saying, " Oh, these archangels! Every day they make life harder and still harder for us angels! "

But the archangel stood there, and once more he bethought him. And he said in his heart, " We have indeed, to be watchful and to keep guard over our guardian angels."

THE STATUE

Once there lived a man among the hills who possessed a statue wrought by an ancient master. It lay at his door face downward and he was not mindful of it.

One day there passed by his house a man from the city, a man of knowledge, and seeing the statue he inquired of the owner if he would sell it.

The owner laughed and said, " And pray who would want to buy that dull and dirty stone? "

The man from the city said, " I will give you this piece of silver for it."

And the other man was astonished and delighted.

The statue was removed to the city, upon the back of an elephant. And after many moons the man from the hills visited the city, and as he walked the streets he saw a crowd before a shop, and a man with a loud voice was crying, " Come ye in and behold the most beautiful, the most wonderful statue in all the world. Only two silver pieces to look upon this most marvelous work of a master."

Thereupon the man from the hills paid two silver pieces and entered the shop to see the statue that he himself had sold for one piece of silver.

THE EXCHANGE

Once upon a crossroad a poor Poet met a rich Stupid, and they conversed. And all that they said revealed but their discontent.

Then the Angel of the Road passed by, and he laid his hand upon the shoulder of the two men. And behold, a miracle: The two men had now exchanged their possessions.

And they parted. But strange to relate, the Poet looked and found naught in his hand but dry moving sand; and the Stupid closed his eyes and felt naught but moving cloud in his heart.

LOVE AND HATE

A woman said unto a man, " I love you." And the man said, " It is in my heart to be worthy of your love."

And the woman said, " You love me not? " And the man only gazed upon her and said nothing.

Then the woman cried aloud, " I hate you." And the man said, " Then it is also in my heart to be worthy of your hate."

DREAMS

A man dreamed a dream, and when he awoke he went to his soothsayer and desired that his dream be made plain unto him.

And the soothsayer said to the man, "Come to me with the dreams that you behold in your wakefulness and I will tell you their meaning. But the dreams of your sleep belong neither to my wisdom nor to your imagination."

THE MADMAN

It was in the garden of a madhouse that I met a youth with a face pale and lovely and full of wonder.

And I sat beside him upon the bench, and I said, " Why are you here? "

And he looked at me in astonishment, and he said, " It is an unseemly question, yet I will answer you. My father would make of me a reproduction of himself; so also would my uncle. My mother would have me the image of her illustrious father. My sister would hold up her seafaring husband as the perfect example for me to follow. My brother thinks I should be like him, a fine athlete.

" And my teachers also, the doctor of philosophy, and the music-master, and the logician, they too were determined, and each would have me but a reflection of his own face in a mirror.

" Therefore I came to this place. I find it more sane here. At least, I can be myself."

Then of a sudden he turned to me and he said, " But tell me, were you also driven to this place by education and good counsel? "

And I answered, " No, I am a visitor."

And he said, " Oh, you are one of those who live in the madhouse on the other side of the wall."

THE FROGS

Upon a summer day a frog said to his mate, "I fear those people living in that house on the shore are disturbed by our night-songs."

And his mate answered and said, "Well, do they not annoy our silence during the day with their talking?"

The frog said, "Let us not forget that we may sing too much in the night."

And his mate answered, "Let us not forget that they chatter and shout overmuch during the day."

Said the frog, "How about the bullfrog who disturbs the whole neighborhood with his God-forbidden booming?"

And his mate replied, "Aye, and what say you of the politician and the priest and the scientist who come to these shores and fill the air with noisy and rhymeless sound?"

Then the frog said, "Well, let us be better than

these human beings. Let us be quiet at night, and keep our songs in our hearts, even though the moon calls for our rhythm and the stars for our rhyme. At least, let us be silent for a night or two, or even for three nights."

And his mate said, " Very well, I agree. We shall see what your bountiful heart will bring forth."

That night the frogs were silent; and they were silent the following night also, and again upon the third night.

And strange to relate, the talkative woman who lived in the house beside the lake came down to breakfast on that third day and shouted to her husband, " I have not slept these three nights. I was secure with sleep when the noise of the frogs was in my ear. But something must have happened. They have not sung now for three nights; and I am almost maddened with sleeplessness."

The frog heard this and turned to his mate and said, winking his eye, " And we were almost maddened with our silence, were we not? "

And his mate answered, " Yes, the silence of

the night was heavy upon us. And I can see now that there is no need for us to cease our singing for the comfort of those who must needs fill their emptiness with noise."

And that night the moon called not in vain for their rhythm nor the stars for their rhyme.

LAWS AND LAW-GIVING

Ages ago there was a great king, and he was wise. And he desired to lay laws unto his subjects.

He called upon one thousand wise men of one thousand different tribes to come to his capitol and lay down the laws.

And all this came to pass.

But when the thousand laws written upon parchment were put before the king and he read them, he wept bitterly in his soul, for he had not known that there were one thousand forms of crime in his kingdom.

Then he called his scribe, and with a smile upon his mouth he himself dictated laws. And his laws were but seven.

And the one thousand wise men left him in anger and returned to their tribes with the laws they had laid down. And every tribe followed the laws of its wise men.

Therefore they have a thousand laws even to our own **day**.

It is a great country, but it has one thousand prisons, and the prisons are full of women and men, breakers of a thousand laws.

It is indeed a great country, but the people thereof are descendants of one thousand law-givers and of only one wise king.

YESTERDAY, TODAY AND TOMORROW

I said to my friend, " You see her leaning upon the arm of that man. It was but yesterday that she leaned thus upon my arm."

And my friend said, " And tomorrow she will lean upon mine."

I said, " Behold her sitting close at his side. It was but yesterday she sat close beside me."

And he answered, " Tomorrow she will sit beside me."

I said, " See, she drinks wine from his cup, and yesterday she drank from mine."

And he said, " Tomorrow, from my cup."

Then I said, " See how she gazes at him with love, and with yielding eyes. Yesterday she gazed thus upon me."

And my friend said, " It will be upon me she gazes tomorrow."

I said, " Do you not hear her now murmuring

songs of love into his ears? Those very songs of love she murmured but yesterday into my ears."

And my friend said, " And tomorrow she will murmur them in mine."

I said, " Why see, she is embracing him. It was but yesterday that she embraced me."

And my friend said, " She will embrace me tomorrow."

Then I said, " What a strange woman."

But he answered, " She is like unto life, possessed by all men; and like death, she conquers all men; and like eternity, she enfolds all men."

THE PHILOSOPHER AND THE
COBBLER

There came to a cobbler's shop a philosopher with worn shoes. And the philosopher said to the cobbler, " Please mend my shoes."

And the cobbler said, " I am mending another man's shoes now, and there are still other shoes to patch before I can come to yours. But leave your shoes here, and wear this other pair today, and come tomorrow for your own."

Then the philosopher was indignant, and he said, " I wear no shoes that are not mine own."

And the cobbler said, " Well then, are you in truth a philosopher, and cannot enfold your feet with the shoes of another man? Upon this very street there is another cobbler who understands philosophers better than I do. Go you to him for mending."

BUILDERS OF BRIDGES

In Antioch where the river Assi goes to meet the sea, a bridge was built to bring one half of the city nearer to the other half. It was built of large stones carried down from among the hills, on the backs of the mules of Antioch.

When the bridge was finished, upon a pillar thereof was engraven in Greek and in Aramaic, " This bridge was builded by King Antiochus II."

And all the people walked across the good bridge over the goodly river Assi.

And upon an evening, a youth, deemed by some a little mad, descended to the pillar where the words were engraven, and he covered over the graving with charcoal, and above it he wrote, " The stones of this bridge were brought down from the hills by the mules. In passing to and fro over it you are riding upon the backs of the mules of Antioch, builders of this bridge."

And when the people read what the youth had

written, some of them laughed and some mar-veled. And some said, " Ah yes, we know who has done this. Is he not a little mad? "

But one mule said, laughing, to another mule, " Do you not remember that we did carry those stones? And yet until now it has been said that the bridge was builded by King Antiochus."

THE FIELD OF ZAAD

Upon the road of Zaad a traveler met a man who lived in a nearby village, and the traveler, pointing with his hand to a vast field, asked the man saying, " Was not this the battle-ground where King Ahlam overcame his enemies? "

And the man answered and said, " This has never been a battle-ground. There once stood on this field the great city of Zaad, and it was burnt down to ashes. But now it is a good field, is it not? "

And the traveler and the man parted.

Not a half mile farther the traveler met another man, and pointing to the field again, he said, " So that is where the great city of Zaad once stood? "

And the man said, " There has never been a city in this place. But once there was a monastery here, and it was destroyed by the people of the South Country."

Shortly after, on that very road of Zaad, the

traveler met a third man, and pointing once more to the vast field he said, " Is it not true that this is the place where once there stood a great monastery? "

But the man answered, " There has never been a monastery in this neighborhood, but our fathers and our forefathers have told us that once there fell a great meteor on this field."

Then the traveler walked on, wondering in his heart. And he met a very old man, and saluting him he said, " Sir, upon this road I have met three men who live in the neighborhood and I have asked each of them about this field, and each one denied what the other had said, and each one told me a new tale that the other had not told."

Then the old man raised his head, and answered, " My friend, each and every one of these men told you what was indeed so; but few of us are able to add fact to different fact and make a truth thereof."

THE GOLDEN BELT

Once upon a day two men who met on the road were walking together toward Salamis, the City of Columns. In mid-afternoon they came to a wide river and there was no bridge to cross it. They must needs swim, or seek another road unknown to them.

And they said to one another, " Let us swim. After all, the river is not so wide." And they threw themselves into the water and swam.

And one of the men who had always known rivers and the ways of rivers, in mid-stream suddenly began to lose himself, and to be carried away by the rushing waters; while the other who had never swum before crossed the river straightway and stood upon the farther bank. Then seeing his companion still wrestling with the stream, he threw himself again into the waters and brought him also safely to the shore.

And the man who had been swept away by

the current said, " But you told me you could not swim. How then did you cross that river with such assurance? "

And the second man answered, " My friend, do you see this belt which girdles me? It is full of golden coins that I have earned for my wife and my children, a full year's work. It is the weight of this belt of gold that carried me across the river, to my wife and my children. And my wife and my children were upon my shoulders as I swam."

And the two men walked on together toward Salamis.

THE RED EARTH

Said a tree to a man, " My roots are in the deep red earth, and I shall give you of my fruit."

And the man said to the tree, " How alike we are. My roots are also deep in the red earth. And the red earth gives you power to bestow upon me of your fruit, and the red earth teaches me to receive from you with thanksgiving."

THE FULL MOON

The full **moon rose** in glory upon the town, and all the **dogs of that** town began to bark at the moon.

Only one dog did not bark, and he said to them in a grave voice, " Awake not stillness from her sleep, nor bring you the moon to the earth with your barking."

Then **all** the dogs ceased barking, in awful silence. But the dog who had spoken to them continued barking for silence, the rest of the night.

THE HERMIT PROPHET

Once there lived a hermit prophet, and thrice a moon he would go down to the great city and in the market places he would preach giving and sharing to the people. And he was eloquent, and his fame was upon the land.

Upon an evening three men came to his hermitage and he greeted them. And they said, " You have been preaching giving and sharing, and you have sought to teach those who have much to give unto those who have little; and we doubt not that your fame has brought you riches. Now come and give us of your riches, for we are in need."

And the hermit answered and said, " My friends, I have naught but this bed and this mat and this jug of water. Take them if it is in your desire. I have neither gold nor silver."

Then they looked down with disdain upon him, and turned their faces from him; and the last man stood at the door for a moment, and said, "Oh, you cheat! You fraud! You teach and preach that which you yourself do not perform."

THE OLD, OLD WINE

Once there lived a rich man who was justly proud of his cellar and the wine therein. And there was one jug of ancient vintage kept for some occasion known only to himself.

The governor of the state visited him, and he bethought him and said, " That jug shall not be opened for a mere governor."

And a bishop of the diocese visited him, but he said to himself, " Nay, I will not open that jug. He would not know its value, nor would its aroma reach his nostrils."

The prince of the realm came and supped with him. But he thought, " It is too royal a wine for a mere princeling."

And even on the day when his own nephew was married, he said to himself, " No, not to these guests shall that jug be brought forth."

And the years passed by, and he died, an old

man, and he was buried like unto every seed and acorn.

And upon the day that he was buried the ancient jug was brought out together with other jugs of wine, and it was shared by the peasants of the neighborhood. And none knew its great age.

To them, all that is poured into a cup is only wine.

THE TWO POEMS

Many centuries ago, on a road to Athens, two poets met, and they were glad to see one another.

And one poet asked the other saying, " What have you composed of late, and how goes it with your lyre? "

And the other poet answered and said with pride, " I have but now finished the greatest of my poems, perchance the greatest poem yet written in Greek. It is an invocation to Zeus the Supreme."

Then he took from beneath his cloak a parchment, saying, " Here, behold, I have it with me, and I would fain read it to you. Come, let us sit in the shade of that white cypress."

And the poet read his poem. And it was a long poem.

And the other poet said in kindliness, " This is a great poem. It will live through the ages, and in it you shall be glorified."

And the first poet said calmly, " And what have you been writing these late days? "

And the other answered, " I have written but little. Only eight lines in remembrance of a child playing in a garden." And he recited the lines.

The first poet said, " Not so bad; not so bad."

And they parted.

And now after two thousand years the eight lines of the one poet are read in every tongue, and are loved and cherished.

And though the other poem has indeed come down through the ages in libraries and in the cells of scholars, and though it is remembered, it is neither loved nor read.

Three men once looked from afar upon a white house that stood alone on a green hill. One of them said, " That is the house of Lady Ruth. She is an old witch."

The second man said, " You are wrong. Lady Ruth is a beautiful woman who lives there consecrated unto her dreams."

The third man said, " You are both wrong. Lady Ruth is the holder of this vast land, and she draws blood from her serfs."

And they walked on discussing Lady Ruth.

Then when they came to a crossroad they met an old man, and one of them asked him, saying, " Would you please tell us about Lady Ruth who lives in that white house upon the hill? "

And the old man raised his head and smiled upon them, and said, " I am ninety of years, and I remember Lady Ruth when I was but a boy. But Lady Ruth died eighty years ago, and now the house is empty. The owls hoot therein, sometimes, and people say the place is haunted."

THE MOUSE AND THE CAT

Once on an evening a poet met a peasant. The poet was distant and the peasant was shy, yet they conversed.

And the peasant said, " Let me tell you a little story which I heard of late. A mouse was caught in a trap, and while he was happily eating the cheese that lay therein, a cat stood by. The mouse trembled awhile, but he knew he was safe within the trap.

" Then the cat said, ' You are eating your last meal, my friend.'

" ' Yes,' answered the mouse, ' one life have I, therefore one death. But what of you? They tell me you have nine lives. Doesn't that mean that you will have to die nine times? ' "

And the peasant looked at the poet and he said, " Is not this a strange story? "

And the poet answered him not, but he walked away saying in his soul, " To be sure, nine lives have we, nine lives to be sure. And we shall die nine times, nine times shall we die. Perhaps it were better to have but one life, caught in a trap — the life of a peasant with a bit of cheese for the last meal. And yet, are we not kin unto the lions of the desert and the jungle? "

THE CURSE

An old man of the sea once said to me, " It was thirty years ago that a sailor ran away with my daughter. And I cursed them both in my heart, for of all the world I loved but my daughter.

" Not long after that, the sailor youth went down with his ship to the bottom of the sea, and with him my lovely daughter was lost unto me.

" Now therefore behold in me the murderer of a youth and a maid. It was my curse that destroyed them. And now on my way to the grave I seek God's forgiveness."

This the old man said. But there was a tone of bragging in his words, and it seems that he is still proud of the power of his curse.

THE POMEGRANATES

There was once a man who had many pomegranate trees in his orchard. And for many an autumn he would put his pomegranates on silvery trays outside of his dwelling, and upon the trays he would place signs upon which he himself had written, "Take one for aught. You are welcome."

But people passed by and no one took of the fruit.

Then the man bethought him, and one autumn he placed no pomegranates on silvery trays outside of his dwelling, but he raised this sign in large lettering: " Here we have the best pomegranates in the land, but we sell them for more silver than any other pomegranates."

And now behold, all the men and women of the neighborhood came rushing to buy.

GOD AND MANY GODS

In the city of Kilafis a sophist stood on the steps of the Temple and preached many gods. And the people said in their hearts, " We know all this. Do they not live with us and follow us wherever we go? "

Not long after, another man stood in the market place and spoke unto the people and said, " There is no god." And many who heard him were glad of his tidings, for they were afraid of gods.

And upon another day there came a man of great eloquence, and he said, " There is but one God." And now the poeple were dismayed for in their hearts they feared the judgment of one God more than that of many gods.

That same season there came yet another man, and he said to the people, " There are three gods, and they dwell upon the wind as one, and they have a vast and gracious mother who is also their mate and their sister."

Then everyone was comforted, for they said in their secret, "Three gods in one must needs disagree over our failings, and besides, their gracious mother will surely be an advocate for us poor weaklings."

Yet even to this day there are those in the city of Kilafis who wrangle and argue with each other about many gods and no god, and one god and three gods in one, and a gracious mother of gods.

SHE WHO WAS DEAF

Once there lived a rich man who had a young wife, and she was stone deaf.

And upon a morning when they were breaking their fast, she spoke to him and she said, "Yesterday I visited the market place, and there were exhibited silken raiment from Damascus, and coverchiefs from India, necklaces from Persia, and bracelets from Yamman. It seems that the caravans had but just brought these things to our city. And now behold me, in rags, yet the wife of a rich man. I would have some of those beautiful things."

The husband, still busy with his morning coffee said, "My dear, there is *no* reason why you should not go down to the Street and buy all that your heart may desire."

And the deaf wife said, "' *No!* ' You always say, 'No, no.' Must I needs appear in tatters among our friends to shame your wealth and my people? "

And the husband said, "I did not say, ' *No.*' You may go forth freely to the market place and purchase the most beautiful apparel and jewels that have come to our city."

But again the wife mis-read his words, and she replied, " Of all rich men you are the most miserly. You would deny me everything of beauty and loveliness, while other women of my age walk the gardens of the city clothed in rich raiment."

And she began to weep. And as her tears fell upon her breast she cried out again, " You always say, ' Nay, nay ' to me when I desire a garment or a jewel."

Then the husband was moved, and he stood up and took out of his purse a handful of gold and placed it before her, saying in a kindly voice, " Go down to the market place, my dear, and buy all that you will."

From that day onward the deaf young wife, whenever she desired anything, would appear before her husband with a pearly tear in her eye, and he in silence would take out a handful of gold and place it in her lap.

Now, it chanced that the young woman fell in love with a youth whose habit it was to make long journeys. And whenever he was away she would sit in her casement and weep.

When her husband found her thus weeping, he would say in his heart, " There must be some new caravan, and some silken garments and rare jewels in the Street."

And he would take a handful of gold and place it before her.

THE QUEST

A thousand years ago two philosophers met on a slope of Lebanon, and one said to the other, " Where goest thou? "

And the other answered, " I am seeking after the fountain of youth which I know wells out among these hills. I have found writings which tell of that fountain flowering toward the sun. And you, what are you seeking? "

The first man answered, " I am seeking after the mystery of death."

Then each of the two philosophers conceived that the other was lacking in his great science, and they began to wrangle, and to accuse each other of spiritual blindness.

Now while the two philosophers were loud upon the wind, a stranger, a man who was deemed a simpleton in his own village, passed by, and when he heard the two in hot dispute, he stood awhile and listened to their argument.

Then he came near to them and said, " My good men, it seems that you both really belong to the same school of philosophy, and that you are speaking of the same thing, only you speak in different words. One of you seeks the fountain of youth, and the other seeks the mystery of death. Yet indeed they are but one, and as one they dwell in you both."

Then the stranger turned away saying, " Farewell, sages." And as he departed he laughed a patient laughter.

The two philosophers looked at each other in silence for a moment, and then they laughed also. And one of them said, " Well now, shall we not walk and seek together? "

THE SCEPTRE

Said a king to his wife, " Madame, you are not truly a queen. You are too vulgar and ungracious to be my mate."

Said his wife, " Sir, you deem yourself king, but indeed you are only a poor soundling."

Now these words angered the king, and he took his sceptre with his hand, and struck the queen upon her forehead with his golden sceptre.

At that moment the lord chamberlain entered, and he said, " Well, well, Majesty! That sceptre was fashioned by the greatest artist of the land. Alas! Some day you and the queen shall be forgotten, but this sceptre shall be kept, a thing of beauty from generation to generation. And now that you have drawn blood from her Majesty's head, Sire, the sceptre shall be the more considered and remembered."

THE PATH

There lived among the hills a woman and her son, and he was her first-born and her only child.

And the boy died of a fever whilst the physician stood by.

The mother was distraught with sorrow, and she cried to the physician and besought him saying, " Tell me, tell me, what was it that made quiet his striving and silent his song? "

And the physician said, " It was the fever."

And the mother said, " What is the fever? "

And the physician answered, " I cannot explain it. It is a thing infinitely small that visits the body, and we cannot see it with our human eye."

Then the physician left her. And she kept repeating to herself, " something infinitely small. We cannot see it with our human eye."

And at evening the priest came to console her. And she wept and she cried out saying, " Oh, why have I lost my son, my only son, my first-born? "

And the priest answered, " My child, it is the will of God."

And the woman said, " What is God and where is God? I would see God that I may tear my bosom before Him, and pour the blood of my heart at His feet. Tell me where I shall find Him."

And the priest said, " God is infinitely vast. He is not to be seen with our human eye."

Then the woman cried out, " The infinitely small has slain my son through the will of the infinitely great! Then what are we? What are we? "

At that moment the woman's mother came into the room with the shroud for the dead boy, and she heard the words of the priest and also her daughter's cry. And she laid down the shroud, and took her daughter's hand in her own hand, and she said, " My daughter, we ourselves are the infinitely small and the infinitely great; and we are the path between the two."

THE WHALE
AND THE BUTTERFLY

Once on an evening a man and a woman found themselves together in a stagecoach. They had met before.

The man was a poet, and as he sat beside the woman he sought to amuse her with stories, some that were of his own weaving, and some that were not his own.

But even while he was speaking the lady went to sleep. Then suddenly the coach lurched, and she awoke, and she said, " I admire your interpretation of the story of Jonah and the whale."

And the poet said, " But Madame, I have been telling you a story of mine own about a butterfly and a white rose, and how they behaved the one to the other! "

PEACE CONTAGIOUS

One branch in bloom said to his neighboring branch, " This is a dull and empty day." And the other branch answered, " It is indeed empty and dull."

At that moment a sparrow alighted on one of the branches, and then another sparrow, nearby.

And one of the sparrows chirped and said, " My mate has left me."

And the other sparrow cried, " My mate has also gone, and she will not return. And what care I? "

Then the two began to twitter and scold, and soon they were fighting and making harsh noise upon the air.

All of a sudden two other sparrows came sailing from the sky, and they sat quietly beside the restless two. And there was calm, and there was peace.

Then the four flew away together in pairs.

And the first branch said to his neighboring branch, " That was a mighty zig-zag of sound." And the other branch answered, " Call it what you will, it is now both peaceful and spacious. And if the upper air makes peace it seems to me that those who dwell in the lower might make peace also. Will you not wave in the wind a little nearer to me? "

And the first branch said, " Oh, perchance, for peace' sake, ere the Spring is over."

And then he waved himself with the strong wind to embrace her.

THE SHADOW

Upon a June day the grass said to the shadow of an elm tree, " You move to right and left over-often, and you disturb my peace."

And the shadow answered and said, " Not I, not I. Look skyward. There is a tree that moves in the wind to the east and to the west, between the sun and the earth."

And the grass looked up, and for the first time beheld the tree. And it said in its heart, " Why, behold, there is a larger grass than myself."

And the grass was silent.

SEVENTY

The poet youth said to the princess, "I love you." And the princess answered, "And I love you too, my child."

"But I am not your child. I am a man and I love you."

And she said, "I am the mother of sons and daughters, and they are fathers and mothers of sons and daughters; and one of the sons of my sons is older than you."

And the poet youth said, "But I love you."

It was not long after that the princess died. But ere her last breath was received again by the greater breath of earth, she said within her soul, "My beloved, mine only son, my youth-poet, it may yet be that some day we shall meet again, and I shall not be seventy."

FINDING GOD

Two men were walking in the valley, and one man pointed with his finger toward the mountain side, and said, " See you that hermitage? There lives a man who has long divorced the world. He seeks but after God, and naught else upon this earth."

And the other man said, " He shall not find God until he leaves his hermitage, and the aloneness of his hermitage, and returns to our world, to share our joy and pain, to dance with our dancers at the wedding feast, and to weep with those who weep around the coffins of our dead."

And the other man was convinced in his heart, though in spite of his conviction he answered, " I agree with all that you say, yet I believe the hermit is a good man. And may it not well be that one good man by his absence does better than the seeming goodness of these many men? "

THE RIVER

In the valley of Kadisha where the mighty river flows, two little streams met and spoke to one another.

One stream said, " How came you, my friend, and how was your path? "

And the other answered, " My path was most encumbered. The wheel of the mill was broken, and the master farmer who used to conduct me from my channel to his plants, is dead. I struggled down oozing with the filth of those who do naught but sit and bake their laziness in the sun. But how was your path, my brother? "

And the other stream answered and said, " Mine was a different path. I came down the hills among fragrant flowers and shy willows; men and women drank of me with silvery cups, and little children paddled their rosy feet at my edges, and there was laughter all about me, and there were sweet songs. What a pity that your path was not so happy."

At that moment the river spoke with a loud voice and said, " Come in, come in, we are going to the sea. Come in, come in, speak no more. Be with me now. We are going to the sea. Come in, come in, for in me you shall forget your wanderings, sad or gay. Come in, come in. And you and I will forget all our ways when we reach the heart of our mother the sea."

THE TWO HUNTERS

Upon a day in May, Joy and Sorrow met beside a lake. They greeted one another, and they sat down near the quiet waters and conversed.

Joy spoke of the beauty which is upon the earth, and of the daily wonder of life in the forest and among the hills, and of the songs heard at dawn and eventide.

And Sorrow spoke, and agreed with all that Joy had said; for Sorrow knew the magic of the hour and the beauty thereof. And Sorrow was eloquent when he spoke of May in the fields and among the hills.

And Joy and Sorrow talked long together, and they agreed upon all things of which they knew.

Now there passed by on the other side of the lake two hunters. And as they looked across the water one of them said, " I wonder who are those two persons? " And the other said, " Did you say two? I see only one."

The first hunter said, " But there are two." And the second said, " There is only one that I can see, and the reflection in the lake is only one."

" Nay, there are two," said the first hunter, " and the reflection in the still water is of two persons."

But the second man said again, " Only one do I see." And again the other said, " But I see two so plainly."

And even to this day one hunter says that the other sees double; while the other says, " My friend is somewhat blind."

THE OTHER WANDERER

Once on a time I met another man of the roads. He too was a little mad, and thus he spoke to me: " I am a wanderer. Oftentimes it seems that I walk the earth among pygmies. And because my head is seventy cubits farther from the earth than theirs, it creates higher and freer thoughts.

" But in truth I walk not among men but above them, and all they can see of me is my footprints in their open fields.

" And often have I heard them discuss and disagree over the shape and size of my footprints. For there are some who say, ' These are the tracks of a mammoth that roamed the earth in the far past.' And others say, ' Nay, these are places where meteors have fallen from the distant stars.'

" But you, my friend, you know full well that they are naught save the footprints of a wanderer."

BOOK THREE

BOOK THREE

SAND AND FOAM

I am forever walking upon these shores,
Betwixt the sand and the foam.
The high tide will erase my foot-prints,
And the wind will blow away the foam.
But the sea and the shore will remain
Forever.

Once I filled my hand with mist.

Then I opened it and lo, the mist was a worm.

And I closed and opened my hand again, and behold there was a bird.

And again I closed and opened my hand, and in its hollow stood a man with a sad face, turned upward.

And again I closed my hand, and when I opened it there was naught but mist.

But I heard a song of exceeding sweetness.

It was but yesterday I thought myself a fragment quivering without rhythm in the sphere of life.

Now I know that I am the sphere, and all life in rhythmic fragments moves within me.

They say to me in their awakening, "You and the world you live in are but a grain of sand upon the infinite shore of an infinite sea."

And in my dream I say to them, "I am the infinite sea, and all worlds are but grains of sand upon my shore."

Only once have I been made mute. It was when a man asked me, "Who are you?"

The first thought of God was an angel.
The first word of God was a man.

We were fluttering, wandering, longing creatures a thousand thousand years
before the sea and the wind in the forest
gave us words.

Now how can we express the ancient of
days in us with only the sounds of our yesterdays?

The Sphinx spoke only once, and the
Sphinx said, "A grain of sand is a desert,
and a desert is a grain of sand; and now
let us all be silent again."

I heard the Sphinx, but I did not understand.

3

Once I saw the face of a woman, and I beheld all her children not yet born.

And a woman looked upon my face and she knew all my forefathers, dead before she was born.

Now would I fulfill myself. But how shall I unless I become a planet with intelligent lives dwelling upon it?

Is not this every man's goal?

A pearl is a temple built by pain around a grain of sand.

What longing built our bodies and around what grains?

When God threw me, a pebble, into this wondrous lake I disturbed its surface with countless circles.

But when I reached the depths I became very still.

Give me silence and I will outdare the night.

I had a second birth when my soul and my body loved one another and were married.

Once I knew a man whose ears were exceedingly keen, but he was dumb. He had lost his tongue in a battle.

I know now what battles that man fought before the great silence came. I am glad he is dead.

The world is not large enough for two of us.

Long did I lie in the dust of Egypt, silent and unaware of the seasons.

Then the sun gave me birth, and I rose and walked upon the banks of the Nile,

Singing with the days and dreaming with the nights.

And now the sun treads upon me with a thousand feet that I may lie again in the dust of Egypt.

But behold a marvel and a riddle!

The very sun that gathered me cannot scatter me.

Still erect am I, and sure of foot do I walk upon the banks of the Nile

Remembrance is a form of meeting.

Forgetfulness is a form of freedom.

6

We measure time according to the movement of countless suns; and they measure time by little machines in their little pockets.

Now tell me, how could we ever meet at the same place and the same time?

Space is not space between the earth and the sun to one who looks down from the windows of the Milky Way.

Humanity is a river of light running from ex-eternity to eternity.

Do not the spirits who dwell in the ether envy man his pain?

On my way to the Holy City I met another pilgrim and I asked him, "Is this indeed the way to the Holy City?"

And he said, "Follow me, and you will reach the Holy City in a day and a night."

And I followed him. And we walked many days and many nights, yet we did not reach the Holy City.

And what was to my surprise he became angry with me because he had misled me.

Make me, oh God, the prey of the lion, ere You make the rabbit my prey.

One may not reach the dawn save by the path of the night.

My house says to me, "Do not leave me, for here dwells your past."

And the road says to me, "Come and follow me, for I am your future."

And I say to both my house and the road, "I have no past, nor have I a future. If I stay here, there is a going in my staying; and if I go there is a staying in my going. Only love and death change all things."

How can I lose faith in the justice of life, when the dreams of those who sleep upon feathers are not more beautiful than the dreams of those who sleep upon the earth?

Strange, the desire for certain pleasures is a part of my pain.

Seven times have I despised my soul:

The first time when I saw her being meek that she might attain height.

The second time when I saw her limping before the crippled.

The third time when she was given to choose between the hard and the easy, and she chose the easy.

The fourth time when she committed a wrong, and comforted herself that others also commit wrong.

The fifth time when she forbore for weakness, and attributed her patience to strength.

The sixth time when she despised the ugliness of a face, and knew not that it was one of her own masks.

And the seventh time when she sang a song of praise, and deemed it a virtue.

I am ignorant of absolute truth. But I am humble before my ignorance and therein lies my honor and my reward.

There is a space between man's imagination and man's attainment that may only be traversed by his longing.

Paradise is there, behind that door, in the next room; but I have lost the key. Perhaps I have only mislaid it.

You are blind and I am deaf and dumb, so let us touch hands and understand.

The significance of man is not in what he attains, but rather in what he longs to attain.

Some of us are like ink and some like paper.

And if it were not for the blackness of some of us, some of us would be dumb;

And if it were not for the whiteness of some of us, some of us would be blind.

Give me an ear and I will give you a voice.

Our mind is a sponge; our heart is a stream.

Is it not strange that most of us choose sucking rather than running?

When you long for blessings that you may not name, and when you grieve knowing not the cause, then indeed you are growing with all things that grow, and rising toward your greater self.

When one is drunk with a vision, he deems his faint expression of it the very wine.

You drink wine that you may be intoxicated; and I drink that it may sober me from that other wine.

When my cup is empty I resign myself to its emptiness; but when it is half full I resent its half-fulness.

The reality of the other person is not in what he reveals to you, but in what he cannot reveal to you.

Therefore, if you would understand him, listen not to what he says but rather to what he does not say.

Half of what I say is meaningless; but I say it so that the other half may reach you.

A sense of humor is a sense of proportion.

My loneliness was born when men praised my talkative faults and blamed my silent virtues.

When Life does not find a singer to sing her heart she produces a philosopher to speak her mind.

A truth is to be known always, to be uttered sometimes.

The real in us is silent; the acquired is talkative.

The voice of life in me cannot reach the ear of life in you; but let us talk that we may not feel lonely.

When two women talk they say nothing; when one woman speaks she reveals all of life.

Frogs may bellow louder than bulls, but they cannot drag the plough in the field nor turn the wheel of the winepress, and of their skins you cannot make shoes.

Only the dumb envy the talkative.

If winter should say, "Spring is in my heart," who would believe winter?

Every seed is a longing.

Should you really open your eyes and see, you would behold your image in all images.

And should you open your ears and listen, you would hear your own voice in all voices.

It takes two of us to discover truth: one to utter it and one to understand it.

Though the wave of words is forever upon us, yet our depth is forever silent.

Many a doctrine is like a window pane. We see truth through it but it divides us from truth.

Now let us play hide and seek. Should you hide in my heart it would not be difficult to find you. But should you hide behind your own shell, then it would be useless for anyone to seek you.

A woman may veil her face with a smile.

How noble is the sad heart who would sing a joyous song with joyous hearts.

He who would understand a woman, or dissect genius, or solve the mystery of silence is the very man who would wake from a beautiful dream to sit at a breakfast table.

I would walk with all those who walk.
I would not stand still to watch **the** procession passing by.

You owe more than gold to him who
serves you. Give him of your heart or
serve him.

Nay, we have not lived in vain. Have
they not built towers of our bones?

Let us not be particular and sectional.
The poet's mind and the scorpion's tail
rise in glory from the same earth.

Every dragon gives birth to a St. George
who slays it.

19

Trees are poems that the earth writes upon the sky. We fell them down and turn them into paper that we may record our emptiness.

Should you care to write (and only the saints know why you should) you must needs have knowledge and art and magic —the knowledge of the music of words, the art of being artless, and the magic of loving your readers.

They dip their pens in our hearts and think they are inspired.

Should a tree write its autobiography it would not be unlike the history of a race.

If I were to choose between the power of writing a poem and the ecstasy of a poem unwritten, I would choose the ecstasy. It is better poetry.

But you and all my neighbors agree that I always choose badly.

Poetry is not an opinion expressed. It is a song that rises from a bleeding wound or a smiling mouth.

Words are timeless. You should utter them or write them with a knowledge of their timelessness.

A poet is a dethroned king sitting among the ashes of his palace trying to fashion an image out of the ashes.

Poetry is a deal of joy and pain and wonder, with a dash of the dictionary.

In vain shall a poet seek the mother of the songs of his heart.

Once I said to a poet, "We shall not know your worth until you die."

And he answered saying, "Yes, death is always the revealer. And if indeed you would know my worth it is that I have more in my heart than upon my tongue, and more in my desire than in my hand."

If you sing of beauty though alone in the heart of the desert you will have an audience.

Poetry is wisdom that enchants the heart.

Wisdom is poetry that sings in the mind.

If we could enchant man's heart and at the same time sing in his mind,

Then in truth he would live in the shadow of God.

Inspiration will always sing; inspiration will never explain.

We often sing lullabyes to our children that we ourselves may sleep.

All our words are but crumbs that fall down from the feast of the mind.

Thinking is always the stumbling stone to poetry.

A great singer is he who sings our silences.

How can you sing if your mouth be filled with food?

How shall your hand be raised in blessing if it is filled with gold?

They say the nightingale pierces his bosom with a thorn when he sings his love song.

So do we all. How else should we sing?

Genius is but a robin's song at the beginning of a slow spring.

Even the most winged spirit cannot escape physical necessity.

A madman is not less a musician than you or myself; only the instrument on which he plays is a little out of tune.

The song that lies silent in the heart of a mother sings upon the lips of her child.

No longing remains unfulfilled.

I have never agreed with my other self wholly. The truth of the matter seems to lie between us.

Your other self is always sorry for you. But your other self grows on sorrow; so all is well.

There is no struggle of soul and body save in the minds of those whose souls are asleep and whose bodies are out of tune.

When you reach the heart of life you shall find beauty in all things, even in the eyes that are blind to beauty.

We live only to discover beauty. All else is a form of waiting.

Sow a seed and the earth will yield you a flower. Dream your dream to the sky and it will bring you your beloved.

The devil died the very day you were born.

Now you do not have to go through hell to meet an angel.

Many a woman borrows a man's heart; very few could possess it.

If you would possess you must not claim.

When a man's hand touches the hand of a woman they both touch the heart of eternity.

Love is the veil between lover and lover.

Every man loves two women; the one is the creation of his imagination, and the other is not yet born.

Men who do not forgive women their little faults will never enjoy their great virtues.

Love that does not renew itself every day becomes a habit and in turn a slavery.

28

Lovers embrace that which is between them rather than each other.

Love and doubt have never been on speaking terms.

Love is a word of light, written by a hand of light, upon a page of light.

Friendship is always a sweet responsibility, never an opportunity.

If you do not understand your friend under all conditions you will never understand him.

Your most radiant garment is of the other person's weaving;

Your most savory meal is that which you eat at the other person's table;

Your most comfortable bed is in the other person's house.

Now tell me, how can you separate yourself from the other person?

Your mind and my heart will never agree until your mind ceases to live in numbers and my heart in the mist.

We shall never understand one another until we reduce the language to seven words.

How shall my heart be unsealed unless it be broken?

Only great sorrow or great joy can reveal your truth.

If you would be revealed you must either dance naked in the sun, or carry your cross.

Should nature heed what we say of contentment no river would seek the sea, and no winter would turn to Spring. Should she heed all we say of thrift, how many of us would be breathing this air?

You see but your shadow when you turn your back to the sun.

31

You are free before the sun of the day, and free before the stars of the night;

And you are free when there is no sun and no moon and no star.

You are even free when you close your eyes upon all there is.

But you are a slave to him whom you love because you love him,

And a slave to him who loves you because he loves you.

We are all beggars at the gate of the temple, and each one of us receives his share of the bounty of the King when he enters the temple, and when he goes out.

But we are all jealous of one another, which is another way of belittling the King.

You cannot consume beyond your appetite. The other half of the loaf belongs to the other person, and there should remain a little bread for the chance guest.

If it were not for guests all houses would be graves.

Said a gracious wolf to a simple sheep, "Will you not honor our house with a visit?"

And the sheep answered: "We would have been honored to visit your house if it were not in your stomach."

I stopped my guest on the threshold and said, "Nay, wipe not your feet as you enter, but as you go out."

Generosity is not in giving me that which I need more than you do, but it is in giving me that which you need more than I do.

You are indeed charitable when you give, and while giving, turn your face away so that you may not see the shyness of the receiver.

The difference between the richest man and the poorest is but a day of hunger and an hour of thirst.

We often borrow from our tomorrows to pay our debts to our yesterdays.

I too am visited by angels and devils,
but I get rid of them.

When it is an angel I pray an old
prayer, and he is bored;

When it is a devil I commit an old sin,
and he passes me by.

After all this is not a bad prison; but I
do not like this wall between my cell and
the next prisoner's cell;

Yet I assure you that I do not wish to
reproach the warder nor the Builder of the
prison.

Those who give you a serpent when you
ask for a fish, may have nothing but serpents to give. It is then generosity on
their part.

Trickery succeeds sometimes, but it always commits suicide.

You are truly a forgiver when you forgive murderers who never spill blood, thieves who never steal, and liars who utter no falsehood.

He who can put his finger upon that which divides good from evil is he who can touch the very hem of the garment of God.

If your heart is a volcano how shall you expect flowers to bloom in your hands?

A strange form of self-indulgence! There are times when I would be wronged and cheated, that I may laugh at the expense of those who think I do not know I am being wronged and cheated.

What shall I say of him who is the pursuer playing the part of the pursued?

Let him who wipes his soiled hands with your garment take your garment. He may need it again; surely you would not.

It is a pity that money-changers cannot be good gardners.

Please do not whitewash your inherent
faults with your acquired virtues. I
would have the faults; they are like mine
own.

How often have I attributed to myself
crimes I have never committed, so that the
other person may feel comfortable in my
presence.

Even the masks of life are masks of
deeper mystery.

You may judge others only according
to your knowledge of yourself.

Tell me now, who among us is guilty
and who is unguilty?

The truly just is he who feels half guilty of your misdeeds.

Only an idiot and a genius break man-made laws; and they are the nearest to the heart of God.

It is only when you are pursued that you become swift.

I have no enemies, O God, but if I am to have an enemy
Let his strength be equal to mine,
That truth alone may be the victor.

You will be quite friendly with your enemy when you both die.

Perhaps a man may commit suicide in self-defense.

Long ago there lived a Man who was crucified for being too loving and too lovable.

And strange to relate I met him thrice yesterday.

The first time He was asking a policeman not to take a prostitute to prison; the second time He was drinking wine with an outcast; and the third time He was having a fist-fight with a promoter inside a church.

If all they say of good and evil were true, then my life is but one long crime.

Pity is but half justice.

The only one who has been unjust to
me is the one to whose brother I have been
unjust.

When you see a man led to prison say
in your heart, "Mayhap he is escaping
from a narrower prison."

And when you see a man drunken say
in your heart, "Mayhap he sought escape
from something still more unbeautiful."

Oftentimes I have hated in self-
defense; but if I were stronger I would
not have used such a weapon.

How stupid is he who would patch the
hatred in his eyes with the smile of his
lips.

41

Only those beneath me can envy or hate me.

I have never been envied nor hated; I am above no one.

Only those above me can praise or belittle me.

I have never been praised nor belittled; I am below no one.

Your saying to me, "I do not understand you," is praise beyond my worth, and an insult you do not deserve.

How mean am I when life gives me gold and I give you silver, and yet I deem myself generous.

When you reach the heart of life you will find yourself not higher than the felon, and not lower than the prophet.

Strange that you should pity the slow-footed and not the slow-minded,

And the blind-eyed rather than the blind-hearted.

It is wiser for the lame not to break his crutches upon the head of his enemy.

How blind is he who gives you out of his pocket that he may take out of your heart.

Life is a procession.   The slow of foot finds it too swift and he steps out;

And the swift of foot finds it too slow and he too steps out.

If there is such a thing as sin some of us commit it backward following our forefathers footsteps;

And some of us commit it forward by overruling our children.

The truly good is he who is one with all those who are deemed bad.

We are all prisoners but some of us are in cells with windows and some without.

Strange that we all defend our wrongs with more vigor than we do our rights.

Should we all confess our sins to one another we would all laugh at one another for our lack of originality.

Should we all reveal our virtues we would also laugh for the same cause.

An individual is above man-made laws until he commits a crime against man-made conventions;
After that he is neither above anyone nor lower than anyone.

Government is an agreement between you and myself. You and myself are often wrong.

Crime is either another name of need or an aspect of a disease.

Is there a greater fault than being conscious of the other person's faults?

If the other person laughs at you, you can pity him; but if you laugh at him you may never forgive yourself.

If the other person injures you, you may forget the injury; but if you injure him you will always remember.

In truth the other person is your most sensitive self given another body.

How heedless you are when you would have men fly with your wings and you cannot even give them a feather.

Once a man sat at my board and ate my bread and drank my wine and went away laughing at me.

Then he came again for bread and wine, and I spurned him;

And the angels laughed at me.

Hate is a dead thing. Who of you would be a tomb?

It is the honor of the murdered that he is not the murderer.

The tribune of humanity is in its silent heart never its talkative mind.

They deem me mad because I will not sell my days for gold;

And I deem them mad because they think my days have a price.

They spread before us their riches of gold and silver, of ivory and ebony, and we spread before them our hearts and our spirits;

And yet they deem themselves the hosts and us the guests.

I would be the least among men with dreams and the desire to fulfill them, rather than the greatest with no dreams and no desires.

The most pitiful among men is he who turns his dreams into silver and gold.

~⚜~⚜~⚜~

We are all climbing toward the summit of our hearts' desire. Should the other climber steal your sack and your purse and wax fat on the one and heavy on the other, you should pity him;

The climbing will be harder for his flesh, and the burden will make his way longer.

And should you in your leanness see his flesh puffing upward, help him a step; it will add to your swiftness.

~⚜~⚜~

You cannot judge any man beyond your knowledge of him, and how small is your knowledge.

49

I would not listen to a conqueror preaching to the conquered.

The truly free man is he who bears the load of the bond slave patiently.

A thousand years ago my neighbor said to me, "I hate life, for it is naught but a thing of pain."

And yesterday I passed by a cemetery and saw life dancing upon his grave.

Strife in nature is but disorder longing for order.

Solitude is a silent storm that breaks down all our dead branches;

Yet it sends our living roots deeper into the living heart of the living earth.

Once I spoke of the sea to a brook, and the brook thought me but an imaginative exaggerator;

And once I spoke of a brook to the sea, and the sea thought me but a depreciative defamer.

How narrow is the vision that exalts the busyness of the ant above the singing of the grasshopper.

The highest virtue here may be the least in another world.

The deep and the high go to the depth or to the height in a straight line; only the spacious can move in circles.

If it were not for our conception of weights and measures we would stand in awe of the firefly as we do before the sun.

A scientist without imagination is a butcher with dull knives and out-worn scales.

But what would you, since we are not all vegetarians?

When you sing the hungry hears you with his stomach.

Death is not nearer to the aged than to the new-born; neither is life.

If indeed you must be candid, be candid beautifully; otherwise keep silent, for there is a man in our neighborhood who is dying.

Mayhap a funeral among men is a wedding feast among the angels.

A forgotten reality may die and leave in its will seven thousand actualities and facts to be spent in its funeral and the b ilding of a tomb.

In truth we talk only to ourselves, but sometimes we talk loud enough that others may hear us.

The obvious is that which is never seen until someone expresses it simply.

If the Milky Way were not within me how should I have seen it or known it?

Unless I am a physician among physicians they would not believe that I am an astronomer.

Perhaps the sea's definition of a shell is the pearl.

Perhaps time's definition of coal is the diamond.

Fame is the shadow of passion standing in the light.

A root is a flower that disdains fame.

There is neither religion nor science beyond beauty.

Every great man I have known had
something small in his make-up; and it
was that small something which prevented
inactivity or madness or suicide.

The truly great man is he who would
master no one, and who would be mas-
tered by none.

I would not believe that man is a medi-
ocre simply because he kills the criminals
and the prophets.

Tolerance is love sick with the sickness
of haughtiness.

Worms will turn; but is it not strange that even elephants will yield?

A disagreement may be the shortest cut between two minds.

I am the flame and I am the dry brush, and one part of me consumes the other part.

We are all seeking the summit of the holy mountain; but shall not our road be shorter if we consider the past a chart and not a guide?

Wisdom ceases to be wisdom when it becomes too proud to weep, too grave to laugh, and too self-ful to seek other than itself.

Had I filled myself with all that you know what room should I have for all that you do not know?

I have learned silence from the talkative, toleration from the intolerant, and kindness from the unkind; yet strange, I am ungrateful to these teachers.

A bigot is a stone-deaf orator.

The silence of the envious is too noisy.

When you reach the end of what you should know, you will be at the beginning of what you should sense.

An exaggeration is a truth that has lost its temper.

If you can see only what light reveals and hear only what sound announces,

Then in truth you do not see nor do you hear.

A fact is a truth unsexed.

You cannot laugh and be unkind at the same time.

The nearest to my heart are a king without a kingdom and a poor man who does not know how to beg.

A shy failure is nobler than an immodest success.

Dig anywhere in the earth and you will find a treasure, only you must dig with the faith of a peasant.

Said a hunted fox followed by twenty horsemen and a pack of twenty hounds, "Of course they will kill me. But how poor and how stupid they must be. Surely it would not be worth while for twenty foxes riding on twenty asses and accompanied by twenty wolves to chase and kill one man."

It is the mind in us that yields to the laws made by us, but never the spirit in us.

A traveler am I and a navigator, and every day I discover a new region within my soul.

A woman protested saying, "Of course it was a righteous war. My son fell in it."

I said to Life, "I would hear Death speak."

And Life raised her voice a little higher and said, "You hear him now."

When you have solved all the mysteries of life you long for death, for it is but another mystery of life.

Birth and death are the two noblest expressions of bravery.

My friend, you and I shall remain strangers unto life,

And unto one another, and each unto himself,

Until the day when you shall speak and and I shall listen

Deeming your voice my own voice;

And when I shall stand before you

Thinking myself standing before a mirror.

They say to me, "Should you know yourself you would know all men."

And I say, "Only when I seek all men shall I know myself."

Man is two men; one is awake in darkness, the other is asleep in light.

A hermit is one who renounces the world of fragments that he may enjoy the world wholly and without interruption.

There lies a green field between the scholar and the poet; should the scholar cross it he becomes a wise man; should the poet cross it, he becomes a prophet.

Yestereve I saw philosophers in the market-place carrying their heads in baskets, and crying aloud, "Wisdom! Wisdom for sale!"

Poor philosophers! They must needs sell their heads to feed their hearts.

Said a philosopher to a street sweeper, "I pity you. Yours is a hard and dirty task."

And the street sweeper said, "Thank you, sir. But tell me what is your task?"

And the philosopher answered saying, "I study man's mind, his deeds and his desires."

Then the street sweeper went on with his sweeping and said with a smile, "I pity you too."

He who listens to truth is not less than he who utters truth.

No man can draw the line between necessities and luxuries. Only the angels can do that, and the angels are wise and wistful.

Perhaps the angels are our better thoughts in space.

He is the true prince who finds his throne in the heart of the dervish.

Generosity is giving more than you can, and pride is taking less than you need.

In truth you owe naught to any man. You owe all to all men.

All those who have lived in the past live with us now. Surely none of us would be an ungracious host.

He who longs the most lives the longest.

They say to me, "A bird in the hand is worth ten in the bush."

But I say, "A bird and a feather in the bush is worth more than ten birds in the hand."

Your seeking after *that feather* is life with winged feet; nay, it is life itself.

There are only two elements here, beauty and truth; beauty in the hearts of lovers, and truth in the arms of the tillers of the soil.

Great beauty captures me, but a beauty still greater frees me even from itself.

Beauty shines brighter in the heart of him who longs for it than in the eyes of him who sees it.

67

I admire the man who reveals his mind to me; I honor him who unveils his dreams. But why am I shy, and even a little ashamed before him who serves me?

The gifted were once proud in serving princes.

Now they claim honor in serving paupers.

The angels know that too many practical men eat their bread with the sweat of the dreamer's brow.

Wit is often a mask. If you could tear it you would find either a genius irritated or cleverness juggling.

The understanding attributes to me understanding and the dull, dullness. I think they are both right.

Only those with secrets in their hearts could divine the secrets in our hearts.

He who would share your pleasure but not your pain shall lose the key to one of the seven gates of Paradise.

Yes, there is a Nirvanah; it is in leading your sheep to a green pasture, and in putting your child to sleep, and in writing the last line of your poem.

We choose our joys and our sorrows
long before we experience them.

Sadness is but a wall between two gardens.

When either your joy or your sorrow
becomes great the world becomes small.

Desire is half of life; indifference is
half of death.

The bitterest thing in our today's sorrow is the memory of our yesterday's joy.

They say to me, "You must needs choose between the pleasures of this world and the peace of the next world."

And I say to them, "I have chosen both the delights of this world and the peace of the next. For I know in my heart that the Supreme Poet wrote but one poem, and it scans perfectly, and it also rhymes perfectly."

Faith is an oasis in the heart which will never be reached by the caravan of thinking.

When you reach your height you shall desire but only for desire; and you shall hunger, for hunger; and you shall thirst for greater thirst.

If you reveal your secrets to the wind you should not blame the wind for revealing them to the trees.

The flowers of spring are winter's dreams related at the breakfast table of the angels.

Said a skunk to a tube-rose, "See how swiftly I run, while you cannot walk nor even creep."

Said the tube-rose to the skunk, "Oh, most noble swift runner, please run swiftly!"

Turtles can tell more about the roads than hares.

Strange that creatures without backbones have the hardest shells.

The most talkative is the least intelligent, and there is hardly a difference between an orator and an auctioneer.

Be grateful that you do not have to live down the renown of a father nor the wealth of an uncle.

But above all be grateful that no one will have to live down either your renown or your wealth.

Only when a juggler misses catching his ball does he appeal to me.

The envious praises me unknowingly.

Long were you a dream in your mother's sleep, and then she woke to give you birth.

The germ of the race is in your mother's longing.

My father and mother desired a child and they begot me.

And I wanted a mother and a father and I begot night and the sea.

Some of our children are our justifications and some are but our regrets.

When night comes and you too are dark, lie down and be dark with a will.

And when morning comes and you are still dark stand up and say to the day with a will, "I am still dark."

It is stupid to play a rôle with the night and the day.

They would both laugh at you.

The mountain veiled in mist is not a hill; an oak tree in the rain is not a weeping willow.

Behold here is a paradox: the deep and high are nearer to one another than the mid-level to either.

When I stood a clear mirror before you,
you gazed into me and saw your image.
Then you said, "I love you."
But in truth you loved yourself in me.

When you enjoy loving your neighbor
it ceases to be a virtue.

Love which is not always springing is
always dying.

You cannot have youth and the knowledge of it at the same time;
For youth is too busy living to know,
and knowledge is too busy seeking itself
to live.

You may sit at your window watching the passersby. And watching you may see a nun walking toward your right hand, and a prostitute toward your left hand.

And you may say in your innocence, "How noble is the one and how ignoble is the other."

But should you close your eyes and listen awhile you would hear a voice whispering in the ether, "One seeks me in prayer, and the other in pain. And in the spirit of each there is a bower for my spirit."

Once every hundred years Jesus of Nazareth meets Jesus of the Christian in a garden among the hills of Lebanon. And they talk long; and each time Jesus of Nazareth goes away saying to Jesus of the Christian, "My friend, I fear we shall never, never agree."

May God feed the over-abundant!

A great man has two hearts; one bleeds and the other forbears.

Should one tell a lie which does not hurt you nor anyone else, why not say in your heart that the house of his facts is too small for his fancies, and he had to leave it for larger space?

Behind every closed door is a mystery sealed with seven seals.

Waiting is the hoofs of time.

What if trouble should be a new window in the Eastern wall of your house?

You may forget the one with whom you have laughed, but never the one with whom you have wept.

There must be something strangely sacred in salt. It is in our tears and in the sea.

Our God in His gracious thirst will drink us all, the dewdrop and the tear.

You are but a fragment of your giant self, a mouth that seeks bread, and a blind hand that holds the cup for a thirsty mouth.

If you would rise but a cubit above race and country and self you would indeed become godlike.

If I were you I would not find fault with the sea at low tide.

It is a good ship and our Captain is able; it is only your stomach that is in disorder.

What we long for and cannot attain is dearer than what we have already attained.

Should you sit upon a cloud you would not see the boundary line between one country and another, nor the boundary stone between a farm and a farm.

It is a pity you cannot sit upon a cloud.

Seven centuries ago seven white doves rose from a deep valley flying to the snow-white summit of the mountain. One of the seven men who watched the flight said, "I see a black spot on the wing of the seventh dove."

Today the people in that valley tell of seven black doves that flew to the summit of the snowy mountain.

In the autumn I gathered all my sorrows and buried them in my garden.

And when April returned and spring came to wed the earth, there grew in my garden beautiful flowers unlike all other flowers.

And my neighbors came to behold them, and they all said to me, "When autumn comes again, at seeding time, will you not give us of the seeds of these flowers that we may have them in our gardens?"

It is indeed misery if I stretch an empty hand to men and receive nothing; but it is hopelessness if I stretch a full hand and find none to receive.

I long for eternity because there I shall meet my unwritten poems and my unpainted pictures.

Art is a step from nature toward the Infinite.

A work of art is a mist carved into an image.

Even the hands that make crowns of thorns are better than idle hands.

Our most sacred tears never seek our eyes.

Every man is the descendant of every king and every slave that ever lived.

If the great-grandfather of Jesus had known what was hidden within him, would he not have stood in awe of himself?

Was the love of Judas' mother for her son less than the love of Mary for Jesus?

There are three miracles of our Brother Jesus not yet recorded in the Book: the first that He was a man like you and me; the second that He had a sense of humor; and the third that He knew He was a conqueror though conquered.

Crucified One, you are crucified upon my heart; and the nails that pierce your hands pierce the walls of my heart.

And tomorrow when a stranger passes by this Golgotha he will not know that two bled here.

He will deem it the blood of one man.

You may have heard of the Blessed Mountain.

It is the highest mountain in our world.

Should you reach the summit you would have only one desire, and that to descend and be with those who dwell in the deepest valley.

That is why it is called the Blessed Mountain.

Every thought I have imprisoned in expression I must free by my deeds.

BOOK FOUR

BOOK FOUR

THE MADMAN
His Parables and Poems

You ask me how I became a madman. It happened thus: One day, long before many gods were born, I woke from a deep sleep and found all my masks were stolen, —the seven masks I have fashioned and worn in seven lives,—I ran maskless through the crowded streets shouting, "Thieves, thieves, the cursèd thieves."

Men and women laughed at me and some ran to their houses in fear of me.

And when I reached the market place, a youth standing on a house-top cried, "He is a madman." I looked up to behold him; the sun kissed my own naked face for the first time. For the first time the sun kissed my own naked face and my soul was inflamed with love for the sun, and I wanted my masks no more. And as if in a trance I cried, "Blessed, blessed are the thieves who stole my masks."

Thus I became a madman.

And I have found both freedom and safety in my madness; the freedom of loneliness and the safety from being understood, for those who understand us enslave something in us.

But let me not be too proud of my safety. Even a Thief in a jail is safe from another thief.

GOD

IN the ancient days, when the first quiver of speech came to my lips, I ascended the holy mountain and spoke unto God, saying, "Master, I am thy slave. Thy hidden will is my law and I shall obey thee for ever more."

But God made no answer, and like a mighty tempest passed away.

And after a thousand years I ascended the holy mountain and again spoke unto God, saying, "Creator, I am thy creation. Out of clay hast thou fashioned me and to thee I owe mine all."

And God made no answer, but like a thousand swift wings passed away.

And after a thousand years I climbed the holy mountain and spoke unto God again, saying, "Father, I am thy son. In pity and love thou hast given me birth, and through love and worship I shall inherit thy kingdom."

And God made no answer, and like the mist that veils the distant hills he passed away.

And after a thousand years I climbed the sacred mountain and again spoke unto God, saying, "My God, my aim and my fulfilment; I am thy yesterday and thou art my tomorrow. I am thy root in the earth and thou art my flower in the sky, and together we grow before the face of the sun."

Then God leaned over me, and in my ears whispered words of sweetness, and even as the sea that enfoldeth a brook that runneth down to her, he enfolded me.

And when I descended to the valleys and the plains God was there also.

MY FRIEND

My friend, I am not what I seem. Seeming is but a garment I wear—a care-woven garment that protects me from thy questionings and thee from my negligence.

The "I" in me, my friend, dwells in the house of silence, and therein it shall remain for ever more, unperceived, unapproachable.

I would not have thee believe in what I say nor trust in what I do—for my words are naught but thy own thoughts in sound and my deeds thy own hopes in action.

When thou sayest, "The wind bloweth eastward," I say, "Aye, it doth blow eastward"; for I would not have thee know that my mind doth not dwell upon the wind but upon the sea.

Thou canst not understand my seafaring thoughts, nor would I have thee understand. I would be at sea alone.

When it is day with thee, my friend, it is night with me; yet even then I speak of the noontide that dances upon the hills and of the purple shadow that steals its way across the valley; for thou canst not hear the songs of my darkness nor see my wings beating against the stars—and I fain would not have thee hear or see. I would be with night alone.

When thou ascendest to thy Heaven I descend to my Hell—even then thou callest to me across the unbridgeable gulf, "My companion, my comrade," and I call back to thee, "My comrade, my companion"—for I would not have thee see my Hell. The flame would burn thy eyesight and the smoke would crowd thy nostrils. And I love my Hell too well to have thee visit it. I would be in Hell alone.

[12]

Thou lovest Truth and Beauty and Righteousness; and I for thy sake say it is well and seemly to love these things. But in my heart I laugh at thy love. Yet I would not have thee see my laughter. I would laugh alone.

My friend, thou art good and cautious and wise; nay, thou art perfect—and I, too, speak with thee wisely and cautiously. And yet I am mad. But I mask my madness. I would be mad alone.

My friend, thou art not my friend, but how shall I make thee understand? My path is not thy path, yet together we walk, hand in hand.

THE SCARECROW

Once I said to a scarecrow, "You must be tired of standing in this lonely field,"

And he said, "The joy of scaring is a deep and lasting one, and I never tire of it."

Said I, after a minute of thought, "It is true; for I too have known that joy."

Said he, "Only those who are stuffed with straw can know it."

Then I left him, not knowing whether he had complimented or belittled me.

A year passed, during which the scarecrow turned philosopher.

And when I passed by him again I saw two crows building a nest under his hat.

THE SLEEP-WALKERS

In the town where I was born lived a woman and her daughter, who walked in their sleep.

One night, while silence enfolded the world, the woman and her daughter, walking, yet asleep, met in their mist-veiled garden.

And the mother spoke, and she said: "At last, at last, my enemy! You by whom my youth was destroyed—who have built up your life upon the ruins of mine! Would I could kill you!"

And the daughter spoke, and she said: "O hateful woman, selfish and old! Who stand between my freer self and me! Who would have my life an echo of your own faded life! Would you were dead!"

[15]

At that moment a cock crew, and both women awoke. The mother said gently, "Is that you, darling?" And the daughter answered gently, "Yes, dear."

THE WISE DOG

ONE day there passed by a company of cats a wise dog.

And as he came near and saw that they were very intent and heeded him not, he stopped.

Then there arose in the midst of the company a large, grave cat and looked upon them and said, "Brethren, pray ye; and when ye have prayed again and yet again, nothing doubting, verily then it shall rain mice."

And when the dog heard this he laughed in his heart and turned from them saying, "O blind and foolish cats, has it not been written and have I not known and my fathers before me, that that which raineth for prayer and faith and supplication is not mice but bones."

[17]

THE TWO HERMITS

Upon a lonely mountain, there lived two hermits who worshipped God and loved one another.

Now these two hermits had one earthen bowl, and this was their only possession.

One day an evil spirit entered into the heart of the older hermit and he came to the younger and said, "It is long that we have lived together. The time has come for us to part. Let us divide our possessions."

Then the younger hermit was saddened and he said, "It grieves me, Brother, that thou shouldst leave me. But if thou must needs go, so be it," and he brought the earthen bowl and gave it to him saying,

"We cannot divide it, Brother, let it be thine."

Then the older hermit said, "Charity I will not accept. I will take nothing but mine own. It must be divided."

And the younger one said, "If the bowl be broken, of what use would it be to thee or to me? If it be thy pleasure let us rather cast a lot."

But the older hermit said again, "I will have but justice and mine own, and I will not trust justice and mine own to vain chance. The bowl must be divided."

Then the younger hermit could reason no further and he said, "If it be indeed thy will, and if even so thou wouldst have it let us now break the bowl."

But the face of the older hermit grew exceeding dark, and he cried, "O thou cursed coward, thou wouldst not fight."

ON GIVING AND TAKING

ONCE there lived a man who had a valley-ful of needles. And one day the mother of Jesus came to him and said: "Friend, my son's garment is torn and I must needs mend it before he goeth to the temple. Wouldst thou not give me a needle?"

And he gave her not a needle, but he gave her a learned discourse on Giving and Taking to carry to her son before he should go to the temple.

THE SEVEN SELVES

In the stillest hour of the night, as I lay half asleep, my seven selves sat together and thus conversed in whispers:

First Self: Here, in this madman, I have dwelt all these years, with naught to do but renew his pain by day and recreate his sorrow by night. I can bear my fate no longer, and now I rebel.

Second Self: Yours is a better lot than mine, brother, for it is given me to be this madman's joyous self. I laugh his laughter and sing his happy hours, and with thrice winged feet I dance his brighter thoughts. It is I that would rebel against my weary existence.

Third Self: And what of me, the love-ridden self, the flaming brand of wild pas-

[21]

sion and fantastic desires? It is I the love-sick self who would rebel against this madman.

Fourth Self: I, amongst you all, am the most miserable, for naught was given me but odious hatred and destructive loathing. It is I, the tempest-like self, the one born in the black caves of Hell, who would protest against serving this madman.

Fifth Self: Nay, it is I, the thinking self, the fanciful self, the self of hunger and thirst, the one doomed to wander without rest in search of unknown things and things not yet created; it is I, not you, who would rebel.

Sixth Self: And I, the working self, the pitiful labourer, who, with patient hands, and longing eyes, fashion the days into images and give the formless elements new and eternal forms—it is I, the solitary one, who would rebel against this restless madman.

[22]

Seventh Self: How strange that you all would rebel against this man, because each and every one of you has a preordained fate to fulfil. Ah! could I but be like one of you, a self with a determined lot! But I have none, I am the do-nothing self, the one who sits in the dumb, empty nowhere and nowhen, while you are busy re-creating life. Is it you or I, neighbours, who should rebel?

When the seventh self thus spake the other six selves looked with pity upon him but said nothing more; and as the night grew deeper one after the other went to sleep enfolded with a new and happy submission.

But the seventh self remained watching and gazing at nothingness, which is behind all things.

WAR

ONE night a feast was held in the palace, and there came a man and prostrated himself before the prince, and all the feasters looked upon him; and they saw that one of his eyes was out and that the empty socket bled. And the prince inquired of him, "What has befallen you?" And the man replied, "O prince, I am by profession a thief, and this night, because there was no moon, I went to rob the money-changer's shop, and as I climbed in through the window I made a mistake and entered the weaver's shop, and in the dark I ran into the weaver's loom and my eye was plucked out. And now, O prince, I ask for justice upon the weaver."

Then the prince sent for the weaver and

[24]

he came, and it was decreed that one of his eyes should be plucked out.

"O prince," said the weaver, "the decree is just. It is right that one of my eyes be taken. And yet, alas! both are necessary to me in order that I may see the two sides of the cloth that I weave. But I have a neighbour, a cobbler, who has also two eyes, and in his trade both eyes are not necessary."

Then the prince sent for the cobbler. And he came. And they took out one of the cobbler's two eyes.

And justice was satisfied.

THE FOX

A FOX looked at his shadow at sunrise and said, "I will have a camel for lunch today." And all morning he went about looking for camels.   But at noon he saw his shadow again—and he said, "A mouse will do."

THE WISE KING

ONCE there ruled in the distant city of Wirani a king who was both mighty and wise. And he was feared for his might and loved for his wisdom.

Now, in the heart of that city was a well, whose water was cool and crystalline, from which all the inhabitants drank, even the king and his courtiers; for there was no other well.

One night when all were asleep, a witch entered the city, and poured seven drops of strange liquid into the well, and said, "From this hour he who drinks this water shall become mad."

Next morning all the inhabitants, save the king and his lord chamberlain, drank from the well and became mad, even as the witch had foretold.

And during that day the people in the narrow streets and in the market places did naught but whisper to one another, "The king is mad. Our king and his lord chamberlain have lost their reason. Surely we cannot be ruled by a mad king. We must dethrone him."

That evening the king ordered a golden goblet to be filled from the well. And when it was brought to him he drank deeply, and gave it to his lord chamberlain to drink.

And there was great rejoicing in that distant city of Wirani, because its king and its lord chamberlain had regained their reason.

AMBITION

THREE men met at a tavern table. One was a weaver, another a carpenter and the third a ploughman.

Said the weaver, "I sold a fine linen shroud today for two pieces of gold. Let us have all the wine we want."

"And I," said the carpenter, "I sold my best coffin. We will have a great roast with the wine."

"I only dug a grave," said the ploughman, "but my patron paid me double. Let us have honey cakes too."

And all that evening the tavern·was busy, for they called often for wine and meat and cakes. And they were merry.

And the host rubbed his hands and smiled at his wife; for his guests were spending freely.

When they left the moon was high, and they walked along the road singing and shouting together.

The host and his wife stood in the tavern door and looked after them.

"Ah!" said the wife, "these gentlemen! So freehanded and so gay! If only they could bring us such luck every day! Then our son need not be a tavern-keeper and work so hard. We could educate him, and he could become a priest."

THE NEW PLEASURE

LAST night I invented a new pleasure, and as I was giving it the first trial an angel and a devil came rushing toward my house. They met at my door and fought with each other over my newly created pleasure; the one crying, "It is a sin!"—the other, "It is a virtue!"

THE OTHER LANGUAGE

THREE days after I was born, as I lay in my silken cradle, gazing with astonished dismay on the new world round about me, my mother spoke to the wet-nurse, saying, "How does my child?"

And the wet-nurse answered, "He does well, madame, I have fed him three times; and never before have I seen a babe so young yet so gay."

And I was indignant; and I cried, "It is not true, mother; for my bed is hard, and the milk I have sucked is bitter to my mouth, and the odour of the breast is foul in my nostrils, and I am most miserable."

But my mother did not understand, nor did the nurse; for the language I spoke was that of the world from which I came.

[32]

And on the twenty-first day of my life, as I was being christened, the priest said to my mother, "You should indeed be happy, madame, that your son was born a christian."

And I was surprised,—and I said to the priest, "Then your mother in Heaven should be unhappy, for you were not born a christian."

But the priest too did not understand my language.

And after seven moons, one day a soothsayer looked at me, and he said to my mother, "Your son will be a statesman and a great leader of men."

But I cried out,—"That is a false prophecy; for I shall be a musician, and naught but a musician shall I be."

But even at that age my language was not understood—and great was my astonishment.

And after three and thirty years, during which my mother, and the nurse, and the

[33]

priest have all died, (the shadow of God be upon their spirits) the soothsayer still lives. And yesterday I met him near the gate of the temple; and while we were talking together he said, "I have always known you would become a great musician. Even in your infancy I prophesied and foretold your future."

And I believed him—for now I too have forgotten the language of that other world.

THE POMEGRANATE

ONCE when I was living in the heart of a pomegranate, I heard a seed saying, "Someday I shall become a tree, and the wind will sing in my branches, and the sun will dance on my leaves, and I shall be strong and beautiful through all the seasons."

Then another seed spoke and said, "When I was as young as you, I too held such views; but now that I can weigh and measure things, I see that my hopes were vain."

And a third seed spoke also, "I see in us nothing that promises so great a future."

And a fourth said, "But what a mockery our life would be, without a greater future!"

Said a fifth, "Why dispute what we shall be, when we know not even what we are."

But a sixth replied, "Whatever we are, that we shall continue to be."

And a seventh said, "I have such a clear idea how everything will be, but I cannot put it into words."

Then an eighth spoke—and a ninth—and a tenth—and then many—until all were speaking, and I could distinguish nothing for the many voices.

And so I moved that very day into the heart of a quince, where the seeds are few and almost silent.

THE TWO CAGES

IN my father's garden there are two cages. In one is a lion, which my father's slaves brought from the desert of Ninavah; in the other is a songless sparrow.

Every day at dawn the sparrow calls to the lion, "Good morrow to thee, brother prisoner."

THE THREE ANTS·

THREE ants met on the nose of a man who was lying asleep in the sun. And after they had saluted one another, each according to the custom of his tribe, they stood there conversing.

The first ant said, "These hills and plains are the most barren I have known. I have searched all day for a grain of some sort, and there is none to be found."

Said the second ant, "I too have found nothing, though I have visited every nook and glade. This is, I believe, what my people call the soft, moving land where nothing grows."

Then the third ant raised his head and said, "My friends, we are standing now on the nose of the Supreme Ant, the mighty and infinite Ant, whose body is so great that we cannot see it, whose shadow is so vast that we cannot trace it, whose voice is so loud that we cannot hear it; and He is omnipresent."

When the third ant spoke thus the other ants looked at each other and laughed.

At that moment the man moved and in his sleep raised his hand and scratched his nose, and the three ants were crushed.

THE GRAVE-DIGGER

ONCE, as I was burying one of my dead selves, the grave-digger came by and said to me, "Of all those who come here to bury, you alone I like."

Said I, "You please me exceedingly, but why do you like me?"

"Because," said he, "They come weeping and go weeping—you only come laughing and go laughing."

ON THE STEPS OF THE TEMPLE

YESTEREVE, on the marble steps of the Temple, I saw a woman sitting between two men. One side of her face was pale, the other was blushing.

THE BLESSED CITY

IN my youth I was told that in a certain city every one lived according to the Scriptures.

And I said, "I will seek that city and the blessedness thereof." And it was far. And I made great provision for my journey. And after forty days I beheld the city and on the forty-first day I entered into it.

And lo! the whole company of the inhabitants had each but a single eye and but one hand. And I was astonished and said to myself, "Shall they of this so holy city have but one eye and one hand?"

Then I saw that they too were astonished, for they were marvelling greatly at my two hands and my two eyes. And as they were speaking together I inquired of them saying, "Is this indeed the Blessed City, where each man lives according to the Scriptures?" And they said, "Yes, this is that city."

"And what," said I, "hath befallen you, and where are your right eyes and your right hands?"

And all the people were moved. And they said, "Come thou and see."

And they took me to the temple in the midst of the city. And in the temple I saw a heap of hands and eyes. All withered. Then said I, "Alas! what conqueror hath committed this cruelty upon you?"

And there went a murmur amongst them. And one of their elders stood forth and said, "This doing is of ourselves. God hath made us conquerors over the evil that was in us."

And he led me to a high altar, and all the people followed. And he showed me above the altar an inscription graven, and I read:

[43]

"If thy right eye offend thee, pluck it out and cast it from thee; for it is profitable for thee that one of thy members should perish, and not that thy whole body should be cast into hell. And if thy right hand offend thee, cut it off and cast it from thee; for it is profitable for thee that one of thy members should perish, and not that thy whole body should be cast into hell."

Then I understood. And I turned about to all the people and cried, "Hath no man or woman among you two eyes or two hands?"

And they answered me saying, "No, not one. There is none whole save such as are yet too young to read the Scripture and to understand its commandment."

And when we had come out of the temple, I straightway left that Blessed City; for I was not too young, and I could read the scripture.

THE GOOD GOD AND THE EVIL GOD

The Good God and the Evil God met on the mountain top.

The Good God said, "Good day to you, brother."

The Evil God made no answer.

And the Good God said, "You are in a bad humour today."

"Yes," said the Evil God, "for of late I have been often mistaken for you, called by your name, and treated as if I were you, and it ill-pleases me."

And the Good God said. "But I too have been mistaken for you and called by your name."

The Evil God walked away cursing the stupidity of man.

[45]

"DEFEAT"

Defeat, my Defeat, my solitude and my
    aloofness;
You are dearer to me than a thousand tri-
    umphs.
And sweeter to my heart than all world-
    glory.

Defeat, my Defeat, my self-knowledge
    and my defiance,
Through you I know that I am yet young
    and swift of foot
And not to be trapped by withering
    laurels.
And in you I have found aloneness
And the joy of being shunned and scorned.

Defeat, my Defeat, my shining sword and
    shield,

[46]

In your eyes I have read
That to be enthroned is to be enslaved,
And to be understood is to be levelled
    down,
And to be grasped is but to reach one's
    fulness
And like a ripe fruit to fall and be con-
    sumed.

Defeat, my Defeat, my bold companion,
You shall hear my songs and my cries and
    my silences,
And none but you shall speak to me of the
    beating of wings,
And urging of seas,
And of mountains that burn in the night,
And you alone shall climb my steep and
    rocky soul.

Defeat, my Defeat, my deathless courage,
You and I shall laugh together with the
    storm,

And together we shall dig graves for all
    that die in us,
And we shall stand in the sun with a will,
And we shall be dangerous.

NIGHT AND THE MADMAN

"I am like thee, O, Night, dark and naked;
I walk on the flaming path which is above
my day-dreams, and whenever my foot
touches earth a giant oaktree comes forth."

"Nay, thou art not like me, O, Madman, for thou still lookest backward to
see how large a foot-print thou leavest
on the sand."

"I am like thee, O, Night, silent and deep;
and in the heart of my loneliness lies a
Goddess in child-bed; and in him who is
being born Heaven touches Hell."

"Nay, thou art not like me, O, Madman, for thou shudderest yet before
pain, and the song of the abyss terrifies
thee."

"I am like thee, O, Night, wild and terri-

[49]

ble; for my ears are crowded with cries of conquered nations and sighs for forgotten lands."

"Nay, thou art not like me, O, Madman, for thou still takest thy little-self for a comrade, and with thy monster-self thou canst not be friend."

"I am like thee, O, Night, cruel and awful; for my bosom is lit by burning ships at sea, and my lips are wet with blood of slain warriors."

"Nay, thou art not like me, O, Madman; for the desire for a sister-spirit is yet upon thee, and thou hast not become a law unto thyself."

"I am like thee, O, Night, joyous and glad; for he who dwells in my shadow is now drunk with virgin wine, and she who follows me is sinning mirthfully."

"Nay, thou art not like me, O, Madman, for thy soul is wrapped in the veil of seven folds and thou holdest not thy heart in thine hand."

[50]

"I am like thee, O, Night, patient and passionate; for in my breast a thousand dead lovers are buried in shrouds of withered kissses."

"Yea, Madman, art thou like me? Art thou like me? And canst thou ride the tempest as a steed, and grasp the lightning as a sword?"

"Like thee, O, Night, like thee, mighty and high, and my throne is built upon heaps of fallen Gods; and before me too pass the days to kiss the hem of my garment but never to gaze at my face."

"Art thou like me, child of my darkest heart? And dost thou think my untamed thoughts and speak my vast language?"

"Yea, we are twin brothers, O, Night; for thou revealest space and I reveal my soul."

FACES

I HAVE seen a face with a thousand countenances, and a face that was but a single countenance as if held in a mould.

I have seen a face whose sheen I could look through to the ugliness beneath, and a face whose sheen I had to lift to see how beautiful it was.

I have seen an old face much lined with nothing, and a smooth face in which all things were graven.

I know faces, because I look through the fabric my own eye weaves, and behold the reality beneath.

THE GREATER SEA

My soul and I went to the great sea to bathe. And when we reached the shore, we went about looking for a hidden and lonely place.

But as we walked, we saw a man sitting on a grey rock taking pinches of salt from a bag and throwing them into the sea.

"This is the pessimist," said my soul, "Let us leave this place. We cannot bathe here."

We walked on until we reached an inlet. There we saw, standing on a white rock, a man holding a bejewelled box, from which he took sugar and threw it into the sea.

"And this is the optimist," said my soul,

"And he too must not see our naked bodies.

Further on we walked. And on a beach we saw a man picking up dead fish and tenderly putting them back into the water.

"And we cannot bathe before him," said my soul. "He is the humane philanthropist."

And we passed on.

Then we came where we saw a man tracing his shadow on the sand. Great waves came and erased it. But he went on tracing it again and again.

"He is the mystic," said my soul, "Let us leave him."

And we walked on, till in a quiet cove we saw a man scooping up the foam and putting it into an alabaster bowl.

"He is the idealist," said my soul, "Surely he must not see our nudity."

And on we walked. Suddenly we heard a voice crying, "This is the sea.

This is the deep sea. This is the vast and mighty sea." And when we reached the voice it was a man whose back was turned to the sea, and at his ear he held a shell, listening to its murmur.

And my soul said, "Let us pass on. He is the realist, who turns his back on the whole he cannot grasp, and busies himself with a fragment."

So we passed on. And in a weedy place among the rocks was a man with his head buried in the sand. And I said to my soul, "We can bathe here, for he cannot see us."

"Nay," said my soul, "For he is the most deadly of them all. He is the puritan."

Then a great sadness came over the face of my soul, and into her voice.

"Let us go hence," she said, "For there is no lonely, hidden place where we can bathe. I would not have this wind lift my golden hair, or bare my white bosom in this air, or let the light disclose my sacred nakedness."

Then we left that sea to seek the Greater Sea.

CRUCIFIED

I CRIED to men, "I would be crucified!"

And they said, "Why should your blood be upon our heads?

And I answered, "How else shall you be exalted except by crucifying madmen?"

And they heeded and I was crucified. And the crucifixion appeased me.

And when I was hanged between earth and heaven they lifted up their heads to see me. And they were exalted, for their heads had never before been lifted.

But as they stood looking up at me one called out, "For what art thou seeking to atone?"

And another cried, "In what cause dost thou sacrifice thyself?"

And a third said, "Thinkest thou with this price to buy world glory?"

Then said a fourth, "Behold, how he smiles! Can such pain be forgiven?"

And I answered them all, and said:

"Remember only that I smiled. I do not atone—nor sacrifice—nor wish for glory; and I have nothing to forgive. I thirsted—and I besought you to give me my blood to drink. For what is there can quench a madman's thirst but his own blood? I was dumb—and I asked wounds of you for mouths. I was imprisoned in your days and nights—and I sought a door into larger days and nights.

And now I go—as others already crucified have gone. And think not we are weary of crucifixion. For we must be crucified by larger and yet larger men, between greater earths and greater heavens."

THE ASTRONOMER

In the shadow of the temple my friend and I saw a blind man sitting alone. And my friend said, "Behold the wisest man of our land."

Then I left my friend and approached the blind man and greeted him. And we conversed.

After a while I said, "Forgive my question; but since when hast thou been blind?"

"From my birth," he answered.

Said I, "And what path of wisdom followest thou?"

Said he, "I am an astronomer."

Then he placed his hand upon his breast saying, "I watch all these suns and moons and stars."

THE GREAT LONGING

HERE I sit between my brother the mountain and my sister the sea.

We three are one in loneliness, and the love that binds us together is deep and strong and strange. Nay, it is deeper than my sister's depth and stronger than my brother's strength, and stranger than the strangeness of my madness.

Aeons upon aeons have passed since the first grey dawn made us visible to one another; and though we have seen the birth and the fulness and the death of many worlds, we are still eager and young.

We are young and eager and yet we are mateless and unvisited, and though we lie in unbroken half embrace, we are uncomforted. And what comfort is there for

[60]

controlled desire and unspent passion?
Whence shall come the flaming god to
warm my sister's bed? And what she-
torrent shall quench my brother's fire?
And who is the woman that shall command
my heart?

In the stillness of the night my sister
murmurs in her sleep the fire-god's unknown name, and my brother calls afar
upon the cool and distant goddess. But
upon whom I call in my sleep I know not.

.   .   .   .   .   .

Here I sit between my brother the mountain and my sister the sea. We three are
one in loneliness, and the love that binds
us together is deep and strong and strange.

SAID A BLADE OF GRASS

SAID a blade of grass to an autumn leaf, "You make such a noise falling! You scatter all my winter dreams."

Said the leaf indignant, "Low-born and low-dwelling! Songless, peevish thing! You live not in the upper air and you cannot tell the sound of singing."

Then the autumn leaf lay down upon the earth and slept. And when spring came she waked again—and she was a blade of grass.

And when it was autumn and her winter sleep was upon her, and above her through all the air the leaves were falling, she muttered to herself, "O these autumn leaves! They make such a noise! They scatter all my winter dreams."

[62]

THE EYE

SAID the Eye one day, "I see beyond these valleys a mountain veiled with blue mist. Is it not beautiful?"

The Ear listened, and after listening intently awhile, said, "But where is any mountain? I do not hear it."

Then the Hand spoke and said, "I am trying in vain to feel it or touch it, and I can find no mountain."

And the Nose said, "There is no mountain, I cannot smell it."

Then the Eye turned the other way, and they all began to talk together about the Eye's strange delusion. And they said, "Something must be the matter with the Eye."

THE TWO LEARNED MEN

ONCE there lived in the ancient city of Afkar two learned men who hated and belittled each other's learning. For one of them denied the existence of the gods and the other was a believer.

One day the two met in the marketplace, and amidst their followers they began to dispute and to argue about the existence or the non-existence of the gods. And after hours of contention they parted.

That evening the unbeliever went to the temple and prostrated himself before the altar and prayed the gods to forgive his wayward past.

And the same hour the other learned man, he who had upheld the gods, burned his sacred books. For he had become an unbeliever.

WHEN MY SORROW
WAS BORN

WHEN my Sorrow was born I nursed it
with care, and watched over it with loving
tenderness.

And my Sorrow grew like all living
things, strong and beautiful and full of
wondrous delights.

And we loved one another, my Sorrow
and I, and we loved the world about us;
for Sorrow had a kindly heart and mine
was kindly with Sorrow.

And when we conversed, my Sorrow and
I, our days were winged and our nights
were girdled with dreams; for Sorrow had
an eloquent tongue, and mine was eloquent with Sorrow.

And when we sang together, my Sorrow

[65]

and I, our neighbours sat at their windows and listened; for our songs were deep as the sea and our melodies were full of strange memories.

And when we walked together, my Sorrow and I, people gazed at us with gentle eyes and whispered in words of exceeding sweetness. And there were those who looked with envy upon us, for Sorrow was a noble thing and I was proud with Sorrow.

But my Sorrow died, like all living things, and alone I am left to muse and ponder.

And now when I speak my words fall heavily upon my ears.

And when I sing my songs my neighbours come not to listen.

And when I walk the streets no one looks at me.

Only in my sleep I hear voices saying in pity, "See, there lies the man whose Sorrow is dead."

AND WHEN MY JOY
WAS BORN

AND when my Joy was born, I held it in my arms and stood on the house-top shouting, "Come ye, my neighbours, come and see, for Joy this day is born unto me. Come and behold this gladsome thing that laugheth in the sun."

But none of my neighbours came to look upon my Joy, and great was my astonishment.

And every day for seven moons I proclaimed my Joy from the house-top—and yet no one heeded me. And my Joy and I were alone, unsought and unvisited.

Then my Joy grew pale and weary because no other heart but mine held its loveliness and no other lips kissed its lips.

[67]

Then my Joy died of isolation.

And now I only remember my dead Joy in remembering my dead Sorrow. But memory is an autumn leaf that murmurs a while in the wind and then is heard no more.

"THE PERFECT WORLD"

GOD of lost souls, thou who art lost amongst the gods, hear me:

Gentle Destiny that watchest over us, mad, wandering spirits, hear me:

I dwell in the midst of a perfect race, I the most imperfect.

I, a human chaos, a nebula of confused elements, I move amongst finished worlds —peoples of complete laws and pure order, whose thoughts are assorted, whose dreams are arranged, and whose visions are enrolled and registered.

Their virtues, O God, are measured, their sins are weighed, and even the countless things that pass in the dim twilight of neither sin nor virtue are recorded and catalogued.

Here days and nights are divided into

[69]

seasons of conduct and governed by rules of blameless accuracy.

To eat, to drink, to sleep, to cover one's nudity, and then to be weary in due time.

To work, to play, to sing, to dance, and then to lie still when the clock strikes the hour.

To think thus, to feel thus much, and then to cease thinking and feeling when a certain star rises above yonder horizon.

To rob a neighbour with a smile, to bestow gifts with a graceful wave of the hand, to praise prudently, to blame cautiously, to destroy a soul with a word, to burn a body with a breath, and then to wash the hands when the day's work is done.

To love according to an established order, to entertain one's best self in a preconceived manner, to worship the gods becomingly, to intrigue the devils artfully —and then to forget all as though memory were dead.

To fancy with a motive, to contemplate with consideration, to be happy sweetly, to suffer nobly—and then to empty the cup so that tomorrow may fill it again.

All these things, O God, are conceived with forethought, born with determination, nursed with exactness, governed by rules, directed by reason, and then slain and buried after a prescribed method. And even their silent graves that lie within the human soul are marked and numbered.

It is a perfect world, a world of consummate excellence, a world of supreme wonders, the ripest fruit in God's garden, the master-thought of the universe.

But why should I be here, O God, I a green seed of unfulfilled passion, a mad tempest that seeketh neither east nor west, a bewildered fragment from a burnt planet?

Why am I here, O God of lost souls, thou who art lost amongst the gods?

BOOK FIVE

THE FORERUNNER
HIS PARABLES AND POEMS

THE FORERUNNER

YOU are your own forerunner, and the towers you have builded are but the foundation of your giant-self. And that self too shall be a foundation.

And I too am my own forerunner, for the long shadow stretching before me at sunrise shall gather under my feet at the noon hour. Yet another sunrise shall lay another shadow before me, and that also shall be gathered at another noon.

Always have we been our own forerunners, and always shall we be. And all that we have gathered and shall gather shall be but seeds for fields yet unploughed. We are the fields and the ploughmen, the gatherers and the gathered.

When you were a wandering desire in the mist, I too was there, a wandering desire. Then we sought one another, and out of our eagerness dreams were born. And dreams were time limitless, and dreams were space without measure.

I

And when you were a silent word upon Life's quivering lips, I too was there, another silent word. Then Life uttered us and we came down the years throbbing with memories of yesterday and with longing for tomorrow, for yesterday was death conquered and tomorrow was birth pursued.

And now we are in God's hands. You are a sun in His right hand and I am earth in His left hand. Yet you are not more, shining, than I, shone upon.

And we, sun and earth, are but the beginning of a greater sun and a greater earth. And always shall we be the beginning.

You are your own forerunner, you the stranger passing by the gate of my garden.

And I too am my own forerunner, though I sit in the shadows of my trees and seem motionless.

GOD'S FOOL

ONCE there came from the desert to the great city of Sharia a man who was a dreamer, and he had naught but his garment and a staff.

And as he walked through the streets he gazed with awe and wonder at the temples and towers and palaces, for the city of Sharia was of surpassing beauty. And he spoke often to the passers-by, questioning them about their city—but they understood not his language, nor he their language.

At the noon hour he stopped before a vast inn. It was built of yellow marble, and people were going in and coming out unhindered.

"This must be a shrine," he said to himself, and he too went in. But what was his surprise to find himself in a hall of great splendour and a large company of men and women seated about many tables. They were eating and drinking and listening to the musicians.

3

"Nay," said the dreamer. "This is no worshipping. It must be a feast given by the prince to the people, in celebration of a great event."

At that moment a man, whom he took to be the slave of the prince, approached him, and bade him be seated. And he was served with meat and wine and most excellent sweets.

When he was satisfied, the dreamer rose to depart. At the door he was stopped by a large man magnificently arrayed.

"Surely this is the prince himself," said the dreamer in his heart, and he bowed to him and thanked him.

Then the large man said in the language of the city:

"Sir, you have not paid for your dinner." And the dreamer did not understand, and again thanked him heartily. Then the large man bethought him, and he looked more closely upon the dreamer. And he saw that he was a stranger, clad in but a poor garment, and that indeed he had not wherewith to pay for his meal. Then the large man clapped his

4

hands and called—and there came four watchmen of
the city. And they listened to the large man. Then
they took the dreamer between them, and they were
two on each side of him. And the dreamer noted the
ceremoniousness of their dress and of their manner
and he looked upon them with delight.

"These," said he, "are men of distinction."

And they walked all together until they came to
the House of Judgment and they entered.

The dreamer saw before him, seated upon a throne,
a venerable man with flowing beard, robed majestically. And he thought he was the king. And he
rejoiced to be brought before him.

Now the watchmen related to the judge, who was
the venerable man, the charge against the dreamer;
and the judge appointed two advocates, one to
present the charge and the other to defend the
stranger. And the advocates rose, the one after the
other, and delivered each his argument. And the
dreamer thought himself to be listening to addresses
of welcome, and his heart filled with gratitude to the
king and the prince for all that was done for him.

Then sentence was passed upon the dreamer, that upon a tablet hung about his neck his crime should be written, and that he should ride through the city on a naked horse, with a trumpeter and a drummer before him. And the sentence was carried out forthwith.

Now as the dreamer rode through the city upon the naked horse, with the trumpeter and the drummer before him, the inhabitants of the city came running forth at the sound of the noise, and when they saw him they laughed one and all, and the children ran after him in companies from street to street. And the dreamer's heart was filled with ecstasy, and his eyes shone upon them. For to him the tablet was a sign of the king's blessing and the procession was in his honour.

Now as he rode, he saw among the crowd a man who was from the desert like himself and his heart swelled with joy, and he cried out to him with a shout:

"Friend! Friend! Where are we? What city of the heart's desire is this? What race of lavish hosts?— who feast the chance guest in their palaces, whose

6

princes companion him, whose king hangs a token upon his breast and opens to him the hospitality of a city descended from heaven."

And he who was also of the desert replied not. He only smiled and slightly shook his head. And the procession passed on.

And the dreamer's face was uplifted and his eyes were overflowing with light.

LOVE

THEY say the jackal and the mole
Drink from the self-same stream
Where the lion comes to drink.

And they say the eagle and the vulture
Dig their beaks into the same carcass,
And are at peace, one with the other,
In the presence of the dead thing.

O love, whose lordly hand
Has bridled my desires,
And raised my hunger and my thirst
To dignity and pride,
Let not the strong in me and the constant
Eat the bread or drink the wine
That tempt my weaker self.
Let me rather starve,

8

And let my heart parch with thirst,
And let me die and perish,
Ere I stretch my hand
To a cup you did not fill,
Or a bowl you did not bless.

THE KING-HERMIT

THEY told me that in a forest among the mountains lives a young man in solitude who once was a king of a vast country beyond the Two Rivers. And they also said that he, of his own will, had left his throne and the land of his glory and come to dwell in the wilderness.

And I said, "I would seek that man, and learn the secret of his heart; for he who renounces a kingdom must needs be greater than a kingdom."

On that very day I went to the forest where he dwells. And I found him sitting under a white cypress, and in his hand a reed as if it were a sceptre. And I greeted him even as I would greet a king. And he turned to me and said gently, "What would you in this forest of serenity? Seek you a lost self in the green shadows, or is it a home-coming in your twilight?"

And I answered, "I sought but you—for I fain would know that which made you leave a kingdom for a forest."

And he said, "Brief is my story, for sudden was the bursting of the bubble. It happened thus: One day as I sat at a window in my palace, my chamberlain and an envoy from a foreign land were walking in my garden. And as they approached my window, the lord chamberlain was speaking of himself and saying, 'I am like the king; I have a thirst for strong wine and a hunger for all games of chance. And like my lord the king I have storms of temper.' And the lord chamberlain and the envoy disappeared among the trees. But in a few minutes they returned, and this time the lord chamberlain was speaking of me, and he was saying, 'My lord the king is like myself—a good marksman; and like me he loves music and bathes thrice a day.'"

After a moment he added, "On the eve of that day I left my palace with but my garment, for I would no longer be ruler over those who assume my vices and attribute to me their virtues."

And I said, "This is indeed a wonder, and passing strange."

And he said, "Nay, my friend, you knocked at the gate of my silences and received but a trifle. For who would not leave a kingdom for a forest where the seasons sing and dance ceaselessly? Many are those who have given their kingdom for less than solitude and the sweet fellowship of aloneness. Countless are the eagles who descend from the upper air to live with moles that they may know the secrets of the earth. There are those who renounce the kingdom of dreams that they may not seem distant from the dreamless. And those who renounce the kingdom of nakedness and cover their souls that others may not be ashamed in beholding truth uncovered and beauty unveiled. And greater yet than all of these is he who renounces the kingdom of sorrow that he may not seem proud and vainglorious."

Then rising he leaned upon his reed and said, "Go now to the great city and sit at its gate and watch all those who enter into it and those who go out. And see that you find him who, though born a king, is without kingdom; and him who though ruled in flesh rules in spirit—though neither he nor his subjects know this; and him also who but seems to rule yet is in truth slave of his own slaves."

After he had said these things he smiled on me, and there were a thousand dawns upon his lips. Then he turned and walked away into the heart of the forest.

And I returned to the city, and I sat at its gate to watch the passers-by even as he had told me. And from that day to this numberless are the kings whose shadows have passed over me and few are the subjects over whom my shadow has passed.

THE LION'S DAUGHTER

FOUR slaves stood fanning an old queen who was asleep upon her throne. And she was snoring. And upon the queen's lap a cat lay purring and gazing lazily at the slaves.

The first slave spoke, and said, "How ugly this old woman is in her sleep. See her mouth droop; and she breathes as if the devil were choking her."

Then the cat said, purring, "Not half so ugly in her sleep as you in your waking slavery."

And the second slave said, "You would think sleep would smooth her wrinkles instead of deepening them. She must be dreaming of something evil."

And the cat purred, "Would that you might sleep also and dream of your freedom."

And the third slave said, "Perhaps she is seeing the procession of all those that she has slain."

And the cat purred, "Aye, she sees the procession of your forefathers and your descendants."

15

And the fourth slave said, "It is all very well to talk about her, but it does not make me less weary of standing and fanning."

And the cat purred, "You shall be fanning to all eternity; for as it is on earth so it is in heaven."

At this moment the old queen nodded in her sleep, and her crown fell to the floor.

And one of the slaves said, "That is a bad omen."

And the cat purred, "The bad omen of one is the good omen of another."

And the second slave said, "What if she should wake, and find her crown fallen! She would surely slay us."

And the cat purred, "Daily from your birth she has slain you and you know it not."

And the third slave said, "Yes, she would slay us and she would call it making sacrifice to the gods."

And the cat purred, "Only the weak are sacrificed to the gods."

And the fourth slave silenced the others, and softly he picked up the crown and replaced it, without waking her, on the old queen's head.

And the cat purred, "Only a slave restores a crown that has fallen."

And after a while the old queen woke, and she looked about her and yawned. Then she said, "Methought I dreamed, and I saw four caterpillars chased by a scorpion around the trunk of an ancient oak tree. I like not my dream."

Then she closed her eyes and went to sleep again. And she snored. And the four slaves went on fanning her.

And the cat purred, "Fan on, fan on, stupids. You fan but the fire that consumes you."

TYRANNY

THUS sings the She-Dragon that guards the seven caves by the sea:

"My mate shall come riding on the waves. His thundering roar shall fill the earth with fear, and the flames of his nostrils shall set the sky afire. At the eclipse of the moon we shall be wedded, and at the eclipse of the sun I shall give birth to a Saint George, who shall slay me."

Thus sings the She-Dragon that guards the seven caves by the sea.

THE SAINT

IN my youth I once visited a saint in his silent grove
beyond the hills; and as we were conversing upon
the nature of virtue a brigand came limping wearily
up the ridge. When he reached the grove he knelt
down before the saint and said, "O saint, I would be
comforted! My sins are heavy upon me."

And the saint replied, "My sins, too, are heavy
upon me."

And the brigand said, "But I am a thief and a
plunderer."

And the saint replied, "I too am a thief and a
plunderer."

And the brigand said, "But I am a murderer, and
the blood of many men cries in my ears."

And the saint replied, "I too am a murderer, and
in my ears cries the blood of many men."

And the brigand said, "I have committed countless
crimes."

And the saint replied, "I too have committed crimes without number."

Then the brigand stood up and gazed at the saint, and there was a strange look in his eyes. And when he left us he went skipping down the hill.

And I turned to the saint and said, "Wherefore did you accuse yourself of uncommitted crimes? See you not that this man went away no longer believing in you?"

And the saint answered, "It is true he no longer believes in me. But he went away much comforted.'

At that moment we heard the brigand singing in the distance, and the echo of his song filled the valley with gladness.

THE PLUTOCRAT

IN my wanderings I once saw upon an island a man-headed, iron-hoofed monster who ate of the earth and drank of the sea incessantly. And for a long while I watched him. Then I approached him and said, "Have you never enough; is your hunger never satisfied and your thirst never quenched?"

And he answered saying, "Yes, I am satisfied, nay, I am weary of eating and drinking; but I am afraid that tomorrow there will be no more earth to eat and no more sea to drink."

THE GREATER SELF

THIS came to pass. After the coronation of
Nufsibaäl, King of Byblus, he retired to his bed
chamber—the very room which the three hermit-
magicians of the mountain had built for him. He took
off his crown and his royal raiment, and stood in the
centre of the room thinking of himself, now the
all-powerful ruler of Byblus.

Suddenly he turned; and he saw stepping out of
the silver mirror which his mother had given him,
a naked man.

The king was startled, and he cried out to the man,
"What would you?"

And the naked man answered, "Naught but this:
Why have they crowned you king?"

And the king answered, "Because I am the noblest
man in the land."

Then the naked man said, "If you were still more
noble, you would not be king."

And the king said, "Because I am the mightiest man in the land they crowned me."

And the naked man said, "If you were mightier yet, you would not be king."

Then the king said, "Because I am the wisest man they crowned me king."

And the naked man said, "If you were still wiser you would not choose to be king."

Then the king fell to the floor and wept bitterly.

The naked man looked down upon him. Then he took up the crown and with tenderness replaced it upon the king's bent head.

And the naked man, gazing lovingly upon the king, entered into the mirror.

And the king roused, and straightway he looked into the mirror. And he saw there but himself crowned.

WAR AND THE SMALL NATIONS

ONCE, high above a pasture, where a sheep and a lamb were grazing, an eagle was circling and gazing hungrily down upon the lamb. And as he was about to descend and seize his prey, another eagle appeared and hovered above the sheep and her young with the same hungry intent. Then the two rivals began to fight filling the sky with their fierce cries.

The sheep looked up and was much astonished. She turned to the lamb and said,

"How strange, my child, that these two noble birds should attack one another. Is not the vast sky large enough for both of them? Pray, my little one, pray in your heart that God may make peace between your winged brothers."

And the lamb prayed in his heart.

CRITICS

ONE nightfall a man travelling on horseback toward the sea reached an inn by the roadside. He dismounted, and confident in man and night like all riders toward the sea, he tied his horse to a tree beside the door and entered into the inn.

At midnight, when all were asleep, a thief came and stole the traveller's horse.

In the morning the man awoke, and discovered that his horse was stolen. And he grieved for his horse, and that a man had found it in his heart to steal.

Then his fellow-lodgers came and stood around him and began to talk.

And the first man said, "How foolish of you to tie your horse outside the stable."

And the second said, "Still more foolish, without even hobbling the horse!"

And the third man said, "It is stupid at best to travel to the sea on horseback."

And the fourth said, "Only the indolent and the slow of foot own horses."

Then the traveller was much astonished. At last he cried, "My friends, because my horse is stolen, you have hastened one and all to tell me my faults and my shortcomings. But strange, not one word of reproach have you uttered about the man who stole my horse."

POETS

FOUR poets were sitting around a bowl of
punch that stood on a table.

Said the first poet, "Methinks I see with my third
eye the fragrance of this wine hovering in space like
a cloud of birds in an enchanted forest."

The second poet raised his head and said, "With
my inner ear I can hear those mist-birds singing.
And the melody holds my heart as the white rose
imprisons the bee within her petals."

The third poet closed his eyes and stretched his
arm upward, and said, "I touch them with my hand.
I feel their wings, like the breath of a sleeping fairy,
brushing against my fingers."

Then the fourth poet rose and lifted up the bowl,
and he said, "Alas, friends! I am too dull of sight and
of hearing and of touch. I cannot see the fragrance of
this wine, nor hear its song, nor feel the beating of its
wings. I perceive but the wine itself. Now therefore

must I drink it, that it may sharpen my senses and raise me to your blissful heights."

And putting the bowl to his lips, he drank the punch to the very last drop.

The three poets, with their mouths open, looked at him aghast, and there was a thirsty yet unlyrical hatred in their eyes.

28

THE WEATHER-COCK

SAID the weather-cock to the wind, "How tedious and monotonous you are! Can you not blow any other way but in my face? You disturb my God-given stability."

And the wind did not answer. It only laughed in space.

THE KING OF ARADUS

ONCE the elders of the city of Aradus presented themselves before the king, and besought of him a decree to forbid to men all wine and all intoxicants within their city.

And the king turned his back upon them and went out from them laughing.

Then the elders departed in dismay.

At the door of the palace they met the lord chamberlain. And the lord chamberlain observed that they were troubled, and he understood their case.

Then he said, "Pity, my friends! Had you found the king drunk, surely he would have granted you your petition."

OUT OF MY DEEPER HEART

OUT of my deeper heart a bird rose and flew skyward.

Higher and higher did it rise, yet larger and larger did it grow.

At first it was but like a swallow, then a lark, then an eagle, then as vast as a spring cloud, and then it filled the starry heavens.

Out of my heart a bird flew skyward. And it waxed larger as it flew. Yet it left not my heart.

O my faith, my untamed knowledge, how shall I fly to your height and see with you man's larger self pencilled upon the sky?

How shall I turn this sea within me into mist, and move with you in space immeasurable?

How can a prisoner within the temple behold its golden domes?

How shall the heart of a fruit be stretched to envelop the fruit also?

O my faith, I am in chains behind these bars of silver and ebony, and I cannot fly with you.

Yet out of my heart you rise skyward, and it is my heart that holds you, and I shall be content.

DYNASTIES

THE Queen of Ishana was in travail of child-birth; and the King and the mighty men of his court were waiting in breathless anxiety in the great hall of the Winged Bulls.

At eventide there came suddenly a messenger in haste and prostrated himself before the King, and said, "I bring glad tidings unto my lord the King, and unto the kingdom and the slaves of the King. Mihrab the Cruel, thy life-long enemy, the King of Bethroun, is dead."

When the King and the mighty men heard this, they all rose and shouted for joy; for the powerful Mihrab, had he lived longer, had assuredly overcome Ishana and carried the inhabitants captive.

At this moment the court physician also entered the hall of Winged Bulls, and behind him came the royal midwives. And the physician prostrated himself before the king, and said, "My lord the King shall live for ever, and through countless generations shall he rule over the people of Ishana. For unto thee, O King, is born this very hour a son, who shall be thy heir."

Then indeed was the soul of the King intoxicated with joy, that in the same moment his foe was dead and the royal line was established.

Now in the City of Ishana lived a true prophet. And the prophet was young, and bold of spirit. And the King that very night ordered that the prophet should be brought before him. And when he was brought, the King said unto him, "Prophesy now, and foretell what shall be the future of my son who is this day born unto the kingdom."

And the prophet hesitated not, but said, "Hearken, O King, and I will indeed prophesy of the future of thy son, that is this day born. The soul of thy enemy, even of thy enemy King Mihrab, who died yester-eve, lingered but a day upon the wind. Then it sought for itself a body to enter into. And that which it entered into was the body of thy son that is born unto thee this hour."

Then the King was enraged, and with his sword he slew the prophet.

And from that day to this, the wise men of Ishana say one to another secretly, "Is it not known, and has it not been said from of old, that Ishana is ruled by an enemy."

KNOWLEDGE AND HALF-KNOWLEDGE

FOUR frogs sat upon a log that lay floating on the edge of a river. Suddenly the log was caught by the current and swept slowly down the stream. The frogs were delighted and absorbed, for never before had they sailed.

At length the first frog spoke, and said, "This is indeed a most marvellous log. It moves as if alive. No such log was ever known before."

Then the second frog spoke, and said, "Nay, my friend, the log is like other logs, and does not move. It is the river, that is walking to the sea, and carries us and the log with it."

And the third frog spoke, and said, "It is neither the log nor the river that moves. The moving is in our thinking. For without thought nothing moves."

And the three frogs began to wrangle about what was really moving. The quarrel grew hotter and louder, but they could not agree.

Then they turned to the fourth frog, who up to this time had been listening attentively but holding his peace, and they asked his opinion.

And the fourth frog said, "Each of you is right, and none of you is wrong. The moving is in the log and the water and our thinking also."

And the three frogs became very angry, for none of them was willing to admit that his was not the whole truth, and that the other two were not wholly wrong.

Then the strange thing happened. The three frogs got together and pushed the fourth frog off the log into the river.

"SAID A SHEET OF SNOW-WHITE PAPER..."

SAID a sheet of snow-white paper, "Pure was I created, and pure will I remain for ever. I would rather be burnt and turn to white ashes than suffer darkness to touch me or the unclean to come near me."

The ink-bottle heard what the paper was saying, and it laughed in its dark heart; but it never dared to approach her. And the multicoloured pencils heard her also, and they too never came near her.

And the snow-white sheet of paper did remain pure and chaste for ever— pure and chaste—and empty.

THE SCHOLAR AND THE POET

SAID the serpent to the lark, "Thou flyest, yet thou canst not visit the recesses of the earth where the sap of life moveth in perfect silence."

And the lark answered, "Aye, thou knowest over much, nay thou art wiser than all things wise—pity thou canst not fly."

And as if he did not hear, the serpent said, "Thou canst not see the secrets of the deep, nor move among the treasures of the hidden empire. It was but yesterday I lay in a cave of rubies. It is like the heart of a ripe pomegranate, and the faintest ray of light turns it into a flame-rose. Who but me can behold such marvels?"

And the lark said, "None, none but thee can lie among the crystal memories of the cycles: pity thou canst not sing."

And the serpent said, "I know a plant whose root

descends to the bowels of the earth, and he who eats of that root becomes fairer than Ashtarte."

And the lark said, "No one, no one but thee could unveil the magic thought of the earth—pity thou canst not fly."

And the serpent said, "There is a purple stream that runneth under a mountain, and he who drinketh of it shall become immortal even as the gods. Surely no bird or beast can discover that purple stream."

And the lark answered, "If thou willest thou canst become deathless even as the gods—pity thou canst not sing."

And the serpent said, "I know a buried temple, which I visit once a moon: It was built by a forgotten race of giants, and upon its walls are graven the secrets of time and space, and he who reads them shall understand that which passeth all understanding."

And the lark said, "Verily, if thou so desirest thou canst encircle with thy pliant body all knowledge of time and space—pity thou canst not fly."

Then the serpent was disgusted, and as he turned

and entered into his hole he muttered, "Empty headed songster!"

And the lark flew away singing, "Pity thou canst not sing. Pity, pity, my wise one, thou canst not fly."

VALUES

ONCE a man unearthed in his field a marble statue of great beauty. And he took it to a collector who loved all beautiful things and offered it to him for sale, and the collector bought it for a large price. And they parted.

And as the man walked home with his money he thought, and he said to himself, "How much life this money means! How can any one give all this for a dead carved stone buried and undreamed of in the earth for a thousand years?"

And now the collector was looking at his statue, and he was thinking, and he said to himself, "What beauty! What life! The dream of what a soul!—and fresh with the sweet sleep of a thousand years. How can any one give all this for money, dead and dreamless?"

OTHER SEAS

A FISH said to another fish, "Above this sea of ours there is another sea, with creatures swimming in it—and they live there even as we live here."

The fish replied, "Pure fancy! Pure fancy! When you know that everything that leaves our sea by even an inch, and stays out of it, dies. What proof have you of other lives in other seas?"

REPENTANCE

On a moonless night a man entered into his neighbour's garden and stole the largest melon he could find and brought it home.

He opened it and found it still unripe.

Then behold a marvel!

The man's conscience woke and smote him with remorse; and he repented having stolen the melon.

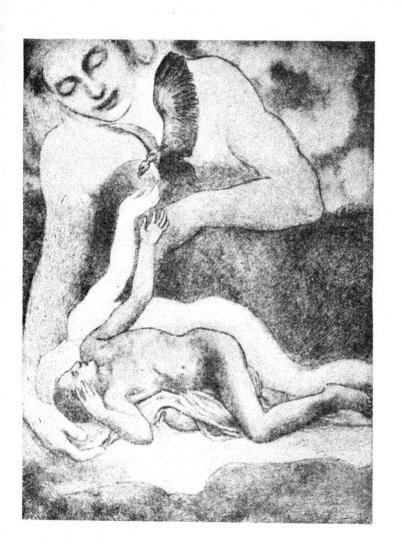

THE DYING MAN AND THE VULTURE

WAIT, wait yet awhile, my eager friend.
I shall yield but too soon this wasted thing,
Whose agony overwrought and useless
Exhausts your patience.
I would not have your honest hunger
Wait upon these moments:
But this chain, though made of a breath,
Is hard to break.
And the will to die,
Stronger than all things strong,
Is stayed by a will to live
Feebler than all things feeble.
Forgive me comrade; I tarry too long.
It is memory that holds my spirit;
A procession of distant days,
A vision of youth spent in a dream,
A face that bids my eyelids not to sleep,

A voice that lingers in my ears,
A hand that touches my hand.
Forgive me that you have waited too long.
It is over now, and all is faded:—
The face, the voice, the hand and the mist that
brought them hither.
The knot is untied.
The cord is cleaved.
And that which is neither food nor drink is
withdrawn.
Approach, my hungry comrade;
The board is made ready,
And the fare, frugal and spare,
Is given with love.
Come, and dig your beak here, into the left side,
And tear out of its cage this smaller bird,
Whose wings can beat no more:
I would have it soar with you into the sky.
Come now, my friend, I am your host tonight,
And you my welcome guest.

BEYOND MY SOLITUDE

BEYOND my solitude is another solitude, and to him who dwells therein my aloneness is a crowded market-place and my silence a confusion of sounds.

Too young am I and too restless to seek that above-solitude. The voices of yonder valley still hold my ears, and its shadows bar my way and I cannot go.

Beyond these hills is a grove of enchantment and to him who dwells therein my peace is but a whirl-wind and my enchantment an illusion.

Too young am I and too riotous to seek that sacred grove. The taste of blood is clinging in my mouth, and the bow and the arrows of my fathers yet linger in my hand and I cannot go.

Beyond this burdened self lives my freer self; and to him my dreams are a battle fought in twilight and my desires the rattling of bones.

Too young am I and too outraged to be my freer self.

And how shall I become my freer self unless I slay my burdened selves, or unless all men become free?

How shall my leaves fly singing upon the wind unless my roots shall wither in the dark?

How shall the eagle in me soar against the sun until my fledglings leave the nest which I with my own beak have built for them?

THE LAST WATCH

AT the high-tide of night, when the first breath
of dawn came upon the wind, the Forerunner,
he who calls himself echo to a voice yet unheard,
left his bed-chamber and ascended to the roof of his
house. Long he stood and looked down upon the
slumbering city. Then he raised his head, and even
as if the sleepless spirits of all those asleep had
gathered around him, he opened his lips and spoke,
and he said:

"My friends and my neighbours and you who daily
pass my gate, I would speak to you in your sleep,
and in the valley of your dreams I would walk naked
and unrestrained; far heedless are your waking hours
and deaf are your sound-burdened ears.

"Long did I love you and overmuch.

"I love the one among you as though he were all,
and all as if you were one. And in the spring of my
heart I sang in your gardens, and in the summer of

53

my heart I watched at your threshing-floors.

"Yea, I loved you all, the giant and the pigmy, the leper and the anointed, and him who gropes in the dark even as him who dances his days upon the mountains.

"You, the strong, have I loved, though the marks of your iron hoofs are yet upon my flesh; and you the weak, though you have drained my faith and wasted my patience.

"You the rich have I loved, while bitter was your honey to my mouth; and you the poor, though you knew my empty-handed shame.

"You the poet with the barrowed lute and blind fingers, you have I loved in self indulgence; and you the scholar, ever gathering rotted shrouds in potters' fields.

"You the priest I have loved, who sit in the silences of yesterday questioning the fate of my tomorrow; and you the worshippers of gods the images of your own desires.

"You the thirsting woman whose cup is ever full, I have loved in understanding; and you the woman of restless nights, you too I have loved in pity.

"You the talkative have I loved, saying, 'Life hath much to say'; and you the dumb have I loved, whispering to myself, 'Says he not in silence that which I fain would hear in words?'

"And you the judge and the critic, I have loved also; yet when you have seen me crucified, you said, 'He bleeds rhythmically, and the pattern his blood makes upon his white skin is beautiful to behold.'

"Yea, I have loved you all, the young and the old, the trembling reed and the oak.

"But alas! it was the over-abundance of my heart that turned you from me. You would drink love from a cup, but not from a surging river. You would hear love's faint murmur, but when love shouts you would muffle your ears.

"And because I have loved you all you have said, 'Too soft and yielding is his heart, and too undiscerning is his path. It is the love of a needy one, who picks crumbs even as he sits at kingly feasts. And it is the love of a weakling, for the strong loves only the strong.'

"And because I have loved you overmuch you

have said, 'It is but the love of a blind man who knows not the beauty of one nor the ugliness of another. And it is the love of the tasteless who drinks vinegar even as wine. And it is the love of the impertinent and the overweening, for what stranger could be our mother and father and sister and brother?'

"This you have said, and more. For often in the market-place you pointed your fingers at me and said mockingly, 'There goes the ageless one, the man without seasons, who at the noon hour plays games with our children and at eventide sits with our elders and assumes wisdom and understanding.'

"And I said 'I will love them more. Aye, even more. I will hide my love with seeming to hate, and disguise my tenderness as bitterness. I will wear an iron mask, and only when armed and mailed shall I seek them.'

"Then I laid a heavy hand upon your bruises, and like a tempest in the night I thundered in your ears

"From the housetop I proclaimed you hypocrites pharisees, tricksters, false and empty earth-bubbles

"The short-sighted among you I cursed for blind bats, and those too near the earth I likened to soulless moles.

"The eloquent I pronounced fork-tongued, the silent, stone-lipped, and the simple and artless I called, the dead never weary of death.

"The seekers after world knowledge I condemned as offenders of the holy spirit and those who would naught but the spirit I branded as hunters of shadows who cast their nets in flat waters and catch but their own images.

"Thus with my lips have I denounced you, while my heart, bleeding within me, called you tender names.

"It was love lashed by its own self that spoke. It was pride half slain that fluttered in the dust. It was my hunger for your love that raged from the house-top, while my own love, kneeling in silence, prayed your forgiveness.

"But behold a miracle!

"It was my disguise that opened your eyes, and my seeming to hate that woke your hearts.

"And now you love me.

"You love the swords that strike you and the arrows that crave your breast. For it comforts you to be wounded and only when you drink of your own blood can you be intoxicated.

"Like moths that seek destruction in the flame you gather daily in my garden: and with faces uplifted and eyes enchanted you watch me tear the fabric of your days. And in whispers you say the one to the other, 'He sees with the light of God. He speaks like the prophets of old. He unveils our souls and unlocks our hearts, and like the eagle that knows the way of foxes he knows our ways.'

"Aye, in truth, I know your ways, but only as an eagle knows the ways of his fledglings. And I fain would disclose my secret. Yet in my need for your nearness I feign remoteness, and in fear of the ebb-tide of your love I guard the floodgates of my love."

After saying these things the Forerunner covered his face with his hands and wept bitterly. For he knew in his heart that love humiliated in its nakedness is greater than love that seeks triumph in disguise; and he was ashamed.

But suddenly he raised his head, and like one waking from sleep he outstretched his arms and said, "Night is over, and we children of night must die when dawn comes leaping upon the hills; and out of our ashes a mightier love shall rise. And it shall laugh in the sun, and it shall be deathless."

BOOK SIX

BOOK SIX

THE EARTH GODS

WHEN the night of the twelfth æon fell,
And silence, the high tide of night, swallowed the
    hills,
The three earth-born gods, the Master Titans of
    life,
Appeared upon the mountains.

Rivers ran about their feet;
The mist floated across their breasts,
And their heads rose in majesty above the world.

Then they spoke, and like distant thunder
Their voices rolled over the plains.

FIRST GOD

The wind blows eastward;
I would turn my face to the south,
For the wind crowds my nostrils with the odors of
   dead things.

SECOND GOD

It is the scent of burnt flesh, sweet and bountiful.
I would breathe it.

FIRST GOD

It is the odor of mortality parching upon its own
   faint flame.
Heavily does it hang upon the air,
And like foul breath of the pit
It offends my senses.
I would turn my face to the scentless north.

SECOND GOD

It is the inflamed fragrance of brooding life
4

That I would breathe now and forever.
Gods live upon sacrifice,
Their thirst quenched by blood,
Their hearts appeased with young souls,
Their sinews strengthened by the deathless sighs
Of those who dwell with death;
Their thrones are built upon the ashes of genera-
tions.

FIRST GOD

Weary is my spirit of all there is.
I would not move a hand to create a world
Nor to erase one.

I would not live could I but die,
For the weight of æons is upon me,
And the ceaseless moan of the seas exhausts my
sleep.
Could I but lose the primal aim
And vanish like a wasted sun;
Could I but strip my divinity of its purpose

5

And breathe my immortality into space,
And be no more;
Could I but be consumed and pass from time's memory
Into the emptiness of nowhere!

THIRD GOD

Listen my brothers, my ancient brothers.
A youth in yonder vale
Is singing his heart to the night.
His lyre is gold and ebony.
His voice is silver and gold.

SECOND GOD

I would not be so vain as to be no more.
I could not but choose the hardest way;
To follow the seasons and support the majesty of
    the years;
To sow the seed and to watch it thrust through the
    soil;
To call the flower from its hiding place

6

And give it strength to nestle its own life,
And then to pluck it when the storm laughs in the
    forest;
To raise man from secret darkness,
Yet keep his roots clinging to the earth;
To give him thirst for life, and make death his cup-
    bearer;
To endow him with love that waxeth with pain,
And exalts with desire, and increases with longing,
And fadeth away with the first embrace;
To girdle his nights with dreams of higher days,
And infuse his days with visions of blissful nights,
And yet to confine his days and his nights
To their immutable resemblance;
To make his fancy like the eagle of the mountain,
And his thought as the tempests of the seas,
And yet to give him hands slow in decision,
And feet heavy with deliberation;
To give him gladness that he may sing before us,
And sorrow that he may call unto us,
And then to lay him low,

7

When the earth in her hunger cries for food;
To raise his soul high above the firmament
That he may foretaste our tomorrow,
And to keep his body groveling in the mire
That he may not forget his yesterday.

Thus shall we rule man unto the end of time,
Governing the breath that began with his mother's
    crying,
And ends with the lamentation of his children.

FIRST GOD

My heart thirsts, yet I would not drink the faint
    blood of a feeble race,
For the cup is tainted, and the vintage therein is
    bitter to my mouth.
Like thee I have kneaded the clay and fashioned it
    to breathing forms
That crept out of my dripping fingers unto the
    marshes and the hills.

Like thee I have kindled the dark depths of beginning life
And watched it crawl from caves to rocky heights.
Like thee I have summoned spring and laid the beauty thereof
For a lure that seizes youth and binds it to generate and multiply.
Like thee I have led man from shrine to shrine,
And turned his mute fear of things unseen
To tremulous faith in us, the unvisited and the unknown.
Like thee I have ridden the wild tempest over his head
That he might bow before us,
And shaken the earth beneath him until he cried unto us;
And like thee, led the savage ocean against his nested isle,
·Till he hath died calling upon us.
All this have I done, and more.
And all that I have done is empty and vain.

9

Vain is the waking and empty is the sleep,
And thrice empty and vain is the dream.

THIRD GOD

Brothers, my august brothers,
Down in the myrtle grove
A girl is dancing to the moon,
A thousand dew-stars are in her hair,
About her feet a thousand wings.

SECOND GOD

We have planted man, our vine, and tilled the soil
In the purple mist of the first dawn.
We watched the lean branches grow,
And through the days of seasonless years
We nursed the infant leaves.
From the angry element we shielded the bud,
And against all dark spirits we guarded the flower.
And now that our vine hath yielded the grape
You will not take it to the winepress and fill the
     cup.

10

Whose mightier hand than yours shall reap the
    fruit?

And what nobler end than your thirst awaits the
    wine?

Man is food for the gods,

And the glory of man begins

When his aimless breath is sucked by gods' hal-
    lowed lips.

All that is human counts for naught if human it re-
    main;

The innocence of childhood, and the sweet ecstasy
    of youth,

The passion of stern manhood, and the wisdom of
    old age;

The splendor of kings and the triumph of warriors,

The fame of poets and the honor of dreamers and
    saints;

All these and all that lieth therein is bread for gods.

And naught but bread ungraced shall it be

If the gods raise it not to their mouths.

And as the mute grain turns to love songs when

swallowed by the nightingale,
Even so as bread for gods shall man taste godhead.

FIRST GOD

Aye, man is meat for gods!
And all that is man shall come upon the gods' eternal board!
The pain of child-bearing and the agony of childbirth,
The blind cry of the infant that pierces the naked night,
And the anguish of the mother wrestling with the sleep she craves,
To pour life exhausted from her breast;
The flaming breath of youth tormented,
And the burdened sobs of passion unspent;
The dripping brows of manhood tilling the barren land,
And the regret of pale old age when life against life's will
Calls to the grave.

12

Behold this is man!

A creature bred on hunger and made food for hungry gods.

A vine that creeps in dust beneath the feet of deathless death.

The flower that blooms in nights of evil shadows;

The grape of mournful days, and days of terror and shame.

And yet you would have me eat and drink.

You would bid me sit amongst shrouded faces

And draw my life from stony lips

And from withered hands receive my eternity.

THIRD GOD

Brothers, my dreaded brothers,

Thrice deep the youth is singing,

And thrice higher is his song.

His voice shakes the forest

And pierces the sky,

And scatters the slumbering of earth.

13

SECOND GOD (*Always unhearing*)

The bee hums harshly in your ears,
And foul is the honey to your lips.
Fain would I comfort you,
But how shall I?
Only the abyss listens when gods call unto gods,
For measureless is the gulf that lies between divini-
  ties,
And windless is the space.
Yet I would comfort you,
I would make serene your clouded sphere;
And though equal we are in power and judgment,
I would counsel you.

When out of chaos came the earth, and we, sons
of the beginning, beheld each other in the lustless
light, we breathed the first hushed, tremulous sound
that quickened the currents of air and sea.

Then we walked, hand in hand, upon the gray infant world, and out of the echoes of our first drowsy
steps time was born, a fourth divinity, that sets his

14

feet upon our footprints, shadowing our thoughts and desires, and seeing only with our eyes.

And unto earth came life, and unto life came the spirit, the winged melody of the universe. And we ruled life and spirit, and none save us knew the measure of the years nor the weight of years' nebulous dreams, till we, at noontide of the seventh æon, gave the sea in marriage to the sun.

And from the inner chamber of their nuptial ecstasy, we brought man, a creature who, though yielding and infirm, bears ever the marks of his parentage.

Through man who walks earth with eyes upon the stars, we find pathways to earth's distant regions; and of man, the humble reed growing beside dark waters, we make a flute through whose hollowed heart we pour our voice to the silence-bound world. From the sunless north to the sun-smitten sand of
the south.
From the lotus land where days are born
To perilous isles where days are slain,

Man, the faint hearted, overbold by our purpose,
Ventures with lyre and sword.
Ours is the will he heralds,
And our the sovereignty he proclaims,
And his love trodden courses are rivers, to the sea of
  our desires.
We, upon the heights, in man's sleep dream our
  dreams.
We urge his days to part from the valley of twilights
And seek their fullness upon the hills.
Our hands direct the tempests that sweep the world
And summon man from sterile peace to fertile strife,
And on to triumph.
In our eyes is the vision that turns man's soul to
  flame,
And leads him to exalted loneliness and rebellious
  prophecy,
And on to crucifixion.
Man is born to bondage,
And in bondage is his honor and his reward.
In man we seek a mouthpiece,
16

And in his life our self fulfillment.

Whose heart shall echo our voice if the human heart
is deafened with dust?

Who shall behold our shining if man's eye is blinded
with night?

And what would you do with man, child of our
earliest heart, our own self image?

THIRD GOD

Brothers, my mighty brothers,
The dancer's feet are drunk with songs.
They set the air a-throbbing,
And like doves her hands fly upward.

FIRST GOD

The lark calls to the lark,
But upward the eagle soars,
Nor tarries to hear the song.
You would teach me self love fulfilled in man's
worship,
And content with man's servitude.

17

But my self love is limitless and without measure.
I would rise beyond my earthbound mortality
And throne me upon the heavens.
My arms would girdle space and encompass the
    spheres.
I would take the starry way for a bow,
And the comets for arrows,
And with the infinite would I conquer the infinite.

But you would not do this, were it in your power.
For even as man is to man,
So are gods to gods.
Nay, you would bring to my weary heart
Remembrance of cycles spent in mist,
When my soul sought itself among the mountains
And mine eyes pursued their own image in slumber-
    ing waters;
Though my yesterday died in child-birth
And only silence visits her womb,
And the wind strewn sand nestles at her breast.

18

Oh yesterday, dead yesterday,
Mother of my chained divinity,
What super-god caught you in your flight
And made you breed in the cage?
What giant sun warmed your bosom
To give me birth?
I bless you not, yet I would not curse you;
For even as you have burdened me with life
So I have burdened man.
But less cruel have I been.
I, immortal, made man a passing shadow;
And you, dying, conceived me deathless.

Yesterday, dead yesterday,
Shall you return with distant tomorrow,
That I may bring you to judgment?
And will you wake with life's second dawn
That I may erase your earth-clinging memory from
        the earth?
Would that you might rise with all the dead of yore,
Till the land choke with its own bitter fruit,

And all the seas be stagnant with the slain,
And woe upon woe exhaust earth's vain fertility.

THIRD GOD

Brother, my sacred brothers,
The girl has heard the song,
And now she seeks the singer.
Like a fawn in glad surprise
She leaps over rocks and streams
And turns her to every side.
Oh, the joy in mortal intent,
The eye of purpose half-born;
The smile on lips that quiver
With foretaste of promised delight!
What flower has fallen from heaven,
What flame has risen from hell,
That startled the heart of silence
To this breathless joy and fear?
What dream dreamt we upon the height,
What thought gave we to the wind
That woke the drowsing valley
And made watchful the night?

20

SECOND GOD

The sacred loom is given you,
And the art to weave the fabric.
The loom and the art shall be yours forevermore,
And yours the dark thread and the light,
And yours the purple and the gold.
Yet you would grudge yourself a raiment.
Your hands have spun man's soul
From living air and fire,
Yet now you would break the thread,
And lend your versèd fingers to an idle eternity.

FIRST GOD

Nay, unto eternity unmoulded I would give my
    hands,
And to untrodden fields assign my feet.
What joy is there in songs oft heard,
Whose tune the remembering ear arrests
Ere the breath yields it to the wind?
My heart longs for what my heart conceives not,

21

And unto the unknown where memory dwells not
I would command my spirit.
Oh, tempt me not with glory possessed,
And seek not to comfort me with your dream or
    mine,
For all that I am, and all that there is on earth,
And all that shall be, inviteth not my soul.

    Oh my soul,
    Silent is thy face,
    And in thine eyes the shadows of night are sleep-
        ing.
    But terrible is thy silence,
    And thou art terrible.

THIRD GOD

Brothers, my solemn brothers,
The girl has found the singer.
She sees his raptured face.
Panther-like she slips with subtle steps
Through rustling vine and fern.
And now amid his ardent cries

22

He gazes full on her.

Oh my brothers, my heedless brothers,
Is it some other god in passion
Who has woven this web of scarlet and white?
What unbridled star has gone astray?
Whose secret keepeth night from morning?
And whose hand is upon our world?

FIRST GOD

Oh my soul, my soul,
Thou burning sphere that girdles me,
How shall I guide thy course,
And unto what space direct thy eagerness?

Oh my mateless soul,
In thy hunger thou preyest upon thyself,
And with thine own tears thou wouldst quench thy
        thirst;
For night gathers not her dew into thy cup,
And the day brings thee no fruit.

23

Oh my soul, my soul,
Thou grounded ship laden with desire,
Whence shall come the wind to fill thy sail,
And what higher tide shall release thy rudder?
Weighed is thine anchor and thy wings would
      spread,
But the skies are silent above thee,
And the still sea mocks at thy immobility.

And what hope is there for thee and me?
What shifting of worlds, what new purpose in the
      heavens,
That shall claim thee?
Does the womb of the virgin infinite
Bear the seed of thy Redeemer,
One mightier than thy vision
Whose hand shall deliver thee from thy captivity?

SECOND GOD

Hold your importunate cry,
And the breath of your burning heart,

24

For deaf is the ear of the infinite,
And heedless is the sky.
We are the beyond and we are the Most High,
And between us and boundless eternity
Is naught save our unshaped passion
And the motive thereof.

You invoke the unknown,
And the unknown clad with moving mist
Dwells in your own soul.
Yea, in your own soul your Redeemer lies asleep,
And in sleep sees what your waking eye does not see.
And that is the secret of our being.
Would you leave the harvest ungathered,
In haste to sow again the dreaming furrow?
And wherefore spread you your cloud in trackless
    fields and desolate,
When your own flock is seeking you,
And would fain gather in your shadow?
Forbear and look down upon the world.
Behold the unweaned children of your love.

The earth is your abode, and the earth is your
　　throne;
And high beyond man's furtherest hope
Your hand upholds his destiny.
You would not abandon him
Who strives to reach you through gladness and
　　through pain.
You would not turn away your face from the need
　　in his eye.

FIRST GOD

Does dawn hold the heart of night unto her heart?
Or shall the sea heed the bodies of her dead?
Like dawn my soul rises within me
Naked and unencumbered.
And like the unresting sea
My heart casts out a perishing wrack of man and
　　earth.
I would not cling to that that clings to me.
But unto that that rises beyond my reach I would
　　arise.

26

Brothers, behold, my brothers,
They meet, two star-bound spirits in the sky encountering.
In silence they gaze the one upon the other.
He sings no more,
And yet his sunburnt throat throbs with the song;
And in her limbs the happy dance is stayed
But not asleep.

Brothers, my strange brothers,
The night waxeth deep,
And brighter is the moon,
And twixt the meadow and the sea
A voice in rapture calleth you and me.

SECOND GOD

To be, to rise, to burn before the burning sun,
To live, and to watch the nights of the living
As Orion watches us!

27

To face the four winds with a head crowned and
    high,
And to heal the ills of man with our tideless breath!
The tentmaker sits darkly at his loom,
And the potter turns his wheel unaware;
But we, the sleepless and the knowing,
We are released from guessing and from chance.
We pause not nor do we wait for thought.
We are beyond all restless questioning.
Be content and let the dreaming go.
Like rivers let us flow to ocean
Unwounded by the edges of the rocks;
And when we reach her heart and are merged,
No more shall we wrangle and reason of tomorrow.

FIRST GOD

Oh, this ache of ceaseless divining,
This vigil of guiding the day unto twilight,
And the night unto dawn;
This tide of ever remembering and forgetting;
This ever sowing destinies and reaping but hopes;

This changeless lifting of self from dust to mist,
Only to long for dust, and to fall down with long-
    ing unto dust,
And still with greater longing to seek the mist again.
And this timeless measuring of time.
Must my soul needs to be a sea whose currents for-
    ever confound one another,
Or the sky where the warring winds turn hurricane?

Were I man, a blind fragment,
I could have met it with patience.
Or if I were the Supreme Godhead,
Who fills the emptiness of man and of gods,
I would be fulfilled.
But you and I are neither human,
Nor the Supreme above us.
We are but twilights ever rising and ever fading
Between horizon and horizon.
We are but gods holding a world and held by it,
Fates that sound the trumpets
Whilst the breath and the music come from beyond.

And I rebel.
I would exhaust myself to emptiness.
I would dissolve myself afar from your vision,
And from the memory of this silent youth, our
    younger brother,
Who sits beside us gazing into yonder valley,
And though his lips move, utters not a word.

THIRD GOD

I speak, my unheeding brothers,
I do indeed speak,
But you hear only your own words.
I bid you see your glory and mine,
But you turn, and close your eyes,
And rock your thrones.
Ye sovereigns who would govern the above world
    and the world beneath,
Gods self-bent, whose yesterday is ever jealous of
    your tomorrow,
Self-weary, who would unleash your temper with
    speech

And lash our orb with thunderings!
Your feud is but the sounding of an Ancient Lyre
Whose strings have been half forgotten by His
 fingers
Who has Orion for a harp and the Pleiades for
 cymbals.
Even now, while you are muttering and rumbling,
His harp rings, His cymbals clash,
And I beseech you hear His song.

 Behold, man and woman,
 Flame to flame,
 In white ecstasy.
Roots that suck at the breast of purple earth,
Flame flowers at the breasts of the sky.
And we are the purple breast,
And we are the enduring sky.
Our soul, even the soul of life, your soul and mine,
Dwells this night in a throat enflamed,
And garments the body of a girl with beating waves.
Your sceptre cannot sway this destiny,

Your weariness is but ambition.
This and all is wiped away
In the passion of a man and a maid.

SECOND GOD

Yea, what of this love of man and woman?
See how the east wind dances with her dancing feet,
And the west wind rises singing with his song.
Behold our sacred purpose now enthroned,
In the yielding of a spirit that sings to a body that
　　dances.

FIRST GOD

I will not turn my eyes downward to the conceit of
　　earth,
Nor to her children in their slow agony that you call
　　love.
And what is love,
But the muffled drum that leads the long procession
　　of sweet uncertainty
To another slow agony?
I will not look downward.

32

What is there to behold
Save a man and a woman in the forest that grew to
    trap them
That they might renounce self
And parent creatures for our unborn tomorrow?

THIRD GOD

Oh, the affliction of knowing,
The starless veil of prying and questioning
Which we have laid upon the world;
And the challenge to human forbearance!
We would lay under a stone a waxen shape
And say, It is a thing of clay,
And in clay let it find its end.
We would hold in our hands a white flame
And say in our heart,
It is a fragment of ourselves returning,
A breath of our breath that had escaped,
And now haunts our hands and lips for more fra-
    grance.
Earth gods, my brothers,

33

High upon the mountain,
We are still earth-bound,
Through man desiring the golden hours of man's
    destiny.
Shall our wisdom ravish beauty from his eyes?
Shall our measures subdue his passion to stillness,
Or to our own passion?

What would your armies of reasoning
Where love encamps his host?
They who are conquered by love,
And upon whose bodies love's chariot ran
From sea to mountain
And again from mountain to the sea,
Stand even now in a shy half-embrace.
Petal unto petal they breathe the sacred perfume,
Soul to soul they find the soul of life,
And upon their eyelids lies a prayer
Unto you and unto me.
Love is a night bent down to a bower anointed,
A sky turned meadow, and all the stars to fireflies.

34

True it is, we are the beyond,
And we are the Most High.
But love is beyond our questioning,
And love outsoars our song.

SECOND GOD

Seek you a distant orb,
And would not consider this star
Where your sinews are planted?
There is no centre in space
Save where self is wedded to self,
And beauty is the witness and the priest.
And see and behold beauty scattered about our feet,
And beauty filling our hands to shame our lips.
The most distant is the most near.
And where beauty is, there are all things.

Oh, lofty dreaming brother,
Return to us from time's dim borderland!
Unlace your feet from no-where and no-when,
And dwell with us in this security

35

Which your hand interwined with ours
Has builded stone upon stone.
Cast off your mantle of brooding,
And comrade us, masters of the young earth green
     and warm.

FIRST GOD

Eternal Altar! Wouldst thou indeed this night
A god for sacrifice?
Now then, I come, and coming I offer up
My passion and my pain.
Lo, there is the dancer, carved out of our ancient
     eagerness,
And the singer is crying mine own songs unto the
     wind.
And in that dancing and in that singing
A god is slain within me.
My god-heart within my human ribs
Shouts to my god-heart in mid-air.
The human pit that wearied me calls to divinity.
36

The beauty that we have sought from the beginning
Calls unto divinity.
I heed, and I have measured the call,
And now I yield.
Beauty is a path that leads to self self-slain.
Beat your strings.
I will to walk the path.
It stretches ever to another dawn.

THIRD GOD

Love triumphs.
The white and green of love beside a lake,
And the proud majesty of love in tower or balcony;
Love in a garden or in the desert untrodden,
Love is our lord and master.
It is not a wanton decay of the flesh,
Nor the crumbling of desire
When desire and self are wrestling;
Nor is it flesh that takes arms against the spirit.
Love rebels not.

37

It only leaves the trodden way of ancient destinies
    for the sacred grove,
To sing and dance its secret to eternity.
Love is youth with chains broken,
Manhood made free from the sod,
And womanhood warmed by the flame
And shining with the light of heaven deeper than
    our heaven.
Love is a distant laughter in the spirit.
It is a wild assault that hushes you to your awaken-
    ing.
It is a new dawn upon the earth,
A day not yet achieved in your eyes or mine,
But already achieved in its own greater heart.

Brothers, my brothers,
The bride comes from the heart of dawn,
And the bridegroom from the sunset.
There is a wedding in the valley.
A day too vast for recording.

Thus has it been since the first morn
Discharged the plains to hill and vale,
And thus shall it be to the last even-tide.
Our roots have brought forth the dancing branches
     in the valley,
And we are the flowering of the song-scent that rises
     to the heights.
Immortal and mortal, twin rivers calling to the sea.
There is no emptiness between call and call,
But only in the ear.
Time maketh our listening more certain,
And giveth it more desire.
Only doubt in mortal hushes the sound.
We have outsoared the doubt.
Man is a child of our younger heart.
Man is god in slow arising;
And betwixt his joy and his pain
Lies our sleeping, and the dreaming thereof.

39

FIRST GOD

Let the singer cry, and let the dancer whirl her feet
And let me be content awhile.
Let my soul be serene this night.
Perchance I may drowse, and drowsing
Behold a brighter world
And creatures more starry supple to my mind.

THIRD GOD

Now I will rise and strip me of time and space,
And I will dance in that field untrodden,
And the dancer's feet will move with my feet;
And I will sing in that higher air,
And a human voice will throb within my voice.

We shall pass into the twilight;
Perchance to wake to the dawn of another world.
But love shall stay,
And his finger-marks shall not be erased.

The blessed forge burns,
40

The sparks rise, and each spark is a sun.
Better it is for us, and wiser,
To seek a shadowed nook and sleep in our earth
    divinity,
And let love, human and frail, command the com-
    ing day.

BOOK SEVEN

BOOK SEVEN

NYMPHS

OF THE VALLEY

MARTHA

MARTHA

Her father died whilst she was still in the cradle, and her mother before she was ten years old. She was left an orphan in the house of a poor neighbor who lived with his wife and children and existed on the fruits of the soil in a small isolated hamlet amidst the beautiful valleys of Lebanon.

Her father died and bequeathed to her nothing save his name and a poor hut standing among the nut trees and poplars. From her mother she inherited only tears of grief and her orphan state. She sojourned a stranger in the land of her birth; alone among the intertwining trees and towering rocks. Each morning she walked barefooted in a tattered dress behind a milch cow to a part of the valley where the pasture was rich, and sat in the shade of a tree. She sang with the birds and wept with the brook while she envied the cow its abundance of food. She looked at the flowers and watched the fluttering butterflies. When the sun sank below the horizon and hunger overtook her she returned to the hut and sat beside her guardian's daughter and ate greedily of the maize bread with a little dried fruit and beans dipped in vinegar and olive oil. After the meal she spread some dry straw on the ground and laid herself down, her head resting on her arms. She slept and sighed, wishing that life were one long deep sleep undisturbed by dreams or awakening. At the approach of dawn her guardian roused her roughly to attend to his needs and she awoke from her slumbers afraid and trembling at his harshness and anger. Thus passed the years for Martha, the unfortunate, amongst those distant hills and valleys.

Soon she began to feel in her heart the stirring of emotions she had never before known; it was like becoming aware of the perfume in the heart of a flower. Dreams and strange thoughts crowded upon her like a flock that comes across a watercourse. She became a woman, and she likened herself in some vague manner to fresh virgin soil that is yet to be planted with the

4

seeds of knowledge and feel upon it the imprints of experience. A girl profound and pure of soul whom a decree of fate had exiled to that farmstead where life passed through its appointed phases with the seasons of the year. It was as though she were a shadow of an unknown god residing between the earth and the sun.

Those of us who have spent the greater part of our existence in crowded cities know little of the life of the inhabitants of the villages and hamlets tucked away in Lebanon. We are carried along on the current of modern civilization. We have forgotten — or so we tell ourselves — the philosophy of that beautiful and simple life of purity and spiritual cleanliness. If we turned and looked we would see it smiling in the spring; drowsing with the summer sun; harvesting in the autumn, and in the winter at rest; like our mother Nature in all her moods. We are richer in material wealth than those villagers; but their spirit is a nobler spirit than ours. We sow much but reap nothing. But what they sow they also reap. We are the slaves of our appetites; they, the children of their contentment. We drink the cup of life, a liquid clouded with bitterness, despair, fear, weariness. They drink of it clear.

Martha reached the age of sixteen years. Her soul was a polished mirror reflecting all the loveliness of the fields, and her heart was like the wide valleys which threw back voices in echo.

One autumn day when nature seemed filled with sadness she sat by a spring, freed from its earthly prison like thoughts from the imagination of a poet, looking at the fluttering of yellowed leaves as they fell from the trees. She watched the wind playing with them as Death plays with the souls of men. She gazed on the flowers and saw that they were withered and their hearts dried up and broken into little pieces. They were storing their seeds in the earth as women their trinkets and jewelry during times of war and disturbance.

While she sat thus looking at the flowers and trees and sharing with them their pain at the passing of summer, she heard the sounds of hoofs on the broken stones of the valley. She turned round and beheld a horseman riding

6

slowly toward her; his bearing and dress told of ease and wealth. He dismounted from his horse and greeted her gently, in a manner no man had ever used to her before.

"I have strayed from the road leading down to the coast. Could you direct me to it?" he asked.

She stood upright by the edge of the spring, straight like a young branch, and answered him: "I do not know, my master, but I will go and ask my guardian; for he knows." She uttered these words, at the same time feeling a little afraid, with a shyness and modesty that heightened her tenderness and beauty. She was about to go when the man stopped her. The red wine of his youth coursed strongly through his veins. His look toward her changed as he said: "No, do not go." She remained standing and wondering, for she felt in his voice a force that prevented her from movement. She stole a glance at him. He was looking at her carefully; a look whose meaning she could not understand. Then he smiled at her in so bewitching a manner as to make her want to weep at its very sweetness.

He let his eye rest with affection on her bare feet, her pretty wrists, her smooth neck, her soft thick hair. He noted, with a rising passion, her gleaming skin given her by the sun, and her arms, which nature had made strong. But she stayed silent and ashamed. She did not want to go away, nor, for reasons she was unable to divine, could she find power to speak.

The milch cow returned that evening to the enclosure without her mistress; for Martha did not go back. When her guardian came home from the fields, he sought her in all the hollows but did not find her. He called her by name but there came no answer save echoes from the cave and the soughing of the wind in the trees. He returned sorrowing to his hut and told his wife. She wept silently throughout that night, saying within herself: "I have seen her in a dream in the claws of a wild beast, who tore her body to pieces the while she smiled and wept."

That is what I gleaned of the life of Martha in that pretty hamlet. I learned it of an old villager who had known her since the days of her childhood. She had disappeared from those places leaving nothing behind her save a few tears in the eyes of the guardian's woman, and a pathetic memory that rode on the morning breeze over the valley and then, like the breath of a child on a windowpane, faded.

II

I returned to Beirut in the autumn of 1900 after having passed my college vacation in North Lebanon. Before returning to my studies I spent a week wandering around in the town with some of my fellow students, savoring with them the delights of freedom, for which youth hungers and which is denied it at home and within the four walls of a classroom. It is like a bird that, finding its cage door open, flies to and fro, its heart swelling with song and the joy of escape.

Youth is a beautiful dream, but its sweetness is enslaved by the dullness of books and its awakening is a harsh one.

Shall there come a day when wise men are able to unite the dreams of youth and the delights of learning as reproach brings together hearts in conflict? Shall there come a day when man's teacher is nature, and humanity is his book and life his school? Will that day be?

We know not, but we feel the urgency that moves us ever upwards toward a spiritual progress, and that progress is an understanding of the beauty of all creation through the kindness of ourselves and the dissemination of happiness through our love of that beauty.

That evening as I sat in the porch of my lodgings watching the moving crowds and listening to the cries of the street venders, each extolling the excellence of his wares and foods, a boy came up to me. He was about five years of age and clad in rags and tatters, and on his shoulder he carried a tray filled with bunches of flowers. In a voice broken and feeble, as though handed down to him as a heritage of long suffering, he asked me to buy a flower from him.

I looked into his small pale face and remarked his eyes, dark with the shadows of weariness and poverty; his mouth, open a little like a wound in a scarred breast; his emaciated bare arms and his puny little body bent over the tray of flowers like a rose-plant yellowed and

withered among fresh green plants. I saw all
these things as it were at one glance, and in my
pity I smiled, a smile in which was something
of tears. Those smiles that break forth from the
depths of our hearts and rise to our lips. Should
we heed them not, they find outlet through our
eyes.

I bought some of his flowers, but it was his
speech that I wished to buy, for I felt that behind his wistful looks was curtained off the act
of a tragedy — a tragedy of the poor, playing
perpetually upon the stage of the days. An act
seldom seen because it is a tragedy. When I spoke
to him with kind words, he grew friendly as
though having found a body in whom he could
seek protection and safety. He gazed at me in
wonder, for he and his like are accustomed only
to rough words from those other boys who look
upon boys of the streets as things defiled and of
no account and not as little souls wounded by
the arrows of fortune. I then asked him his
name.

"Fouad," he answered, with his eyes averted
to the ground.

"The son of whom, and where are your people?"

"I am the son of Martha, woman of Ban."

"And your father?" I asked.

He shook his small head as one who knows not what a father is.

"Then where is your mother, Fouad?"

"At home, ill."

These few words from the boy's lips smote my ears, and out of them my inmost feelings fashioned strange and melancholy forms and figures for I knew, at once, that the unfortunate Martha whose story I had heard from the villager was now ill in Beirut. That girl who yesterday was among the trees and valleys away from harm was today suffering the harshness of hunger and pain in a city. The orphan girl who passed the days of her childhood with nature, tending her cows in the beautiful fields, had been carried away on the tide of corrupt civilization to become a prey in the grasp of misery and misfortune.

As these things passed through my mind the boy continued to gaze at me as though he saw

13

with the eye of his innocent spirit my broken heart.

He made as if to go away but I seized his hand and said: "Take me to your mother; I want to see her."

He led the way, walking before me silent and wondering. From time to time he looked back to see if in truth I was following behind him. With feelings of fear and dread I walked on through dirty streets wherein the air was leavened with the breath of death, past tumble-down houses wherein evil men practiced their evil deeds behind the curtains of night. Through winding alleyways that twisted and writhed like vipers I walked behind that boy of tender years and innocent heart and unvoiced courage. The courage of those acquainted with the wiles and tricks of the dregs in the midst of a city known to the East as the "Bride of Syria" and the pearl in the crown of kings. We reached the outskirts of the quarter at last, and the boy entered a mean dwelling to which the passage of years had left only a crumbling side.

I went in after him, my heart beating rapidly as I approached the room. I found myself in the middle of a room the air of which was damp. It possessed no furniture save a lamp whose feeble light cut the gloom with its yellow rays, and a couch whose appearance spoke of dire poverty, and destitution and want. Upon the couch was a sleeping woman with her face turned to the wall as though taking refuge in it from the cruelties of the world; or mayhap seeing in its stones a heart more tender and compassionate than the hearts of men. The boy went up to her crying: "Mother, Mother." She turned round and saw him pointing at me. At this she made a movement beneath the tattered bed-coverings and, in a voice rendered bitter by the sufferings of a spirit in agony, cried:

"What do you want, O man? Do you come to purchase the last shreds of my life so that you might defile it with your lust? Go from me, for the streets are filled with women ready to sell their bodies and souls cheaply. But I, I have naught for sale save a few gasps of breath, and those will Death soon buy with the peace of the grave."

I moved near to the bed. Her words moved me to the depths of my heart for they were the epitome or her tale of sorrow. I spoke to her and wished that my feelings might flow with my words.

"Be not afraid of me, Martha. I come not to you as a ravening beast but as a sorrowing man. I am of Lebanon and long have I dwelt in the midst of those valleys and villages by the forest of the cedars. Fear not, then, Martha."

She listened to my words and knew in her being that they rose from the deepnesses of a spirit that wept with her, for she shook and trembled upon her bed like a naked branch before the winter wind. She put her hands over her face as though she would hide herself from that memory, frightening in its sweetness, bitter in its beauty. After a silence in which was a sighing her face reappeared between her trembling shoulders. I saw her sunken eyes gaze at an unseen thing standing in the emptiness of the room, and her dry lips quiver with the quiver of despair. In her throat the approach of death rattled and with it a deep and broken moaning. Then she spoke. Entreaty and supplication gave her utterance, and weakness and pain brought back her voice:

"You have come here from kindness and compassion, and if pity for the sinful be deemed a pious deed, and compassion on those who have gone astray a meritorious act, then shall Heaven reward you for me. I pray you go from here and return whence you come, for your presence in this place will earn for you shame, and your pity for me will bring insult and contempt upon you. Go, go ere anybody see you in this foul room, filthy with the filth of swine. Walk swiftly and cover your face with your cloak so that no passer-by may know you. The compassion that fills you will not bring back my purity, neither will it wipe out my sin, nor stay the strong hand of Death from me. My wretchedness and guilt have banished me to these dark depths. Let not your pity bring you near to blemish. I am a leper dwelling amidst graves. Do not approach me lest people hold you unclean and draw away from you. Return now, but mention not my name in those sacred valleys, for the shepherd will deny the diseased lamb in fear for his flock. If you should make mention of me say that Martha, woman of Ban, is dead; say naught else."

She then took her son's two small hands and kissed them sadly. She sighed and spoke again:

"People will look upon my child with contempt and a mocking, saying this one is the offshoot of sin; this is the son of Martha, the harlot; this is the child of shame, of chance. They will say of him more than that, for they are blind and will not see and know not that his mother has purified his childhood with her agony and tears and atoned for his life with her sorrow and misfortune. I shall die leaving him an orphan among the children of the streets, alone in this pitiless existence, bequeathing to him naught save a terrible memory. If he be a coward and a weakling, he will be ashamed before this memory; if he be courageous and just, then will his blood be stirred. If Heaven should perchance preserve him and let him grow to be a man in strength, then will he be helped by Heaven against those who have wronged him and his mother. If he should die and be delivered from the snare of years, he shall find me beyond, where all is light and rest, awaiting his coming."

My heart inspired me to speak:

18

"You are no leper, Martha, even if you dwelt among graves. You are not unclean even if life has put you in the hands of the unclean. The dross of the flesh cannot reach out its hand to the pure spirit, and the masses of snow cannot kill the living seeds. What is this life except a threshing-floor of sorrows upon which the sheaves of souls are trodden ere giving up their yield? But woe to those ears that are left without the threshing-floor, for the ants of the earth shall carry them away and the birds of the sky shall take them up and they shall not enter into the storehouses of the master of the field.

"You are oppressed, Martha, and he who has oppressed you is a child of the palaces, great of wealth and little of soul. You are persecuted and despised, but it were better that a person should be the oppressed than that he should be the oppressor; and fitter that he should be a victim to the frailty of human instincts than that he should be powerful and crush the flowers of life and disfigure the beauties of feeling with his desire. The soul is a link in the divine chain. The fiery heat may twist and distort this link and destroy the beauty of its roundness, but it cannot transmute its gold to another metal; rather will it become even more glittering. But woe to the bruised and the weak when the fire shall consume him and make him ashes to be blown by the winds and scattered over the face of the desert! Ay, Martha, you are a flower crushed beneath the feet of the animal that is concealed in a human being. Heavy-shod feet have trodden you down, but they have not destroyed that fragrance which goes up with the widow's lament and the orphan's cry and the poor man's sigh toward Heaven, the fount of justice and mercy. Take comfort, Martha, in that you are the flower crushed and not the foot that has crushed it."

She listened with intentness as I spoke, and her face was lighted up with solace as the clouds are illuminated by the soft rays of the setting sun. She motioned me to sit beside her. I did so, seeking to learn from her eloquent features of the hidden things of her sad spirit. She had the look of one who knows that he is about to die. It was the look of a girl yet in the spring-time of life who felt the footfalls of Death by her broken-down bed. The look of a woman forsaken who yesteryear stood in the beautiful valleys of Lebanon filled with life and strength, but now exhausted and awaiting deliverance from the bonds of existence.

After a moving silence she gathered together the remnants of her strength. She started to speak, her tears adding meaning to the words, her very soul in every breath she took:

"Yes, I am oppressed. I am the prey to the animal in men. I am a flower trodden underfoot. . . . I was sitting by the edge of the spring as he rode by. He spoke kindly to me and said that I was beautiful, that he loved me and would not forsake me. He said that the wide spaces were places of desolation and the valleys the abode of birds and jackals. . . . He took me and drew me to his breast and kissed me. Until then I knew not the taste of kisses, for I was an orphan and outcast. He mounted me behind him on the back of his horse and took me to a fine house standing alone. There he gave me garments of silk and perfumes and rich food and drink. . . . All this did he do, smiling, and behind soft words and loving gestures did he conceal his lust and animal desires. After

he had satisfied himself of my body and brought
low my spirit in humility he went away, leaving inside me a living flame fed by my liver,
and it grew in swiftness. Then I went out into
this darkness from between the embers of pain
and the bitterness of weeping. . . . So was life
cut into two parts; one weak and grieving, and
the other small and crying into the silences of
the night, seeking return to the vast emptiness.
In that lonely house my oppressor left me and
my suckling child to endure the cruelties of
hunger and cold and aloneness. No companion
had we save fear and haunting; neither had we
helper save weeping and lament. His friends
came to learn of my place and know of my need
and weakness. They came to me, one following
upon another. They wanted to buy me with
wealth and give me bread against my honor.
. . . Ah, many times did my own hand determine to set free my spirit. But I turned from
that, for my life belonged not to me alone; my
child had part in it. My child, whom Heaven
had thrust aside from it into this life as it had
exiled me from life and cast me into the depths
of the abyss. . . . Behold now, the hour is at

hand and my bridegroom Death is come after long absence to lead me to his soft bed."

After a deep silence that was like the presence of spirits in flight, she lifted up eyes veiled by the shadows of death and in a gentle voice said:

"O Justice who are hidden, concealed behind these terrifying images, you, and you alone, hear the cry of my departing spirit and the call of my neglected heart. You alone do I pray and beseech to have mercy on me and guard with your right hand my child and with your left receive my spirit."

Her strength ebbed and her sighing grew weak. She looked toward her son with grief and tenderness, then lowered her eyes slowly and in a voice that was almost a silence recited:

"Our Father which art in heaven, hallowed be Thy name. . . . Thy kingdom come. Thy will be done on earth as it is in heaven. . . . Forgive us our transgressions. . . ."

Her voice ceased, but her lips still moved for a while. When they grew still, all movement left her body. A shudder ran through her and she sighed and her face became pale. Her spirit departed and her eyes remained gazing at the unseen.

With the coming of dawn Martha's body was laid in a wooden coffin and carried on the shoulders of two poor persons. We buried her in a deserted field far out from the town, for the priests would not pray over her remains, neither would they let her bones rest in the cemetery, wherein the cross stood guard over the graves. No mourners went to that distant burial-ground save her son and another boy whom the adversities of existence had taught compassion.

DUST OF THE AGES AND THE ETERNAL FIRE

DUST OF THE AGES
AND THE ETERNAL FIRE

I

[*Autumn,* 116 B.C.]

The night was still and all life slept in the
City of the Sun.[1] The lamps in the houses scattered around the great temples in the midst of
olive and laurel trees had long been extinguished. The rising moon spilled its rays over
the whiteness of the tall marble columns which
stood upright like giant sentinels in the tranquil
night over the shrines of the gods. They looked
in wonder and awe toward the towers of Lebanon, dwelling in rugged places on distant
heights.

---

[1] I.e., Baalbek, city of Baal, the sun god. The ancients
knew it as Heliopolis; it was one of the loveliest cities of
Syria, and its ruins still stand.

At that magic hour poised between the spirits of the sleeping and dreams of the infinite, Nathan, son of the priest, entered the temple of Astarte.[1] He carried in his trembling hand a torch and kindled with it the lamps and the censers. The sweet smell of frankincense and myrrh rose in the air, and the image of the goddess was adorned with a delicate veil like the veil of desire and longing that enshrines the human heart. He prostrated himself before an altar overlaid with ivory and gold, raised his hands in supplication, and lifted eyes filled with tears to the heavens. In a voice strangled with grief and broken by harsh sobs, he cried:

"Mercy, O great Astarte. Mercy, O goddess of love and beauty. Have pity on me and lift the hand of death from off my beloved, whom my soul has chosen to do your will. The potions and powders of the physicians have availed nothing, and the charms of the priests and wise men are in vain. There remains but your sacred

---

[1] Goddess of love and beauty among the ancient Phœnicians, who worshipped her in Tyre, Sidon, Byblos, and Baalbek. The Greek Aphrodite and the Roman Venus.

name to help and succor me. Answer, then, my prayer; look to my contrite heart and agony of spirit, and let her that is the part of my soul live so that we may rejoice in the secrets of your love and exult in the beauty of youth, which proclaims your glory. . . . From the depths do I cry unto you, sacred Astarte. From out of the darkness of this night do I seek the protection of your mercy. . . . Hear my cry! I am your servant Nathan, son of Hiram the priest, who has dedicated his life to the service of your altar. I love a maiden and have taken her for my own, but the brides of the Jinn have breathed upon her beautiful body the breath of a strange disease. They have sent the messenger of death to lead her to their enchanted caves. He now lies like a roaring hungry beast by her couch, spreading his black wings over her and stretching out his defiled hands to wrest her from me. Because of this have I come to you. Take pity on me and let her live. She is a flower that has not lived to enjoy the summer of its life; a bird whose joyful song greeting the dawn is cut off. Save her from the clutches of death and we will sing praises and make burnt offerings to the glory of your name. We will bring sacrifices to your altar and fill your vessels with wine and sweet scented oil and spread your tabernacle with roses and jasmine. We will burn incense and sweet-smelling aloe wood before your image. . . . Save her, O goddess of miracles, and let love conquer death, for you are the mistress of love and death."

He stopped speaking, weeping and sighing in his agony. Then he continued: "Alas, sacred Astarte, my dreams are shattered and the last breath of my life is fast ebbing; my heart is dying within me and my eyes are burned with tears. Sustain me through your compassion and let my beloved remain with me."

At that moment one of his slaves entered, came slowly toward him, and whispered in his ear: "She has opened her eyes, my lord, and looks around her couch but does not see you. I come to call you, for she cries for you continually."

Nathan rose and went out quickly, the slave following. On reaching his palace he entered the room of the sick girl and stood over her bed. He took her thin hand in his and kissed her lips repeatedly as though he would breathe new life into her emaciated body. She turned her face, which had been hidden among the silken pillows, toward him and opened her eyes a little. Upon her lips appeared the shadow of a smile — all that remained of life in her beautiful body; the last ray of light from a departing spirit; the echo from the cry of a heart fast approaching its end. She spoke, and her breath came in short gasps like that of a starveling child.

"The gods call me, betrothed of my soul, and Death has come to part us. . . . Grieve not, for the will of the gods is sacred and the demands of Death are just. . . . I am going now, but the twin cups of love and youth are still full in our hands and the ways of sweet life lie before us. . . . I am going, my beloved, to the meadows of the spirits, but I shall return to this world. Astarte brings back to this life the souls of lovers who have gone to the infinite before they have tasted of the delights of love and the joys of youth. . . . We shall meet again, Nathan, and together drink of the morning dew from the cups of the narcissus and re-

joice in the sun with the birds of the fields.
. . . Farewell, my beloved."

Her voice grew low and her lips began to
tremble like the petals of a flower before the
dawn breeze. Her lover clasped her to him,
wetting her neck with his tears. When his lips
touched her mouth they found it cold like ice.
He gave a terrible cry, rent his garments, and
threw himself upon her dead body, while his
spirit in its agony hovered between the deep
sea of life and the abyss of death.

In the stillness of that night the eyelids of
those who slept trembled, and the women of
the quarter grieved, and the souls of children
were afraid, for the darkness was rent by loud
cries of mourning and bitter weeping rising
from the palace of Astarte's priest. When
morning came the people sought Nathan to
console him and soothe him in his affliction, but
they did not find him.

Many days later, when the caravan from the
east arrived, its leader related how he had seen
Nathan far off in the wilderness wandering like
a stricken soul with the gazelles of the deserts.

Centuries passed and the feet of time obliterated the work of the ages. The gods went from the land, and other gods came in their stead — gods of anger wedded to destruction and ruin. They razed the fine temple of the City of the Sun and destroyed its beautiful palaces. Its verdant gardens became dry, and drought overtook its fertile fields. Nothing remained in that valley except decaying ruins to haunt the memory with ghosts of yesterday and recall the faint echo of psalms chanted to a past glory. But the ages that pass on and sweep away the works of man cannot destroy his dreams, nor can they weaken his innermost feelings and emotions; for these endure as long as the immortal spirit. Here, perhaps, they are concealed; there they may go into hiding like the sun at eventide or the moon with the approach of the morning.

II

[*Spring*, A.D. 1890]

Day was waning and the light was fading as the sun gathered up her garments from the plains of Baalbek. Ali Al-Husaini[1] turned with his flock toward the ruins of the temple and sat down by the fallen pillars. They looked like ribs of a long-forgotten soldier that had been broken in battle and rendered naked by the elements. The sheep gathered around him browsing, lulled into safety by the melodies of his pipe.

Midnight came and the heavens cast the seeds of the morrow into its dark depths. The eyelids of Ali grew tired with the specters of wakefulness. His mind became weary with the passing of the processions of imagination marching through the awful silence amidst the

---

[1] The Husainis are an Arab tribe dwelling in tents around Baalbek.

34

ruined walls. He supported himself on his arm while sleep crept upon him and covered his wakefulness lightly with the folds of its veil as the fine mist touches the surface of a calm lake.

Forgotten was his earthly self as he met his spiritual self; his hidden self filled with dreams transcending the laws and teachings of men. A vision appeared before his eyes and things hidden revealed themselves to him. His spirit stood apart from the procession of time ever hurrying on toward nothingness. It stood alone before the serried ranks of thoughts and contending emotions. He knew, or he was about to know, for the first time in his life, the causes of this spiritual hunger overtaking his youth. A hunger uniting all the bitterness and sweetness in existence. A thirst bringing together a cry of yearning and the serenity of fulfillment. A longing that all the glory of this world cannot blot out nor the course of life conceal.

For the first time in his life Ali Al-Husaini felt a strange sensation awakened in him by the ruins of the temple. A feeling without form of the remembrance of incense from the censers.

A haunting feeling that played unceasingly upon his senses as the fingertips of a musician play upon the strings of his lute. A new feeling welled up from out of nothingness — or perhaps it was from something. It grew and developed until it embraced the whole of his spiritual being. It filled his soul with an ecstasy near to death in its kindness, with a pain sweet in its bitterness, agreeable in its harshness. A feeling born of the vast spaces of a minute filled with sleepiness. A minute that gave birth to the patterns of the ages as the nations grow from one seed.

Ali looked toward the ruined shrine, and his weariness gave place to an awakening of the spirit. The ruined remains of the altar appeared to his sight and the places of the fallen pillars and the foundations of the crumbling walls grew clear and sharp. His eyes became glazed and his heart beat violently, and then suddenly, as with one who was till then sightless, the light returned to his eyes and he began to see — and he thought and reflected. And out of the chaos of thought and confusion of reflection were born the phantoms of memory, and he remembered. He remembered those pillars standing upright in greatness and pride. He recalled the silver lamps and censers surrounding the image of an awe-inspiring goddess. He recalled the venerable priests laying their offerings before an altar overlaid with ivory and gold. He recalled the maidens beating their tambourines and the youths chanting praises to the goddess of love and beauty. He remembered, and saw these figures becoming clear before his gaze. He felt the impressions of sleeping things stirring in the silences of his depths. But remembrance brings back naught save shadowy forms, which we see from the past of our lives; neither does it bring back to our ears except the echoes of voices that they once heard. What then was the link joining these haunting memories to the past life of a youth reared among the tents, who passed the springtime of his life tending his sheep in the wilderness?

Ali rose and walked among the ruins and broken stones. Those distant remembrances raised the covering of forgetfulness from his mind's eyes as a woman brushes away a cobweb

from the glass of her mirror. And so it was
until he reached the heart of the temple and
then stood still as though a magnetic attraction
in the earth were drawing his feet. And then
he suddenly saw before him a broken statue
lying on the ground. Involuntarily he prostrated himself before it. His feelings over-
flowed within him like the flowing of blood
from an open wound; his heartbeats rose and
fell, like the rise and fall of sea waves. He was
humbled in its sight and he sighed a bitter sigh
and wept in his grief, for he felt an aloneness
that wounded and a distance that annhilated,
separating his spirit from the beautiful spirit
that was by his side ere he entered this life. He
felt his very essence as naught save part of a
burning flame that God had separated from his
self before the beginning of time. He felt the
light fluttering of wings in his burning bones,
and around the relaxed cells of his brain a
strong and mighty love taking possession of his
heart and soul. A love that revealed the hidden
things of the spirit to the spirit, and by its actions separated the mind from the regions of
measurement and weight. A love that we hear

speaking when the tongues of life are silent; that we behold standing as a pillar of fire when darkness hides all things. That love, that god, had fallen in this hour upon the spirit of Ali Al-Husaini and awakened in it feelings bitter and sweet as the sun brings forth the flowers side by side with thorns.

What thing is this love? Whence does it come? What does it want of a youth resting with his flock among the ruined shrines? What is this wine which courses through the veins of one whom maidens' glances left unmoved? What are these heavenly melodies that rise and fall upon the ears of a bedouin who heard not yet the sweet songs of women?

What thing is this love and whence does it come? What does it want of Ali, busied with his sheep and his flute away from men? Is it something sowed in his heart by man-wrought beauties without the awareness of his senses? Or is it a bright light veiled by the mist and now breaking forth to illumine the emptiness of his soul? Is it perchance a dream come in the stillness of the night to mock at him, or a truth that was and will be to the end of time?

Ali closed his tear-filled eyes and stretched out his hands like a beggar seeking pity. His spirit trembled within him, and out of its trembling came broken sobs in which were both whining complaint and the fire of longing. In a voice that only the faint sound of words lifted above a sigh he called:

"Who are you that are so close to my heart yet unseen by my eyes, separating myself from my self, linking my present to distant and forgotten ages? Are you a nymph, a sprite, come from the world of immortals to speak to me of the vanity of life and the frailty of the flesh? Are you mayhap the spirit of the queen of the Jinn risen from the bowels of the earth to enslave my senses and make of me a laughing-stock among the young men of my tribe? Who are you and what thing is this temptation, quickening and destroying, which has seized hold of my heart? What feelings are these that fill me with fire and light? Who am I and what is this new self I call 'I' yet which is a stranger to me? Is the spring water of life swallowed up with the particles of air and I am become an angel that sees and hears all things secret? Am I drunk of the Devil's brew and become blinded to real things?"

He fell silent for a little while. His emotion grew in strength and his spirit grew in stature. He spoke again:

"O one whom the spirit reveals and brings near and whom the night conceals and makes distant, O beautiful spirit hovering in the spaces of my dreams, you have awakened within my being feelings that were aslumber like flower seeds hidden beneath the snow, and passed as the breeze, the bearer of the breath of the fields. And touched my senses so that they are shaken and disturbed as the leaves of a tree. Let me look upon you, if you be then of body and substance. Command sleep to close my eyelids that I might see you in my dreaming, if you be free of the earth. Let me touch you; let me hear your voice. Tear aside the veil that covers my whole being and destroy the fabric that conceals my divineness. Grant me wings that I might fly after you to the regions of the assembly on high, if you be of those that inhabit there. Touch with magic my eyelids and I shall follow you to the secret places of the Jinn, if you be one of their nymphs. Put your unseen hand upon my heart and possess me, if you be free to let follow whom you will."

So did Ali whisper into the ears of darkness words moving up from the echo of a melody in the depths of his heart. Between his vision and his surroundings flowed phantoms of the night as though they were incense rising out of his hot tears. Upon the walls of the temple appeared enchanted pictures in the colors of the rainbow.

So passed the hour. He rejoiced in his tears and was glad in his grief. He listened to the beating of his heart. He looked to beyond all things as though seeing the pattern of this life slowly fading and in its place a dream wonderful in its beauties, awful in its thought-images. As a prophet who looks to the stars of the heavens watching for divine inspiration, so he awaited the comings of the minutes. His quick sighing stopped his quiet breathing and his spirit forsook him to hover around him and then return as though it were seeking among those ruins a lost loved one.

The dawn broke and the silence trembled at the passing of the breeze. The vast spaces smiled the smiles of a sleeper who has seen in his sleep the image of his beloved. The birds appeared from out of clefts in the ruined walls and moved about among the pillars, singing and calling out one to the others and heralding the approach of day. Ali rose to his feet and put his hand to his hot brow. He looked about him with dull eyes. Then like Adam when his eyes were opened by the breath of God, he looked at all before him and wondered. He approached his sheep and called them; they rose and shook themselves and trotted quietly behind him toward the green pastures.

Ali walked on before his flock, his large eyes looking into the serene atmosphere. His inmost feelings took flight from reality to reveal to him the secrets and closed things of existence; to show him that which had passed with the ages and that which yet remained, as it were in one flash; and in one flash to make him forget it all and bring back to him his yearning and longing. And he found between himself and the spirit of his spirit a veil like a veil between the eye and the light. He sighed, and with his sigh was a flame stripped from his burning heart.

He came to the brook whose babblings proclaimed the secrets of the fields, and he sat him down on its bank beneath a willow tree whose boughs hung down into the water as though they would suck up its sweetness. The sheep cropped the grass with bent heads, the morning dew gleaming on the whiteness of their wool.

After the passing of a minute Ali began to feel the swift beating of his heart and the renewed quaking of his spirit. Like a sleeper whom the sun's rays have startled into wakefulness he moved and looked about him. He beheld a girl coming out from among the trees carrying a jar upon her shoulder. Slowly she walked toward the water; her bare feet were wet with dew. When she came to the edge of the stream and bent to fill her jar she looked toward the opposite bank and her eyes met the eyes of Ali. She gave a cry and threw the jar to the ground and drew back a little. It was the act of one who finds an acquaintance who has been lost.

A minute passed by and its seconds were as lamps lighting the way between their two hearts; creating from the silence strange melodies to bring back to these two the echo of vague remembrances, and show to each one the other in another place, surrounded by shadows and figures, far from that stream and those trees. The one looked at the other with imploring in the eyes of each; and each one found favor in the eyes of the other; each listened to the sighing of the other with ears of love.

They communed, the one with the other, in all the tongues of the spirit. And when full understanding and knowledge possessed their two souls, Ali crossed the stream, drawn thither by an invisible power. He drew nigh to the girl, embraced her, and kissed her lips and her neck and her eyes. She made no movement in his arms, as though the sweetness of the embrace had robbed her of her will and the lightness of touch taken from her all strength. She yielded as the fragrance of the jasmine gives itself up to the currents of air. She dropped her head upon his breast like one exhausted who has found rest, and sighed deeply. A sigh telling of the birth of contentment in a constricted heart and the stirring of life within that had been sleeping and was now awakened. She raised her head and looked into his eyes, the look of one who despises the speech customary among men by the side of silence — the language of the spirit; the look of one who is not content that love should be a soul in a body of words.

The two lovers walked among the willow trees, and the oneness of each was a language speaking of the oneness of both; and an ear listening in silence to the inspiration of love; and a seeing eye seeing the glory of happiness. The sheep followed them, eating the tops of flowers and herbs, and the birds met them from all sides with songs of enchantment.

When they came to the end of the valley, which time the sun had risen and cast upon the heights a golden mantle, they sat down by a rock that protected the violets with its shadow. After a time the girl looked into the black eyes of Ali while the breeze played in her hair as though it were invisible lips that would kiss her. She felt bewitched fingertips caressing her

46

tongue and lips, and her will was a prisoner. She spoke and said in a voice of wounding sweetness:

"Astarte has brought back our souls to this life so that the delights of love and the glory of youth might not be forbidden us, my beloved."

Ali closed his eyes, for the music of her words had made clear the patterns of a dream that he saw ofttimes in his sleep. He felt that unseen wings were bearing him away from that place to a room of strange form. He was standing by the side of a couch on which lay the body of a beautiful woman whose beauty death had taken with the warmth of her lips. He cried out in his anguish at this terrible scene. Then he opened his eyes and found sitting beside him the maiden; upon her lips was a smile of love and in her glance the rays of life. His face lighted up and his spirit was refreshed, the visions were scattered, and he forgot both the past and the future. . . .

The lovers embraced and drank of the wine of kisses until they were satisfied. They slept

47

each enfolded in the arms of the other until the shade moved away and the sun's heat awakened them.

YUHANNA THE MAD

YUHANNA THE MAD

And in the summer Yuhanna went out every
morning to the field leading his oxen and his
calves and carrying his plow over his shoulder,
the while listening to the songs of the thrushes
and the rustling of the leaves in the trees. At
noontide he sat beside the dancing stream that
wound its way through the lowland of the
green meadows, where he ate his food, leaving
unfinished morsels of bread on the grass for the
birds. In the evening, when the setting sun took
with it the light of day, he returned to his
humble dwelling, which looked out over the
villages and hamlets of North Lebanon. There,
as he sat with his aged parents and listened in
silence to their conversation and their talk about
happenings of the times, a feeling of sleepiness
and restfulness gradually overtook him.

During the winter days he crouched by the
fireside for warmth and listened to the sough-

ing of the wind and the cry of the elements, pondering the way the seasons followed one upon another. He looked out of the window toward the valleys under their garment of snow, and the trees denuded of their leaves like a crowd of poor people left outside to the mercy of the harsh cold and the violent winds. Throughout the long nights he stayed up until after his parents had gone to sleep. Then he would open a wooden chest and take out of it the book of the Gospels to read from it in secret by the feeble glow of a lamp, looking stealthily from time to time in the direction of his slumbering father, who had forbidden him to read the Book. It was forbidden because the priests did not allow the simple in mind to probe the secrets of the teachings of Jesus. If they did so, then the church would excommunicate them. Thus did Yuhanna pass the days of his youth between that field of wonder and beauty and the book of Jesus, filled with the light and the spirit. Whenever his father spoke he remained silent and in thought, listening to him, but never a word would he utter. Ofttimes he would sit with companions of his own age, silent and looking beyond them to where the evening twilight met the blue of the sky. Whenever he went to church he returned with a feeling of sorrow because the teachings that he heard from the pulpit and altar were not those that he read about in the Gospel. And the life led by the faithful and their leaders was not the beautiful life of which Jesus of Nazareth spoke in His book.

Spring returned to the fields and the meadows, and the snows melted away. On the mountaintops some snow still remained until it in turn melted and ran down the mountainsides and became streams twisting and winding in the valleys below. Soon they met and joined one another until they were swift-flowing rivers, their roaring announcing to all that Nature had awakened from her sleep. The apple and the walnut trees blossomed and the poplar and the willow bore new leaves; and on the heights appeared grass and flowers. Yuhanna grew weary of his existence by the fireside; his calves fretted in their narrow enclosure and hungered for the green pastures, for their store of barley and straw was almost consumed. So he set them free of their manger and led them out to the countryside. He carried his Bible under his cloak so that nobody should see it, until he reached the meadow that rested on the shoulder of the valley near the fields of a monastery which stood up grimly like a tower in the midst of the hillocks.[1] There his calves dispersed to pasture on the grass. Yuhanna sat him down against a rock, now looking across the valley in all its beauty, now reading the words in his book that spoke to him of the Kingdom of Heaven.

It was a day toward the end of Lent, when the villagers, who were abstaining from the eating of meats, awaited impatiently the coming of Easter. But Yuhanna, like all the poor farmers, knew no difference between days of fasting and days of feasting; to him life itself was one long fast-day. His food was never more than bread kneaded with the sweat of his brow and fruits purchased with his heart's blood. For him

---

[1] This is a wealthy monastery in North Lebanon, owning extensive lands. It is known as the Deir Elisha Al-Nabi (i.e., Monastery of the Prophet Elisha). — Author's note.

abstention from meats and rich foods was a natural thing. Fasting brought him not hunger of the body but hunger of the spirit; for it brought to him the sorrow of the Son of Man and the close of His life upon earth.

Around Yuhanna the birds fluttered, calling out one to another, and flocks of doves flew swiftly overhead; the flowers swayed gently to and fro in the breeze as though bathing themselves in the warming rays of the sun. He read the while, immersed in his book, and then lifted up his head. He saw the church domes in the towns and villages scattered around the valley and heard the pealing of the bells. He closed his eyes and let his spirit soar high across the centuries to old Jerusalem, there to follow in the footsteps of Jesus in the streets, inquiring of the passers-by about Him. They answered and said: "Here did He cure the blind and make the halt to rise. There did they make for Him a crown of thorns and place it upon His head. In this street He stopped and addressed the crowd in parables. In that place they bound Him to a pillar and spat in His face and whipped Him. In this lane did He forgive the harlot her sins. Yonder fell He to the ground under the weight of His cross."

The hours passed, the while Yuhanna suffered with the God-man in agony of body and was exalted with Him in spirit. When he rose from his place the midday sun was high. He looked around him but did not see his calves; he sought them everywhere, perplexed at their disappearance in those flat meadows. When he reached the road that wound across the fields like lines on the palm of a hand, he saw from afar a man clothed in black standing in the midst of the gardens. He hastened toward him and on drawing near perceived that it was one of the monks from the monastery. Yuhanna bowed his head in greeting and asked him if he had seen his calves in the gardens.

The monk, trying to conceal his anger, looked at him and answered roughly: "Yes, I have seen them, they are yonder; come, and thou shalt see them." Yuhanna followed the monk until they came to the monastery. There he saw his calves tethered by ropes within a wide enclosure and guarded by another monk.

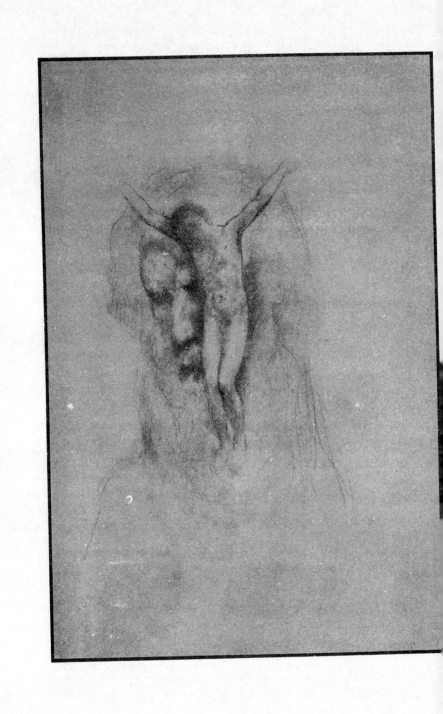

In his hand was a heavy stick with which he belabored the beasts whenever they moved. When Yuhanna made as if to lead them away, the monk seized him by his cloak and, turning in the direction of the doorway of the monastery, shouted in a loud voice: "Here is the guilty shepherd boy; I have caught him." At his cry priests and monks ran from all directions toward him, led by their Superior, a man distinguished from his companions by his dress of fine material and his soured features. They surrounded Yuhanna like soldiers scrambling after loot. He looked at the Superior and in a gentle voice said: "What have I done that you call me a criminal and why have you seized me?" The Superior answered him in a voice that rasped like a saw: "Thou hast pastured these cattle on land that is the monastery's land and they have nibbled and gnawed at our vines. We have seized them because the shepherd is responsible for the damage wrought by his flock." His angry face grew hard as he spoke. Then spoke Yuhanna with pleading in his voice: "Father," he said, "they are but dumb creatures without intelligence, and I am a poor man and possess naught except the strength of my forearm and these beasts. Let me take them away and I shall promise not to come to these meadows again."

The Father Superior moved a step forward, raised his hand toward the heavens, and again spoke: "God has put us in this place and He has entrusted to us the guardianship of this land, the land of His chosen, the great Elisha. Day and night do we guard it with all our might, for it is sacred; those who approach it will it consume with fire. If thou refusest to render account to the monastery, then shall the very grass turn to poison in the bellies of thy beasts. There is no escape for thee for we shall keep the calves here in our enclosure until thou hast paid the last fils."[1]

The Superior was about to go when Yuhanna stopped him and said in a voice of supplication: "I entreat you, my lord, for the sake of these sacred days wherein Jesus suffered and Mary wept in sorrow, to let me go with my calves. Harden not your heart against me; I am poor and the monastery is rich and powerful. It will

[1] Coin of fractional value.

58

assuredly forgive my foolishness and have pity upon my father's years." The Superior looked at him, mocking, and said: "The monastery will not excuse thee, not even to the amount of one grain, stupid one; it matters not whether thou be rich or poor. Who art thou to adjure me by things sacred since it is we alone that know their secrets and hidden things? If thou wouldst take away the calves from these pastures, then shalt thou redeem them in the sum of three dinars to pay for what they have consumed of the crops." Said Yuhanna in a choking voice: "I have nothing, father, not even a para piece. Have compassion on me and my poverty."

The Superior caressed his thick beard with his fingers. "Then go thou and sell part of thy field and return with three dinars. Is it not better for thee to enter heaven and possess no field than to earn Elisha's wrath with thy ceaseless arguing before his altar and thus go down into hell, where all is eternal fire?"

Yuhanna remained silent for a while. From his eyes shone a light and his features expanded with joy. His bearing changed from one of entreaty and pleading to one of strength and resolve. When he spoke it was in a voice in which were knowledge and the determination of youth:

"Must the poor sell the fields that earn them their bread and maintain their existence in order to fill further the coffers of the monastery, heavy with gold and silver? Is it just that the poor should be yet poorer and the wretched die of hunger that great Elisha may forgive the sins of hungry beasts? " The Superior shook his head haughtily. "Jesus the Christ said: For unto everyone that hath shall be given and he shall have abundance; but from him that hath not shall be taken away even that which he hath."

As Yuhanna heard these words his heart beat faster in his breast, he grew in spirit and increased in stature. It was as though the earth were developing at his feet. From his pocket he drew out his Bible as the warrior draws his sword to defend himself, and cried: "Thus do you make a mockery of the teachings of this Book, O hypocrites, and use that which is most sacred in life to spread the evils therein. Woe to you when the Son of Man shall come a second time and lay in ruins your monasteries and scat-

ter their stones across the valley and burn with
fire your altars and images! Woe to you by the
innocent blood of Jesus and the tears of His
mother's weeping, for they shall overwhelm you
as a flood and carry you down to the depths of
the abyss! Woe to you who prostrate yourselves
before the idols of your greed and conceal beneath your black raiment the blackness of your
deeds! Woe to you who move your lips in prayer
while your hearts are yet hard as rock; who
bend low in humility before the altar yet in your
souls rebel against your God! In your harshness
you have brought me to this place and seized
hold of me as a transgressor for the sake of a
little pasture land that the sun has nourished for
us equally. When I entreat you in the name of
Jesus and adjure you by the days of His sorrow
and pain, you scoff at me as one who speaks in
ignorance. Take then this Book, look into it,
and show me when Jesus was not forgiving.
Read this divine tragedy and tell me where He
speaks without mercy and compassion. Was it
in His Sermon on the Mount or in His teachings in the temple before the persecutors of the
wretched harlot or upon Golgotha as He opened

wide His arms on the cross to embrace all mankind? Look down, all you hard of heart, upon these poor towns and villages in whose dwellings the sick writhe in agony on beds of pain; in whose prisons the unfortunate pass their days in despair; at whose gates the beggars beg; on whose highways the stranger makes his bed, and in whose cemeteries the widow and the orphan weep. But you are here living in sloth and idleness and comfort, enjoying the yield of the fields and the grapes of the vine. You visit not the sick and the imprisoned; nor do you feed the hungry or give refuge to the stranger or comfort to the mourner. Would that you were content with what you hold and that which you have plundered from our forefathers! You stretch out your hands as the viper its head and rob the widow of the labor of her hands and the peasant of his store against old age."

Yuhanna ceased from talking in order to regain his breath. Then he went on, his head lifted proudly and said in a gentle voice:

"You are many and I am one. Do to me as you wish. The ewe may fall as prey to the wolves in the darkness of the night, but her blood will stain the stones of the valley until the coming of dawn and the rising of the sun."

Yuhanna spoke these words, and in his voice was a strength inspired, a force that restrained the monks from all movement and caused anger and harshness to rise within them. They trembled in their rage and ground their teeth like caged and hungry lions, awaiting a sign from their chief to tear the youth to pieces. So they were until Yuhanna had ceased speaking and became silent like the calm after the storm has wrought destruction on the topmost branches of a tree and the strongest of plants. Then cried the Superior: "Seize this miserable sinner; take from him the Book and drag him away to a dark cell. Those who would curse God's elect shall receive pardon neither here nor in the hereafter." The monks fell upon Yuhanna as the lion falls upon his prey; they pinioned his arms and led him away to a narrow chamber. Before locking the door on him they belabored his body with blows and kicks.

In that dark place stood Yuhanna, the victor whom fortune has given to the foe as captive. Through a small opening in the wall he looked out on the valley reposing in the sunlight. His face became illumined and his spirit felt the embrace of a divine content; a sweet tranquillity took possession of him. The narrow cell imprisoned his body, but his spirit was free to roam with the breeze among the meadows and ruins. The hands of the monks had bruised his limbs, but they had not touched his inmost feelings; in those he rested in safety with Jesus the Nazarene. Persecution harms not the just man nor does oppression destroy one who is on the side of truth. Socrates drank of the hemlock smiling; Paul was stoned rejoicing. When we oppose the hidden conscience, it does us hurt. When we betray it, it judges us.

The parents of Yuhanna came to know of what had befallen their only child. His mother came to the monastery walking with the aid of her stick and threw herself at the feet of the Superior. She wept and kissed his hands and beseeched him to have pity on her son and pardon his ignorance. The Superior lifted his eyes heavenwards like one raised above worldly affairs and said to the woman: "We can forgive the playfulness of thy son and show tolerance toward his foolishness, but the monastery possesses sacred rights to which account must be rendered. We in our humility forgive the transgressions of men, but great Elisha forgives not nor pardons the trespassers on his vineyards and those who put to pasture their beasts on his land."

The mother looked up at him while the tears ran down her withered old cheeks. Then from around her neck she took a silver collar and put it in his hand, saying: "I have naught except this collar, father. It is a gift of my mother, given me on the day of my marriage. Perchance the monastery will accept it as an atonement for the guilt of my only son."

The Superior took the collar and put it in his pocket and addressed the mother, the while she kissed his hands in gratitude and thankfulness: "Woe to this generation, for the verses of the Book have become contrariwise and the children have eaten of sour grapes and the fathers' teeth are set on edge! Go now, good woman, and pray for thy foolish son that Heaven may cure him and give back his reason."

Yuhanna went out from his prison and walked

slowly before his calves by the side of his mother as she leaned on her staff, bowed down under the weight of her years. When he reached the hut, he left the calves to browse and sat beside the window in silence, looking at the fading light of day. After a little time he heard his father whisper these words into his mother's ear: "Many times have I told thee, Sarah, that our son is weak in mind, but never didst thou agree with me. Now thou dost no longer contradict me, for his actions have justified my words. What the reverend father told thee today have I been telling thee for years."

Yuhanna remained looking toward the west, where the rays of the setting sun put color to the close-packed masses of cloud.

II

It was Easter-tide and fasting gave place to feasting. The building of the new church was completed and it rose above the houses of Besharry, in whose midst it stood, like the palace of a prince among the mean dwellings of his subjects. The people stood and watched for the coming of the bishop to dedicate their sanctuary and consecrate its altars. And when they felt that the time of his arrival was near they went out from the town in processions and he entered with them to songs of praise from the young men and the chanting of the priests, and the clashing of cymbals and ringing of bells. When he dismounted from his horse, adorned with decorated saddle and silver bridle, he was met by men of religion and notable persons who welcomed him with pomp and fitting words and verse and songs of praise. When he reached the new church he was invested with a priestly robe

67

embroidered in gold, and a jewel-encrusted crown was put upon his head. Then he was girded with the shepherd's crook of cunning workmanship and precious stones. He made a circuit of the church, singing and chanting orisons with the priests, while around him rose and swirled goodly-smelling incense and the flickering flames of many candles.

At that hour Yuhanna was standing among the shepherds and tillers of the soil on a raised platform observing this spectacle through his sad eyes. He sighed bitterly in his pain and grief as he saw on the one side silken clothes and gold vessels, censers and costly silver lamps; and on the other, crowds of poor and wretched people who had come up from little villages and hamlets to assist at the rejoicings of this festival and the ceremony of consecration. On the one side, power in its velvets and satins; on the other, misery in its rags and tatters. Here wealth and power personifying the religion with its songs and chants; there an enfeebled people, humble and poor, rejoicing in its secret soul in the Resurrection. Praying in silence and sighing sighs that rose from the bottom of broken hearts to

68

float on the ether and whisper into the ears of the air. Here the leaders and headmen to whom power gave life like the life of the evergreen cypress tree. There the peasants who submit, whose existence is a ship with Death for its captain; whose rudder is broken by the waves and whose sails are torn by the winds; now rising, now sinking between the anger of the deep and the terror of the storm. Here harsh tyranny; there blind obedience. Which one is parent to the other? Is tyranny a strong tree that grows not except on low ground? Or is submission an abandoned field in which naught lives but thorns?

With these sorrowful reflections and torturing thoughts did Yuhanna occupy himself. He pressed his arms against his breast as if his throat were closing in upon his breathing, in fear that his breast were being rent asunder to let go his breath. In this manner he remained until the ceremony of dedication was at an end, when the people dispersed and went their diverse ways.

Soon he began to feel as though there were a spirit in the air urging him to arise and speak in its name; and in the crowd a power moving him

69

to come forth as a preacher before heaven and earth.

He came to the end of the platform and, lifting up his eyes, made a sign with his hand to the heavens. In a strong voice that compelled the ears and eyes to give attention he cried:

"Behold thou, O Jesus, Man of Nazareth, who sittest within the circle of light on high. Look down from beyond the blue dome of heaven upon this earth; whose elements Thou didst wear yesterday as a cloak. Look, O faithful Tiller, for the thorns of the thicket have strangled the flowers whose seeds did quicken into life by the sweat of Thy brow. Look, O good Shepherd, for the weak lamb Thou didst carry on Thy shoulder is torn to pieces by wild beasts. Thine innocent blood is sucked into the earth, and Thy hot tears are dried up in the hearts of men. The warmth of Thy breath is scattered before desert winds. This field hallowed by Thy feet is become a battleground where the feet of the strong grind the ribs of the outcast, where the hand of the oppressor blights the spirit of the weak. The persecuted cry out from the darkness, and those who sit upon

70

thrones in Thy name heed not their cries. Neither is the weeping of the bereaved heard by those who preach Thy words from pulpits. The lamb that Thou didst send for the sake of the Lord of Life is become a rampaging beast tearing to pieces the wings of the Lamb enfolded by Thine arms. The word of life that Thou didst bring down from the heart of God is concealed and hidden within the pages of books, and in its place is a terrible shouting, putting fear and dread into all hearts. These people, O Jesus, have raised temples and tabernacles to the glory of Thy name and adorned them with woven silk and molten gold. They have left naked the bodies of Thy chosen poor in the cold streets: yet do they fill the air with the smoke of incense and candles. Those who believe in Thy godlike state have they robbed of bread. Though the air echoes to their psalms and hymns, yet they hear not the orphan's cry, neither the widow's lamentation. Come then, O Jesus, a second time, and drive out from the temple those who trade in religion, for they have made of it a nest of vipers with their cunning and guile. Come, and do reckoning with these Cæsars who have wrested from the weak that which is theirs and God's. Behold the vine that Thy right hand did plant. The worms have eaten of its shoots, and its grapes are trampled beneath the feet of the passer-by. Consider those upon whom Thou didst enjoin peace and see how they are divided, contending among themselves. Our troubled souls and oppressed hearts have they made as victims of their wars. On their feast-days and holy days they lift up their voices saying glory to God in His heaven, peace upon earth, and joy to all men. Is Thy heavenly Father glorified when corrupt lips and lying tongues utter His name? Is there peace upon earth when the children of sorrow toil in the fields and see their strength ebbing away in the light of the sun to feed the mouth of the strong and fill the tyrant's belly? Is there rejoicing among men when the outcast look with their broken eyes toward death as the conquered looks to his deliverer? What is peace, gentle Jesus? Is it in the eyes of children at the breasts of hungry mothers in cold dark dwellings? Or in the bodies of the needy who sleep in their beds of stone wishing for the food that comes

72

not to them but is thrown by the priests to their fattened swine? What is joy, O Jesus? Does it exist when a prince can buy the strength of men and the honor of women for a few pieces of silver? Is it in those silent ones that are slaves in body and soul to whosoever dazzles their eyes with the gleam of bejeweled orders and the flash of stones in rings and the silk of their garments? Is there rejoicing in the cries of the oppressed and downtrodden when tyrants fall upon them with the sword and crush the bodies of their women and young ones under horses' hoofs and make drunk the earth with their blood? Stretch forth Thy strong hand, Jesus, and save us, for the oppressor's hand is heavy upon us. Or send to us Death, that he might lead us to the grave, wherein we shall sleep in peace against the second coming, secure in the shadow of Thy cross. For verily our life is naught but a darkness whose inhabitants are evil spirits, and a valley wherein snakes and dragons make sport. What are our days except whetted swords concealed by night between our bed-coverings and revealed by the morning light hanging over our heads whenever the love of existence leads us

73

to the fields? Have mercy, O Jesus, on these multitudes joined together as one by Thy name on the day of the Resurrection. Have compassion on their weakness and humility."

Thus did Yuhanna hold converse with the heavens while the people stood around him. Some were pleased and praised him; others were angry and reviled him. One shouted: "He says aright and speaks for us before Heaven, for we are oppressed." Another said: "He is possessed and speaks with the tongue of an evil spirit." That one cried: "We never heard such foolishness from our fathers before us; neither do we wish to hear it now." Yet another whispered into his neighbor's ear, saying: "At the sound of his voice I felt within me an awful trembling that shook my very heart, for he spoke with a strange power." Answered his friend: "It is so; but our leaders are more knowledgeable in these affairs than are we. It is wrong to doubt them."

As the cries rose from all sides and swelled into a roar like the sea only to be scattered and lost in the ether, a priest appeared, seized hold of Yuhanna, and delivered him up to the police. They led him away to the Governor's house.

When they asked him questions he answered not a word, for he remembered that Jesus was silent too before His persecutors. So they threw him into the dark prison house and there he slept, gently leaning against the stone wall.

And on the morning of the following day came Yuhanna's father to testify before the Governor to his son's madness.

"My lord," he said, "often have I heard him babbling in his solitude and talking of strange things that have no existence. Night after night has he spoken into the silence in unknown words, calling upon the shadows of darkness in a terrible voice like that of sorcerers uttering incantations. Ask of the boys of the quarter who used to sit with him, for they know how his mind was attracted by another world beyond. When they spoke to him, seldom did he answer. And when he did speak, his words were confused and without relation to their conversation. Ask of his mother, for more than all others was she aware of a soul stripped of all its senses. Ofttimes did she see him looking toward the horizon with eyes staring and glazed, and hear him speaking with passion of the trees and brooks and flowers and stars in the way children prattle of trifles. Ask of the monks in the monastery with whom he contended yesterday, mocking at their godliness and scorning their sacred way of life. He is mad, my lord, but to his mother and me he is kind. He sustains us in our old age and fulfills our wants with the sweat of his brow. Show him mercy through your compassion upon us and forgive his foolishness for the sake of his parents."

Yuhanna was set free and the story of his madness spread abroad. The young men spoke of him with mocking. But the maidens looked at him with sad eyes and said: "For much that is strange in men are the heavens accountable. So in this youth is beauty united with madness, and the light of his beautiful eyes wedded to the darkness of his sick soul."

Between the meadows and the heights, clothed in their garments of flowers and plants, sat Yuhanna by the calves, who had fled from the stress and strife of men to the good pastures. He looked with tear-dimmed eyes toward the villages and hamlets scattered upon the shoulders of the valley and, sighing deeply, repeated these words:

"You are many and I am one. Say what you will of me and do to me as you wish. The ewe may fall as prey to the wolves in the darkness of the night, but her blood will stain the stones of the valley until the coming of the dawn and the rising of the sun."

BOOK EIGHT

TEARS AND LAUGHTER

THE CREATION

THE GOD separated a spirit from Himself and fashioned it into beauty. He showered upon her all the blessings of gracefulness and kindness. He gave her the cup of happiness and said, "Drink not from this cup unless you forget the past and the future, for happiness is naught but the moment." And He also gave her a cup of sorrow and said, "Drink from this cup and you will understand the meaning of the fleeting instants of the joy of life, for sorrow ever abounds."

And the God bestowed upon her a love that would desert her forever upon her first sigh of earthly satisfaction, and a sweetness that would vanish with her first awareness of flattery.

And He gave her wisdom from heaven to lead her to the all-righteous path, and placed in the depth of her heart an eye that sees the unseen, and created in her an affection and goodness toward all things. He dressed her with raiment of hopes spun by the angels of heaven from the sinews of the rainbow. And He cloaked her in the shadow of confusion, which is the dawn of life and light.

3

Then the God took consuming fire from the furnace of anger, and searing wind from the desert of ignorance, and sharp cutting sands from the shore of selfishness, and coarse earth from under the feet of ages, and combined them all and fashioned Man. He gave to Man a blind power that rages and drives him into a madness which extinguishes only before gratification of desire, and placed life in him which is the spectre of death.

And the God laughed and cried. He felt an overwhelming love and pity for Man, and sheltered him beneath His guidance.

HAVE MERCY ON ME,
MY SOUL!

WHY ARE you weeping, my Soul?
Knowest thou my weakness?
Thy tears strike sharp and injure,
For I know not my wrong.
Until when shalt thou cry?
I have naught but human words
To interpret your dreams,
Your desires, and your instructions.

Look upon me, my Soul; I have
Consumed my full life heeding
Your teachings. Think of how
I suffer! I have exhausted my
Life following you.

My heart was glorying upon the
Throne, but is now yoked in slavery;
My patience was a companion, but
Now contends against me;
My youth was my hope, but
Now reprimands my neglect.

5

Why, my Soul, are you all-demanding?
I have denied myself pleasure
And deserted the joy of life
Following the course which you
Impelled me to pursue.
Be just to me, or call Death
To unshackle me,
For justice is your glory.

Have mercy on me, my Soul.
You have laden me with Love until
I cannot carry my burden. You and
Love are inseparable might; Substance
And I are inseparable weakness.
Will e'er the struggle cease
Between the strong and the weak?

Have mercy on me, my Soul.
You have shown me Fortune beyond
My grasp. You and Fortune abide on
The mountain top; Misery and I are
Abandoned together in the pit of
The valley. Will e'er the mountain
And the valley unite?

Have mercy on me, my Soul.
You have shown me Beauty, but then
Concealed her You and Beauty live
In the light; Ignorance and I are
Bound together in the dark. Will
E'er the light invade darkness?

Your delight comes with the Ending,
And you revel now in anticipation;
But this body suffers with life
While in life.
This, my Soul, is perplexing.

You are hastening toward Eternity,
But this body goes slowly toward
Perishment. You do not wait for him,
And he cannot go quickly.
This, my Soul, is sadness.

You ascend high, through heaven's
Attraction, but this body falls by
Earth's gravity. You do not console
Him, and he does not appreciate you.
This, my Soul, is misery.

You are rich in wisdom, but this
Body is poor in understanding.
You do not compromise
And he does not obey.
This, my Soul, is extreme suffering.

In the silence of the night you visit
The Beloved and enjoy the sweetness of
His presence. This body ever remains
The bitter victim of hope and separation.
This, my Soul, is agonizing torture.
Have mercy on me, my Soul!

TWO INFANTS

A PRINCE stood on the balcony of his palace addressing a great multitude summoned for the occasion and said, "Let me offer you and this whole fortunate country my congratulations upon the birth of a new prince who will carry the name of my noble family, and of whom you will be justly proud. He is the new bearer of a great and illustrious ancestry, and upon him depends the brilliant future of this realm. Sing and be merry!" The voices of the throngs, full of joy and thankfulness, flooded the sky with exhilarating song, welcoming the new tyrant who would affix the yoke of oppression to their necks by ruling the weak with bitter authority, and exploiting their bodies and killing their souls. For that destiny, the people were singing and drinking ecstatically to the health of the new Emir.

Another child entered life and that kingdom at the same time. While the crowds were glorifying the strong and belittling themselves by singing praise to a potential despot, and while the angels of heaven were weeping over the people's weakness and servitude, a sick woman was thinking. She lived in an old, deserted hovel and, lying in her hard bed beside her newly-born infant wrapped with ragged swaddles, was starving to death. She was a penurious and miserable young wife neglected by humanity; her husband had fallen into the trap of death set by the prince's oppression, leaving a solitary woman to whom God had sent, that night, a tiny companion to prevent her from working and sustaining life.

As the mass dispersed and silence was restored to the vicinity, the wretched woman placed the infant on her lap and looked into his face and wept as if she were to baptize him with tears. And with a hunger-weakened voice she spoke to the child saying, "Why have you left the spiritual world and come to share with me the bitterness of earthly life? Why have you deserted the angels and the spacious firmament and come to this miserable land of humans, filled with agony, oppression, and heartlessness? I have nothing to give you except tears; will you be nourished on tears instead of milk? I have no silk clothes to put on you; will my naked, shivering arms give you warmth? The little animals graze in the pasture and return safely to their shed; and the small birds pick the seeds and sleep placidly between the branches. But you, my beloved, have naught save a loving but destitute mother."

Then she took the infant to her withered breast and clasped her arms around him as if wanting to join the two bodies in one, as before. She lifted her burning eyes slowly toward heaven and cried, "God! Have mercy on my unfortunate countrymen!"

At that moment the clouds floated from the face of the moon, whose beams penetrated the transom of that poor home and fell upon two corpses.

THE LIFE OF LOVE

SPRING

COME, my beloved; let us walk amidst the knolls,
For the snow is water, and Life is alive from its
Slumber and is roaming the hills and valleys.
Let us follow the footprints of Spring into the
Distant fields, and mount the hilltops to draw
Inspiration high above the cool green plains.

Dawn of Spring has unfolded her winter-kept gar-
ment
And placed it on the peach and citrus trees; and
They appear as brides in the ceremonial custom of
The Night of Kedre.

The sprigs of grapevine embrace each other like
Sweethearts, and the brooks burst out in dance
Between the rocks, repeating the song of joy;
And the flowers bud suddenly from the heart of
Nature, like foam from the rich heart of the sea.

Come, my beloved; let us drink the last of Winter's
Tears from the cupped lilies, and soothe our spirits

With the shower of notes from the birds, and wander
In exhilaration through the intoxicating breeze.

Let us sit by that rock, where violets hide; let us
Pursue their exchange of the sweetness of kisses.

SUMMER

Let us go into the fields, my beloved, for the
Time of harvest approaches, and the sun's eyes
Are ripening the grain.
Let us tend the fruit of the earth, as the
Spirit nourishes the grains of Joy from the
Seeds of Love, sowed deep in our hearts.
Let us fill our bins with the products of
Nature, as life fills so abundantly the
Domain of our hearts with her endless bounty.
Let us make the flowers our bed, and the
Sky our blanket, and rest our heads together
Upon pillows of soft hay.
Let us relax after the day's toil, and listen
To the provoking murmur of the brook.

AUTUMN

Let us go and gather the grapes of the vineyard
For the winepress, and keep the wine in old
Vases, as the spirit keeps Knowledge of the
Ages in eternal vessels.

Let us return to our dwelling, for the wind has
Caused the yellow leaves to fall and shroud the
Withering flowers that whisper elegy to Summer.

12

Come home, my eternal sweetheart, for the birds
Have made pilgrimage to warmth and left the chilled
Prairies suffering pangs of solitude. The jasmine
And myrtle have no more tears.

Let us retreat, for the tired brook has
Ceased its song; and the bubblesome springs
Are drained of their copious weeping; and
The cautious old hills have stored away
Their colourful garments.

Come, my beloved; Nature is justly weary
And is bidding her enthusiasm farewell
With quiet and contented melody.

WINTER

Come close to me, oh companion of my full life;
Come close to me and let not Winter's touch
Enter between us. Sit by me before the hearth,
For fire is the only fruit of Winter.

Speak to me of the glory of your heart, for
That is greater than the shrieking elements
Beyond our door.
Bind the door and seal the transoms, for the
Angry countenance of the heaven depresses my
Spirit, and the face of our snow-laden fields
Makes my soul cry.

Feed the lamp with oil and let it not dim, and
Place it by you, so I can read with tears what
Your life with me has written upon your face.

Bring Autumn's wine. Let us drink and sing the
Song of remembrance to Spring's carefree sowing,
And Summer's watchful tending, and Autumn's
Reward in harvest.

Come close to me, oh beloved of my soul; the
Fire is cooling and fleeing under the ashes.
Embrace me, for I fear loneliness; the lamp is
Dim, and the wine which we pressed is closing
Our eyes. Let us look upon each other before
They are shut.
Find me with your arms and embrace me; let
Slumber then embrace our souls as one.
Kiss me, my beloved, for Winter has stolen
All but our moving lips.

You are close by me, My Forever.
How deep and wide will be the ocean of Slumber,
And how recent was the dawn!

14

THE HOUSE OF FORTUNE

MY WEARIED heart bade me farewell and left for the House of Fortune. As he reached that holy city which the soul had blessed and worshipped, he commenced wondering, for he could not find what he had always imagined would be there. The city was empty of power, money, and authority.

And my heart spoke to the daughter of Love saying, "Oh Love, where can I find Contentment? I heard that she had come here to join you."

And the daughter of Love responded, "Contentment has already gone to preach her gospel in the city, where greed and corruption are paramount; we are not in need of her."

Fortune craves not Contentment, for it is an earthly hope, and its desires are embraced by union with objects, while Contentment is naught but heartfelt.

The eternal soul is never contented; it ever seeks exaltation. Then my heart looked upon Life of Beauty and said, "Thou art all knowledge; enlighten me as to the mystery of Woman." And he answered, "Oh human heart, woman is your own reflection, and whatever you are, she is; wherever you live, she lives; she is like religion if not interpreted by the ignorant, and like a moon, if not veiled with clouds, and like a breeze, if not poisoned with impurities."

And my heart walked toward Knowledge, the daughter of Love and Beauty, and said, "Bestow upon me wisdom, that I might share it with the people." And she responded, "Say not wisdom, but rather fortune, for real fortune comes not from outside, but begins in the Holy of Holies of life. Share of thyself with the people."

SONG OF THE WAVE

THE STRONG SHORE is my beloved
And I am his sweetheart.
We are at last united by love, and
Then the moon draws me from him.
I go to him in haste and depart
Reluctantly, with many
Little farewells.

I steal swiftly from behind the
Blue horizon to cast the silver of
My foam upon the gold of his sand, and
We blend in melted brilliance.

I quench his thirst and submerge his
Heart; he softens my voice and subdues
My temper.
At dawn I recite the rules of love upon
His ears, and he embraces me longingly.

At eventide I sing to him the song of
Hope, and then print smooth kisses upon
His face; I am swift and fearful, but he
Is quiet, patient, and thoughtful. His
Broad bosom soothes my restlessness.

As the tide comes we caress each other,
When it withdraws, I drop to his feet in
Prayer.

Many times have I danced around mermaids
As they rose from the depths and rested
Upon my crest to watch the stars;
Many times have I heard lovers complain
Of their smallness, and I helped them to sigh.

Many times have I teased the great rocks
And fondled them with a smile, but never
Have I received laughter from them;
Many times have I lifted drowning souls
And carried them tenderly to my beloved
Shore. He gives them strength as he
Takes mine.

Many times have I stolen gems from the
Depths and presented them to my beloved
Shore. He takes in silence, but still
I give for he welcomes me ever.

In the heaviness of night, when all
Creatures seek the ghost of Slumber, I
Sit up, singing at one time and sighing
At another. I am awake always.

Alas! Sleeplessness has weakened me!
But I am a lover, and the truth of love
Is strong.
I may weary, but I shall never die.

A POET'S DEATH IS HIS LIFE

THE DARK WINGS of night enfolded the city upon which Nature had spread a pure and white garment of snow; and men deserted the streets for their houses in search of warmth, while the north wind probed in contemplation of laying waste the gardens. There in the suburb stood an old hut heavily laden with snow and on the verge of falling. In a dark recess of that hovel was a poor bed in which a dying youth was lying, staring at the dim light of his oil lamp, made to flicker by the entering winds. He was a man in the spring of life who foresaw fully that the peaceful hour of freeing himself from the clutches of life was fast nearing. He was awaiting Death's visit gratefully, and upon his pale face appeared the dawn of hope; and on his lips a sorrowful smile; and in his eyes forgiveness.

He was a poet perishing from hunger in the city of living rich. He was placed in the earthly world to enliven the heart of man with his beautiful and profound sayings. He was a noble soul, sent by the Goddess of Understanding to soothe and make gentle the human spirit. But alas! He gladly bade the cold earth farewell without receiving a smile from its strange occupants.

He was breathing his last and had no one at his bedside save the oil lamp, his only companion, and some parchments upon which he had inscribed his heart's feeling. As he salvaged the remnants of his withering strength he lifted his hands heavenward; he moved his eyes hopelessly, as if wanting to pene- trate the ceiling in order to see the stars from behind the veil of clouds.

And he said, "Come, oh beautiful Death; my soul is longing for you. Come close to me and unfasten the irons of life, for I am weary of dragging them. Come, oh sweet Death, and deliver me from my neighbours who looked upon me as a stranger be- cause I interpret to them the language of the angels. Hurry, oh peaceful Death, and carry me from these multitudes who left me in the dark corner of ob- livion because I do not bleed the weak as they do. Come, oh gentle Death, and enfold me under your white wings, for my fellowmen are not in want of me. Embrace me, oh Death, full of love and mercy; let your lips touch my lips which never tasted a mother's kiss, nor touched a sister's cheeks, nor caressed a sweetheart's fingertips. Come and take me, my beloved Death."

Then, at the bedside of the dying poet appeared an angel who possessed a supernatural and divine beauty, holding in her hand a wreath of lilies. She embraced him and closed his eyes so he could see no more, except with the eye of his spirit. She impressed a deep and long and gently withdrawn kiss that left an eternal smile of fulfillment upon his lips. Then the hovel became empty and nothing was left save parchments and papers which the poet had strewn about with bitter futility.

Hundreds of years later, when the people of the city arose from the diseased slumber of ignorance and saw the dawn of knowledge, they erected a monument in the most beautiful garden of the city and celebrated a feast every year in honour of that poet, whose writings had freed them. Oh, how cruel is man's ignorance!

PEACE

THE TEMPEST calmed after bending the branches of the trees and leaning heavily upon the grain in the field. The stars appeared as broken remnants of the lightning, but now silence prevailed over all, as if Nature's war had never been fought.

At that hour a young woman entered her chamber and knelt by her bed sobbing bitterly. Her heart flamed with agony but she could finally open her lips and say, "Oh Lord, bring him home safely to me. I have exhausted my tears and can offer no more, oh Lord, full of love and mercy. My patience is drained and calamity is seeking possession of my heart. Save him, oh Lord, from the iron paws of War; deliver him from such unmerciful Death, for he is weak, governed by the strong. Oh Lord, save my beloved, who is Thine own son, from the foe, who is thy foe. Keep him from the forced pathway to Death's door; let him see me, or come and take me to him."

Quietly a young man entered. His head was wrapped in bandage soaked with escaping life.

He approached her with a greeting of tears and laughter, then took her hand and placed against it his flaming lips. And with a voice which bespoke past sorrow, and joy of union, and uncertainty of her reaction, he said, "Fear me not, for I am the object of your plea. Be glad, for Peace has carried me back safely to you, and humanity has restored what greed essayed to take from us. Be not sad, but smile, my beloved. Do not express bewilderment, for Love has power that dispels Death; charm that conquers the enemy. I am your one. Think me not a spectre emerging from the House of Death to visit your Home of Beauty.

"Do not be frightened, for I am now Truth, spared from swords and fire to reveal to the people the triumph of Love over War. I am Word uttering introduction to the play of happiness and peace."

Then the young man became speechless and his tears spoke the language of the heart; and the angels of Joy hovered about that dwelling, and the two hearts restored the singleness which had been taken from them.

At dawn the two stood in the middle of the field, contemplating the beauty of Nature injured by the tempest. After a deep and comforting silence, the soldier looked to the east and said to his sweetheart, "Look at the Darkness, giving birth to the Sun."

THE CRIMINAL

$\mathbb{A}$ YOUNG man of strong body, weakened by hunger, sat on the walker's portion of the street stretching his hand toward all who passed, begging and repeating the sad song of his defeat in life, while suffering from hunger and from humiliation.

When night came, his lips and tongue were parched, while his hand was still as empty as his stomach.

He gathered himself and went out from the city, where he sat under a tree and wept bitterly. Then he lifted his puzzled eyes to heaven while hunger was eating his inside, and he said, "Oh Lord, I went to the rich man and asked for employment, but he turned away because of my shabbiness; I knocked at the school door, but was forbidden solace because I was empty-handed; I sought any occupation that would give me bread, but all to no avail. In desperation I asked alms, but Thy worshippers saw me and said, "He is strong and lazy, and he should not beg."

"Oh Lord, it is Thy will that my mother gave

birth unto me, and now the earth offers me back to You before the Ending."

His expression then changed. He arose and his eyes now glittered in determination. He fashioned a thick and heavy stick from the branch of the tree, and pointed it toward the city, shouting, "I asked for bread with all the strength of my voice, and was refused. Now I shall obtain it by the strength of my muscles! I asked for bread in the name of mercy and love, but humanity did not heed. I shall take it now in the name of evil!"

The passing years rendered the youth a robber, killer, and destroyer of souls; he crushed all who opposed him; he amassed fabulous wealth with which he won himself over to those in power. He was admired by colleagues, envied by other thieves, and feared by the multitudes.

His riches and false position prevailed upon the Emir to appoint him deputy in that city—the sad process pursued by unwise governors. Thefts were then legalized; oppression was supported by authority; crushing of the weak became commonplace; the throngs curried and praised.

Thus does the first touch of humanity's selfishness make criminals of the humble, and make killers of the sons of peace; thus does the early greed of humanity grow and strike back at humanity a thousandfold!

THE PLAYGROUND OF LIFE

ONE HOUR devoted to the pursuit of Beauty
And Love is worth a full century of glory
Given by the frightened weak to the strong.

From that hour comes man's Truth; and
During that century Truth sleeps between
The restless arms of disturbing dreams.

In that hour the soul sees for herself
The Natural Law, and for that century she
Imprisons herself behind the law of man;
And she is shackled with irons of oppression.

That hour was the inspiration of the Songs
Of Solomon, and that century was the blind
Power which destroyed the temple of Baalbek.

That hour was the birth of the Sermon on the
Mount, and that century wrecked the castles of
Palmyra and the tower of Babylon.

That hour was the Hegira of Mohammed, and that
Century forgot Allah, Golgotha, and Sinai.

One hour devoted to mourning and lamenting the
Stolen equality of the weak is nobler than a
Century filled with greed and usurpation.

It is at that hour when the heart is
Purified by flaming sorrow, and
Illuminated by the torch of Love.
And in the century, desires for Truth
Are buried in the bosom of the earth.
That hour is the root which must flourish.
That hour is the hour of contemplation,
The hour of meditation, the hour of
Prayer, and the hour of a new era of good.

And that century is a life of Nero spent
On self-investment taken solely from
Earthly substance.

This is life.
Portrayed on the stage for ages;
Recorded earthily for centuries;
Lived in strangeness for years;
Sung as a hymn for days;
Exalted for but an hour, but the
Hour is treasured by Eternity as a jewel.

SONG OF FORTUNE

MAN and I are sweethearts
He craves me and I long for him,
But alas! Between us has appeared
A rival who brings us misery.
She is cruel and demanding,
Possessing empty lure.
Her name is Substance.
She follows wherever we go
And watches like a sentinel, bringing
Restlessness to my lover.

I ask for my beloved in the forest,
Under the trees, by the lakes.
I cannot find him, for Substance
Has spirited him to the clamourous
City and placed him on the throne
Of quaking, metal riches.

I call for him with the voice of
Knowledge and the song of Wisdom.
He does not hearken, for Substance
Has enticed him into the dungeon
Of selfishness, where avarice dwells.

I seek him in the field of Contentment,
But I am alone, for my rival has
Imprisoned him in the cave of gluttony
And greed, and locked him there
With painful chains of gold.

I call to him at dawn, when Nature smiles,
But he does not hear, for excess has
Laden his drugged eyes with sick slumber.

I beguile him at eventide, when Silence rules
And the flowers sleep. But he responds not,
For his fear over what the morrow will
Bring, shadows his thoughts.

He yearns to love me;
He asks for me in his own acts. But he
Will find me not except in God's acts.
He seeks me in the edifices of his glory
Which he has built upon the bones of others;
He whispers to me from among
His heaps of gold and silver;
But he will find me only by coming to
The house of Simplicity which God has built
At the brink of the stream of affection.

He desires to kiss me before his coffers,
But his lips will never touch mine except
In the richness of the pure breeze.

He asks me to share with him his
Fabulous wealth, but I will not forsake God's
Fortune; I will not cast off my cloak of beauty.

He seeks deceit for medium; I seek only
The medium of his heart.
He bruises his heart in his narrow cell;
I would enrich his heart with my love.

My beloved has learned how to shriek and
Cry for my enemy, Substance; I would
Teach him how to shed tears of affection
And mercy from the eyes of his soul
For all things,
And utter sighs of contentment through
Those tears.

Man is my sweetheart;
I want to belong to him.

THE CITY OF THE DEAD

Yesterday I drew myself from the noisome throngs and proceeded into the field until I reached a knoll upon which Nature had spread her comely garments. Now I could breathe.

I looked back, and the city appeared with its magnificent mosques and stately residences veiled by the smoke of the shops.

I commenced analyzing man's·mission, but could conclude only that most of his life was identified with struggle and hardship. Then I tried not to ponder over what the sons of Adam had done, and centered my eyes on the field which is the throne of God's glory. In one secluded corner of the field I observed a burying ground surrounded by poplar trees.

There, between the city of the dead and the city of the living, I meditated. I thought of the eternal silence in the first and the endless sorrow in the second.

In the city of the living I found hope and despair, love and hatred, joy and sorrow, wealth and poverty, faith and infidelity.

In the city of the dead there is buried earth in earth that Nature converts, in the night's silence, into vegetation, and then into animal, and then into man. As my mind wandered in this fashion, I saw a procession moving slowly and reverently, accompanied by pieces of music that filled the sky with sad melody. It was an elaborate funeral. The dead was followed by the living who wept and lamented his going. As the cortege reached the place of interment the priests commenced praying and burning incense, and the musicians blowing and plucking their instruments, mourning the departed. Then the leaders came forward one after the other and recited their eulogies with fine choice of words.

At last the multitude departed, leaving the dead resting in a most spacious and beautiful vault, expertly designed in stone and iron, and surrounded by the most expensively-entwined wreaths of flowers.

The farewell-bidders returned to the city and I remained, watching them from a distance and speaking softly to myself while the sun was descending to the horizon and Nature was making her many preparations for slumber.

Then I saw two men labouring under the weight of a wooden casket, and behind them a shabby-appearing woman carrying an infant on her arms. Following last was a dog who, with heartbreaking eyes, stared first at the woman and then at the casket.

It was a poor funeral This guest of Death left to cold society a miserable wife and an infant to share her sorrows, and a faithful dog whose heart knew of his companion's departure.

As they reached the burial place they deposited the casket into a ditch away from the tended shrubs and marble stones, and retreated after a few simple words to God. The dog made one last turn to look at his friend's grave as the small group disappeared behind the trees.

I looked at the city of the living and said to myself, "That place belongs to the few." Then I looked upon the trim city of the dead and said, "That place, too, belongs to the few. Oh Lord, where is the haven of all people?"

As I said this, I looked toward the clouds, mingled with the sun's longest and most beautiful golden rays. And I heard a voice within me saying, "Over there!"

SONG OF THE RAIN

I AM dotted silver threads dropped from heaven
By the gods. Nature then takes me, to adorn
Her fields and valleys.

I am beautiful pearls, plucked from the
Crown of Ishtar by the daughter of Dawn
To embellish the gardens.

When I cry the hills laugh;
When I humble myself the flowers rejoice;
When I bow, all things are elated.

The field and the cloud are lovers
And between them I am a messenger of mercy.
I quench the thirst of the one;
I cure the ailment of the other.

The voice of thunder declares my arrival;
The rainbow announces my departure.
I am like earthly life, which begins at
The feet of the mad elements and ends
Under the upraised wings of death.

I emerge from the heart of the sea and
Soar with the breeze. When I see a field in
Need, I descend and embrace the flowers and
The trees in a million little ways.

I touch gently at the windows with my
Soft fingers, and my announcement is a
Welcome song. All can hear, but only
The sensitive can understand.

The heat in the air gives birth to me,
But in turn I kill it,
As woman overcomes man with
The strength she takes from him.

I am the sigh of the sea;
The laughter of the field;
The tears of heaven.

So with love—
Sighs from the deep sea of affection;
Laughter from the colourful field of the spirit;
Tears from the endless heaven of memories.

THE WIDOW AND HER SON

Night fell over North Lebanon and snow was covering the villages surrounded by the Kadeesha Valley, giving the fields and prairies the appearance of a great sheet of parchment upon which the furious Nature was recording her many deeds. Men came home from the streets while silence engulfed the night.

In a lone house near those villages lived a woman who sat by her fireside spinning wool, and at her side was her only child, staring now at the fire and then at his mother.

A terrible roar of thunder shook the house and the little boy took fright. He threw his arms about his mother, seeking protection from Nature in her affection. She took him to her bosom and kissed him; then she sat him on her lap and said, "Do not fear, my son, for Nature is but comparing her great power to man's weakness. There is a Supreme Being beyond the falling snow and the heavy clouds and the blowing wind, and He knows the needs of the earth, for He made it; and He looks upon the weak with merciful eyes.

"Be brave, my boy. Nature smiles in Spring and laughs in Summer and yawns in Autumn, but now she is weeping; and with her tears she waters life, hidden under the earth.

"Sleep, my dear child; your father is viewing us from Eternity. The snow and thunder bring us closer to him at this time.

"Sleep, my beloved, for this white blanket which makes us cold, keeps the seeds warm, and these war-like things will produce beautiful flowers when Nisan comes.

"Thus, my child, man cannot reap love until after sad and revealing separation, and bitter patience, and desperate hardship. Sleep, my little boy; sweet dreams will find your soul who is unafraid of the terrible darkness of night and the biting frost."

The little boy looked upon his mother with sleep-laden eyes and said, "Mother, my eyes are heavy, but I cannot go to sleep without saying my prayer."

The woman looked at his angelic face, her vision blurred by misted eyes, and said, "Repeat with me, my boy—'God, have mercy on the poor and protect them from the winter; warm their thin-clad bodies with Thy merciful hands; look upon the orphans who are sleeping in wretched houses, suffering from hunger and cold. Hear, oh Lord, the call of widows who are helpless and shivering with fear for their young. Open, oh Lord, the hearts of all humans,

37

that they may see the misery of the weak. Have mercy upon the sufferers who knock on doors, and lead the wayfarers into warm places. Watch, oh Lord, over the little birds and protect the trees and fields from the anger of the storm; for Thou art merciful and full of love.' "

As Slumber captured the boy's spirit, his mother placed him in the bed and kissed his eyes with quivering lips. Then she went back and sat by the hearth, spinning the wool to make him raiment.

THE POET

HE IS link between this and the coming world.
   He is
A pure spring from which all thirsty souls may
   drink.

He is a tree watered by the River of Beauty, bearing
Fruit which the hungry heart craves;
He is a nightingale, soothing the depressed
Spirit with his beautiful melodies;
He is a white cloud appearing over the horizon,
Ascending and growing until it fills the face of the
   sky.
Then it falls on the flowers in the Field of Life,
Opening their petals to admit the light.

He is an angel, sent by the goddess to
Preach the Deity's gospel;
He is a brilliant lamp, unconquered by darkness
And inextinguishable by the wind. It is filled with
Oil by Ishtar of Love, and lighted by Apollon of
   Music.

He is a solitary figure, robed in simplicity and
Kindness; He sits upon the lap of Nature to draw his
Inspiration, and stays up in the silence of the night,
Awaiting the descending of the spirit.

He is a sower who sows the seeds of his heart in the
Prairies of affection, and humanity reaps the
Harvest for her nourishment.

This is the poet—whom the people ignore in this
   life,
And who is recognized only after he bids the earthly
World farewell and returns to his arbor in heaven.

This is the poet—who asks naught of
Humanity but a smile.
This is the poet—whose spirit ascends and
Fills the firmament with beautiful sayings;
Yet the people deny themselves his radiance.

Until when shall the people remain asleep?
Until when shall they continue to glorify those
Who attained greatness by moments of advantage?
How long shall they ignore those who enable
Them to see the beauty of their spirit,
Symbol of peace and love?
Until when shall human beings honor the dead
And forget the living, who spend their lives
Encircled in misery, and who consume themselves
Like burning candles to illuminate the way
For the ignorant and lead them into the path of
   light?

Poet, you are the life of this life, and you have
Triumphed over the ages despite their severity.

Poet, you will one day rule the hearts, and
Therefore, your kingdom has no ending.

Poet, examine your crown of thorns; you will
Find concealed in it a budding wreath of laurel.

SONG OF THE SOUL

IN THE DEPTH of my soul there is
A wordless song—a song that lives
In the seed of my heart.
It refuses to melt with ink on
Parchment; it engulfs my affection
In a transparent cloak and flows,
But not upon my lips.

How can I sigh it? I fear it may
Mingle with earthly ether;
To whom shall I sing it? It dwells
In the house of my soul, in fear of
Harsh ears.

When I look into my inner eyes
I see the shadow of its shadow;
When I touch my fingertips
I feel its vibrations.

The deeds of my hands heed its
Presence as a lake must reflect
The glittering stars; my tears

Reveal it, as bright drops of dew
Reveal the secret of a withering rose.

It is a song composed by contemplation,
And published by silence,
And shunned by clamour,
And folded by truth,
And repeated by dreams,
And understood by love,
And hidden by awakening,
And sung by the soul.

It is the song of love;
What Cain or Esau could sing it?

It is more fragrant than jasmine;
What voice could enslave it?

It is heartbound, as a virgin's secret;
What string could quiver it?

Who dares unite the roar of the sea
And the singing of the nightingale?
Who dares compare the shrieking tempest
To the sigh of an infant?
Who dares speak aloud the words
Intended for the heart to speak?
What human dares sing in voice
The song of God?

LAUGHTER AND TEARS

As the Sun withdrew his rays from the garden, and the moon threw cushioned beams upon the flowers, I sat under the trees pondering upon the phenomena of the atmosphere, looking through the branches at the strewn stars which glittered like chips of silver upon a blue carpet; and I could hear from a distance the agitated murmur of the rivulet singing its way briskly into the valley.

When the birds took shelter among the boughs and the flowers folded their petals, and tremendous silence descended, I heard a rustle of feet through the grass. I took heed and saw a young couple approaching my arbor. They sat under a tree where I could see them without being seen.

After he looked about in every direction, I heard the young man saying, "Sit by me, my beloved, and listen to my heart; smile, for your happiness is a symbol of our future; be merry, for the sparkling days rejoice with us.

"My soul is warning me of the doubt in your heart, for doubt in love is a sin.

"Soon you will be the owner of this vast land,

lighted by this beautiful moon; soon you will be the mistress of my palace, and all the servants and maids will obey your commands.

"Smile, my beloved, like the gold smiles from my father's coffers.

"My heart refuses to deny you its secret. Twelve months of comfort and travel await us; for a year we will spend my father's gold at the blue lakes of Switzerland, and viewing the edifices of Italy and Egypt, and resting under the Holy Cedars of Lebanon; you will meet the princesses who will envy you for your jewels and clothes.

"All these things I will do for you; will you be satisfied?"

In a little while I saw them walking and stepping on flowers as the rich step upon the hearts of the poor. As they disappeared from my sight, I commenced to make comparison between love and money, and to analyze their position in my heart.

Money! The source of insincere love; the spring of false light and fortune; the well of poisoned water; the desperation of old age!

I was still wandering in the vast desert of contemplation when a forlorn and spectre-like couple passed by me and sat on the grass; a young man and a young woman who had left their farming shacks in the nearby fields for this cool and solitary place.

After a few moments of complete silence, I heard the following words uttered with sighs from weather-bitten lips, "Shed not tears, my beloved; love that opens our eyes and enslaves our hearts can give us the blessings of patience. Be consoled in our delay, for we have taken an oath and entered Love's shrine; for our love will ever grow in adversity; for it is in Love's name that we are suffering the obstacles of poverty and the sharpness of misery and the emptiness of separation. I shall attack these hardships until I triumph and place in your hands a strength that will help over all things to complete the journey of life.

"Love—which is God—will consider our sighs and tears as incense burned at His altar and He will reward us with fortitude. Good-bye, my beloved; I must leave before the heartening moon vanishes."

A pure voice, combined of the consuming flame of love, and the hopeless bitterness of longing and the resolved sweetness of patience, said, "Good-bye, my beloved."

They separated, and the elegy to their union was smothered by the wails of my crying heart.

I looked upon slumbering Nature, and with deep reflection discovered the reality of a vast and infinite thing—something no power could demand, influence acquire, nor riches purchase. Nor could it be effaced by the tears of time or deadened by sorrow; a thing which cannot be discovered by the blue lakes of Switzerland or the beautiful edifices of Italy.

It is something that gathers strength with patience, grows despite obstacles, warms in winter, flourishes in spring, casts a breeze in summer, and bears fruit in autumn—I found Love.

SONG OF THE FLOWER

I AM A KIND WORD uttered and repeated
By the voice of Nature;
I am a star fallen from the
Blue tent upon the green carpet.
I am the daughter of the elements
With whom Winter conceived;
To whom Spring gave birth; I was
Reared in the lap of Summer and I
Slept in the bed of Autumn.

At dawn I unite with the breeze
To announce the coming of light;
At eventide I join the birds
In bidding the light farewell.

The plains are decorated with
My beautiful colours, and the air
Is scented with my fragrance.

As I embrace Slumber the eyes of
Night watch over me, and as I
Awaken I stare at the sun, which is
The only eye of the day.

47

I drink dew for wine, and hearken to
The voices of the birds, and dance
To the rhythmic swaying of the grass.

I am the lover's gift; I am the wedding wreath;
I am the memory of a moment of happiness;
I am the last gift of the living to the dead;
I am a part of joy and a part of sorrow.

But I look up high to see only the light,
And never look down to see my shadow.
This is wisdom which man must learn.

VISION

THERE in the middle of
the field, by the side of a crystalline stream, I saw a
bird-cage whose rods and hinges were fashioned by
an expert's hands. In one corner lay a dead bird, and
in another were two basins—one empty of water and
the other of seeds. I stood there reverently, as if the
lifeless bird and the murmur of the water were
worthy of deep silence and respect—something
worthy of examination and meditation by the heart
and conscience.

As I engrossed myself in view and thought, I
found that the poor creature had died of thirst
beside a stream of water, and of hunger in the midst
of a rich field, cradle of life; like a rich man locked
inside his iron safe, perishing from hunger amid
heaps of gold.

Before my eyes I saw the cage turned suddenly
into a human skeleton, and the dead bird into a
man's heart which was bleeding from a deep wound
that looked like the lips of a sorrowing woman. A
voice came from that wound saying, "I am the

human heart, prisoner of substance and victim of earthly laws.

"In God's field of Beauty, at the edge of the stream of life, I was imprisoned in the cage of laws made by man.

"In the center of beautiful Creation I died neglected because I was kept from enjoying the freedom of God's bounty.

"Everything of beauty that awakens my love and desire is a disgrace, according to man's conceptions; everything of goodness that I crave is but naught, according to his judgment.

"I am the lost human heart, imprisoned in the foul dungeon of man's dictates, tied with chains of earthly authority, dead and forgotten by laughing humanity whose tongue is tied and whose eyes are empty of visible tears."

All these words I heard, and I saw them emerging with a stream of ever-thinning blood from that wounded heart.

More was said, but my misted eyes and crying soul prevented further sight or hearing.

SONG OF LOVE

I AM the lover's eyes, and the spirit's
Wine, and the heart's nourishment.
I am a rose. My heart opens at dawn and
The virgin kisses me and places me
Upon her breast.

I am the house of true fortune, and the
Origin of pleasure, and the beginning
Of peace and tranquility. I am the gentle
Smile upon the lips of beauty. When youth
Overtakes me he forgets his toil, and his
Whole life becomes reality of sweet dreams.

I am the poet's elation,
And the artist's revelation,
And the musician's inspiration.

I am a sacred shrine in the heart of a
Child, adored by a merciful mother.

I appear to a heart's cry; I shun a demand;
My fullness pursues the heart's desire;
It shuns the empty claim of the voice.

I appeared to Adam through Eve
And exile was his lot;
Yet I revealed myself to Solomon, and
He drew wisdom from my presence.

I smiled at Helena and she destroyed Tarwada;
Yet I crowned Cleopatra and peace dominated
The Valley of the Nile.

I am like the ages—building today
And destroying tomorrow;
I am like a god, who creates and ruins;
I am sweeter than a violet's sigh;
I am more violent than a raging tempest.

Gifts alone do not entice me;
Parting does not discourage me;
Poverty does not chase me;
Jealousy does not prove my awareness;
Madness does not evidence my presence.

Oh seekers, I am Truth, beseeching Truth;
And your Truth in seeking and receiving
And protecting me shall determine my
Behaviour.

TWO WISHES

IN THE silence of the night Death descended from God toward the earth. He hovered above a city and pierced the dwellings with his eyes. He saw the spirits floating on wings of dreams, and the people who were surrendered to the mercy of Slumber.

When the moon fell below the horizon and the city became black, Death walked silently among the houses—careful to touch nothing—until he reached a palace. He entered through the bolted gates undisturbed, and stood by the rich man's bed; and as Death touched his forehead, the sleeper's eyes opened, showing great fright.

When he saw the spectre, he summoned a voice mingled with fear and anger, and said, "Go away, oh horrible dream; leave me, you dreadful ghost. Who are you? How did you enter this place? What do you want? Leave this place at once, for I am the lord of the house and will call my slaves and guards, and order them to kill you!"

Then Death spoke, softly but with smouldering thunder, "I am Death. Stand and bow!"

The man responded, "What do you want? Why have you come here when I have not yet finished my affairs? What seek you from strength such as mine? Go to the weak man, and take him away!

"I loathe the sight of your bloody paws and hollow face, and my eyes take sick at your horrible ribbed wings and cadaverous body."

After a quiet moment of fearful realization he added, "No, no, oh merciful Death! Mind not my talk, for fear reveals what the heart forbids.

"Take a bushelful of my gold, or a handful of my slaves' souls, but leave me. I have accounts with Life requiring settling; I have due from the people much gold; my ships have not reached the harbour; my wheat has not been harvested. Take anything you demand, but spare my life. Death, I own harems of supernatural beauty; your choice is my gift to you. Give heed, Death—I have but one child, and I love him dearly for he is my only joy in this life. I offer supreme sacrifice—take him, but spare me!"

Death murmured, "You are not rich, but pitifully poor." Then Death took the hand of that earthly slave, removed his reality, and gave to the angels the heavy task of correction.

And Death walked slowly amidst the dwellings of the poor until he reached the most miserable he could find. He entered and approached a bed upon which a youth slept fitfully. Death touched his eyes;

the lad sprang up as he saw Death standing by, and, with a voice full of love and hope he said, "Here I am, my beautiful Death. Accept my soul, for you are the hope of my dreams. Be their accomplishment! Embrace me, oh beloved Death! You are merciful; do not leave me. You are God's messenger; deliver me to Him. You are the right hand of Truth and the heart of Kindness; do not neglect me.

"I have begged for you many times, but you did not come; I have sought you, but you avoided me; I called out to you, but you listened not. You hear me now—embrace my soul, beloved Death!"

Death placed his softened hand upon the trembling lips, removed all reality, and enfolded it beneath his wings for secure conduct. And returning to the sky, Death looked back and whispered his warning:

"Only those return to Eternity
Who on earth seek out Eternity."

SONG OF MAN

I WAS HERE from the moment of the
Beginning, and here I am still. And
I shall remain here until the end
Of the world, for there is no
Ending to my grief-stricken being.

I roamed the infinite sky, and
Soared in the ideal world, and
Floated through the firmament. But
Here I am, prisoner of measurement.

I heard the teachings of Confucius;
I listened to Brahma's wisdom;
I sat by Buddha under the Tree of Knowledge.
Yet here am I, existing with ignorance
And heresy.

I was on Sinai when Jehovah approached Moses;
I saw the Nazarene's miracles at the Jordan;
I was in Medina when Mohammed visited.
Yet here I am, prisoner of bewilderment.

Then I witnessed the might of Babylon;
I learned of the glory of Egypt;
I viewed the warring greatness of Rome.
Yet my earlier teachings showed the
Weakness and sorrow of those achievements.

I conversed with the magicians of Ain Dour;
I debated with the priests of Assyria;
I gleaned depth from the prophets of Palestine.
Yet, I am still seeking the truth.

I gathered wisdom from quiet India;
I probed the antiquity of Arabia;
I heard all that can be heard.
Yet, my heart is deaf and blind.

I suffered at the hands of despotic rulers;
I suffered slavery under insane invaders;
I suffered hunger imposed by tyranny;
Yet, I still possess some inner power
With which I struggle to greet each day.

My mind is filled, but my heart is empty;
My body is old, but my heart is an infant.
Perhaps in youth my heart will grow, but I
Pray to grow old and reach the moment of
My return to God. Only then will my heart fill!

I was here from the moment of the
Beginning, and here I am still. And
I shall remain here until the end
Of the world, for there is no
Ending to my grief-stricken being.

YESTERDAY AND TODAY

THE GOLD-HOARDER WALKED in his palace park and with him walked his troubles. And over his head hovered worries as a vulture hovers over a carcass, until he reached a beautiful lake surrounded by magnificent marble statuary.

He sat there pondering the water which poured from the mouths of the statues like thoughts flowing freely from a lover's imagination, and contemplating heavily his palace which stood upon a knoll like a birth-mark upon the cheek of a maiden. His fancy revealed to him the pages of his life's drama which he read with falling tears that veiled his eyes and prevented him from viewing man's feeble additions to Nature.

He looked back with piercing regret to the images of his early life, woven into pattern by the gods, until he could no longer control his anguish. He said aloud, "Yesterday I was grazing my sheep in the green valley, enjoying my existence, sounding my flute, and holding my head high. Today I am a prisoner of greed. Gold leads into gold, then into restlessness, and finally into crushing misery.

"Yesterday I was like a singing bird, soaring freely here and there in the fields. Today I am a slave to fickle wealth, society's rules, the city's customs, and purchased friends, pleasing the people by conforming to the strange and narrow laws of man. I was born to be free and enjoy the bounty of life, but I find myself like a beast of burden so heavily laden with gold that his back is breaking.

"Where are the spacious plains, the singing brooks, the pure breeze, the closeness of Nature? Where is my deity? I have lost all! Naught remains save loneliness that saddens me, gold that ridicules me, slaves who curse to my back, and a palace that I have erected as a tomb for my happiness, and in whose greatness I have lost my heart.

"Yesterday I roamed the prairies and the hills together with the Bedouin's daughter; Virtue was our companion, Love our delight, and the moon our guardian. Today I am among women with shallow beauty who sell themselves for gold and diamonds.

"Yesterday I was carefree, sharing with the shepherds all the joy of life; eating, playing, working, singing, and dancing together to the music of the heart's truth. Today I find myself among the people like a frightened lamb among the wolves. As I walk in the roads, they gaze at me with hateful eyes and point at me with scorn and jealousy, and as I steal through the park I see frowning faces all about me.

"Yesterday I was rich in happiness and today I am poor in gold.

"Yesterday I was a happy shepherd looking upon my herd as a merciful king looks with pleasure upon his contented subjects. Today I am a slave standing before my wealth, my wealth which robbed me of the beauty of life I once knew.

"Forgive me, my Judge! I did not know that riches would put my life in fragments and lead me into the dungeons of harshness and stupidity. What I thought was glory is naught but an eternal inferno."

He gathered himself wearily and walked slowly toward the palace, sighing and repeating, "Is this what people call wealth? Is this the god I am serving and worshipping? Is this what I seek of the earth? Why can I not trade it for one particle of contentment? Who would sell me one beautiful thought for a ton of gold? Who would give me one moment of love for a handful of gems? Who would grant me an eye that can see others' hearts, and take all my coffers in barter?"

As he reached the palace gates he turned and looked toward the city as Jeremiah gazed toward Jerusalem. He raised his arms in woeful lament and shouted, "Oh people of the noisome city, who are living in darkness, hastening toward misery, preaching falsehood, and speaking with stupidity . . until when shall you remain ignorant? Until when shall you abide in the filth of life and continue to desert its gardens? Why wear you tattered robes of narrowness while the silk raiment of Nature's beauty is fashioned for you? The lamp of wisdom is dimming;

it is time to furnish it with oil. The house of true fortune is being destroyed; it is time to rebuild it and guard it. The thieves of ignorance have stolen the treasure of your peace; it is time to retake it!"

At that moment a poor man stood before him and stretched forth his hand for alms. As he looked at the beggar, his lips parted, his eyes brightened with a softness, and his face radiated kindness. It was as if the yesterday he had lamented by the lake had come to greet him. He embraced the pauper with affection and filled his hand with gold, and with a voice sincere with the sweetness of love he said, "Come back tomorrow and bring with you your fellow sufferers. All your possessions will be restored."

He entered his palace saying, "Everything in life is good; even gold, for it teaches a lesson. Money is like a stringed instrument; he who does not know how to use it properly will hear only discordant music. Money is like love; it kills slowly and painfully the one who withholds it, and it enlivens the other who turns it upon his fellow men."

BEFORE THE THRONE
OF BEAUTY

ONE HEAVY day I ran away from the grim face of society and the dizzying clamour of the city and directed my weary steps to the spacious valley. I pursued the beckoning course of the rivulet and the musical sounds of the birds until I reached a lonely spot where the flowing branches of the trees prevented the sun from touching the earth.

I stood there, and it was entertaining to my soul—my thirsty soul who had seen naught but the mirage of life instead of its sweetness.

I was engrossed deeply in thought and my spirits were sailing the firmament when a Houri, wearing a sprig of grapevine that covered part of her naked body, and a wreath of poppies about her golden hair, suddenly appeared to me. As she realized my astonishment, she greeted me saying, "Fear me not; I am the Nymph of the Jungle."

"How can beauty like yours be committed to live in this place? Please tell me who you are and whence you come?" I asked. She sat gracefully on the green grass and responded, "I am the symbol of Nature! I am the Ever-Virgin your forefathers worshipped, and to my honour they erected shrines and temples at Baalbek and Djabeil." And I dared say, "But those temples and shrines were laid waste and the bones of my adoring ancestors became a part of the earth; nothing was left to commemorate their goddess save a pitiful few and forgotten pages in the book of history."

She replied, "Some goddesses live in the lives of their worshippers and die in their death, while some live an eternal and infinite life. My life is sustained by the world of Beauty which you will see wherever you rest your eyes, and this Beauty is Nature itself; it is the beginning of the shepherd's joy among the hills, and a villager's happiness in the fields, and the pleasure of the awe-filled tribes between the mountains and the plains. This Beauty promotes the wise into the throne of Truth."

Then I said, "Beauty is a terrible power!" And she retorted, "Human beings fear all things, even yourselves. You fear heaven, the source of spiritual peace; you fear Nature, the haven of rest and tranquility; you fear the God of goodness and accuse him of anger, while he is full of love and mercy."

After a deep silence, mingled with sweet dreams, I asked, "Speak to me of that Beauty which the people interpret and define, each one according to his own conception; I have seen her honoured and worshipped in different ways and manners."

She answered, "Beauty is that which attracts your soul, and that which loves to give and not to receive. When you meet Beauty, you feel that the hands deep within your inner self are stretched forth to bring her into the domain of your heart. It is a magnificence combined of sorrow and joy; it is the Unseen which you see, and the Vague which you understand, and the Mute which you hear—it is the Holy of Holies that begins in yourself and ends vastly beyond your earthly imagination."

Then the Nymph of the Jungle approached me and laid her scented hand upon my eyes. And as she withdrew, I found me alone in the valley. When I returned to the city, whose turbulence no longer vexed me, I repeated her words:

"Beauty is that which attracts your soul,
And that which loves to give and not to receive."

LEAVE ME, MY BLAMER

Leave me, my blamer,
For the sake of the love
Which unites your soul with
That of your beloved one;
For the sake of that which
Joins spirit with mother's
Affection, and ties your
Heart with filial love. Go,
And leave me to my own
Weeping heart.

Let me sail in the ocean of
My dreams; wait until Tomorrow
Comes, for Tomorrow is free to
Do with me as he wishes. Your
Flaying is naught but shadow
That walks with the spirit to
The tomb of abashment, and shows
Her the cold, solid earth.

I have a little heart within me
And I like to bring him out of

His prison and carry him on the
Palm of my hand to examine him
In depth and extract his secret.
Aim not your arrows at him, lest
He take fright and vanish ere he
Pours the secret's blood as a
Sacrifice at the altar of his
Own faith, given him by Deity
When He fashioned him of Love and **Beauty.**

The sun is rising and the nightingale
Is singing, and the myrtle is
Breathing its fragrance into space.
I want to free myself from the
Quilted slumber of wrong. Do not
Detain me, my blamer!

Cavil me not by mention of the
Lions of the forest or the
Snakes of the valley, for
My soul knows no fear of earth and
Accepts no warning of evil before
Evil comes.

Advise me not, my blamer, for
Calamities have opened my heart and
Tears have cleansed my eyes, and
Errors have taught me the language
Of the hearts.

Talk not of banishment, for Conscience
Is my judge and he will justify me

And protect me if I am innocent, and
Will deny me of life if I am a criminal.

Love's procession is moving;
Beauty is waving her banner;
Youth is sounding the trumpet of joy;
Disturb not my contrition, my blamer.
Let me walk, for the path is rich
With roses and mint, and the air
Is scented with cleanliness.

Relate not the tales of wealth and
Greatness, for my soul is rich
With bounty and great with God's glory.

Speak not of peoples and laws and
Kingdoms, for the whole earth is
My birthplace and all humans are
My brothers.

Go from me, for you are taking away
Life-giving repentance and bringing
Needless words.

A LOVER'S CALL

WHERE are you, my beloved? Are you in that little
Paradise, watering the flowers who look upon you
As infants look upon the breast of their mothers?

Or are you in your chamber where the shrine of
Virtue has been placed in your honour, and upon
Which you offer my heart and soul as sacrifice?

Or amongst the books, seeking human knowledge,
While you are replete with heavenly wisdom?

Oh companion of my soul, where are you? Are you
Praying in the temple? Or calling Nature in the
Field, haven of your dreams?

Are you in the huts of the poor, consoling the
Broken-hearted with the sweetness of your soul, and
Filling their hands with your bounty?

You are God's spirit everywhere;
You are stronger than the ages.

Do you have memory of the day we met, when the
  halo of
Your spirit surrounded us, and the Angels of Love
Floated about, singing the praise of the soul's deeds?

Do you recollect our sitting in the shade of the
Branches, sheltering ourselves from Humanity, as
  the ribs
Protect the divine secret of the heart from injury?

Remember you the trails and forest we walked, with
  hands
Joined, and our heads leaning against each other,
  as if
We were hiding ourselves within ourselves?

Recall you the hour I bade you farewell,
And the Miriamite kiss you placed on my lips?
That kiss taught me that joining of lips in Love
Reveals heavenly secrets which the tongue cannot
  utter!

That kiss was introduction to a great sigh,
Like the Almighty's breath that turned earth into
  man.

That sigh led my way into the spiritual world,
Announcing the glory of my soul; and there
It shall perpetuate until again we meet.

I remember when you kissed me and kissed me,
With tears coursing your cheeks, and you said,

"Earthly bodies must often separate for earthly purpose,
And must live apart impelled by worldly intent.

"But the spirit remains joined safely in the hands of
Love, until death arrives and takes joined souls to
   God.

"Go, my beloved; Love has chosen you her delegate;
Obey her, for she is Beauty who offers to her fol-
   lower
The cup of the sweetness of life.
As for my own empty arms, your love shall remain
   my
Comforting groom; your memory, my Eternal wed-
   ding."

Where are you now, my other self? Are you awake in
The silence of the night? Let the clean breeze convey
To you my heart's every beat and affection.

Are you fondling my face in your memory? That
   image
Is no longer my own, for Sorrow has dropped his
Shadow on my happy countenance of the past.

Sobs have withered my eyes which reflected your
   beauty
And dried my lips which you sweetened with kisses

Where are you, my beloved? Do you hear my weeping
From beyond the ocean? Do you understand my
need?
Do you know the greatness of my patience?

Is there any spirit in the air capable of conveying
To you the breath of this dying youth? Is there any
Secret communication between angels that will carry
to
You my complaint?

Where are you, my beautiful star? The obscurity of
life
Has cast me upon its bosom; sorrow has conquered
me.
Sail your smile into the air; it will reach and enliven
me!
Breathe your fragrance into the air; it will sustain
me!

Where are you, my beloved?
Oh, how great is Love!
And how little am I!

THE BEAUTY OF DEATH

Dedicated to M. E. H.

PART ONE—THE CALLING

LET ME sleep, for my soul is intoxicated with love, and

Let me rest, for my spirit has had its bounty of days and nights;

Light the candles and burn the incense around my bed, and

Scatter leaves of jasmine and roses over my body;

Embalm my hair with frankincense and sprinkle my feet with perfume,

And read what the hand of Death has written on my forehead.

Let me rest in the arms of Slumber, for my open eyes are tired;

Let the silver-stringed lyre quiver and soothe my spirit;

Weave from the harp and lute a veil around my withering heart.

Sing of the past as you behold the dawn of hope in
my eyes, for
Its magic meaning is a soft bed upon which my
heart rests.

Dry your tears, my friends, and raise your heads as
the flowers
Raise their crowns to greet the dawn.
Look at the bride of Death standing like a column
of light
Between my bed and the infinite;
Hold your breath and listen with me to the beckon-
ing rustle of
Her white wings.

Come close and bid me farewell; touch my eyes
with smiling lips.
Let the children grasp my hands with soft and rosy
fingers;
Let the aged place their veined hands upon my head
and bless me;
Let the virgins come close and see the shadow of
God in my eyes,
And hear the echo of His will racing with my breath.

PART TWO—THE ASCENDING

I have passed a mountain peak and my soul is soaring in the
Firmament of complete and unbound freedom;
I am far, far away, my companions, and the clouds
are

73

Hiding the hills from my eyes.
The valleys are becoming flooded with an ocean of
  silence, and the
Hands of oblivion are engulfing the roads and the
  houses;
The prairies and fields are disappearing behind a
  white spectre
That looks like the spring cloud, yellow as the
  candlelight
And red as the twilight.

The songs of the waves and the hymns of the streams
Are scattered, and the voices of the throngs reduced
  to silence;
And I can hear naught but the music of Eternity
In exact harmony with the spirit's desires.
I am cloaked in full whiteness;
I am in comfort; I am in peace.

PART THREE—THE REMAINS

Unwrap me from this white linen shroud and clothe
  me
With leaves of jasmine and lilies;
Take my body from the ivory casket and let it rest
Upon pillows of orange blossoms.
Lament me not, but sing songs of youth and joy;
Shed not tears upon me, but sing of harvest and the
  winepress;
Utter no sigh of agony, but draw upon my face with
  your

Finger the symbol of Love and Joy.
Disturb not the air's tranquility with chanting and
    requiems,
But let your hearts sing with me the song of Eternal
    Life;
Mourn me not with apparel of black,
But dress in colour and rejoice with me;
Talk not of my departure with sighs in your hearts;
    close
Your eyes and you will see me with you forever-
    more.

Place me upon clusters of leaves and
Carry me upon your friendly shoulders and
Walk slowly to the deserted forest.
Take me not to the crowded burying ground lest
    my slumber
Be disrupted by the rattling of bones and skulls.
Carry me to the cypress woods and dig my grave
    where violets
And poppies grow not in the other's shadow;
Let my grave be deep so that the flood will not
Carry my bones to the open valley;
Let my grave be wide, so that the twilight shadows
Will come and sit by me.

Take from me all earthly raiment and place me
    deep in my
Mother Earth; and place me with care upon my
    mother's breast.

Cover me with soft earth, and let each handful be mixed
With seeds of jasmine, lilies, and myrtle; and when they
Grow above me and thrive on my body's element they will
Breathe the fragrance of my heart into space;
And reveal even to the sun the secret of my peace;
And sail with the breeze and comfort the wayfarer.

Leave me then, friends—leave me and depart on mute feet,
As the silence walks in the deserted valley;
Leave me to God and disperse yourselves slowly, as the almond
And apple blossoms disperse under the vibration of Nisan's breeze.

Go back to the joy of your dwellings and you will find there
That which Death cannot remove from you and me.
Leave this place, for what you see here is far away in meaning
From the earthly world. Leave me.

THE PALACE AND THE HUT

PART ONE

As night fell and the light glittered in the great house, the servants stood at the massive door awaiting the coming of the guests; and upon their velvet garments shone golden buttons.

The magnificent carriages drew into the palace park and the nobles entered, dressed in gorgeous raiment and decorated with jewels. The instruments filled the air with pleasant melodies while the dignitaries danced to the soothing music.

At midnight the finest and most palatable foods were served on a beautiful table embellished with all kinds of the rarest flowers. The feasters dined and drank abundantly, until the sequence of the wine began to play its part. At dawn the throng dispersed boisterously, after spending a long night of intoxication and gluttony which hurried their worn bodies into their deep beds with unnatural sleep.

PART TWO

At eventide, a man attired in the dress of heavy work stood before the door of his small house and knocked at the door. As it opened, he entered and greeted the occupants in a cheerful manner, and then sat between his children who were playing at the fireplace. In a short time, his wife had the meal prepared and they sat at a wooden table consuming their food. After eating they gathered around the oil lamp and talked of the day's events. When early night had lapsed, all stood silently and surrendered themselves to the King of Slumber with a song of praise and a prayer of gratitude upon their lips.

A POET'S VOICE

PART ONE

THE POWER of charity sows deep in my heart, and I reap and gather the wheat in bundles and give them to the hungry.

My soul gives life to the grapevine and I press its bunches and give the juice to the thirsty.

Heaven fills my lamp with oil and I place it at my window to direct the stranger through the dark.

I do all these things because I live in them; and if destiny should tie my hands and prevent me from so doing, then death would be my only desire. For I am a poet, and if I cannot give, I shall refuse to receive.

Humanity rages like a tempest, but I sigh in silence for I know the storm must pass away while a sigh goes to God.

Human kinds cling to earthly things, but I seek ever to embrace the torch of love so it will purify me by its fire and sear inhumanity from my heart.

Substantial things deaden a man without suffering; love awakens him with enlivening pains.

Humans are divided into different clans and tribes, and belong to countries and towns. But I find myself a stranger to all communities and belong to no settlement. The universe is my country and the human family is my tribe.

Men are weak, and it is sad that they divide amongst themselves. The world is narrow and it is unwise to cleave it into kingdoms, empires, and provinces.

Human kinds unite themselves only to destroy the temples of soul, and they join hands to build edifices for earthly bodies. I stand alone listening to the voice of hope in my deep self saying, "As love enlivens a man's heart with pain, so ignorance teaches him the way to knowledge." Pain and ignorance lead to great joy and knowledge because the Supreme Being has created nothing vain under the sun.

PART TWO

I have a yearning for my beautiful country, and I love its people because of their misery. But if my people rose, stimulated by plunder and motivated by what they call "patriotic spirit" to murder, and invaded my neighbour's country, then upon the committing of any human atrocity I would hate my people and my country.

I sing the praise of my birthplace and long to see the home of my childhood; but if the people in that home refused to shelter and feed the needy wayfarer, I would convert my praise into anger and my longing into forgetfulness. My inner voice would say, "The house that does not comfort the needy is worthy of naught but destruction."

I love my native village with some of my love for my country; and I love my country with part of my love for the earth, all of which is my country; and I love the earth with all of myself because it is the haven of humanity, the manifest spirit of God.

Humanity is the spirit of the Supreme Being on earth, and that humanity is standing amidst ruins, hiding its nakedness behind tattered rags, shedding tears upon hollow cheeks, and calling for its children with pitiful voice. But the children are busy singing their clan's anthem; they are busy sharpening the swords and cannot hear the cry of their mothers.

Humanity appeals to its people but they listen not. Were one to listen, and console a mother by wiping her tears, others would say, "He is weak, affected by sentiment."

Humanity is the spirit of the Supreme Being on earth, and that Supreme Being preaches love and good-will. But the people ridicule such teachings. The Nazarene Jesus listened, and crucifixion was his lot; Socrates heard the voice and followed it, and he too fell victim in body. The followers of The Nazarene and Socrates are the followers of Deity, and since people will not kill them, they deride them, saying, "Ridicule is more bitter than killing."

Jerusalem could not kill The Nazarene, nor

BOOK ONE

Athens Socrates; they are living yet and shall live eternally. Ridicule cannot triumph over the followers of Deity. They live and grow forever.

PART THREE

Thou art my brother because you are a human, and we both are sons of one Holy Spirit; we are equal and made of the same earth.

You are here as my companion along the path of life, and my aid in understanding the meaning of hidden Truth. You are a human, and, that fact sufficing, I love you as a brother. You may speak of me as you choose, for Tomorrow shall take you away and will use your talk as evidence for his judgment, and you shall receive justice.

You may deprive me of whatever I possess, for my greed instigated the amassing of wealth and you are entitled to my lot if it will satisfy you.

You may do unto me whatever you wish, but you shall not be able to touch my Truth.

You may shed my blood and burn my body, but you cannot kill or hurt my spirit.

You may tie my hands with chains and my feet with shackles, and put me in the dark prison, but you shall not enslave my thinking, for it is free, like the breeze in the spacious sky.

You are my brother and I love you. I love you worshipping in your church, kneeling in your temple, and praying in your mosque. You and I and all are children of one religion, for the varied paths of religion are but the fingers of the loving hand of the Supreme Being, extended to all, offering completeness of spirit to all, anxious to receive all.

I love you for your Truth, derived from your knowledge; that Truth which I cannot see because of my ignorance. But I respect it as a divine thing, for it is the deed of the spirit. Your Truth shall meet my Truth in the coming world and blend together like the fragrance of flowers and become one whole and eternal Truth, perpetuating and living in the eternity of Love and Beauty.

I love you because you are weak before the strong oppressor, and poor before the greedy rich. For these reasons I shed tears and comfort you; and from behind my tears I see you embraced in the arms of Justice, smiling and forgiving your persecutors. You are my brother and I love you.

PART FOUR

You are my brother, but why are you quarreling with me? Why do you invade my country and try to subjugate me for the sake of pleasing those who are seeking glory and authority?

Why do you leave your wife and children and follow Death to the distant land for the sake of those who buy glory with your blood, and high honour with your mother's tears?

Is it an honour for a man to kill his brother man? If you deem it an honour, let it be an act of worship, and erect a temple to Cain who slew his brother Abel.

Is self-preservation the first law of Nature? Why, then, does Greed urge you to self-sacrifice in order only to achieve his aim in hurting your brothers? Beware, my brother, of the leader who says, "Love of existence obliges us to deprive the people of their rights!" I say unto you but this: protecting others' rights is the noblest and most beautiful human act; if my existence requires that I kill others, then death is more honourable to me, and if I cannot find someone to kill me for the protection of my honour, I will not hesitate to take my life by my own hands for the sake of Eternity before Eternity comes.

Selfishness, my brother, is the cause of blind superiority, and superiority creates clanship, and clanship creates authority which leads to discord and subjugation.

The soul believes in the power of knowledge and justice over dark ignorance; it denies the authority that supplies the swords to defend and strengthen ignorance and oppression—that authority which destroyed Babylon and shook the foundation of Jerusalem and left Rome in ruins. It is that which made people call criminals great men; made writers respect their names; made historians relate the stories of their inhumanity in manner of praise.

The only authority I obey is the knowledge of guarding and acquiescing in the Natural Law of Justice.

What justice does authority display when it kills the killer? When it imprisons the robber? When it descends on a neighbouring country and slays its people? What does justice think of the authority under which a killer punishes the one who kills, and a thief sentences the one who steals?

You are my brother, and I love you; and Love is justice with its full intensity and dignity. If justice did not support my love for you, regardless of your tribe and community, I would be a deceiver concealing the ugliness of selfishness behind the outer garment of pure love.

CONCLUSION

My soul is my friend who consoles me in misery and distress of life. He who does not befriend his soul is an enemy of humanity, and he who does not find human guidance within himself will perish desperately. Life emerges from within, and derives not from environs.

I came to say a word and I shall say it now. But if death prevents its uttering, it will be said by To-morrow, for Tomorrow never leaves a secret in the book of Eternity.

I came to live in the glory of Love and the light of Beauty, which are the reflections of God. I am here living, and the people are unable to exile me from the domain of life for they know I will live in death. If they pluck my eyes I will hearken to the murmurs of Love and the songs of Beauty.

If they close my ears I will enjoy the touch of the breeze mixed with the incense of Love and the fragrance of Beauty.

If they place me in vacuum, I will live together with my soul, the child of Love and Beauty.

I came here to be for all and with all, and what I do today in my solitude will be echoed by Tomorrow to the people.

What I say now with one heart will be said tomorrow by many hearts.

THE BRIDE'S BED*

THE BRIDE and bride groom, preceded by candle carriers and followed by priests and friends, left the temple accompanied by young men and women who walked by their sides singing and filling the firmament with beautiful and happy melodies.

As the procession reached the bridegroom's residence, the newly wed couple took high seats in the spacious room, and the celebrants seated themselves upon the silken cushions and velvet divans until the place became crowded with multitudes of well wishers. The servants set the tables, and the feasters commenced drinking to the health of the bride and bridegroom, while the musicians were soothing the spirits with their stringed instruments. One could hear the ringing and rattling of the drinking cups in unison with the sound of tambourines. The maidens began to dance gracefully and twist their

* This incident occurred in North Lebanon in the latter part of the nineteenth century and it was conveyed to me by a person who was related to one of the principals in this story, and who attended the function described. (*Kahlil Gibran.*)

flexible bodies to the melodies of the music, while the onlookers watched cheerfully and drank more and more wine.

In a few hours the scene was converted from a gay and pleasant wedding celebration into a coarse and profane orgy of drunkenness. Here is a young man pouring out all of his heart's sentiment and revealing his momentary, questionable love to an attractive maiden. And there is another youth endeavouring to converse with a woman, and having difficulty in bringing to his wine-drugged tongue the beautiful expressions he sought. Now and then you hear an elderly man urging the musicians to repeat a certain song that reminded him of his youthful days. In this group a woman is flirting with a man who, in turn, is looking passionately at her rival. In that corner, a grey-haired woman is watching the maidens smilingly, trying to select a wife for her only son. By the window stands a married woman who affords herself this opportunity to make plans with her lover while her husband is occupied with wine. It seemed that all were reaping the fruits of the present and forgetting the past and the future.

All this was taking place while the beautiful bride watched them with sorrowful eyes. She felt like a miserable prisoner behind the iron bars of a prison, and frequently she glanced across the room toward a young man who was sitting alone and quietly, like a wounded bird left behind by the flock. His arms were folded across his bosom as if he were trying to keep his heart from bursting. He was gazing at something invisible in the sky of the room and seemed to be completely lost in a world of darkness.

Midnight came, and the exultation of the throng mounted higher until it assumed the aspects of unleashed madness, for the minds were free and the tongues were uncontrolled.

The bridegroom, who was an elderly man, already drunk, left the bride to herself and circulated amidst the guests, drinking with the feasters and adding fuel to the flames of his intoxication.

Responding to the bride's signal, a maiden came and sat close by her side, whereupon the bride turned around and looked in every direction before she whispered with a trembling voice, "I beg you, my companion, and appeal to you in the name of our friendship and everything that is dear to you in this world, to go now and tell Saleem to join me in the garden under the willow tree. Please, Susan, beg him for me and ask him to grant my request; remind him of our past and tell him that I will die if I do not see him. Tell him that I must confess my sins to him and ask him to forgive me; tell him that I want to pour out all my heart's secrets before him. Hurry, and do not fear."

Susan dispatched the bride's message with sincerity; Saleem looked at her as a thirsty man looks at a brook far off and he quietly said, "I will wait for her in the garden under the willow tree." He left the house, and a few minutes passed before the bride followed him, stealing her way between the drunken revelers. As she reached the garden, she looked to the rear like a gazelle who is fleeing a wolf, and sped toward the willow tree where the youth awaited her. When she found herself by his side, she threw her arms about him and said tearfully, "My beloved, listen to me; I am sorry for having been hasty and thoughtless. I repented until my heart is crushed with sorrow; I love you and do not love any other; I shall continue to love you to the end of my life. They lied to me and told me that you loved another and Najeebee deceived me when she told me that you had fallen in love with her, and did so in order to induce me to accept her cousin as my bridegroom, as the family had long planned. I am married now but you are the only one I love and you are my bridegroom. Now that the veil has been removed from my eyes and truth is near, I came here to follow you to the end of life, and I will never go back to the man whom falsehood and narrow custom have selected for me as a husband. Let us hurry, my beloved, and leave this place under the protection of night. Let us go to the seacoast and embark upon a ship that will take us to a distant land where we will live together unmolested. Let us start now so when dawn comes we will be safe from the grip of the enemy; I have enough jewelry to take care of us for the rest of our lives . . . Why do you not talk, Saleem? Why do you not look at me? Why do you not kiss me? Are you listening to the wailing of my soul and the crying of my heart? Speak, and let us make haste to leave this place! The minutes we are losing are more precious than diamonds, and dearer than the crowns of the kings."

Her voice was more soothing than Life's whispering, and more anguished than the moaning call of Death, and softer than the rustling of wings, and deeper than the message of the waves . . . it was a voice that vibrated with hope and despair, with pleasure and pain, with happiness and misery, with need for life and desire for death. The youth was listening, but within him Love and Honour fought each other . . . Honour that confronts the spirit, and Love that God places in the human heart . . . After a long silence, the youth raised his head and turned his eyes away from the bride who was quivering with anxiety and he quietly protested, "Return to your destiny, for it is now too late. Sobriety has effaced what intoxication had painted. Go back before the guests see you here and say that you betrayed your husband on the wedding night just as you betrayed me during my absence." When she heard these words, she trembled like a withering flower before a tempest and she said painfully, "I shall never go back to that house which I have left forever. I feel now like a prisoner who leaves his exile . . . do not cast me from you, saying that I betrayed you. The hands that joined your heart and mine are stronger than the Emir's and the priest's hands which committed my body to my revolting bridegroom. There is no power that can take you from me . . . not even Death can separate our souls, for as Heaven has willed it, only Heaven can alter it."

Feigning disinterest and trying to free himself from the grip of her arms around him, Saleem retorted, "Depart from me! I love another with an intensity that causes me to forget you exist in this world. Najeebee was right when she told you that I loved her. Go back to your husband and be a faithful wife to him as the law commands"

The bride desperately protested, "No, no! I do not believe you, Saleem! I know that you love me, and I can read it in your eyes; I sense your love when I am close to you; I shall never leave you for my husband's home as long as my heart beats; I came here to follow you to the end of the world. Lead the way, Saleem, or shed my blood and take my life now." With a voice no stronger than before, Saleem returned, "Leave me, or I will shout and gather the people in this garden and disgrace you before God and man and let my beloved Najeebee laugh at you and be proud of her triumph."

As Saleem was endeavouring to unclasp her arms, she turned from a hopeful, kind, and pleading woman into a furious lioness who had lost her cubs, and she cried out saying, "No one shall ever triumph over me and take my love from me!" Having uttered these words, she drew a dagger from beneath her wedding gown, and swift as lightning, she sheathed it in the youth's heart. He fell upon the ground like a tender branch broken by the storms and she bent over him, holding the blood-stained dagger in her hand. He opened his eyes and his lips vibrated when he faltered, "Come now, my beloved; come, Lyla, and do not leave me. Life is weaker than Death, and Death is weaker than Love. Listen to the cruel laughter of the feasters inside the house, and hear the tinkling and breaking of the drinking cups, my beloved. Lyla, you have rescued me from Life's suffering. Let me kiss the hand that broke the chains and let me free. Kiss me and forgive me, for I have not been truthful.

"Place your blood-cleansed hands upon my withering heart, and when my soul ascends into the spacious sky, place the dagger in my right hand and say that I took my own life." He choked for breath and whispered, "I love you, Lyla, and never loved another. Self-sacrifice is nobler than fleeing with you. Kiss me, oh beloved sweetheart of my soul. Kiss me, oh Lyla . . ." And he placed his hand upon his wounded heart and breathed his last. The bride looked toward the house and cried in piercing agony, "Emerge from your stupor, for here is the wedding! The bride and the bridegroom are awaiting you! Come and see our soft bed! Wake up, you madmen and drunkards; hurry to this place so we can reveal to you the truth of Love, Death and Life!" Her hysterical voice rang through every corner of the house, echoing into the guests' ears. As if

in a trance, they were drawn to the door and they
walked out, looking in every direction. As they approached the scene of tragic beauty, and saw the
bride weeping over Saleem, they retreated in fright
and none dared come close by. It seemed that the
stream of blood from the youth's heart, and the
dagger in the bride's hand, had fascinated them and
frozen the blood in their bodies. The bride looked
at him and moaned bitterly, "Come, you cowards!
Fear not the spectre of Death whose greatness will
refuse to approach your littleness, and dread not
this dagger, for it is a divine instrument which declines to touch your filthy bodies and empty hearts.
Look at this handsome youth . . . he is my beloved,
and I killed him because I loved him . . . he is my
bridegroom and I am his bride. We sought a bed
worthy of our love in this world which you have
made so small with your ignorance and traditions.
But we chose this bed. Where is that wicked woman
who slandered my beloved and said that he loved
her? Where is the one who believed she triumphed
over me? Where is Najeebee, that hell-viper who
deceived me? Where is the woman who gathered
you here to celebrate my beloved's departure and
not the wedding of the man she had chosen for me?
My words are vague to you, for the abyss cannot
understand the song of the stars. You shall tell your
children that I killed my beloved on the wedding
night. My name shall be upon your dirty lips uttered with blasphemy, but your grandchildren shall

bless me, for Tomorrow shall be for the freedom of truth and the spirit. And you, my ignorant husband, who bought my body but not my love, and who owns me but will never possess me, you are the symbol of this miserable nation, seeking light in darkness, and awaiting the coming of water from the rock; you symbolize a country ruled by blindness and stupidity; you represent a false humanity which cuts throats and arms in order to reach for a necklace or bracelet. I forgive you now, for the happy, departing soul forgives the sins of all the people."

Then the bride lifted her dagger toward the sky, and like a thirsty person who brings the edge of a drinking glass to his lips, she brought it down and planted it in her bosom. She fell by the side of her beloved like a lily whose flower was cut off by a sharp scythe. The women gazed upon the horrible scene and cried frightfully; some of them fell into a swoon, and the uproar of the men filled the sky. As they shamefully and reverently approached the victims, the dying bride looked at them, and with blood streaming from her stricken body, she said, "Stay away from us and separate not our bodies, for if you commit such a sin, the spirit that hovers over your heads will grasp you and take your lives. Let this hungry earth swallow our bodies and hide us in its bosom. Let it protect us as it protects the seeds from the snow until Spring comes, and restores pure life and awakening."

She came close to her beloved, placed her lips

upon his cold lips, and uttered her last words, "Look, my forever . . . look at our friends. How the jealous are gathering about our bed! Hear the grating of their teeth and the crushing of their fingers! You have waited for me a long time, Saleem, and here I am, for I have broken the chains and shackles. Let us go toward the sun, for we have been waiting too long in this confining, dark world. All objects are disappearing from my sight and I can see naught but you, my beloved. These are my lips, my greatest earthly possession . . . accept my last human breath. Come, Saleem, let us leave now. Love has lifted his wings and ascended into the great light." She dropped her head upon his bosom and her unseeing eyes were still open and gazing upon him.

Silence prevailed, as if the dignity of death had stolen the people's strength and prevented them from moving. Whereupon the priest who had performed the wedding ceremony came forth and pointed with his forefinger at the death-bound couple shouting, "Cursed are the hands that touch these blood-spattered carcasses that are soaked with sin. And cursed are the eyes that shed tears of sorrow upon these two evil souls. Let the corpse of the son of Sodom and that of the daughter of Gomorrah remain lying in this diseased spot until the beasts devour their flesh and the wind scatters their bones. Go back to your homes and flee from the pollution of these sinners! Disperse now, before the flames of hell sting you, and he who remains here shall be cursed and excommunicated from the Church and shall never again enter the temple and join the Christians in offering prayers to God!"

Susan, who acted as the last messenger between the bride and her beloved, walked forth bravely and stood before the priest. She looked at him with tearful eyes and said, "I shall remain here, you merciless heretic, and I shall guard them until dawn comes. I shall dig a grave for them under these hanging branches and bury them in the garden of their last earthly kiss. Leave this place immediately, for the swine detest the aromatic scent of incense, and the thieves fear the lord of the house and dread the coming of the brilliant sunrise. Hurry to your obscured beds, for the hymns of the angels will not enter your ears, blocked with the hardened cement of cruel and stupid rules."

The throng departed slowly with the stern-faced priest, and Susan remained watching over Lyla and Saleem as a loving mother guards her children in the silence of the night. And when the multitude was gone, she dropped down and wept with the crying angels.

BOOK NINE

BETWEEN
NIGHT & MORN

THE TEMPEST

Yusif El Fakhri was thirty years of age when he withdrew himself from society and departed to live in an isolated hermitage in the vicinity of Kedeesha Valley in North Lebanon. The people of the nearby villages heard various tales concerning Yusif; some related that his was a wealthy and noble family, and that he loved a woman who betrayed him and caused him to lead a solitary life, while others said that he was a poet who deserted the clamourous city and retired to that place in order to record his thoughts and compose his inspiration; and many were sure that he was a mystic who was contented with the spiritual world, although most people insisted that he was a madman.

As for myself, I could not draw any conclusion regarding the man, for I knew that there must be a deep secret within his heart whose revelation I would not trust to mere speculation. I had long hoped for the opportunity to meet this strange man. I had endeavoured in devious ways to win his friendship in order to study his reality and learn his story by inquiring as to his purpose in life, but my efforts were in vain. When I met him for the first time, he was walking by the forest of the Holy Cedars of Lebanon, and I greeted him with the finest choice of words, but he returned my greeting by merely shaking his head and striding off.

On another occasion I found him standing in the midst of a small vineyard by a monastery, and again I approached and greeted him, saying, "It is said by the villagers that this monastery was built by a Syriac group in the Fourteenth Century; do you know anything of its history?" He replied coldly, "I do not know who built this monastery, nor do I care to know." And he turned his back to me and added, "Why do you not ask your grandparents, who are older than I, and who know more of the history of these valleys than I do?" Realizing at once my utter failure, I left him.

Thus did two years pass, and the bizarre life of this strange man preyed on my mind and disturbed my dreams.

PART TWO

One day in Autumn, as I was roaming the hills and knolls adjacent to the hermitage of Yusif El Fakhri, I was suddenly caught in a strong wind and torrent rain, and the tempest cast me here and there like a boat whose rudder has been broken and whose masts have been torn by a gale in a rough sea. I directed my steps with difficulty toward Yusif's place, saying to myself, "This is an opportunity I have long sought, and the tempest will be my excuse for entering, while my wet clothes will serve as good reason for lingering."

I was in a miserable plight when I reached the hermitage, and as I knocked on the door, the man whom I had been longing to see opened it. He was holding in one hand a dying bird whose head had been injured and whose wings had been broken. I greeted him saying, "I beg your forgiveness for this annoying intrusion. The raging tempest trapped me while I was afar from home." He frowned, saying, "There are many caves in this wilderness in which you might have taken refuge." However, he did not close the door, and the beat of my heart quickened in anticipation, for the realization of my great wish was close at hand. He commenced to touch the bird's head gently and with the utmost care and interest, exhibiting a quality important to my heart. I was surprised over the two opponent characteristics I found in that man—mercy and cruelty at the same time. We became aware of the strained silence. He resented my presence, I desired to remain.

It seemed as if he felt my thought, for he looked up and said, "The tempest is clean, and declines to eat soured meat. Why do you seek to escape from it?" And with a touch of humour, I responded, "The tempest may not desire salted or soured things, but she is inclined to chill and tender all things, and undoubtedly she would enjoy consuming me if she grasped me again." His expression was severe when he retorted, "The tempest would have bestowed upon you a great honour, of which you are not worthy, if she had swallowed you." I agreed, "Yes, Sir, I fled the tempest so I might not be awarded an honour which I do not merit." He turned his face from me in an effort to choke his smile, and then motioned toward a wooden bench by the fireplace and invited me to rest and dry my raiment. I could scarcely control my elation.

I thanked him and sat down while he seated himself opposite, on a bench carved of rock. He commenced to dip his finger tips into an earthenware jar containing a kind of oil, applying it softly to the bird's head and wings. Without looking up he said, "The strong winds have caused this bird to fall upon the rocks between Life and Death." I replied, rendering comparison, "And the strong winds have sent me, adrift, to your door, in time to prevent having my head injured and my wings broken."

He looked at me seriously and said, "It is my wish that man would show the bird's instinct, and it is my wish that the tempest would break the people's wings. For man inclines toward fear and cowardice, and as he feels the awakening of the tempest he crawls into the crevices and the caves of the earth and hides himself."

My purpose was to extract the story of his self-imposed exile, and I provoked, "Yes, the birds possess

an honour and courage that man does not possess.
. . . Man lives in the shadow of laws and customs
which he made and fashioned for himself, but the
birds live according to the same free Eternal Law
which causes the earth to pursue its mighty path
about the sun." His eyes and face brightened, as if
he had found in me an understanding disciple, and
he exclaimed, "Well done! If you place belief in
your own words you should leave civilization and its
corrupt laws and traditions, and live like the birds
in a place empty of all things except the magnificent
law of heaven and earth.

"Believing is a fine thing, but placing those beliefs into execution is a test of strength. Many are
those who talk like the roar of the sea, but their
lives are shallow and stagnant, like the rotting
marshes. Many are those who lift their heads above
the mountain tops, but their spirits remain dormant
in the obscurity of the caverns." He rose trembling
from his seat and placed the bird upon a folded
cloth by the window.

He placed a bundle of dry sticks upon the fire,
saying, "Remove your sandals and warm your feet,
for dampness is dangerous to man's health. Dry well
your garments, and be comfortable."

Yusif's continued hospitality kept my hopes high.
I approached near to the fire, and the steam sifted
from my wet robe. While he stood at the door gazing
at the grey skies, my mind searched and scurried for
the opening wedge into his background. I asked

innocently, "Has it been long since you came to this place?"

Without looking at me, he answered quietly, "I came to this place when the earth was without form, and void; and darkness was upon the face of the deep. And the Spirit of God moved upon the face of the waters."

I was aghast at these words! Struggling to gather my shocked and scattered wits, I said to myself, "How fantastic this man is! And how difficult is the path that leads to his reality! But I shall attack cautiously and slowly and patiently, until his reticence turns into communication, and his strangeness into understanding."

PART THREE

Night was spreading her black garment upon those valleys, and the tempest was shrieking dizzily and the rain becoming stronger. I began to fancy that the Biblical flood was coming again, to abolish life and wash man's filth from God's earth.

It seemed that the revolution of elements had created in Yusif's heart a tranquility which often comes as a reaction to temperament and converts aloneness into conviviality. He ignited two candles, and then placed before me a jar of wine and a large tray containing bread, cheese, olives, honey, and some dry fruits. Then he sat near me, and after apologizing for the small quantity—but not for the simplicity—of the food, asked me to join him.

We partook of the repast in understanding silence, listening to the wailing of the wind and the crying of the rain, and at the same time I was contemplating his face and trying to dig out his secrets, meditating the possible motive underlying his unusual existence. Having finished, he took a copper kettle from the fire and poured pure, aromatic coffee into two cups; then he opened a small box and offered me a cigarette, addressing me as "Brother." I took one while drinking my coffee, not believing what my eyes were seeing. He looked at me smilingly, and after he had inhaled deeply of his cigarette and sipped some coffee, he said, "Undoubtedly you are thinking upon the existence here of wine and tobacco and coffee, and you may also be wondering over my food and comforts. Your curiosity is justified in all respects, for you are one of the many who believe that in being away from the people, one is absent from life, and must abstain from all its enjoyment." Quickly I agreed, "Yes, it is related by the wise men that he who deserts the world for the purpose of worshipping God alone will leave behind all the enjoyment and plenty of life, contenting himself with the simple products of God alone, and existing on plants and water."

After a pause, heavy with thought, he mused, "I could have worshipped God while living among His creatures, for worship does not require solitude. I did not leave the people in order to see God, for I had always seen Him at the home of my father and mother. I deserted the people because their natures were in conflict with mine, and their dreams did not agree with my dreams. . . . I left man because I found that the wheel of my soul was turning one way and grinding harshly against the wheels of other souls which were turning in the opposite direction. I left civilization because I found it to be an old and corrupt tree, strong and terrible, whose roots are locked into the obscurity of the earth and whose branches are reaching beyond the cloud; but its blossoms are of greed and evil and crime, and its fruit is of woe and misery and fear. Crusaders have undertaken to blend good into it and change its nature, but they could not succeed. They died disappointed, persecuted and torn."

Yusif leaned toward the side of the fireplace as if awaiting the impression of his Words upon my heart. I thought it best to remain a listener, and he continued, "No, I did not seek solitude to pray and lead a hermit's life . . . for prayer, which is the song of the heart, will reach the ears of God even when mingled with the shout and cry of thousands of voices. To live the life of a recluse is to torture the body and soul and deaden the inclinations, a kind of existence which is repugnant to me, for God has erected the bodies as temples for the spirits, and it is our mission to deserve and maintain the trust reposed in us by God.

"No, my brother, I did not seek solitude for religious purposes, but solely to avoid the people and their laws, their teachings and their traditions, their ideas and their clamour and their wailing.

"I sought solitude in order to keep from seeing the faces of men who sell themselves and buy with the same price that which is lower than they are, spiritually and materially.

"I sought solitude in order that I might not encounter the women who walk proudly, with one thousands smiles upon their lips, while in the depths of their thousands of hearts there is but one purpose.

"I sought solitude in order to conceal myself from those self-satisfied individuals who see the spectre of knowledge in their dreams and believe that they have attained their goal.

"I fled from society to avoid those who see but the phantom of truth in their awakening, and shout to the world that they have acquired completely the essence of truth.

"I deserted the world and sought solitude because I became tired of rendering courtesy to those multitudes who believe that humility is a sort of weakness, and mercy a kind of cowardice, and snobbery a form of strength.

"I sought solitude because my soul wearied of association with those who believe sincerely that the sun and moon and stars do not rise save from their coffers, and do not set except in their gardens.

"I ran from the office-seekers who shatter the earthly fate of the people while throwing into their eyes the golden dust and filling their ears with sounds of meaningless talk.

"I departed from the ministers who do not live according to their sermons, and who demand of the people that which they do not solicit of themselves.

"I sought solitude because I never obtained kindness from a human unless I paid the full price with my heart.

"I sought solitude because I loathe that great and terrible institution which the people call civilization—that symmetrical monstrosity erected upon the perpetual misery of human kinds.

"I sought solitude for in it there is a full life for the spirit and for the heart and for the body. I found the endless prairies where the light of the sun rests, and where the flowers breathe their fragrance into space, and where the streams sing their way to the sea. I discovered the mountains where I found the fresh awakening of Spring, and the colourful longing of Summer, and the rich songs of Autumn, and the beautiful mystery of Winter. I came to this far corner of God's domain for I hungered to learn the secrets of the Universe, and approach close to the throne of God."

Yusif breathed deeply, as if he had been relieved of a heavy burden. His eyes shone with strange and magical rays, and upon his radiant face appeared the signs of pride, will, and contentment.

A few minutes passed, and I was gazing placidly

at him, and pondering the unveiling of what had been hidden from me; then I addressed him, saying, "You are undoubtedly correct in most of the things you have said, but through your diagnosis of the social ailment, you prove at the same time that you are a good doctor. I believe that the sick society is in dire need of such a physician, who should cure it or kill it. This distressed world begs your attention. Is it just or merciful to withdraw yourself from the ailing patient and deny him your benefit?"

He stared at me thoughtfully, and then said with futility, "Since the beginning of the world, the doctors have been trying to save the people from their disorders; some used knives, while others used potions, but pestilence spread hopelessly. It is my wish that the patient would content himself with remaining in his filthy bed, meditating his long-continued sores; but instead, he stretches his hands from under the robe and clutches at the neck of each who comes to visit him, choking him to death. What irony it is! The evil patient kills the doctor, and then closes his eyes and says within himself, 'He was a great physician.' No, Brother, no one on earth can benefit humanity. The sower, however wise and expert he may be, cannot cause the field to sprout in Winter."

And I argued, "The people's Winter will pass away, and then comes the beautiful Spring, and the flowers must surely bloom in the fields, and the brooks will again leap in the valleys."

He frowned, and said bitterly, "Alas! Has God

divided man's life—which is the whole creation—
into seasons like those of the year? Will any tribe
of human beings, living now in God's truth and
spirit, desire to re-appear on the face of this earth?
Will ever the time come when man settles and abides
at the right arm of Life, rejoicing with the brilliant
light of day and the peaceful silence of night? Can
that dream become reality? Can it materialize after
the earth has been covered with human flesh and
drenched with man's blood?"

And Yusif stood and raised his hand toward the
sky, as if pointing at a different world, and he continued, "This is naught but a vain dream for the
world, but I am finding its accomplishment for
myself, and what I am discovering here occupies
every space in my heart and in the valleys and in
the mountains." He now raised his intense voice,
"What I really know to be true is the crying of my
inner self. I am here living, and in the depths of my
existence there is a thirst and hunger, and I find
joy in partaking of the bread and wine of Life from
the vases which I make and fashion by my own hands.
For this reason I abandoned the boards of the people
and came to this place, and I shall remain here until
the Ending!"

He continued walking back and forth across the
room in agitation while I was pondering his sayings
and meditating the description of society's gaping
wounds. I ventured again a tactful criticism. "I hold
the utmost regard for your opinion and intentions,

and I envy and respect your solitude and aloneness, but I know that this miserable nation has sustained a great loss in your expatriation, for she is in need of an understanding healer to help her through her difficulties and awaken her spirit."

He shook his head slowly and said, "This nation is like all the nations. And the people are made of the same element and do not vary except in their exterior appearance, which is of no consequence. The misery of our Oriental nations is the misery of the world, and what you call civilization in the West is naught but another spectre of the many phantoms of tragic deception.

"Hypocrisy will always remain, even if her finger tips are coloured and polished; and Deceit will never change even if her touch becomes soft and delicate; and Falsehood will never turn into Truth even if you dress her with silken robes and place her in the palace; and Greed will not become Contentment; nor will Crime become Virtue. And Eternal Slavery to teachings, to customs, and to history will remain Slavery even if she paints her face and disguises her voice. Slavery will remain Slavery in all her horrible form, even if she calls herself Liberty.

"No, my brother, the West is not higher than the East, nor is the West lower than the East, and the difference that stands between the two is not greater than the difference between the tiger and the lion. There is a just and perfect law that I have found behind the exterior of society, which equalizes misery, prosperity, and ignorance; it does not prefer one nation to another, nor does it oppress one tribe in order to enrich another."

I exclaimed, "Then civilization is vanity, and all in it is vanity!" He quickly responded, "Yes, civilization is vanity and all in it is vanity. . . . Inventions and discoveries are but amusement and comfort for the body when it is tired and weary. The conquest of distance and the victory over the seas are but false fruit which do not satisfy the soul, nor nourish the heart, neither lift the spirit, for they are afar from nature. And those structures and theories which man calls knowledge and art are naught except shackles and golden chains which man drags, and he rejoices with their glittering reflections and ringing sounds. They are strong cages whose bars man commenced fabricating ages ago, unaware that he was building from the inside, and that he would soon become his own prisoner to eternity. Yes, vain are the deeds of man, and vain are his purposes, and all is vanity upon the earth." He paused, then slowly added, "And among all vanities of life, there is only one thing that the spirit loves and craves. One thing dazzling and alone."

"What is it?" I inquired with quivering voice. He looked at me for a long minute and then closed his eyes. He placed his hands on his chest, while his face brightened, and with a serene and sincere voice he said, "It is an awakening in the spirit; it is an awakening in the inner depths of the heart; it is an overwhelming and magnificent power that descends suddenly upon man's conscience and opens his eyes, whereupon he sees Life amid a dizzying shower of brilliant music, surrounded by a circle of great light, with man standing as a pillar of beauty between the earth and the firmament. It is a flame that suddenly rages within the spirit and sears and purifies the heart, ascending above the earth and hovering in the spacious sky. It is a kindness that envelops the individual's heart whereby he would bewilder and disapprove all who opposed it, and revolt against those who refuse to understand its great meaning. It is a secret hand which removed the veil from my eyes while I was a member of society amidst my family, my friends and my countrymen.

"Many times I wondered, and spoke to myself, saying, 'What is this Universe, and why am I different from those people who are looking at me, and how do I know them, and where did I meet them, and why am I living among them? Am I a stranger among them, or is it they who are strange to this earth, built by Life who entrusted me with the keys?' "

He suddenly became silent, as if remembering something he had seen long before, refusing to reveal it. Then he stretched his arms forward and whispered, "That is what happened to me four years ago, when I left the world and came to this void place to live in the awakeness of life and enjoy kind thoughts and beautiful silence."

115

He walked toward the door, looking at the depths of the darkness as if preparing to address the tempest. But he spoke in a vibrating voice, saying, "It is an awakening within the spirit; he who knows it, is unable to reveal it by words; and he who knows it not, will never think upon the compelling and beau tiful mystery of existence."

PART FOUR

An hour had passed and Yusif El Fakhri was striding about the room, stopping at random and gazing at the tremendous grey skies. I remained silent, reflecting upon the strange unison of joy and sorrow in his solitary life.

Later in the night he approached me and stared long into my face, as if wanting to commit to memory the picture of the man to whom he had disclosed the piercing secrets of his life. My mind was heavy with turmoil, my eyes with mist. He said quietly, "I am going now to walk through the night with the tempest, to feel the closeness of Nature's expression; it is a practise that I enjoy greatly in Autumn and Winter. Here is the wine, and there is the tobacco; please accept my home as your own for the night."

He wrapped himself in a black robe and added smilingly, "I beg you to fasten the door against the intruding humans when you leave in the morning, for I plan to spend the day in the forest of the Holy Cedars." Then he walked toward the door, carrying a long walking staff and he concluded, "If the tempest surprises you again while you are in this vicinity, do not hesitate to take refuge in this hermitage. . . . I hope you will teach yourself to love, and not to fear, the tempest. . . . Good night, my brother."

He opened the door and walked out with his head high, into the dark. I stood at the door to see which course he had taken, but he had disappeared from view. For a few minutes I heard the fall of his feet upon the broken stones of the valley.

PART FIVE

Morning came, after a night of deep thought, and the tempest had passed away, while the sky was clear and the mountains and the plains were reveling in the sun's warm rays. On my way back to the city I felt that spiritual awakening of which Yusif El Fakhri had spoken, and it was raging throughout every fibre of my being. I felt that my shivering must be visible. And when I calmed, all about me was beauty and perfection.

As soon as I reached the noisome people and heard their voices and saw their deeds, I stopped and said within myself, "Yes, the spiritual awakening is the most essential thing in man's life, and it is the sole purpose of being. Is not civilization, in all its tragic forms, a supreme motive for spiritual awakening? Then how can we deny existing matter, while its very existence is unwavering proof of its conformability into the intended fitness? The present civilization may possess a vanishing purpose, but the eternal law has offered to that purpose a ladder whose steps can lead to a free substance."

I never saw Yusif El Fakhri again, for through my endeavours to attend the ills of civilization, Life had expelled me from North Lebanon in late Autumn ot that same year, and I was required to live in exile in a distant country whose tempests are domestic. And leading a hermit's life in that country is a sort of glorious madness, for its society, too, is ailing.

SLAVERY

THE PEOPLE are the slaves
of Life, and it is slavery which fills their days with
misery and distress, and floods their nights with tears
and anguish.

Seven thousand years have passed since the day
of my first birth, and since that day I have been
witnessing the slaves of Life, dragging their heavy
shackles.

I have roamed the East and West of the earth and
wandered in the Light and in the Shadow of Life.
I have seen the processions of civilization moving
from light into darkness, and each was dragged down
to hell by humiliated souls bent under the yoke of
slavery. The strong is fettered and subdued, and the
faithful is on his knees worshipping before the idols.
I have followed man from Babylon to Cairo, and
from Ain Dour to Baghdad, and observed the marks
of his chains upon the sand. I heard the sad echoes
of the fickle ages repeated by the eternal prairies and
valleys.

I visited the temples and altars and entered the

palaces, and sat before the thrones. And I saw the apprentice slaving for the artisan, and the artisan slaving for the employer, and the employer slaving for the soldier, and the soldier slaving for the governor, and the governor slaving for the king, and the king slaving for the priest, and the priest slaving for the idol. . . . And the idol is naught but earth fashioned by Satan and erected upon a knoll of skulls.

I entered the mansions of the rich and visited the huts of the poor. I found the infant nursing the milk of slavery from his mother's bosom, and the children learning submission with the alphabet.

The maidens wear garments of restriction and passivity, and the wives retire with tears upon beds of obedience and legal compliance.

I accompanied the ages from the banks of the Kange to the shores of Euphrates; from the mouth of the Nile to the plains of Assyria; from the arenas of Athens to the churches of Rome; from the slums of Constantinople to the palaces of Alexandria. . . . Yet I saw slavery moving over all, in a glorious and majestic procession of ignorance. I saw the people sacrificing the youths and maidens at the feet of the idol, calling her the God; pouring wine and perfume upon her feet, and calling her the Queen; burning incense before her image, and calling her the Prophet; kneeling and worshipping before her, and calling her the Law; fighting and dying for her, and calling her Patriotism; submitting to her will, and calling her the Shadow of God on earth; destroying and demolishing homes and institutions for her sake, and calling her Fraternity; struggling and stealing and working for her, and calling her Fortune and Happiness; killing for her, and calling her Equality.

She possesses various names, but one reality. She has many appearances, but is made of one element. In truth, she is an everlasting ailment bequeathed by each generation unto its successor.

I found the blind slavery, which ties the people's present with their parents' past, and urges them to yield to their traditions and customs, placing ancient spirits in the new bodies.

I found the mute slavery, which binds the life of a man to a wife whom he abhors, and places the woman's body in the bed of a hated husband, deadening both lives spiritually.

I found the deaf slavery, which stifles the soul and the heart, rendering man but an empty echo of a voice, and a pitiful shadow of a body.

I found the lame slavery, which places man's neck under the domination of the tyrant and submits strong bodies and weak minds to the sons of Greed for use as instruments to their power.

I found the ugly slavery, which descends with the infants' spirits from the spacious firmament into the home of Misery, where Need lives by Ignorance, and Humiliation resides beside Despair. And the children grow as miserables, and live as criminals, and die as despised and rejected non-existents.

I found the subtle slavery, which entitles things with other than their names—calling slyness an intelligence, and emptiness a knowledge, and weakness a tenderness, and cowardice a strong refusal.

I found the twisted slavery, which causes the tongues of the weak to move with fear, and speak outside of their feelings, and they feign to be meditating their plight, but they become as empty sacks, which even a child can fold or hang.

I found the bent slavery, which prevails upon one nation to comply with the laws and rules of another nation, and the bending is greater with each day.

I found the perpetual slavery, which crowns the sons of monarchs as kings, and offers no regard to merit.

I found the black slavery, which brands with shame and disgrace forever the innocent sons of the criminals.

Contemplating slavery, it is found to possess the vicious powers of continuation and contagion.

When I grew tired of following the dissolute ages, and wearied of beholding the processions of stoned people, I walked lonely in the Valley of the Shadow of Life, where the past attempts to conceal itself in guilt, and the soul of the future folds and rests itself too long. There, at the edge of Blood and Tears

River, which crawled like a poisonous viper and twisted like a criminal's dreams, I listened to the frightened whisper of the ghosts of slaves, and gazed at nothingness.

When midnight came and the spirits emerged from hidden places, I saw a cadaverous, dying spectre fall to her knees, gazing at the moon. I approached her, asking, "What is your name?"

"My name is Liberty," replied this ghastly shadow of a corpse.

And I inquired, "Where are your children?"

And Liberty, tearful and weak, gasped, "One died crucified, another died mad, and the third one is not yet born."

She limped away and spoke further, but the mist in my eyes and cries of my heart prevented sight or hearing.

SATAN

THE PEOPLE looked upon Father Samaan as their guide in the field of spiritual and theological matters, for he was an authority and a source of deep information on venial and mortal sins, well versed in the secrets of Paradise, Hell, and Purgatory.

Father Samaan's mission in North Lebanon was to travel from one village to another, preaching and curing the people from the spiritual disease of sin, and saving them from the horrible trap of Satan. The Reverend Father waged constant war with Satan. The fellahin honoured and respected this clergyman, and were always anxious to buy his advice or prayers with pieces of gold and silver; and at every harvest they would present him with the finest fruits of their fields.

One evening in Autumn, as Father Samaan walked his way toward a solitary village, crossing those valleys and hills, he heard a painful cry emerging from a ditch at the side of the road. He stopped and looked in the direction of the voice, and saw an unclothed

124

man lying on the ground. Streams of blood oozed from deep wounds in his head and chest. He was moaning pitifully for aid, saying, "Save me, help me. Have mercy on me, I am dying." Father Samaan looked with perplexity at the sufferer, and said within himself, "This man must be a thief. . . . He probably tried to rob the wayfarers and failed. Some one has wounded him, and I fear that should he die I may be accused of having taken his life."

Having thus pondered the situation, he resumed his journey, whereupon the dying man stopped him, calling out, "Do not leave me! I am dying!" Then the Father meditated again, and his face became pale as he realized he was refusing to help. His lips quivered, but he spoke to himself, saying, "He must surely be one of the madmen wandering in the wilderness. The sight of his wounds brings fear into my heart; what shall I do? Surely a spiritual doctor is not capable of treating flesh-wounded bodies." Father Samaan walked ahead a few paces when the near-corpse uttered a painful plaint that melted the heart of the rock and he gasped, "Come close to me! Come, for we have been friends a long time. . . . You are Father Samaan, the Good Shepherd, and I am not a thief nor a madman. . . . Come close, and do not let me die in this deserted place. Come, and I will tell you who I am."

Father Samaan came close to the man, knelt, and stared at him; but he saw a strange face with contrasting features; he saw intelligence with slyness, ugliness with beauty, and wickedness with softness. He withdrew to his feet sharply, and exclaimed, "Who are you?"

With a fainting voice, the dying man said, "Fear me not, Father, for we have been strong friends for long. Help me to stand, and take me to the nearby streamlet and cleanse my wounds with your linens." And the Father inquired, "Tell me who you are, for I do not know you, nor even remember having seen you."

And the man replied with an agonizing voice, "You know my identity! You have seen me one thousand times and you speak of me each day. . . . I am dearer to you than your own life." And the Father reprimanded, "You are a lying imposter! A dying man should tell the truth. . . . I have never seen your evil face in my entire life. Tell me who you are, or I will suffer you to die, soaked in your own escaping life." And the wounded man moved slowly and looked into the clergyman's eyes, and upon his lips appeared a mystic smile; and in a quiet, deep and smooth voice he said, "I am Satan."

Upon hearing the fearful word, Father Samaan uttered a terrible cry that shook the far corners of the valley; then he stared, and realized that the dying man's body, with its grotesque distortions, coincided with the likeness of Satan in a religious picture hanging on the wall of the village church. He trembled and cried out, saying, "God has shown me your hellish image and justly caused me to hate you;

cursed be you forevermore! The mangled lamb must be destroyed by the shepherd lest he will infect the other lambs!"

Satan answered, "Be not in haste, Father, and lose not this fleeting time in empty talk. . . . Come and close my wounds quickly, before Life departs from my body." And the clergyman retorted, "The hands which offer a daily sacrifice to God shall not touch a body made of the secretion of Hell. . . . You must die accursed by the tongues of the Ages, and the lips of Humanity, for you are the enemy of Humanity, and it is your avowed purpose to destroy all virtue."

Satan moved in anguish, raising himself upon one elbow, and responded, "You know not what you are saying, nor understand the crime you are committing upon yourself. Give heed, for I will relate my story. Today I walked alone in this solitary valley. When I reached this place, a group of angels descended to attack, and struck me severely; had it not been for one of them, who carried a blazing sword with two sharp edges, I would have driven them off, but I had no power against the brilliant sword." And Satan ceased talking for a moment, as he pressed a shaking hand upon a deep wound in his side. Then he continued, "The armed angel—I believe he was Michael —was an expert gladiator. Had I not thrown myself to the friendly ground and feigned to have been slain, he would have torn me into brutal death."

With voice of triumph, and casting his eyes heavenward, the Father offered, "Blessed be Michael's name, who has saved Humanity from this vicious enemy."

And Satan protested, "My disdain for Humanity is not greater than your hatred for yourself. . . . You are blessing Michael who never has come to your rescue. . . . You are cursing me in the hour of my defeat, even though I was, and still am, the source of your tranquility and happiness. . . . You deny me your blessing, and extend not your kindness, but you live and prosper in the shadow of my being. . . . You have adopted for my existence an excuse and weapon for your career, and you employ my name in justification for your deeds. Has not my past caused you to be in need of my present and future? Have you reached your goal in amassing the required wealth? Have you found it impossible to extract more gold and silver from your followers, using my kingdom as a threat?

"Do you not realize that you will starve to death if I were to die? What would you do tomorrow if you allowed me to die today? What vocation would you pursue if my name disappeared? For decades you have been roaming these villages and warning the people against falling into my hands. They have bought your advice with their poor denars and with the products of their land. What would they buy from you tomorrow, if they discovered that their wicked enemy no longer existed? Your occupation would die with me, for the people would be safe

from sin. As a clergyman, do you not realize that
Satan's existence alone has created his enemy, the
church? That ancient conflict is the secret hand
which removes the gold and silver from the faithful's
pocket and deposits it forever into the pouch of the
preacher and missionary. How can you permit me
to die here, when you know it will surely cause you
to lose your prestige, your church, your home, and
your livelihood?"

Satan became silent for a moment and his humility
was now converted into a confident independence,
and he continued, "Father, you are proud, but ignorant. I will disclose to you the history of belief, and
in it you will find the truth which joins both of
our beings, and ties my existence with your very
conscience.

"In the first hour of the beginning of time, man
stood before the face of the sun and stretched forth
his arms and cried for the first time, saying, 'Behind
the sky there is a great and loving and benevolent
God.' Then man turned his back to the great circle
of light and saw his shadow upon the earth, and he
hailed, 'In the depths of the earth there is a dark
devil who loves wickedness.'

"And the man walked toward his cave, whispering
to himself, 'I am between two compelling forces, one
in whom I must take refuge, and the other against
whom I must struggle.' And the ages marched in procession while man existed between two powers, one

that he blessed because it exalted him, and one that he cursed because it frightened him. But he never perceived the meaning of a blessing or of a curse; he was between the two, like a tree between Summer, when it blooms, and Winter, when it shivers.

"When man saw the dawn of civilization, which is human understanding, the family as a unit came into being. Then came the tribes, whereupon labour was divided according to ability and inclination; one clan cultivated the land, another built shelters, others wove raiment or hunted food. Subsequently divination made its appearance upon the earth, and this was the first career adopted by man which possessed no essential urge or necessity."

Satan ceased talking for a moment. Then he laughed and his mirth shook the empty valley, but his laughter reminded him of his wounds, and he placed his hand on his side, suffering with pain. He steadied himself and continued, "Divination appeared and grew on earth in strange fashion.

"There was a man in the first tribe called La Wiss. I know not the origin of his name. He was an intelligent creature, but extremely indolent and he detested work in the cultivation of land, construction of shelters, grazing of cattle or any pursuit requiring body movement or exertion. And since food, during that era, could not be obtained except by arduous toil, La Wiss slept many nights with an empty stomach.

"One Summer night, as the members of that clan

were gathered around the hut of their Chief, talking
of the outcome of their day and waiting for their
slumber time, a man suddenly leaped to his feet,
pointed toward the moon, and cried out, saying,
'Look at the Night God! His face is dark, and his
beauty has vanished, and he has turned into a black
stone hanging in the dome of the sky!' The multitude gazed at the moon, shouted in awe, and shook
with fear, as if the hands of darkness had clutched
their hearts, for they saw the Night God slowly
turning into a dark ball which changed the bright
countenance of the earth and caused the hills and
valleys before their eyes to disappear behind a black
veil.

"At that moment, La Wiss, who had seen an
eclipse before, and understood its simple cause,
stepped forward to make much of this opportunity.
He stood in the midst of the throng, lifted his hands
to the sky, and in a strong voice he addressed them,
saying, 'Kneel and pray, for the Evil God of Obscurity is locked in struggle with the Illuminating
Night God; if the Evil God conquers him, we will
all perish, but if the Night God triumphs over him,
we will remain alive. . . . Pray now and worship. . .
Cover your faces with earth. . . . Close your eyes,
and lift not your heads toward the sky, for he who
witnesses the two gods wrestling will lose his sight
and mind, and will remain blind and insane all his
life! Bend your heads low, and with all your hearts

urge the Night God against his enemy, who is our mortal enemy!'

"Thus did La Wiss continue talking, using many cryptic words of his own fabrication which they had never heard. After this crafty deception, as the moon returned to its previous glory, La Wiss raised his voice louder than before and said impressively, 'Rise now, and look at the Night God who has triumphed over his evil enemy. He is resuming his journey among the stars. Let it be known that through your prayers you have helped him to overcome the Devil of Darkness. He is well pleased now, and brighter than ever.'

"The multitude rose and gazed at the moon that was shining in full beam. Their fear became tranquility, and their confusion was now joy. They commenced dancing and singing and striking with their thick sticks upon sheets of iron, filling the valleys with their clamour and shouting.

"That night, the Chief of the tribe called La Wiss and spoke to him, saying, 'You have done something that no man has ever done. . . . You have demonstrated knowledge of a hidden secret that no other among us understands. Reflecting the will of my people, you are to be the highest ranking member, after me, in the tribe. I am the strongest man, and you are the wisest and most learned person. . . . You are the medium between our people and the gods, whose desires and deeds you are to interpret, and you will teach us those things necessary to gain their blessings and love.'

"And La Wiss slyly assured, 'Everything the Human God reveals to me in my divine dreams will be conveyed to you in awakeness, and you may be confident that I will act directly between you and him.' The chief was assured, and gave La Wiss two horses, seven calves, seventy sheep and seventy lambs; and he spoke to him, saying, 'The men of the tribe shall build for you a strong house, and we will give you at the end of each harvest season a part of the crop of the land so you may live as an honourable and respected Master.'

"La Wiss rose and started to leave, but the Chief stopped him, saying, 'Who and what is the one whom you call the Human God? Who is this daring God who wrestles with the glorious Night God? We have never pondered him before.' La Wiss rubbed his forehead and answered him, saying, 'My Honourable Master, in the olden time, before the creation of man, all the Gods were living peacefully together in an upper world behind the vastness of the stars. The God of Gods was their father, and knew what they did not know, and did what they were unable to do. He kept for himself the divine secrets that existed beyond the eternal laws. During the seventh epoch of the twelfth age, the spirit of Bahtaar, who hated the great God, revolted and stood before his father, and said, 'Why do you keep for yourself the power of great authority upon all creatures, hiding away from us the secrets and laws of the Universe? Are we not your children who believe in you and share with you the great understanding and the perpetual being?'

"The God of Gods became enraged and said, 'I shall preserve for myself the primary power and the great authority and the essential secrets, for I am the beginning and the end.'

"And Bahtaar answered him saying, 'Unless you share with me your might and power, I and my children and my children's children will revolt against you!' At that moment, the God of Gods stood upon his throne in the deep heavens, and drew forth a sword, and grasped the Sun as a shield; and with a voice that shook all corners of eternity he shouted out, saying, 'Descend, you evil rebel, to the dismal lower world where darkness and misery exist! There you shall remain in exile, wandering until the Sun turns into ashes and the stars into dispersed particles!' In that hour, Bahtaar descended from the upper world into the lower world, where all the evil spirits dwelt. Thereupon, he swore by the secret of Life that he would fight his father and brothers by trapping every soul who loved them.'

"As the Chief listened, his forehead wrinkled and his face turned pale. He ventured, 'Then the name of the Evil God is Bahtaar?' and La Wiss responded, 'His name was Bahtaar when he was in upper world, but when he entered into the lower world, he adopted successively the names Baalzaboul, Satanail,

Balial, Zamiel, Ahriman, Mara, Abdon, Devil, and finally Satan, which is the most famous.'

"The Chief repeated the word 'Satan' many times with a quivering voice that sounded like the rustling of the dry branches at the passing of the wind; then he asked, 'Why does Satan hate man as much as he hates the gods?'

"And La Wiss responded quickly, 'He hates man because man is a descendant of Satan's brothers and sisters.' The Chief exclaimed, 'Then Satan is the cousin of man!' In a voice mingled with confusion and annoyance, he retorted, 'Yes, Master, but he is their great enemy who fills their days with misery and their nights with horrible dreams. He is the power who directs the tempest toward their hovels, and brings famine upon their plantation, and disease upon them and their animals. He is an evil and powerful god; he is wicked, and he rejoices when we are in sorrow, and he mourns when we are joyous. We must, through my knowledge, examine him thoroughly, in order to avoid his evil; we must study his character, so we will not step upon his trap-laden path.'

"The Chief leaned his head upon his thick stick and whispered, saying, 'I have learned now the inner secret of that strange power who directs the tempest toward our homes and brings the pestilence upon us and our cattle. The people shall learn all that I have comprehended now, and La Wiss will be blessed, honoured and glorified for revealing to them the mystery of their powerful enemy, and directing them away from the road of evil.'

"And La Wiss left the Chief of the tribe and went to his retiring place, happy over his ingenuity, and intoxicated with the wine of his pleasure and fancy. For the first time, the Chief and all the tribe, except La Wiss, spent the night slumbering in beds surrounded by horrible ghosts, fearful spectres, and disturbing dreams."

Satan ceased talking for a moment, while Father Samaan stared at him as one bewildered, and upon the Father's lips appeared the sickly laughter of Death. Then Satan continued, "Thus divination came to this earth, and thus was my existence the cause for its appearance. La Wiss was the first who adopted my cruelty as a vocation. After the death of La Wiss, this occupation circulated through his children and prospered until it became a perfect and divine profession, pursued by those whose minds are ripe with knowledge, and whose souls are noble, and whose hearts are pure, and whose fancy is vast.

"In Babylon, the people bowed seven times in worshipping before a priest who fought me with his chantings. . . . In Nineveh, they looked upon a man, who claimed to have known my inner secrets, as a golden link between God and man. . . . In Tibet, they called the person who wrestled with me The Son of the Sun and Moon. . . . In Byblus, Ephesus and Antioch, they offered their children's lives in sacrifice to my opponents. . . . In Jerusalem and Rome, they placed their lives in the hands of those who claimed they hated me and fought me with all their might.

"In every city under the sun my name was the axis of the educational circle of religion, arts, and philosophy. Had it not been for me, no temples would have been built, no towers or palaces would have been erected. I am the courage that creates resolution in man. . . . I am the source that provokes originality of thought. . . . I am the hand that moves man's hands. . . . I am Satan everlasting. I am Satan whom the people fight in order to keep themselves alive. If they cease struggling against me, slothfulness will deaden their minds and hearts and souls, in accordance with the weird penalties of their tremendous **myth**.

"I am the **enrage**d and mute tempest who agitates the minds of man and the hearts of women. And in fear of me, they will travel to places of worship to condemn me, or to places of vice to make me happy by surrendering to my will. The monk who prays in the silence of the night to keep me away from his bed is like the prostitute who invites me to her chamber. I am Satan everlasting and eternal.

"I am the builder of convents and monasteries upon the foundation of fear. I build wine shops and wicked houses **upon** the foundations of lust and self-gratification. If **I** cease to exist, fear and enjoyment will be abolished from the world, and through their disappearance, desires and hopes will cease to exist in the human heart. Life will become empty and cold, like a harp with broken strings. I am Satan everlasting.

"I am the inspiration for Falsehood, Slander, Treachery, Deceit and Mockery, and if these elements were to be removed from this world, human society would become like a deserted field in which naught would thrive but thorns of virtue. I am Satan everlasting.

"I am the father and mother of sin, and if sin were to vanish, the fighters of sin would vanish with it, along with their families and structures.

"I am the heart of all evil. Would you wish for human motion to stop through cessation of my heartbeats? Would you accept the result after destroying the cause? I am the cause! Would you allow me to die in this deserted wilderness? Do you desire to sever the bond that exists between you and me? Answer me, clergyman!"

And Satan stretched his arms and bent his head forward and gasped deeply; his face turned to grey and he resembled one of those Egyptian statues laid waste by the Ages at the side of the Nile. Then he fixed his glittering eyes upon Father Samaan's face, and said, in a faltering voice, "I am tired and weak. I did wrong by using my waning strength to speak on things you already knew. Now you may do as you please. . . . You may carry me to your home and treat my wounds, or leave me in this place to die."

Father Samaan quivered and rubbed his hands nervously, and with apology in his voice he said, "I know now what I had not known an hour ago. Forgive my ignorance. I know that your existence in this world creates temptation, and temptation is a measurement by which God adjudges the value of human souls. It is a scale which Almighty God uses to weigh the spirits. I am certain that if you die, temptation will die, and with its passing, death will destroy the ideal power which elevates and alerts man.

"You must live, for if you die and the people know it, their fear of hell will vanish and they will cease worshipping, for naught would be sin. You must live, for in your life is the salvation of humanity from vice and sin.

"As to myself, I shall sacrifice my hatred for you on the altar of my love for man."

Satan uttered a laugh that rocked the ground, and he said, "What an intelligent person you are, Father! And what wonderful knowledge you possess in theological facts! You have found, through the power of your knowledge, a purpose for my existence which I had never understood, and now we realize our need for each other.

"Come close to me, my brother; darkness is submerging the plains, and half of my blood has escaped upon the sand of this valley, and naught remains of me but the remnants of a broken body which Death shall soon buy unless you render aid." Father Samaan rolled the sleeves of his robe and approached, and lifted Satan to his back and walked toward his home.

In the midst of those valleys, engulfed with silence and embellished with the veil of darkness, Father Samaan walked toward the village with his back bent under his heavy burden. His black raiment and long beard were spattered with blood streaming from above him, but he struggled forward, his lips moving in fervent prayer for the life of the dying Satan.

THE MERMAIDS

In the depths of the sea, surrounding the nearby islands where the sun rises, there is a profoundness. And there, where the pearl exists in abundance, lay a corpse of a youth encircled by sea maidens of long golden hair; they stared upon him with their deep blue eyes, conversing among themselves with musical voices. And the conversation, heard by the depths and conveyed to the shore by the waves, was brought to me by the frolicsome breeze.

One of them said, "This is a human who entered into our world yesterday, while our sea was raging."

And the second one said, "The sea was not raging. Man, who claims that he is a descendant of the Gods, was making iron war, and his blood is being shed until the colour of the water is now crimson; this human is a victim of war."

The third one ventured, "I do not know what war is, but I do know that man, after having subdued the land, became aggressive and resolved to subdue the sea. He devised a strange object which carried him upon the seas, whereupon our severe Neptune became enraged over his greed. In order to please Neptune, man commenced offering gifts and sacrifices, and the still body before us is the most recent gift of man to our great and terrible Neptune."

The fourth one asserted, "How great is Neptune, and how cruel is his heart! If I were the Sultan of the sea I would refuse to accept such payment. . . . Come now, and let us examine this ransom. Perhaps we may enlighten ourselves as to the human clan."

The mermaids approached the youth, probed the pockets, and found a message close to his heart; one of them read it aloud to the others:

"My Beloved:

"Midnight has again come, and I have no consolation except my pouring tears, and naught to comfort me save my hope in your return to me from between the bloody paws of war. I cannot forget your words when you took departure: 'Every man has a trust of tears which must be returned some day.'

"I know not what to say, My Beloved, but my soul will pour itself into parchment . . . my soul that suffers through separation, but is consoled by Love that renders pain a joy, and sorrow a happiness. When Love unified our hearts, and we looked to the day when our two hearts would be joined by the mighty breath of God, War shouted her horrible call and you followed her, prompted by your duty to the leaders.

"What is this duty that separates the lovers, and causes the women to become widows, and the children to become orphans? What is this patriotism which provokes wars and destroys kingdoms through trifles? And what cause can be more than trifling when compared to but one life? What is this duty which invites poor villagers, who are looked upon as nothing by the strong and by the sons of the inherited nobility, to die for the glory of their oppressors? If duty destroys peace among nations, and patriotism disturbs the tranquility of man's life, then let us say, 'Peace be with duty and patriotism.'

"No, no, My Beloved! Heed not my words! Be courageous and faithful to your country.... Hearken not unto the talk of a damsel, blinded by Love, and lost through farewell and aloneness.... If Love will not restore you to me in this life, then Love will surely join us in the coming life.

Your Forever"

The mermaids replaced the note under the youth's raiment and swam silently and sorrowfully away. As they gathered together at a distance from the body of the dead soldier, one of them said, "The human heart is more severe than the cruel heart of Neptune."

WE AND YOU

WE ARE the sons of Sorrow, and you are the
Sons of Joy. We are the sons of Sorrow,
And Sorrow is the shadow of a God who
Lives not in the domain of evil hearts.

We are sorrowful spirits, and Sorrow is
Too great to exist in small hearts.
When you laugh, we cry and lament; and he
Who is seared and cleansed once with his
Own tears will remain pure forevermore.

You understand us not, but we offer our
Sympathy to you. You are racing with the
Current of the River of Life, and you
Do not look upon us; but we are sitting by
The coast, watching you and hearing your
Strange voices.

You do not comprehend our cry, for the
Clamour of the days is crowding your ears,
Blocked with the hard substance of your
Years of indifference to truth; but we hear
Your songs, for the whispering of the night

Has opened our inner hearts. We see you
Standing under the pointing finger of light,
But you cannot see us, for we are tarrying
In the enlightening darkness.

We are the sons of Sorrow; we are the poets
And the prophets and the musicians. We weave
Raiment for the goddess from the threads of
Our hearts, and we fill the hands of the
Angels with the seeds of our inner selves.

You are the sons of the pursuit of earthly
Gaiety. You place your hearts in the hands
Of Emptiness, for the hand's touch to
Emptiness is smooth and inviting.

You reside in the house of Ignorance, for
In his house there is no mirror in which to
View your souls.

We sigh, and from our sighs arise the
Whispering of flowers and the rustling of
Leaves and the murmur of rivulets.

When you ridicule us your taunts mingle
With the crushing of the skulls and the
Rattling of shackles and the wailing of the
Abyss. When we cry, our tears fall into the
Heart of Life, as dew drops fall from the
Eyes of Night into the heart of Dawn; and
When you laugh, your mocking laughter pours
Down like the viper's venom into a wound.

We cry, and sympathize with the miserable
Wanderer and distressed widow; but you rejoice
And smile at the sight of resplendent gold.

We cry, for we listen to the moaning of the
Poor and the grieving of the oppressed weak,
But you laugh, for you hear naught but the
Happy sound of the wine goblets.

We cry, for our spirits are at the moment
Separated from God; but you laugh, for your
Bodies cling with unconcern to the earth.

We are the sons of Sorrow, and you are the
Sons of Joy. . . . Let us measure the outcome of
Our sorrow against the deeds of your joy
Before the face of the Sun. . . .

You have built the Pyramids upon the hearts
Of slaves, but the Pyramids stand now upon
The sand, commemorating to the Ages our
Immortality and your evanescence.

You have built Babylon upon the bones of the
Weak, and erected the palaces of Nineveh upon
The graves of the miserable. Babylon is now but
The footprint of the camel upon the moving sand
Of the desert, and its history is repeated
To the nations who bless us and curse you.

We have carved Ishtar from solid marble,
And made it to quiver in its solidity and
Speak through its muteness.

146

We have composed and played the soothing
Song of Nahawand upon the strings, and caused
The Beloved's spirit to come hovering in the
Firmament near to us; we have praised the
Supreme Being with words and deeds; the words
Became as the words of God, and the deeds
Became overwhelming love of the angels.

You are following Amusement, whose sharp claws
Have torn thousands of martyrs in the arenas
Of Rome and Antioch. . . . But we are following
Silence, whose careful fingers have woven the
Iliad and the Book of Job and the Lamentations
Of Jeremiah.

You lie down with Lust, whose tempest has
Swept one thousand processions of the soul of
Woman away and into the pit of shame and
Horror. . . . But we embrace Solitude, in whose
Shadow the beauties of Hamlet and Dante arose.

You curry for the favor of Greed, and the sharp
Swords of Greed have shed one thousand rivers
Of blood. . . . But we seek company with Truth,
And the hands of Truth have brought down
Knowledge from the Great Heart of the Circle
Of Light.

We are the sons of Sorrow, and you are the
Sons of Joy; and between our sorrow and your
Joy there is a rough and narrow path which

Your spirited horses cannot travel, and upon
Which your magnificent carriages cannot pass.

We pity your smallness as you hate our
Greatness; and between our pity and your
Hatred, Time halts bewildered. We come to
You as friends, but you attack us as enemies;
And between our friendship and your enmity,
There is a deep ravine flowing with tears
And blood.

We build palaces for you, and you dig graves
For us; and between the beauty of the palace
And the obscurity of the grave, Humanity
Walks as a sentry with iron weapons.

We spread your path with roses, and you cover
Our beds with thorns; and between the roses
And the thorns, Truth slumbers fitfully.

Since the beginning of the world you have
Fought against our gentle power with your
Coarse weakness; and when you triumph over
Us for an hour, you croak and clamour merrily
Like the frogs of the water. And when we
Conquer you and subdue you for an Age, we
Remain as silent giants.

You crucified Jesus and stood below Him,
Blaspheming and mocking at Him; but at last
He came down and overcame the generations,

And walked among you as a hero, filling the
Universe with His glory and His beauty.

You poisoned Socrates and stoned Paul and
Destroyed Ali Talib and assassinated
Madhat Pasha, and yet those immortals are
With us forever before the face of Eternity.

But you live in the memory of man like
Corpses upon the face of the earth; and you
Cannot find a friend who will bury you in
The obscurity of non-existence and oblivion,
Which you sought on earth.

We are the sons of Sorrow, and sorrow is a
Rich cloud, showering the multitudes with
Knowledge and Truth. You are the sons of
Joy, and as high as your joy may reach,
By the Law of God it must be destroyed
Before the winds of heaven and dispersed
Into nothingness, for it is naught but a
Thin and wavering pillar of smoke.

THE LONELY POET

I AM A STRANGER in this world, and there is a severe solitude and painful lonesomeness in my exile. I am alone, but in my aloneness I contemplate an unknown and enchanting country, and this meditation fills my dreams with spectres of a great and distant land which my eyes have never seen.

I am a stranger among my people and I have no friends. When I see a person I say within myself, "Who is he, and in what manner do I know him, and why is he here, and what law has joined me with him?"

I am a stranger to myself, and when I hear my tongue speak, my ears wonder over my voice; I see my inner self smiling, crying, braving, and fearing; and my existence wonders over my substance while my soul interrogates my heart; but I remain unknown, engulfed by tremendous silence.

My thoughts are strangers to my body, and as I stand before the mirror, I see something in my face. which my soul does not see, and I find in my eyes what my inner self does not find.

When I walk vacant-eyed through the streets of the clamourous city, the children follow me, shouting, "Here is a blind man! Let us give him a walking cane to feel his way." When I run from them, I meet with a group of maidens, and they grasp the edges of my garment, saying, "He is deaf like the rock; let us fill his ears with the music of love." And when I flee from them, a throng of aged people point at me with trembling fingers and say, "He is a madman who lost his mind in the world of genii and ghouls."

I am a stranger in this world; I roamed the Universe from end to end, but could not find a place to rest my head; nor did I know any human I confronted, neither an individual who would hearken to my mind.

When I open my sleepless eyes at dawn, I find myself imprisoned in a dark cave from whose ceiling hang the insects and upon whose floor crawl the vipers.

When I go out to meet the light, the shadow of my body follows me, but the shadow of my spirit precedes me and leads the way to an unknown place seeking things beyond my understanding, and grasping objects that are meaningless to me.

At eventide 1 return and lie upon my bed, made of soft feathers and lined with thorns, and I contemplate and feel the troublesome and happy desires, and sense the painful and joyous hopes.

At midnight the ghosts of the past ages and the

spirits of the forgotten civilization enter through the crevices of the cave to visit me . . . I stare at them and they gaze upon me; I talk to them and they answer me smilingly. Then I endeavour to clutch them, but they sift through my fingers and vanish like the mist which rests on the lake.

I am a stranger in this world, and there is no one in the Universe who understands the language I speak. Patterns of bizarre remembrance form suddenly in my mind, and my eyes bring forth queer images and sad ghosts. I walk in the deserted prairies, watching the streamlets running fast, up and up from the depths of the valley to the top of the mountain; I watch the naked trees blooming and bearing fruit, and shedding their leaves in one instant, and then I see the branches fall and turn into speckled snakes. I see the birds hovering above, singing and wailing; then they stop and open their wings and turn into undraped maidens with long hair, looking at me from behind kohled and infatuated eyes, and smiling at me with full lips soaked with honey, stretching their scented hands toward me. Then they ascend and disappear from my sight like phantoms, leaving in the firmament the resounding echo of their taunts and mocking laughter.

I am a stranger in this world . . . I am a poet who composes what life proses, and who proses what life composes.

For this reason I am a stranger, and I shall remain

a stranger until the white and friendly wings of Death carry me home into my beautiful country. There, where light and peace and understanding abide, I will await the other strangers who will be rescued by the friendly trap of time from this narrow, dark world.

ASHES OF THE AGES AND
ETERNAL FIRE

PART ONE

Spring of the Year 116 B.C.

Night had fallen and silence prevailed while life slumbered in the City of the Sun,* and the lamps were extinguished in the scattered houses about the majestic temples amidst the olive and laurel trees. The moon poured its silver rays upon the white marble columns that stood like giants in the silence of the night, guarding the god's temples and looking with perplexity toward the towers of Lebanon that sat bristling upon the foreheads of the distant hills.

At that hour, while souls succumbed to the allure of slumber, Nathan, the son of the High Priest, entered Ishtar's temple, bearing a torch in trembling

---

* Baalbek, or the City of Baal, called by the ancients "The City of the Sun," was built in honor of the Sun God Heliopolis, and historians assert that Baalbek was the most beautiful city in the Middle East. Its ruins, which we observe at present time, indicate that the architecture was largly influenced by the Romans during the occupation of Syria. (*Editor's note.*)

hands. He lighted the lamps and censers until the aromatic scent of myrrh and frankincense reached to the farthest corners; then he knelt before the altar, studded with inlays of ivory and gold, raised his hands toward Ishtar, and with a painful and choking voice he cried out, saying, "Have mercy upon me, O great Ishtar, goddess of Love and Beauty. Be merciful, and remove the hands of Death from my beloved, whom my soul has chosen by thy will. . . . The potions of the physicians and the wizards do not restore her life, neither the enchantments of the priests and the sorcerers. Naught is left to be done except thy holy will. Thou art my guide and my aid. Have mercy on me and grant my prayers! * Gaze upon my crushed heart and aching soul! Spare my beloved's life so that we may rejoice with the secrets of thy love, and glory in the beauty of youth that reveals the mystery of thy strength and wisdom. From the depths of my heart I cry unto thee, O exalted Ishtar, and from behind the darkness of the night I beg thy mercy; hear me, O Ishtar! I am thy good servant Nathan, the son of the High Priest Hiram, and I devote all of my deeds and words to thy greatness at thy altar.

"I love a maiden amongst all maidens and made

* Ishtar was the great goddess of the Phoenicians. They worshipped her in the cities of Tyre, Sidon, Sûr, Djabeil and Baalbek, and described her as the Burner of the Torch of Life, and Guardian of Youth. Greece adored her after Phoenicia, calling her the goddess of Love and Beauty. The Romans called her Venus. (*Editor's note.*)

her my companion, but the genii brides envied her and blew into her body a strange affliction and sent unto her the messenger of Death who is standing by her bed like a hungry spectre, spreading his black ribbed wings over her, stretching forth his sharp claws in readiness to prey upon her. I come here now beseeching you to have mercy upon me and spare that flower who has not yet rejoiced with the summer of Life.

"Save her from the grasp of Death so we may sing joyfully thy praise and burn incense in thine honour and offer sacrifices at thy altar, filling thy vases with perfumed oil and spreading roses and violets upon the portico of thy place of worship, burning frankincense before thy shrine. Save her, O Ishtar, goddess of miracles, and let Love overcome Death in this struggle of Joy against Sorrow." *

Nathan then became silent. His eyes were flooded with tears and his heart was uttering sorrowful sighs; then he continued, "Alas, my dreams are shattered, O Ishtar divine, and my heart is melted within; enliven me with thy mercy and spare my beloved."

At that moment one of his slaves entered the temple, hastened to Nathan, and whispered to him, "She has opened her eyes, Master, and looked about

---

* During the Era of Ignorance, the Arabs believed that if a genie loved a human youth, she would prevent him from marrying, and if he did wed, she would bewitch the bride and cause her to die. This mythological superstition persists today in some small villages in Lebanon. (*Editor's note.*)

her bed, but could not find you; then she called for you, and I used all speed to advise you."

Nathan departed hurriedly and the slave followed him.

When he reached his palace, he entered the chamber of the ailing maiden, leaned over her bed, held her frail hand, and printed several kisses upon her lips as if striving to breathe into her body a new life from his own life. She moved her head on the silk cushions and opened her eyes. And upon her lips appeared the phantom of a smile which was the faint residue of life in her wasted body . . . the echo of the calling of a heart which is racing toward a halt; and with a voice that bespoke the weakening cries of a hungry infant on the breast of a withered mother, she said, "The goddess has called me, Oh Life of my Soul, and Death has come to sever me from you; but fear not, for the will of the goddess is sacred, and the demands of Death are just. I am departing now, and I hear the rustle of the whiteness descending, but the cups of Love and Youth are still full in our hands, and the flowered paths of beautiful Life are extended before us. I am embarking, My Beloved, upon an ark of the spirit, and I shall come back to this world, for great Ishtar will bring back to life those souls of loving humans who departed to Eternity before they enjoyed the sweetness of Love and the happiness of Youth.

"We shall meet again, Oh Nathan, and drink together the dew of the dawn from the cupped petals of the lilies, and rejoice with the birds of the fields over the colours of the rainbow. Until then, My Forever, farewell." *

Her voice lowered and her lips trembled like a lone flower before the gusts of dawn. Nathan embraced her with pouring tears, and as he pressed his lips upon her lips, he found them cold as the stone of the field. He uttered a terrible cry and commenced tearing his raiment; he threw himself upon her dead body while his shivering soul was sailing fitfully between the mountain of Life and the precipice of Death.

In the silence of the night, the slumbering souls were awakened. Women and children were frightened as they heard mighty rumbling and painful wailing and bitter lamentation coming from the corners of the palace of the High Priest of Ishtar.

When the tired morn arrived, the people asked about Nathan to offer their sympathy, but were told that he had disappeared. And after a fortnight, the chief of a caravan arriving from the East related that he had seen Nathan in the distant wilderness, wandering with a flock of gazelles.

The ages passed, crushing with their invisible feet the feeble acts of the civilizations, and the goddess of Love and Beauty had left the country. A strange

* Many Asiatics pursue this belief with conviction, having derived it from their holy writings. Mohammed said, "You were dead and He brought you back to life, and He will deaden you again and

and fickle goddess took her place. She destroyed the magnificent temples of the City of the Sun and demolished its beautiful palaces. The blooming orchards and fertile prairies were laid waste and nothing was left in that spot save ruins commemorating to the aching souls the ghosts of Yesterday, repeating to the sorrowful spirits only the echo of the hymns of glory.

But the severe ages that crushed the deeds of man could not destroy his dreams; nor could they weaken his love, for dreams and affections are ever-living with the Eternal Spirit. They may disappear for a time, pursuing the sun when the night comes, and the stars when morning appears, but like the lights of heaven, they must surely return.

PART TWO

Spring of the Year 1890 A.D.

The day was over, Nature was making her many preparations for slumber, and the sun withdrew its golden rays from the plains of Baalbek. Ali El Hosseini * brought his herd back to the shed in the

then will enliven you, whereupon you shall go back to Him." Buddha said, "Yesterday we existed in this life, and now we came, and we will continue to go back until we become perfect like the God." (*Editor's note.*)

* The Hosseinese are groups comprising an Arabian tribe, at present living in tents pitched in the plains surrounding the ruins of Baalbek. (*Editor's note.*)

midst of the ruins of the temples. He sat there near the ancient columns which symbolized the bones of countless soldiers left behind in the field of battle. The sheep folded around him, charmed with the music of his flute.

Midnight came, and heaven sowed the seeds of the following day in the deep furrows of the darkness. Ali's eyes became tired of the phantoms of awakeness, and his mind was wearied by the procession of ghosts marching in horrible silence amidst the demolished walls. He leaned upon his arm, and sleep captured his senses with the extreme end of its plaited veil, like a delicate cloud touching the face of a calm lake. He forgot his actual self and encountered his invisible self, rich with dreams and ideals higher than the laws and teachings of man. The circle of vision broadened before his eyes, and Life's hidden secrets gradually became apparent to him. His soul abandoned the rapid parade of time rushing toward nothingness; it stood alone before symmetrical thoughts and crystal ideas. For the first time in his life, Ali was aware of the causes for the spiritual famine that had accompanied his youth. . . . The famine which levels away the pit between the sweetness and the bitterness of Life. . . . That thirst which unites into contentment the sighs of Affection and the silence of Satisfaction. . . . That longing which cannot be vanquished by the glory of the world nor twisted by the passing of the ages. Ali felt the surge of a strange affection and a kind tenderness within himself which was Memory, enlivening itself like incense placed upon white firebrands. . . . It was a magic love whose soft fingers had touched Ali's heart as a musician's delicate fingers touch quivering strings. It was a new power emanating from nothingness and growing forcefully, embracing his real self and filling his spirit with ardent love, at once painful and sweet.

Ali looked toward the ruins and his heavy eyes became alert as he fancied the glory of those devastated shrines that stood as mighty, impregnable, and eternal temples long before. His eyes became motionless and the breathing of his heart quickened. And like a blind man whose sight has suddenly been restored, he commenced to see, think and meditate. . . . He recollected the lamps and the silver censers that surrounded the image of an adored and revered goddess. . . . He remembered the priests offering sacrifices before an altar built of ivory and gold. . . . He envisioned the dancing maidens, and the tambourine players, and the singers who chanted the praise of the goddess of Love and Beauty; he saw all this before him, and felt the impression of their obscurity in the choking depths of his heart.

But memory alone brings naught save echoes of voices heard in the depths of the long ago. What, then, is the bizarre relationship between these powerful, weaving memories and the past actual life of a simple youth who was born in a tent and who spent the spring of his life grazing sheep in the valleys?

Ali gathered himself and walked amidst the ruins, and the gnawing memories suddenly tore the veil of oblivion from his thoughts. As he reached the great and cavernous entrance to the temple, he halted as if a magnetic power gripped him and fastened his feet. As he looked downward, he found a smashed statue on the ground. He broke from the grasp of the Unseen and at once his soul's tears unleashed and poured like blood issuing from a deep wound; his heart roared in ebb and flow like the welling waves of the sea. He sighed bitterly and cried painfully, for he felt a stabbing aloneness and a destructive remoteness standing as an abyss between his heart and the heart from whom he was torn before he entered upon this life. He felt that his soul's element was but a flame from the burning torch which God had separated from Himself before the passing of the Ages. He perceived the feathery touch of delicate wings rustling about his flaming heart, and a great love possessing him. . . . A love whose power separates the mind from the world of quantity and measurement. . . . A love that talks when the tongue of Life is muted. . . . A love that stands as a blue beacon to point out the path, guiding with no visible light. That love or that God who descended in that quiet hour upon Ali's heart had seared into his being a bitter and sweet affection, like thorns growing by the side of the flourishing flowers.

But who is this Love and whence did he come? What does he desire of a shepherd kneeling in the midst of those ruins? Is it a seed sown without awareness in the domain of the heart by a Bedouin maiden? Or a beam appeared from behind the dark cloud to illuminate life? Is it a dream that crept close in the silence of the night to ridicule him? Or is it Truth that existed since the Beginning, and shall continue to exist until the Ending?

Ali closed his tearful eyes and stretched forth his arms like a beggar, and exclaimed, "Who are you, standing close to my heart but away from my sight, yet acting as a great wall between me and my real self, binding my today with my forgotten past? Are you the phantom of a spectre from Eternity to show me the vanity of Life and the weakness of mankind? Or the spirit of a genie appeared from the earth's crevices to enslave me and render me an object of mockery amongst the youths of my tribe? Who are you and what is this strange power which at one time deadens and enlivens my heart? Who am I and what is this strange self whom I call "Myself?" Has the Water of Life which I drank made of me an angel, seeing and hearing the mysterious secrets of the Universe, or is it merely an evil wine that intoxicated me and blinded me from myself?"

He became silent, while his anxiety grew and his spirit exulted. Then he continued, "Oh, that which the soul reveals, and the night conceals. . . . Oh, beautiful spirit, hovering in the sky of my dream;

you have awakened in me a dormant fullness, like healthy seeds hidden under the blankets of snow; you have passed me like a frolicsome breeze carrying to my hungry self the fragrance of the flowers of heaven; you have touched my senses and agitated and quivered them like the leaves of the trees. Let me look upon you now if you are a human, or command Slumber to shut my eyes so I can view your vastness through my inner being. Let me touch you; let me hear your voice. Tear away this veil that conceals my entire purpose, and destroy this wall that hides my deity from my clearing eyes, and place upon me a pair of wings so I may fly behind you to the halls of the Supreme Universe. Or bewitch my eyes so I may follow you to the ambush of the genii if you are one of their brides. If I am worthy, place your hand upon my heart and possess me."

Ali was whispering these words into the mystic darkness, and before him crept the ghosts of night, as if they were vapour coming from his boiling tears. Upon the walls of the temple he fancied magical pictures painted with the brush of the rainbow.

Thus did one hour pass, with Ali shedding tears and reveling in his miserable plight and hearing the beats of his heart, looking beyond the objects as if he were observing the images of Life vanishing slowly and being replaced with a dream, strange in its beauty and terrible in enormity. Like a prophet who meditates the stars of heaven awaiting the Descent and Revelation, he pondered the power existing beyond these contemplations. He felt that his spirit left him and probed through the temples for a priceless but unknown segment of himself, lost among the ruins.

Dawn had appeared and silence roared with the passing of the breeze; the first rays of light raced through, illuminating the particles of the ether, and the sky smiled like a dreamer viewing his beloved's phantom. The birds probed from their sanctuary in the crevices of the walls and emerged into the halls of the columns, singing their morning prayers.

Ali placed his cupped hand over his forehead, looking downward with glazed eyes. Like Adam, when God opened his eyes with Almighty breath, Ali saw new objects, strange and fantastic. Then he approached his sheep and called to them, whereupon they followed him quietly toward the lush fields. He led them, as he gazed at the sky like a philosopher divining and meditating the secrets of the Universe. He reached a brook whose murmuring was soothing to the spirit, and he sat by the edge of the spring under the willow tree, whose branches dipped over the water as if drinking from the cool depths. The dew of dawn glistened upon the sheep's wool as they grazed amid flowers and green grass.

In a few moments Ali again felt that his heartbeats were increasing rapidly and his spirit commenced to vibrate violently, almost visibly. Like a mother suddenly awakened from her slumber by the scream of her child, he bolted from his position, and as his eyes were compelled to her, he saw a beautiful maiden carrying an earthenware container upon her shoulder, slowly approaching the far side of the brook. As she reached the edge and leaned forward to fill the jar, she glanced across, and her eyes met Ali's eyes. As if in insanity she cried out, dropped the jar, and withdrew swiftly. Then she turned, gazing at Ali with anxious, agonizing disbelief.

A minute passed, whose seconds were glittering lamps illuminating their hearts and spirits, and silence brought vague remembrance, revealing to them images and scenes far away from that brook and those trees. They heard each other in the understanding silence, listening tearfully to each other's sighs of heart and soul until complete knowing prevailed between the two.

Ali, still compelled by a mysterious power, leaped across the brook and approached the maiden, embraced her and printed a long kiss upon her lips. As if the sweetness of Ali's caress had usurped her will, she did not move, and the kind touch of Ali's arms had stolen her strength. She yielded to him as the fragrance of jasmine concedes to the vibration of the breeze, carrying it into the spacious firmament.

She placed her head upon his chest like a tortured person who has found rest. She sighed deeply . . . a sigh that announced the rebirth of happiness in a torn heart and proclaimed a revolution of wings that had ascended after having been injured and committed to earth.

She raised her head and looked at him with her soul . . . the look of a human which, in mighty silence, belittles the conventional words used amongst mankind; the expression which offers myriads of thoughts in the unspoken language of the hearts. She bore the look of a person who accepts Love not as a spirit in a body of words, but as a reunion occurring long after two souls were divided by earth and joined by God.

The enamoured couple walked amidst the willow trees, and the singleness of two selves was a speaking tongue for their unification; a seeing eye for the glory of Happiness; a silent listener to the tremendous revelation of Love.

The sheep continued grazing, and the birds of the sky still hovered above their heads, singing the song of Dawn, following the emptiness of night. As they reached the end of the valley the sun appeared, spreading a golden garment upon the knolls and the hills, and they sat by the side of a rock where the violets hid. The maiden looked into Ali's black eyes while the breeze caressed her hair, as if the shimmering wisps were fingertips craving for sweet kisses. She felt as though some magic and strong gentleness were touching her lips in spite of her will, and with a serene and charming voice she said, "Ishtar has restored both of our spirits to this life from another, so we may not be denied the joy of Love and the glory of Youth, my beloved."

Ali closed his eyes, as if her musical voice brought to him images of a dream he had seen, and he felt an invisible pair of wings carrying him from that place and depositing him in a strange chamber by the side of a bed upon which lay the corpse of a maiden whose beauty had been claimed by Death. He cried fearfully, then opened his eyes and found that same maiden sitting by his side, and upon her lips appeared a smile. Her eyes shone with the rays of Life. Ali's face brightened and his heart was refreshed. The phantom of his vision withdrew slowly until he forgot completely the past and its cares. The two lovers embraced and drank the wine of sweet kisses together until they became intoxicated. They slumbered, wrapped between each other's arms, until the last remnant of the shadow was dispersed by the Eternal Power which had awakened them.

BETWEEN NIGHT AND MORN

B E SILENT, my heart, for the space cannot
Hear you; be silent, for the ether is
Laden with cries and moans, and cannot
Carry your songs and hymns.

Be silent, for the phantoms of the night
Will not give heed to the whispering of
Your secrets; nor will the processions
Of darkness halt before your dreams.

Be silent, my heart, until Dawn comes,
For he who patiently awaits the morn
Will meet him surely, and he who loves
The light will be loved by the light.

Be silent, my heart, and hearken to my
Story; in my dream I saw a nightingale
Singing over the throat of a fiery
Volcano, and I saw a lily raising her
Head above the snow, and a naked Houri
Dancing in the midst of the graves, and
An infant playing with skulls while
Laughing.

I saw all these images in my dream, and
When I opened my eyes and looked about
Me, I saw the volcano still raging, but
No longer heard the nightingale sing;
Nor did I see him hovering.

I saw the sky spreading snow upon the
Fields and valleys, and concealing under
White shrouds the stilled bodies of the
Lilies. I saw a row of graves before
The silence of the Ages, but there was
No person dancing or praying in their
Midst. I saw a heap of skulls, but no
One was there to laugh, save the wind.

In my awakeness I saw grief and sorrow;
What became of the joy and sweetness of
My dream? Where has the beauty of my
Dream gone, and in what manner did the
Images disappear?

How can the soul be patient until Slumber
Restores the happy phantoms of hope and
Desire?

Give heed, my heart, and hear my story;
Yesterday my soul was like an old and
Strong tree, whose roots grasped into the
Depths of the earth, and whose branches
Reached the Infinite. My soul blossomed
In Spring, and gave fruit in Summer, and

When Autumn came, I gathered the fruit on
A silver tray and placed it by the
Walker's portion of the street; and all
Who passed partook willingly and continued
To walk.

And when Autumn passed away, and submerged
His rejoicing under wailing and lamentation,
I looked upon my tray and found but one
Fruit remaining; I took it and placed it
Into my mouth, but found it bitter as gall,
And sour as the hard grapes, and I said to
Myself, "Woe to me, for I have placed a
Curse in the mouths of the people, and an
Ailment in their bodies. What have you
Done, my soul, with the sweet sap which
Your roots have sucked from the earth, and
The fragrance which you have drawn from
The sky?" In anger did I tear the strong
And old tree of my soul, with each of the
Struggling roots, from the depths of the
Earth.

I uprooted it from the past, and took
From it the memories of one thousand
Springs and one thousand Autumns, and I
Planted the tree of my soul in another
Place. It was now in a field afar from
The path of Time; and I tended it in day
And in night, saying within me, "Wakefulness
Will bring us closer to the stars."

I watered it with blood and tears, saying,
"There is a flavour in blood, and a
Sweetness in tears." When Spring returned,
My tree bloomed again, and in the Summer it
Bore fruit. And when Autumn came, I gathered
All the ripe fruit upon a golden plate and
Offered it in the public path, and the people
Passed but none desired my fruit.

Then I took one fruit and brought it to my
Lips, and it was sweet as the honeycomb
And exhilarating as the wine of Babylon
And fragrant as the jasmine. And I cried
Out, saying, "The people do not want a
Blessing in their mouths, nor a truth in
Their hearts, for Blessing is the daughter
Of Tears, and Truth is the son of Blood."

I left the noisome city to sit in the shadow
Of the solitary tree of my soul, in a
Field far from life's path.

Be silent, my heart, until Dawn comes;
Be silent and attend my story;
Yesterday my thoughts were a boat sailing
Amidst the waves in the sea, and moving
With the winds from one land to another.
And my boat was empty except of seven
Jars of rainbow colours; and the time
Came when I grew weary of moving about
On the face of the sea, and I said to

Myself, "I shall return with the empty
Boat of my thoughts to the harbour of the
Isle of my birth."

And I prepared by colouring my boat yellow
Like the sunset, and green like the heart
Of Spring, and blue like the sky, and red
Like the anemone. And on the masts and
On the rudder I drew strange figures that
Compelled the attention and dazzled the
Eye. And as I ended my task, the boat of
My thoughts seemed as a prophetic vision,
Sailing between the two infinities, the
Sea and the sky.

I entered the harbour of the isle of my
Birth, and the people surged to meet me
With singing and merriment. And the
Throngs invited me to enter the city;
And they were plucking their instruments
And sounding their tambourines.

Such welcome was mine because my boat
Was beautifully decorated, and none
Entered and saw the interior of the
Boat of my thoughts, nor asked what
I had brought from beyond the seas. Nor
Could they observe that I had brought
My boat back empty, for its brilliance
Had rendered them blind. Thereupon I
Said within myself, "I have led the

People astray, and with seven jars of
Colours I have cheated their eyes."

Thereafter, I embarked in the boat of
My thoughts, again to set sail. I
Visited the East Islands and gathered
Myrrh, frankincense and sandalwood, and
Placed them in my boat. . . . I roamed the
West Islands and brought ivory and ruby
And emerald and many rare gems. . . . I
Journeyed the South Islands and carried
Back with me beautiful armours and
Glittering swords and spears and all
Varieties of weapons. . . . I filled the
Boat of my thoughts with the choicest
And most precious things on earth, and
Returned to the harbour of the isle of
My birth, saying, "The people shall again
Glorify me, but with honesty, and they
Shall again invite me to enter their
City, but with merit."

And when I reached the harbour, none
Came to meet me. . . . I walked the streets
Of my earlier glory but no person looked
Upon me. . . . I stood in the market place
Shouting to the people of the treasures
In my boat, and they mocked at me and
Heeded not.

I returned to the harbour with spiritless
Heart and disappointment and confusion.

174

And when I gazed upon my boat, I observed
A thing which I had not seen during my
Voyage, and I exclaimed, "The waves of
The sea have done away with the colours and
The figures on my boat and caused it to look
Like a skeleton." The winds and the spray
Together with the burning sun had effaced
The brilliant hues and my boat looked now
Like tattered grey raiment. I could not
Observe these changes from amid my treasures,
For I had blinded my eyes from the inside.

I had gathered the most precious things on
Earth and placed them in a floating chest
Upon the face of the water and returned to
My people, but they cast me away and could
Not see me, for their eyes had been allured
By empty, shimmering objects.

At that hour I left the boat of my thoughts
For the City of the Dead, and sat in the
Midst of the trim graves, contemplating
Their secrets.

Be silent, my heart, until Dawn comes; be
Silent, for the raging tempest is ridiculing
Your inner whispering, and the caves of
The valleys do not echo the vibration of
Your strings.

Be silent, my heart, until Morn comes,
For he who awaits patiently the coming

175

Of Dawn will be embraced longingly by
Morningtide.

Dawn is breaking. Speak if you are able,
My heart. Here is the procession of
Morningtide. . . .Why do you not speak?
Has not the silence of the night left
A song in your inner depths with which
You may meet Dawn?

Here are the swarms of doves and the
Nightingales moving in the far portion
Of the valley. Are you capable of flying
With the birds, or has the horrible night
Weakened your wings? The shepherds are
Leading the sheep from their folds; has
The phantom of the night left strength
In you so you may walk behind them to
The green prairies? The young men and
Women are walking gracefully toward the
Vineyards. Will you be able to stand
And walk with them? Rise, my heart, and
Walk with Dawn, for the night has passed,
And the fear of darkness has vanished with
Its black dreams and ghastly thoughts and
Insane travels.

Rise, my heart, and raise your voice with
Music, for he who shares not Dawn with
His songs is one of the sons of ever-
Darkness.

BOOK TEN

SECRETS
OF THE HEART

SECRETS OF THE HEART

A MAJESTIC mansion
stood under the wings of the silent night, as Life
stands under the cover of Death. In it sat a maiden
at an ivory desk, leaning her beautiful head on her
soft hand, as a withering lily leans upon its petals.
She looked around, feeling like a miserable prisoner,
struggling to penetrate the walls of the dungeon
with her eyes in order to witness Life walking in the
procession of Freedom.

The hours passed like the ghosts of the night, as
a procession chanting the dirge of her sorrow, and
the maiden felt secure with the shedding of her tears
in anguished solitude. When she could not resist
the pressure of her suffering any longer, and as she
felt that she was in full possession of the treasured
secrets of her heart, she took the quill and commenced mingling her tears with ink upon parchment, and she inscribed:

"My Beloved Sister,
    "When the heart becomes congested with secrets,

179

and the eyes begin to burn from the searing tears, and the ribs are about to burst with the growing of the heart's confinement, one cannot find expression for such a labyrinth except by a surge of release.

"Sorrowful persons find joy in lamentation, and lovers encounter comfort and condolence in dreams, and the oppressed delight in receiving sympathy. I am writing to you now because I feel like a poet who fancies the beauty of objects whose impression he composes in verse while being ruled by a divine power. . . . I am like a child of the starving poor who cries for food, instigated by bitterness of hunger, disregarding the plight of his poor and merciful mother and her defeat in life.

"Listen to my painful story, my dear sister, and weep with me, for sobbing is like a prayer, and the tears of mercy are like a charity because they come forth from a living and sensitive and good soul and they are not shed in vain. It was the will of my father when I married a noble and rich man. My father was like most of the rich, whose only joy in life is to improve their wealth by adding more gold to their coffers in fear of poverty, and curry nobility with grandeur in anticipation of the attacks of the black days. . . . I find myself now, with all my love and dreams, a victim upon a golden altar which I hate, and an inherited honour which I despise.

"I respect my husband because he is generous and kind to all; he endeavours to bring happiness to me, and spends his gold to please my heart, but I have found that the impression of all these things is not worth one moment of a true and divine love. Do not ridicule me, my sister, for I am now a most enlightened person regarding the needs of a woman's heart—that throbbing heart which is like a bird flying in the spacious sky of love. . . . It is like a vase replenished with the wine of the ages that has been pressed for the sipping souls. . . . It is like a book in whose pages one reads the chapters of happiness and misery, joy and pain, laughter and sorrow. No one can read this book except the true companion who is the other half of the woman, created for her since the beginning of the world.

"Yes, I became most knowing amongst all women as to the purpose of the soul and meaning of the heart, for I have found that my magnificent horses and beautiful carriages and glittering coffers of gold and sublime nobility are not worth one glance from the eyes of that poor young man who is patiently waiting and suffering the pangs of bitterness and misery. . . . That youth who is oppressed by the cruelty and will of my father, and imprisoned in the narrow and melancholy jail of Life. . .

"Please, my dear, do not contrive to console me, for the calamity through which I have realized the power of my love is my great consoler. Now I am looking forward from behind my tears and awaiting the coming of Death to lead me to where I will meet the companion of my soul and embrace him as I did before we entered this strange world.

"Do not think evil of me, for I am doing my duty as a faithful wife, and complying calmly and patiently with the laws and rules of man. I honour my husband with my sense, and respect him with my heart, and revere him with my soul, but there is a withholding, for God gave part of me to my beloved before I knew him.

"Heaven willed that I spend my life with a man not meant for me, and I am wasting my days silently according to the will of Heaven; but if the gates of Eternity do not open, I will remain with the beautiful half of my soul and look back to the Past, and that Past is this Present. . . . I shall look at life as Spring looks at Winter, and contemplate the obstacles of Life as one who has climbed the rough trail and reached the mountain top."

At that moment the maiden ceased writing and hid her face with her cupped hands and wept bitterly. Her heart declined to entrust to the pen its most sacred secrets, but resorted to the pouring of dry tears that dispersed quickly and mingled with the gentle ether, the haven of the lovers' souls and the flowers' spirits. After a moment she took the quill and added, "Do you remember that youth? Do you recollect the rays which emanated from his eyes, and the sorrowful signs upon his face? Do you recall that laughter which bespoke the tears of a mother, torn from her only child? Can you retrace his serene voice speaking the echo of a distant valley? Do you remember him meditating and staring longingly and calmly at objects and speaking of them in strange words, and then bending his head and sighing as if fearing to reveal the secrets of his great heart? Do you recall his dreams and beliefs? Do you recollect all these things in a youth whom humanity counts as one of her children and upon whom my father looked with eyes of superiority because he is higher than earthly greed and nobler than inherited grandeur?

"You know, my dear sister, that I am a martyr in this belittling world, and a victim of ignorance. Will you sympathize with a sister who sits in the silence of the horrible night pouring down the contents of her inner self and revealing to you her heart's secrets? I am sure that you will sympathize with me, for I know that Love has visited your heart."

Dawn came, and the maiden surrendered herself to Slumber, hoping to find sweeter and more gentle dreams than those she had encountered in her awakeness. . . .

MY COUNTRYMEN

WHAT do you seek, My Countrymen?
Do you desire that I build for
You gorgeous palaces, decorated
With words of empty meaning, or
Temples roofed with dreams? Or
Do you command me to destroy what
The liars and tyrants have built?
Shall I uproot with my fingers
What the hypocrites and the wicked
Have implanted? Speak your insane
Wish!

What is it you would have me do,
My Countrymen? Shall I purr like
The kitten to satisfy you, or roar
Like the lion to please myself? I
Have sung for you, but you did not
Dance; I have wept before you, but
You did not cry. Shall I sing and
Weep at the same time?

Your souls are suffering the pangs
Of hunger, and yet the fruit of

184

Knowledge is more plentiful than
The stones of the valleys.

Your hearts are withering from
Thirst, and yet the springs of
Life are streaming about your
Homes—why do you not drink?
The sea has its ebb and flow,
The moon has its fullness and
Crescents, and the Ages have
Their winter and summer, and all
Things vary like the shadow of
An unborn God moving between
Earth and sun, but Truth cannot
Be changed, nor will it pass away;
Why, then, do you endeavour to
Disfigure its countenance?

I have called you in the silence
Of the night to point out the
Glory of the moon and the dignity
Of the stars, but you startled
From your slumber and clutched
Your swords in fear, crying,
"Where is the enemy? We must kill
Him first!" At morningtide, when
The enemy came, I called to you
Again, but now you did not wake
From your slumber, for you were
Locked in fear, wrestling with

The processions of spectres in
Your dreams.

And I said unto you, "Let us climb
To the mountain top and view the
Beauty of the world." And you
Answered me, saying, "In the depths
Of this valley our fathers lived,
And in its shadows they died, and in
Its caves they were buried. How can
We depart this place for one which
They failed to honour?"
And I said unto you, "Let us go to
The plain that gives it bounty to
The sea." And you spoke timidly to
Me, saying, "The uproar of the abyss
Will frighten our spirits, and the
Terror of the depths will deaden
Our bodies."

I have loved you, My Countrymen, but
My love for you is painful to me
And useless to you; and today I
Hate you, and hatred is a flood
That sweeps away the dry branches
And quavering houses.

I have pitied your weakness, My
Countrymen, but my pity has but
Increased your feebleness, exalting

And nourishing slothfulness which
Is vain to Life. And today I see
Your infirmity which my soul loathes
And fears.

I have cried over your humiliation
And submission; and my tears streamed
Like crystalline, but could not sear
Away your stagnant weakness; yet they
Removed the veil from my eyes.

My tears have never reached your
Petrified hearts, but they cleansed
The darkness from my inner self.
Today I am mocking at your suffering,
For laughter is a raging thunder that
Precedes the tempest and never comes
After it.

What do you desire, My Countrymen?
Do you wish for me to show you
The ghost of your countenance on
The face of still water? Come,
Now, and see how ugly you are!

Look and meditate! Fear has
Turned your hair grey as the
Ashes, and dissipation has grown
Over your eyes and made them into
Obscured hollows, and cowardice
Has touched your cheeks that now
Appear as dismal pits in the

Valley, and Death has kissed
Your lips and left them yellow
As the Autumn leaves.

What is it that you seek, My
Countrymen? What ask you from
Life, who does not any longer
Count you among her children?

Your souls are freezing in the
Clutches of the priests and
Sorcerers, and your bodies
Tremble between the paws of the
Despots and the shedders of
Blood, and your country quakes
Under the marching feet of the
Conquering enemy; what may you
Expect even though you stand
Proudly before the face of the
Sun? Your swords are sheathed
With rust, and your spears are
Broken, and your shields are
Laden with gaps; why, then, do
You stand in the field of battle?

Hypocrisy is your religion, and
Falsehood is your life, and
Nothingness is your ending; why,
Then, are you living? Is not
Death the sole comfort of the
Miserables?

Life is a resolution that
Accompanies youth, and a diligence
That follows maturity, and a
Wisdom that pursues senility; but
You, My Countrymen, were born old
And weak. And your skins withered
And your heads shrank, whereupon
You became as children, running
Into the mire and casting stones
Upon each other.

Knowledge is a light, enriching
The warmth of life, and all may
Partake who seek it out; but you,
My Countrymen, seek out darkness
And flee the light, awaiting the
Coming of water from the rock,
And your nation's misery is your
Crime. . . . I do not forgive you
Your sins, for you know what you
Are doing.

Humanity is a brilliant river
Singing its way and carrying with
It the mountains' secrets into
The heart of the sea; but you,
My Countrymen, are stagnant
Marshes infested with insects
And vipers.

The Spirit is a sacred blue
Torch, burning and devouring

The dry plants, and growing
With the storm and illuminating
The faces of the goddesses; but
You, My Countrymen . . . your souls
Are like ashes which the winds
Scatter upon the snow, and which
The tempests disperse forever in
The valleys.

Fear not the phantom of Death,
My Countrymen, for his greatness
And mercy will refuse to approach
Your smallness; and dread not the
Dagger, for it will decline to be
Lodged in your shallow hearts.

I hate you, My Countrymen, because
You hate glory and greatness. I
Despise you because you despise
Yourselves. I am your enemy, for
You refuse to realize that you are
The enemies of the goddesses.

JOHN THE MADMAN

IN SUMMER John walked
every morning into the field, driving his oxen and
carrying his plough over his shoulder, hearkening
to the soothing songs of the birds and the rustling of
the leaves and the grass.

At noon he sat beside a brook in the colourful
prairies for repast, leaving a few morsels upon the
green grass for the birds of the sky.

At eventide he returned to his wretched hovel
that stood apart from those hamlets and villages in
North Lebanon. After the evening meal he sat and
listened attentively to his parents, who related tales
of the past ages until sleep allured and captured his
eyes.

In winter he spent his days by the fireside, pondering the wailing of the winds and lamentation of the
elements, meditating upon the phenomena of the
seasons, and looking through the window toward
the snow-laden valleys and leafless trees, symbolizing
a multitude of suffering people left helpless in the
jaws of biting frost and strong wind.

During the long winter nights he sat up until his parents retired, whereupon he opened a rough wooden closet, brought out his New Testament, and read it secretly under the dim light of a flickering lamp. The priests objected to the reading of the Good Book, and John exercised great caution during these fascinating moments of study. The fathers warned the simple-hearted people against its use, and threatened them with excommunication from the church if discovered possessing it.

Thus John spent his youth between the beautiful earth of God and the New Testament, full of light and truth. John was a youth of silence and contemplation; he listened to his parents' conversations and never spoke a word nor asked a question. When sitting with his contemporaries, he gazed steadily at the horizon, and his thoughts were as distant as his eyes. After each visit to the church he returned home with a depressed spirit, for the teachings of the priests were different from the precepts he found in the Gospel, and the life of the faithful was not the beautiful life of which Christ spoke.

Spring came and the snow melted in the fields and valleys. The snow upon the mountain tops was thawing gradually and forming many streamlets in the winding paths leading into the valleys, combining into a torrent whose roaring bespoke the awakening of Nature. The almond and apple trees were in full bloom; the willow and poplar trees were sprouting with buds, and Nature had spread her happy and colourful garments over the countryside.

John, tired of spending his days by the fireside, and knowing that his oxen were longing for the pastures, released his animals from the sheds and led them to the fields, concealing his New Testament under his cloak for fear of detection. He reached a beautiful arbor adjacent to some fields belonging to the St. Elija Monastery * which stood majestically upon a nearby hill. As the oxen commenced grazing, John leaned upon a rock and began to read his New Testament and meditate the sadness of the children of God on earth, and the beauty of the Kingdom of Heaven.

It was the last day of Lent, and the villagers who abstained from eating meat were impatiently awaiting the coming of Easter. John, like the rest of the poor fellahin, never distinguished Lent from any other day of the year, for his whole life was an extended Lent, and his food never exceeded the simple bread, kneaded with the pain of his heart, or the fruits, purchased with the blood of his body. The only nourishment craved by John during Lent was that spiritual food—the heavenly bread that brought into his heart sad thoughts of the tragedy of the Son of Man and the end of His life on earth.

The birds were singing and hovering about him, and large flocks of doves circled in the sky, while the

* A rich abbey in North Lebanon with vast lands, occupied by scores of monks called Alepoans. (*Editor's note.*)

flowers swayed with the breeze as if exhilarated by the brilliant sunshine.

John busied himself absorbing the Book, and between these intense, light-giving sessions, he watched the domes of the churches in the nearby villages and listened to the rhythmic toll of the bells. Occasionally he would close his eyes and fly on the wings of dreams to Old Jerusalem, following Christ's steps and asking the people of the city about the Nazarene, whereupon he would receive the answer, "Here He cured the paralyzed and restored to the blind their sight; and there they braided for Him a wreath of thorns and placed it upon His head; from that portico He spoke to the multitude with beautiful parables; in that palace they tied Him to the marble columns and scourged Him; on this road He forgave the adulteress her sins, and upon that spot He fell under the weight of His Cross."

One hour passed, and John was suffering physically with God and glorifying with Him in spirit. Noon quickly came, and the oxen were beyond the reach of John's sight. He looked in every direction but could not see them, and as he reached the trail that led to the adjacent fields, he saw a man at a distance, standing amidst the orchards. As he approached and saw that the man was one of the Monastery's monks, he greeted him, bowed reverently, and asked him if he had seen the oxen. The monk appeared to be restraining anger, and he said, "Yes, I saw them.

Follow me and I will show them to you." As they reached the Monastery, John found his oxen tied with ropes in a shed. One of the monks was acting as a watchman over them, and each time an animal moved, he struck the ox across the back with a heavy club. John made a frantic attempt to unbind the helpless animals, but the monk took hold of his cloak and withheld him. At the same time he turned toward the Monastery and shouted, saying, "Here is the criminal shepherd! I have found him!" The priests and monks, preceded by the head priest, hurried to the scene and encircled John, who was bewildered, and felt like a captive. "I have done nothing to merit the treatment of a criminal," said John to the head priest. And the leader replied angrily, "Your oxen have ruined our plantation and destroyed our vineyards. Since you are responsible for the damage we will not give up your oxen until you adjust our loss."

John protested, "I am poor and have no money. Please release my oxen and I pledge my honour that I will never again bring them to these lands." The head priest took a step forward, raised his hand toward heaven, and said, "God has appointed us to be the protectors over this vast land of St. Elija, and it is our sacred duty to guard it with all of our might, for this land is holy, and, like fire, it will burn any who trespass upon it. If you refuse to account for your crime against God, the grass that your oxen have eaten will surely turn into poison and destroy them!"

The head priest started to depart, but John touched his robe and humbly begged, "I appeal to you in the name of Jesus and all the saints, to let me and my animals free. Be kind to me, for I am poor, and the coffers of the Monastery are bursting with silver and gold. Have mercy upon my poor and aged parents, whose lives depend on me. God will forgive me if I have harmed you." The head priest looked at him with severity, and said, "Poor or rich, the Monastery cannot forgive you your debts; three denars will free your oxen." John pleaded, "I do not possess a single coin; have mercy on a poor grazier, Father." And the head priest retorted, "Then you must sell a part of your possessions and bring three denars, for it is better to enter the Kingdom of Heaven without property than to bring the wrath of St. Elija upon you and descend to hell." The other monks nodded their accord.

After a short silence, John's face brightened and his eyes shone as if fear and servility had deserted his heart. With his head high, he looked at the head priest and addressed him boldly, saying, "Do the weak poor have to sell their pitiful belongings, the source of their life's bread, in order to add more gold to the Monastery's wealth? Is it just that the poor should be oppressed and made poorer in order that St. Elija may forgive the oxen their innocent wrongs?" The head priest raised his eyes to heaven and intoned, "It is written in the Book of God that he who has plenty shall be given more, and he who has not shall be taken from."

When John heard these words he became furious, and like a soldier who draws his sword in the face of the enemy, he drew the New Testament from his pocket and shouted out, "This is how you twist the teachings of Christ, you hypocrite! And thus do you pervert the most sacred heritage of life in order to spread your evils. . . . Woe to you when the Son of Man comes again and destroys your Monastery and throws its debris in the valley, and burns your shrine and altars into ashes. . . . Woe to you when the wrath of the Nazarene descends upon you and throws you into the depths of the abyss. . . . Woe to you, worshippers of the idols of greed, who hide the ugliness of hatred under your black garments. . . . Woe to you, foes of Jesus, who move your lips with prayers while your hearts are laden with lusts. . . . Woe to you who kneel before the altar in body while your spirits are revolting against God! You are polluted with your own sin of punishing me for approaching your land, paid for by me and my ancestors. You ridiculed me when I asked for mercy in the name of Christ. Take this Book and show your smiling monks where the Son of God ever refused to forgive. . . . Read this heavenly tragedy and tell them where He spoke not of mercy and of kindness, be it in the Sermon of the Mount, or in the temple. Did He not forgive the adulteress her sins? Did He not part his

197

hands upon the Cross to embrace humanity? Look upon our wretched homes, where the sick suffer upon their hard beds. . . . Look behind the prison bars, where the innocent man is victim of oppression and injustice. . . . Look upon the beggars, stretching forth their hands for alms, humiliated in heart and broken in body. . . . Think upon your slaving followers, who are suffering the pangs of hunger while you are living a life of luxury and indifference, and enjoying the fruits of the fields and the wine of the vineyards. You have never visited a sufferer nor consoled the down-hearted nor fed the hungry; neither have you sheltered the wayfarer nor offered sympathy to the lame. Yet you are not satisfied with what you have pilfered from our fathers, but still stretch your hands like vipers' heads, grasping by threats of hell what little a widow has saved through body-breaking toil, or a miserable fellah has stored away to keep his children alive!"

John took a deep breath, then calmed his voice and quietly added, "You are numerous, and I am alone—you may do unto me what you wish; the wolves prey upon the lamb in the darkness of the night, but the blood stains remain upon the stones in the valley until the dawn comes, and the sun reveals the crime to all."

There was a magic power in John's talk that arrested their attention and injected a defensive anger into the monks' hearts. They were shaking with fury and waiting only for their superior's order to fall upon John and bring him to submission. The brief silence was like the heavy quiet of the tempest, after laying waste the gardens. The head priest then commanded the monks, saying, "Bind this criminal and take the Book from him and drag him into a dark cell, for he who blasphemes the holy representatives of God will never be forgiven on this earth, neither in Eternity." The Monks leaped upon John and led him manacled into a narrow prison and barred him there.

The courage shown by John could not be perceived or understood by one who partakes of the submission or the deceit or the tyranny of this enslaved country, called by the Orientals "The Bride of Syria," and "The Pearl of the Sultan's Crown." And in his cell, John thought of the needless misery brought upon his countrymen by the grip of the things he had just learned. He smiled with a sad sympathy and his smile was mingled with suffering and bitterness; the kind that cuts its way through the depths of the heart; the kind that sets the soul to a choking futility; the kind which, if left unsupported, ascends to the eyes and falls down helplessly.

John then stood proudly, and looked through the window-slit facing the sunlit valley. He felt as if a spiritual joy were embracing his soul and a sweet tranquility possessing his heart. They had imprisoned his body, but his spirit was sailing freely with the breeze amidst the knolls and prairies. His love for Jesus never changed, and the torturing hands could not remove his heart's ease, for persecution cannot harm him who stands by Truth. Did not Socrates fall proudly a victim in body? Was not Paul stoned for the sake of the Truth? It is our inner self that hurts us when we disobey and kills us when we betray.

John's parents were informed of his imprisonment and the confiscation of the oxen. His old mother came to the Monastery leaning heavily over her walking stick and she prostrated herself before the head priest, kissing his feet and begging him for mercy upon her only son. The head priest raised his head reverently toward heaven and said, "We will forgive your son for his madness, but St. Elija will not forgive any who trespass upon his land." After gazing at him with tearful eyes, the old lady took a silver locket from her neck and handed it to the head priest, saying, "This is my most precious possession, given to me as a wedding gift by my mother. . . . Will you accept it as atonement for my son's sin?"

The head priest took the locket and placed it in his pocket, whereupon he looked at John's ancient mother who was kissing his hands and expressing to him her thanks and gratitude, and he said, "Woe to this sinful age! You twist the saying of the Good Book and cause the children to eat the sour, and the parents' teeth sit on edge; go now, good woman, and pray to God for your mad son and ask Him to restore his mind."

John left the prison, and walked quietly by the side of his mother, driving the oxen before him. When they reached their wretched hovel, he led the animals into their mangers and sat silently by the window, meditating the sunset. In a few moments he heard his father whispering to his mother, saying, "Sara, many times have I told you that John was mad, and you disbelieved. Now you will agree, after what you have seen, for the head priest has spoken to you today the very words I spoke to you in past years." John continued looking toward the distant horizon, watching the sun descend.

Easter arrived, and at that time the construction of a new church in the town of Bsherri had just been completed. This magnificent place of worship was like a prince's palace standing amidst the huts of poor subjects. The people were scurrying through the many preparations to receive a prelate who was assigned to officiate at the religious ceremonies in-augurating the new temple. The multitudes stood in rows over the roads waiting for His Grace's arrival. The chanting of the priests in unison with cymbal sounds and the hymns of the throngs filled the sky.

The prelate finally arrived, riding a magnificent horse harnessed with a gold-studded saddle, and as he dismounted, the priests and political leaders met him with the most beautiful of welcoming speeches.

He was escorted to the new altar, where he clothed himself in ecclesiastical raiment, decorated with gold threads and encrusted with sparkling gems; he wore the golden crown, and walked in a procession around the altar, carrying his jewelled staff. He was followed by the priests and the carriers of tapers and incense burners.

At that hour, John stood amongst the fellahin at the portico, contemplating the scene with bitter sighs and sorrowful eyes, for it pained him to observe the expensive robes, and precious crown, and staff, and vases and other objects of needless extravagance, while the poor fellahin who came from the surrounding villages to celebrate the occasion were suffering the gnawing pangs of poverty. Their tattered swaddles and sorrowful faces bespoke their miserable plight.

The rich dignitaries, decorated with badges and ribbons, stood aloof praying loudly, while the suffering villagers, in the rear of the scene, beat their bosoms in sincere prayer that came from the depths of their broken hearts.

The authority of those dignitaries and leaders was like the ever-green leaves of the poplar trees, and the life of those fellahin was like a boat whose pilot had met his destiny and whose rudder had been lost and whose sails had been torn by the strong wind and left at the mercy of the furious depths and the raging tempest.

Tyranny and blind submission . . . which one of

these gave birth to the other? Is tyranny a strong
tree that grows not in the low earth, or is it submission, which is like a deserted field where naught but
thorns can grow? Such thoughts and contemplations
preyed on John's mind while the ceremonies were
taking place; he braced his arms about his chest for
fear his bosom would burst with agony over the people's plight in this tragedy of opposites.

He gazed upon the withering creatures of severe
humanity, whose hearts were dry and whose seeds
were now seeking shelter in the bosom of the earth,
as destitute pilgrims seek rebirth in a new realm.

When the pageantry came to an end and the multitude was preparing to disperse, John felt that a
compelling power was urging him to speak in behalf
of the oppressed poor. He proceeded to an extreme
end of the square, raised his hands toward the sky,
and as the throngs gathered about, he opened his
lips and said, "O Jesus, Who art sitting in the heart
of the circle of light, give heed! Look upon this
earth from behind the blue dome and see how the
thorns have choked the flowers which Thy truth
hast planted.

"Oh Good Shepherd, the wolves have preyed upon
the weak lamb which Thou hast carried in Thy
arms. Thy pure blood has been drawn into the
depths of the earth which Thy feet have made sacred.
This good earth has been made by Thine enemies
into an arena where the strong crushes the weak.
The cry of the miserable and the lamentation of the

helpless can no longer be heard by those sitting upon the thrones, preaching Thy word. The lambs which Thou hast sent to this earth are now wolves who eat the one which Thou hast carried and blessed.

"The word of light which sprang forth from Thy heart has vanished from the scripture and is replaced with an empty and terrible uproar that frightens the spirit.

"Oh Jesus, they have built these churches for the sake of their own glory, and embellished them with silk and melted gold. . . . They left the bodies of Thy chosen poor wrapped in tattered raiment in the cold night. . . . They filled the sky with the smoke of burning candles and incense and left the bodies of Thy faithful worshippers empty of bread. . . . They raised their voices with hymns of praise, but deafened themselves to the cry and moan of the widows and orphans.

"Come again, Oh Living Jesus, and drive the vendors of Thy faith from Thy sacred temple, for they have turned it into a dark cave where vipers of hypocrisy and falsehood crawl and abound."

John's words, strong and sincere, brought murmurs of approval, and the approach of the dignitaries quelled him not. With added courage, strengthened by memories of his earlier experience, he continued, "Come, Oh Jesus, and render accounts with those Caesars who usurped from the weak what is the weak's and from God what is God's. The grapevine which Thou hast planted with Thy right hand has been eaten by worms of greed and its bunches have been trampled down. Thy sons of peace are dividing amongst themselves and fighting one with another, leaving poor souls as victims in the wintry field. Before Thy altar, they raise their voices with prayers, saying, 'Glory to God in the highest, and on earth peace, good will toward men.' Will our Father in heaven be glorified when His name is uttered by empty hearts and sinful lips and false tongues? Will peace be on earth while the sons of misery are slaving in the fields to feed the strong and fill the stomachs of the tyrants? Will ever peace come and save them from the clutches of destitution?

"What is peace? Is it in the eyes of those infants, nursing upon the dry breasts of their hungry mothers in cold huts? Or is it in the wretched hovels of the hungry who sleep upon hard beds and crave for one bite of the food which the priests and monks feed to their fat pigs?

"What is joy, Oh Beautiful Jesus? Is it manifest when the Emir buys the strong arms of men and the honour of women for threats of death or for a few pieces of silver? Or is it found in submission, and slaving of body and spirit to those who dazzle our eyes with their glittering badges and golden diadems? Upon each complaint to Thy peace makers, they reward us with their soldiers, armed with swords and spears to step upon our women and children and steal our blood.

"Oh Jesus, full of love and mercy, stretch forth

Thy strong arms and protect us from those thieves or send welcome Death to deliver us and lead us to the graves where we can rest peacefully under the watchful care of Thy Cross; there we shall wait for Thy return. Oh Mighty Jesus, this life is naught but a dark cell of enslavement. . . . It is a playing ground of horrible ghosts, and it is a pit alive with spectres of death. Our days are but sharp words concealed under the ragged quilts of our beds in the fearful darkness of the night. At dawn, these weapons rise above our heads as demons, pointing out to us our whip-driven slavery in the fields.

"Oh Jesus, have mercy upon the oppressed poor who came today to commemorate Thy Resurrection. . . . Pity them, for they are miserable and weak."

John's talk appealed to one group and displeased another. "He is telling the truth, and speaking in our behalf before heaven," one remarked. And another one said, "He is bewitched, for he speaks in the name of an evil spirit." And a third commented, "We have never heard such infamous talk, not even from our fathers! We must bring it to an end!" And a fourth one said, whispering into the next man's ears, "I felt a new spirit in me when I heard him talking." The next man added, "But the priests know our needs more so than he does; it is a sin to doubt them." As the voices grew from every direction like the roar of the sea, one of the priests approached, placed John in restraint and turned him immediately to the law, whereupon he was taken to the Governor's palace for trial.

Upon his interrogation, John uttered not a single word, for he knew that the Nazarene resorted to silence before His persecutors. The governor ordered John to be placed in a prison, where he slept peacefully and heart-cleansed that night, leaning his head on the rock wall of the dungeon.

The next day John's father came and testified before the Governor that his son was mad, and added, sadly, "Many times have I heard him talking to himself and speaking of many strange things that none could see or understand. Many times did he sit talking in the silence of the night, using vague words. I heard him calling the ghosts with a voice like that of a sorcerer. You may ask the neighbors who talked to him and found beyond doubt that he was insane. He never answered when one spoke to him, and when he spoke, he uttered cryptic words and phrases unknown to the listener and out of the subject. His mother knows him well. Many times she saw him gazing at the distant horizon with glazed eyes and speaking with passion, like a small child, about the brooks and the flowers and the stars. Ask the monks whose teachings he ridiculed and criticized during their sacred Lent. He is insane, Your Excellency, but he is very kind to me and to his mother; he does much to help us in our old age, and he works with diligence to keep us fed and warm and alive Pity him, and have mercy on us."

The Governor released John, and the news of his madness spread throughout the village. And when the people spoke of John they mentioned his name with humour and ridicule, and the maidens looked upon him with sorrowful eyes and said, "Heaven has its strange purpose in man. . . . God united beauty and insanity in this youth, and joined the kind brightness of his eyes with the darkness of his unseen self."

In the midst of God's fields and prairies, and by the side of the knolls, carpeted with green grass and beautiful flowers, the ghost of John, alone and restless, watches the oxen grazing peacefully, undisturbed by man's hardships. With tearful eyes he looks toward the scattered villages on both sides of the valley and repeats with deep sighs, "You are numerous and I am alone; the wolves prey upon the lambs in the darkness of the night, but the blood stains remain upon the stones in the valley until the dawn comes, and the sun reveals the crime to all."

THE ENCHANTING HOURI

WHERE are you leading me, Oh Enchanting
Houri, and how long shall I follow you
Upon this hispid road, planted with
Thorns? How long shall our souls ascend
And descend painfully on this twisting
And rocky path?

Like a child following his mother I am
Following you, holding the extreme end
Of your garment, forgetting my dreams
And staring at your beauty, blinding
My eyes under your spell to the
Procession of spectres hovering above
Me, and attracted to you by an inner
Force within me which I cannot deny.

Halt for a moment and let me see your
Countenance; and look upon me for a
Moment; perhaps I will learn your
Heart's secrets through your strange
Eyes. Stop and rest, for I am weary,
And my soul is trembling with fear

Upon this horrible trail. Halt, for
We have reached that terrible crossroad
Where Death embraces Life.

Oh Houri, listen to me! I was as free
As the birds, probing the valleys and
The forests, and flying in the spacious
Sky. At eventide I rested upon the
Branches of the trees, meditating the
Temples and palaces in the City of the
Colourful Clouds which the Sun builds
In the morning and destroys before
Twilight.

I was like a thought, walking alone
And at peace to the East and West of
The Universe, rejoicing with the
Beauty and joy of Life, and inquiring
Into the magnificent mystery of
Existence.

I was like a dream, stealing out under
The friendly wings of the night,
Entering through the closed windows
Into the maidens' chambers, frolicking
And awakening their hopes. . . . Then I
Sat by the youths and agitated their
Desires. . . . Then I probed the elders'
Quarters and penetrated their thoughts
Of serene contentment.

Then you captured my fancy, and since
That hypnotic moment I felt like a
Prisoner dragging his shackles and
Impelled into an unknown place. . . .
I became intoxicated with your sweet
Wine that has stolen my will, and I
Now find my lips kissing the hand
That strikes me sharply. Can you
Not see with your soul's eye, the
Crushing of my heart? Halt for a
Moment; I am regaining my strength
And untying my weary feet from the
Heavy chains. I have crushed the
Cup from which I have drunk your
Tasty venom. . . . But now I am in
A strange land, and bewildered;
Which road shall I follow?

My freedom has been restored; will
You now accept me as a willing
Companion, who looks at the Sun
With glazed eyes and grasps the
Fire with untrembling fingers?

I have unbound my wings and I am
Ready to ascend; will you accompany
A youth who spends his days roaming
The mountains like the lone eagle, and
Wastes his nights wandering in the
Deserts like the restless lion?

Will you content yourself with the
Affection of one who looks upon Love
As but an entertainer, and declines
To accept her as his master?

Will you accept a heart that loves,
But never yields? And burns, but
Never melts? Will you be at ease
With a soul that quivers before the
Tempest, but never surrenders to it?
Will you accept one as a companion
Who makes not slaves, nor will become
One? Will you own me but not possess
Me, by taking my body and not my heart?

Then here is my hand—grasp it with
Your beautiful hand; and here is my
Body—embrace it with your loving
Arms; and here are my lips—bestow
Upon them a deep and dizzying kiss.

BEHIND THE GARMENT

RACHEL woke at midnight and gazed intently at something invisible in the sky of her chamber. She heard a voice more soothing than the whispers of Life, and more dismal than the moaning call of the abyss, and softer than the rustling of white wings, and deeper than the message of the waves. . . . It vibrated with hope and with futility, with joy and with misery, and with affection for life, yet with desire for death. Then Rachel closed her eyes and sighed deeply, and gasped, saying, "Dawn has reached the extreme end of the valley; we should go toward the sun and meet him." Her lips were parted, resembling and echoing a deep wound in the soul.

At that moment the priest approached her bed and felt her hand, but found it as cold as the snow; and when he grimly placed his fingers upon her heart, he determined that it was as immobile as the ages, and as silent as the secret of his heart.

The reverend father bowed his head in deep despair. His lips quivered as if wanting to utter a

213

divine word, repeated by the phantoms of the night in the distant and deserted valleys.

After crossing her arms upon her bosom, the priest looked toward a man sitting in an obscured corner of the room, and with a kind and merciful voice he said, "Your beloved has reached the great circle of light. Come, my brother, let us kneel and pray."

The sorrowful husband lifted his head; his eyes stared, gazing at the unseen, and his expression then changed as if he saw understanding in the ghost of an unknown God. He gathered the remnants of himself and walked reverently toward the bed of his wife, and knelt by the side of the clergyman who was praying and lamenting and making the sign of the cross.

Placing his hand upon the shoulder of the grief-stricken husband, the Father said quietly, "Go to the adjoining room, brother, for you are in great need of rest."

He rose obediently, walked to the room and threw his fatigued body upon a narrow bed, and in a few moments he was sailing in the world of sleep like a little child taking refuge in the merciful arms of his loving mother.

The priest remained standing like a statue in the center of the room, and a strange conflict gripped him. And he looked with tearful eyes first at the cold body of the young woman and then through

the parted curtain at her husband, who had surrendered himself to the allure of slumber. An hour,
longer than an age and more terrible than Death,
had already passed, and the priest was still standing
between two parted souls. One was dreaming as a
field dreams of the coming Spring after the tragedy
of Winter, and the other was resting eternally.

Then the priest came close to the body of the
young woman and knelt as if worshipping before
the altar; he held her cold hand and placed it against
his trembling lips, and looked at her face that was
adorned with the soft veil of Death. His voice was
at the same time calm as the night and deep as the·
chasm and faltering as with the hopes of man. And
in voice he wept, "Oh Rachel, bride of my soul,
hear me! At last I am able to talk! Death has opened
my lips so that I can now reveal to you a secret
deeper than Life itself. Pain has unpinioned my
tongue and I can disclose to you my suffering, more
painful than pain. Listen to the cry of my soul, Oh
Pure Spirit, hovering between the earth and the
firmament. Give heed to the youth who waited for
you to come from the field, gazing upon you from
behind the trees, in fear of your beauty. Hear the
priest, who is serving God, calling to you unashamed,
after you have reached the City of God. I have
proved the strength of my love by concealing it!"

Having thus opened his soul, the Father leaned
over and printed three long, warm, and mute kisses
upon her forehead, eyes and throat, pouring forth

all his heart's secret of love and pain, and the anguish of the years. Then he suddenly withdrew to the dark corner and dropped in agony upon the floor, shaking like an Autumn leaf, as if the touch of her cold face had awakened within him the spirit to repent; whereupon he composed himself and knelt, hiding his face with his cupped hands, and he whispered softly, "God. . . . Forgive my sin; forgive my weakness, Oh Lord. I could no longer resist disclosing that which You knew. Seven years have I kept the deep secrets hidden in my heart from the spoken word, until Death came and tore them from me. Help me, Oh God, to hide this terrible and beautiful memory which brings sweetness from life and bitterness from You. Forgive me, My Lord, and forgive my weakness."

Without looking at the young woman's corpse, he continued suffering and lamenting until Dawn came and dropped a rosy veil upon those two still images, revealing the conflict of Love and Religion to one man; the peace of Life and Death to the other.

DEAD ARE MY PEOPLE

(Written in exile during the famine in Syria)

WORLD WAR I

Gone are my people, but I exist yet,
Lamenting them in my solitude. . . .
Dead are my friends, and in their
Death my life is naught but great
Disaster.

The knolls of my country are submerged
By tears and blood, for my people and
My beloved are gone, and I am here
Living as I did when my people and my
Beloved were enjoying life and the
Bounty of life, and when the hills of
My country were blessed and engulfed
By the light of the sun.

My people died from hunger, and he who
Did not perish from starvation was
Butchered with the sword; and I am
Here in this distant land, roaming
Amongst a joyful people who sleep

Upon soft beds, and smile at the days
While the days smile upon them.

My people died a painful and shameful
Death, and here àm I living in plenty
And in peace. . . . This is deep tragedy
Ever-enacted upon the stage of my
Heart; few would care to witness this
Drama, for my people are as birds with
Broken wings, left behind by the flock.

If I were hungry and living amid my
Famished people, and persecuted among
My oppressed countrymen, the burden
Of the black days would be lighter
Upon my restless dreams, and the
Obscurity of the night would be less
Dark before my hollow eyes and my
Crying heart and my wounded soul.
For he who shares with his people
Their sorrow and agony will feel a
Supreme comfort created only by
Suffering in sacrifice. And he will
Be at peace with himself when he dies
Innocent with his fellow innocents.

But I am not living with my hungry
And persecuted people who are walking
In the procession of death toward
Martyrdom. . . . I am here beyond the
Broad seas living in the shadow of

Tranquility, and in the sunshine of
Peace. . . . I am afar from the pitiful
Arena and the distressed, and cannot
Be proud of aught, not even of my own
Tears.

What can an exiled son do for his
Starving people, and of what value
Unto them is the lamentation of an
Absent poet?

Were I an ear of corn grown in the earth
Of my country, the hungry child would
Pluck me and remove with my kernels
The hand of Death from his soul. Were
I a ripe fruit in the gardens of my
Country, the starving woman would
Gather me and sustain life. Were I
A bird flying in the sky of my country,
My hungry brother would hunt me and
Remove with the flesh of my body the
Shadow of the grave from his body.
But alas! I am not an ear of corn
Grown in the plains of Syria, nor a
Ripe fruit in the valleys of Lebanon;
This is my disaster, and this is my
Mute calamity which brings humiliation
Before my soul and before the phantoms
Of the night. . . . This is the painful
Tragedy which tightens my tongue and
Pinions my arms and arrests me usurped

Of power and of will and of action.
This is the curse burned upon my
Forehead before God and man.

And oftentime they say unto me,
"The disaster of your country is
But naught to the calamity of the
World, and the tears and blood shed
By your people are as nothing to
The rivers of blood and tears
Pouring each day and night in the
Valleys and plains of the earth. . . .'

Yes, but the death of my people is
A silent accusation; it is a crime
Conceived by the heads of the unseen
Serpents. . . . It is a songless and
Sceneless tragedy. . . . And if my
People had attacked the despots
And oppressors and died as rebels,
I would have said, "Dying for
Freedom is nobler than living in
The shadow of weak submission, for
He who embraces death with the sword
Of Truth in his hand will eternalize
With the Eternity of Truth, for Life
Is weaker than Death and Death is
Weaker than Truth.

If my nation had partaken in the war
Of all nations and had died in the

Field of battle, I would say that
The raging tempest had broken with
Its might the green branches; and
Strong death under the canopy of
The tempest is nobler than slow
Perishment in the arms of senility.
But there was no rescue from the
Closing jaws. . . . My people dropped
And wept with the crying angels.

If an earthquake had torn my
Country asunder and the earth had
Engulfed my people into its bosom,
I would have said, "A great and
Mysterious law has been moved by
The will of divine force, and it
Would be pure madness if we frail
Mortals endeavoured to probe its
Deep secrets. . . ."
But my people did not die as rebels;
They were not killed in the field
Of battle; nor did the earthquake
Shatter my country and subdue them.
Death was their only rescuer, and
Starvation their only spoils.

My people died on the cross. . . .
They died while their hands
Stretched toward the East and West,
While the remnants of their eyes

Stared at the blackness of the
Firmament. . . . They died silently,
For humanity had closed its ears
To their cry. They died because
They did not befriend their enemy.
They died because they loved their
Neighbours. They died because
They placed trust in all humanity.
They died because they did not
Oppress the oppressors. They died
Because they were the crushed
Flowers, and not the crushing feet.
They died because they were peace
Makers. They perished from hunger
In a land rich with milk and honey.
They died because the monsters of
Hell arose and destroyed all that
Their fields grew, and devoured the
Last provisions in their bins. . . .
They died because the vipers and
Sons of vipers spat out poison into
The space where the Holy Cedars and
The roses and the jasmine breathe
Their fragrance.

My people and your people, my Syrian
Brother, are dead. . . . What can be
Done for those who are dying? Our
Lamentations will not satisfy their
Hunger, and our tears will not quench

Their thirst; what can we do to save
Them from between the iron paws of
Hunger? My brother, the kindness
Which compels you to give a part of
Your life to any human who is in the
Shadow of losing his life is the only
Virtue which makes you worthy of the
Light of day and the peace of the
Night. . . . Remember, my brother,
That the coin which you drop into
The withered hand stretching toward
You is the only golden chain that
Binds your rich heart to the
Loving heart of God. . . .

THE AMBITIOUS VIOLET

THERE was a beautiful and fragrant violet who lived placidly amongst her friends, and swayed happily amidst the other flowers in a solitary garden. One morning, as her crown was embellished with beads of dew, she lifted her head and looked about; she saw a tall and handsome rose standing proudly and reaching high into space, like a burning torch upon an emerald lamp.

The violet opened her blue lips and said, "What an unfortunate am I among these flowers, and how humble is the position I occupy in their presence! Nature has fashioned me to be short and poor. . . . I live very close to the earth and I cannot raise my head toward the blue sky, or turn my face to the sun, as the roses do."

And the rose heard her neighbour's words; she laughed and commented, "How strange is your talk! You are fortunate, and yet you cannot understand your fortune. Nature has bestowed upon you fragrance and beauty which she did not grant to any other. . . . Cast aside your thoughts and be contented, and remember that he who humbles himself will be exalted, and he who exalts himself will be crushed."

The violet answered, "You are consoling me because you have that which I crave. . . . You seek to embitter me with the meaning that you are great. . . . How painful is the preaching of the fortunate to the heart of the miserable! And how severe is the strong when he stands as advisor among the weak!"

And Nature heard the conversation of the violet and the rose; she approached and said, "What has happened to you, my daughter violet? You have been humble and sweet in all your deeds and words. Has greed entered your heart and numbed your senses?" In a pleading voice, the violet answered her, saying, "Oh great and merciful mother, full of love and sympathy, I beg you, with all my heart and soul, to grant my request and allow me to be a rose for one day."

And Nature responded, "You know not what you are seeking; you are unaware of the concealed disaster behind your blind ambition. If you were a rose you would be sorry, and repentance would avail you but naught." The violet insisted, "Change me into a tall rose, for I wish to lift my head high with pride; and regardless of my fate, it will be my own doing." Nature yielded, saying, "Oh ignorant and rebellious violet, I will grant your request. But if calamity befalls you, your complaint must be to yourself."

And Nature stretched forth her mysterious and magic fingers and touched the roots of the violet, who immediately turned into a tall rose, rising above all other flowers in the garden.

At eventide the sky became thick with black clouds, and the raging elements disturbed the silence of existence with thunder, and commenced to attack the garden, sending forth a great rain and strong winds. The tempest tore the branches and uprooted the plants and broke the stems of the tall flowers, sparing only the little ones who grew close to the friendly earth. That solitary garden suffered greatly from the belligerent skies, and when the storm calmed and the sky cleared, all the flowers were laid waste and none of them had escaped the wrath of Nature except the clan of small violets, hiding by the wall of the garden.

Having lifted her head and viewed the tragedy of the flowers and trees, one of the violet maidens smiled happily and called to her companions, saying, "See what the tempest has done to the haughty flowers!" Another violet said, "We are small, and live close to the earth, but we are safe from the wrath of the skies." And a third one added, "Because we are poor in height the tempest is unable to subdue us."

At that moment the queen of violets saw by her

side the converted violet, hurled to earth by the storm and distorted upon the wet grass like a limp soldier in a battle field. The queen of the violets lifted her head and called to her family, saying, "Look, my daughters, and meditate upon that which Greed has done to the violet who became a proud rose for one hour. Let the memory of this scene be a reminder of your good fortune."

And the dying rose moved and gathered the remnants of her strength, and quietly said, "You are contented and meek dullards; I have never feared the tempest. Yesterday I, too, was satisfied and contented with Life, but Contentment has acted as a barrier between my existence and the tempest of Life, confining me to a sickly and sluggish peace and tranquility of mind. I could have lived the same life you are living now by clinging with fear to the earth. . . . I could have waited for winter to shroud me with snow and deliver me to Death, who will surely claim all violets. . . . I am happy now because I have probed outside my little world into the mystery of the Universe . . . something which you have not yet done. I could have overlooked Greed, whose nature is higher than mine, but as I hearkened to the silence of the night, I heard the heavenly world talking to this earthly world, saying, 'Ambition beyond existence is the essential purpose of our being.' At that moment my spirit revolted and my heart longed for a position higher than my limited existence. I realized that the abyss cannot hear the song

of the stars, and at that moment I commenced fighting against my smallness and craving for that which
did not belong to me, until my rebelliousness turned
into a great power, and my longing into a creating
will. . . . Nature, who is the great object of our
deeper dreams, granted my request and changed me
into a rose with her magic fingers."

The rose became silent for a moment, and in a
weakening voice, mingled with pride and achieve-
ment, she said, "I have lived one hour as a proud
rose; I have existed for a time like a queen; I have
looked at the Universe from behind the eyes of the
rose; I have heard the whisper of the firmament
through the ears of the rose and touched the folds of
Light's garment with rose petals. Is there any here
who can claim such honour?" Having thus spoken,
she lowered her head, and with a choking voice she
gasped, "I shall die now, for my soul has attained
its goal. I have finally extended my knowledge to a
world beyond the narrow cavern of my birth. This
is the design of Life. . . . This is the secret of Existence." Then the rose quivered, slowly folded her
petals, and breathed her last with a heavenly smile
upon her lips . . . a smile of fulfillment of hope and
purpose in Life . . . a smile of victory . . . a God's
smile.

THE CRUCIFIED

(WRITTEN ON GOOD FRIDAY)

TODAY, and on this same day of each year, man is startled from his deep slumber and stands before the phantoms of the Ages, looking with tearful eyes toward Mount Calvary to witness Jesus the Nazarene nailed on the Cross. . . . But when the day is over and eventide comes, human kinds return and kneel praying before the idols, erected upon every hilltop, every prairie, and every barter of wheat.

Today, the Christian souls ride on the wing of memories and fly to Jerusalem. There they will stand in throngs, beating upon their bosoms, and staring at Him, crowned with a wreath of thorns, stretching His arms before heaven, and looking from behind the veil of Death into the depths of Life. . . .

But when the curtain of night drops over the stage of the day and the brief drama is concluded, the Christians will go back in groups and lie down in the shadow of oblivion between the quilts of ignorance and slothfulness.

On this one day of each year, the philosophers leave their dark caves, and the thinkers their cold cells, and the poets their imaginary arbors, and all stand reverently upon that silent mountain, listening to the voice of a young man saying of His killers, "Oh Father, forgive them, for they know not what they are doing."

But as dark silence chokes the voices of the light, the philosophers and the thinkers and the poets return to their narrow crevices and shroud their souls with meaningless pages of parchment.

The women who busy themselves in the splendour of Life will bestir themselves today from their cushions to see the sorrowful woman standing before the Cross like a tender sapling before the raging tempest; and when they approach near to her, they will hear a deep moaning and a painful grief.

The young men and women who are racing with the torrent of modern civilization will halt today for a moment, and look backward to see the young Magdalen washing with her tears the blood stains from the feet of a Holy Man suspended between Heaven and Earth; and when their shallow eyes weary of the scene they will depart and soon laugh.

On this day of each year, Humanity wakes with the awakening of the Spring, and stands crying below the suffering Nazarene; then she closes her eyes and surrenders herself to a deep slumber. But

Spring will remain awake, smiling and progressing until merged into Summer, dressed in scented golden raiment. Humanity is a mourner who enjoys lamenting the memories and heroes of the Ages. . . . If Humanity were possessed of understanding, there would be rejoicing over their glory. Humanity is like a child standing in glee by a wounded beast. Humanity laughs before the strengthening torrent which carries into oblivion the dry branches of the trees, and sweeps away with determination all things not fastened to strength.

Humanity looks upon Jesus the Nazarene as a poor-born Who suffered misery and humiliation with all of the weak. And He is pitied, for Humanity believes He was crucified painfully. . . . And all that Humanity offers to Him is crying and wailing and lamentation. For centuries Humanity has been worshipping weakness in the person of the Saviour.

The Nazarene was not weak! He was strong and is strong! But the people refuse to heed the true meaning of strength.

Jesus never lived a life of fear, nor did He die suffering or complaining. . . . He lived as a leader; He was crucified as a crusader; He died with a heroism that frightened His killers and tormentors.

Jesus was not a bird with broken wings; He was a raging tempest who broke all crooked wings. He feared not His persecutors nor His enemies. He suffered not before His killers. Free and brave and daring He was. He defied all despots and oppressors.

He saw the contagious pustules and amputated them. . . . He muted Evil and He crushed False-hood and He choked Treachery.

Jesus came not from the heart of the circle of Light to destroy the homes and build upon their ruins the convents and monasteries. He did not per-suade the strong man to become a monk or a priest, but He came to send forth upon this earth a new spirit, with power to crumble the foundation of any monarchy built upon human bones and skulls. . . . He came to demolish the majestic palaces, con-structed upon the graves of the weak, and crush the idols, erected upon the bodies of the poor. Jesus was not sent here to teach the people to build magnificent churches and temples amidst the cold wretched huts and dismal hovels. . . . He came to make the human heart a temple, and the soul an altar, and the mind a priest.

These were the missions of Jesus the Nazarene, and these are the teachings for which He was cruci-fied. And if Humanity were wise, she would stand today and sing in strength the song of conquest and the hymn of triumph.

Oh, Crucified Jesus, Who are looking sorrowfully from Mount Calvary at the sad procession of the Ages, and hearing the clamour of the dark nations, and understanding the dreams of Eternity . . . Thou art, on the Cross, more glorious and dignified than one thousand kings upon one thousand thrones in one thousand empires. . . .

Thou art, in the agony of death, more powerful than one thousand generals in one thousand wars. . . .

With Thy sorrows, Thou art more joyous than Spring with its flowers. . . .

With Thy suffering, Thou art more bravely silent than the crying angels of heaven. . . .

Before Thy lashers, Thou art more resolute than the mountain of rock. . . .

Thy wreath of thorns is more brilliant and sublime than the crown of Bahram. . . . The nails piercing Thy hands are more beautiful than the sceptre of Jupiter. . . .

The spatters of blood upon Thy feet are more resplendent than the necklace of Ishtar.

Forgive the weak who lament Thee today, for they do not know how to lament themselves. . . .

Forgive them, for they do not know that Thou hast conquered death with death, and bestowed life upon the dead. . . .

Forgive them, for they do not know that Thy strength still awaits them. . . .

Forgive them, for they do not know that every.day is Thy day.

233

EVENTIDE OF THE FEAST

NIGHT had fallen and obscurity engulfed the city while the lights glittered in the palaces and the huts and the shops. The multitudes, wearing their festive raiment, crowded the streets and upon their faces appeared the signs of celebration and contentment.

I avoided the clamour of the throngs and walked alone, contemplating the Man Whose greatness they were honouring, and meditating the Genius of the Ages Who was born in poverty, and lived virtuously, and died on the Cross.

I was pondering the burning torch which was lighted in this humble village in Syria by the Holy Spirit. . . . The Holy Spirit Who hovers over all the ages, and penetrates one civilization and then another through His truth.

As I reached the public garden, I seated myself on a rustic bench and commenced looking between the naked trees toward the crowded streets; I listened to the hymns and songs of the celebrants.

After an hour of deep thinking, I looked sidewise

and was surprised to find a man sitting by me, holding a short branch with which he engraved vague figures on the ground. I was startled, for I had not seen nor heard his approach, but I said within myself, "He is solitary, as I am." And after looking thoroughly at him, I saw that in spite of his old-fashioned raiment and long hair, he was a dignified man, worthy of attention. It seemed that he detected the thoughts within me, for in a deep and quiet voice he said, "Good evening, my son."

"Good evening to you," I responded with respect.

And he resumed his drawing while the strangely soothing sound of his voice was still echoing in my ears. And I spoke to him again, saying, "Are you a stranger in this city?"

"Yes, I am a stranger in this city and every city," he replied. I consoled him, adding, "A stranger should forget that he is an outsider in these holidays, for there is kindness and generosity in the people." He replied wearily, "I am more a stranger in these days than in any other." Having thus spoken, he looked at the clear skies; his eyes probed the stars and his lips quivered as if he had found in the firmament an image of a distant country. His queer statement aroused my interest, and I said, "This is the time of the year when the people are kind to all other people. The rich remember the poor and the strong have compassion for the weak."

He returned, "Yes, the momentary mercy of the rich upon the poor is bitter, and the sympathy of the strong toward the weak is naught but a reminder of superiority."

I affirmed, "Your words have merit, but the weak poor do not care to know what transpires in the heart of the rich, and the hungry never think of the method by which the bread he is craving is kneaded and baked."

And he responded, "The one who receives is not mindful, but the one who gives bears the burden of cautioning himself that it is with a view to brotherly love, and toward friendly aid, and not to self-esteem."

I was amazed at his wisdom, and again commenced to meditate upon his ancient appearance and strange garments. Then I returned mentally and said, "It appears that you are in need of help; will you accept a few coins from me?" And with a sad smile he answered me, saying, "Yes, I am in desperate need, but not of gold or silver."

Puzzled, I asked, "What is it that you require?"

"I am in need of shelter. I am in need of a place where I can rest my head and my thoughts."

"Please accept these two denars and go to the inn for lodging," I insisted.

Sorrowfully he answered, "I have tried every inn, and knocked at every door, but in vain. I have entered every food shop, but none cared to help me. I am hurt, not hungry; I am disappointed, not tired; I seek not a roof, but human shelter."

I said within myself, "What a strange person he

is! Once he talks like a philosopher and again like a madman!" As I whispered these thoughts into the ears of my inner self, he stared at me, lowered his voice to a sad level, and said, "Yes, I am a madman, but even a madman will find himself a stranger without shelter and hungry without food, for the heart of man is empty."

I apologized to him, saying, "I regret my unwitting thought. Would you accept my hospitality and take shelter in my quarters?"

"I knocked at your door and all the doors one thousand times, and received no answer," he answered severely.

Now I was convinced that he was truly a madman, and I suggested, "Let us go now, and proceed to my home."

He lifted his head slowly and said, "If you were aware of my identity you would not invite me to your home."

"Who are you?" I inquired, fearfully, slowly.

With a voice that sounded like the roar of the ocean, he thundered, bitterly, "I am the revolution who builds what the nations destroy. . . . I am the tempest who uproots the plants, grown by the ages. . . . I am the one who came to spread war on earth and not peace, for man is content only in misery!"

And, with tears coursing down his cheeks, he stood up high, and a mist of light grew about him, and he stretched forth his arms, and I saw the marks of the nails in the palms of his hands; I prostrated

237

myself before him convulsively and cried out, saying, "Oh Jesus, the Nazarene!"

And He continued, in anguish, "The people are
celebrating in My honour, pursuing the tradition
woven by the ages around My name, but as to Myself, I am a stranger wandering from East to West
upon this earth, and no one knows of Me. The foxes
have their holes, and the birds of the skies their
nests, but the Son of Man has no place to rest His
head."

At that moment, I opened my eyes, lifted my head,
and looked around, but found naught except a column of smoke before me, and I heard only the shivering voice of the silence of the night, coming from
the depths of Eternity. I collected myself and looked
again to the singing throngs in the distance, and a
voice within me said, "The very strength that protects the heart from injury is the strength that prevents the heart from enlarging to its intended greatness within. The song of the voice is sweet, but the
song of the heart is the pure voice of heaven."

THE GRAVE DIGGER

In the terrible silence of the night, as all heavenly things disappeared behind the grasping veil of thick clouds, I walked lonely and afraid in the Valley of the Phantoms of Death.

As midnight came, and the spectres leaped about me with their horrible, ribbed wings, I observed a giant ghost standing before me, fascinating me with his hypnotic ghastliness. In a thundering voice he said, "Your fear is two-fold! You fear being in fear of me! You cannot conceal it, for you are weaker than the thin thread of the spider. What is your earthly name?"

I leaned against a great rock, gathered myself from this sudden shock, and in a sickly, trembling voice replied, "My name is Abdallah, which means 'slave of God.'" For a few moments he remained silent with a frightening silence. I grew accustomed to his appearance, but was again shaken by his weird thoughts and words, his strange beliefs and contemplations.

He rumbled, "Numerous are the slaves of God,

and great are God's woes with His slaves. Why did not your father call you 'Master of Demons' instead, adding one more disaster to the huge calamity of earth? You cling with terror to the small circle of gifts from your ancestors, and your affliction is caused by your parents' bequest, and you will remain a slave of death until you become one of the dead.

"Your vocations are wasteful and deserted, and your lives are hollow. Real life has never visited you, nor will it; neither will your deceitful self realize your living death. Your illusioned eyes see the people quivering before the tempest of life and you believe them to be alive, while in truth they have been dead since they were born. There were none who would bury them, and the one good career for you is that of grave digger, and as such you may rid the few living of the corpses heaped about the homes, the paths, and the churches."

I protested, "I cannot pursue such a vocation. My wife and children require my support and companionship."

He leaned toward me, showing his braided muscles that seemed as the roots of a strong oak tree, abounding with life and energy, and he bellowed, "Give to each a spade and teach them to dig graves; your life is naught but black misery hidden behind walls of white plaster. Join us, for we genii are the only possessors of reality! The digging of graves brings a slow but positive benefit which causes the vanishing of the dead creatures who tremble with the storm and never walk with it." He mused and then inquired, "What is your religion?"

Bravely I stated, "I believe in God and I honour His prophets; I love virtue and I have faith in eternity."

With remarkable wisdom and conviction he responded, "These empty words were placed on human lips by past ages and not by knowledge, and you actually believe in yourself only; and you honour none but yourself, and you have faith only in the eternity of your desires. Man has worshipped his own self since the beginning, calling that self by appropriate titles, until now, when he employs the word 'God' to mean that same self." Then the giant roared with laughter, the echoes reverberating through the hollows of the caverns, and he taunted, "How strange are those who worship their own selves, their real existence being naught but earthly carcasses!"

He paused, and I contemplated his sayings and meditated their meanings. He possessed a knowledge stranger than life and more terrible than death, and deeper than truth. Timidly, I ventured, "Do you have a religion or a God?"

"My name is The Mad God," he offered, "and I was born at all times, and I am the god of my own self. I am not wise, for wisdom is a quality of the weak. I am strong, and the earth moves under the steps of my feet, and when I stop, the procession of stars stops with me. I mock at the people. . . . I accompany the giants of night. . . . I mingle with the great kings of the genii. . . . I am in possession of the secrets of existence and non-existence.

"In the morning I blaspheme the sun . . . at noontide I curse humanity . . . at eventide I submerge nature . . . at night I kneel and worship myself. I never sleep, for I am time, the sea, and myself. . . . I eat human bodies for food, drink their blood to quench my thirst, and use their dying gasps to draw my breath. Although you deceive yourself, you are my brother and you live as I do. Begone . . . hypocrite! Crawl back to earth and continue to worship your own self amid the living dead!"

I staggered from the rocky, cavernous valley in narcotic bewilderment, scarcely believing what my ears had heard and my eyes had seen! I was torn in pain by some of the truths he had spoken, and wandered trough the fields all that night in melancholy contemplation.

I procured a spade and said within myself, "Dig deeply the graves. . . . Go, now, and wherever you find one of the living dead, bury him in the earth."

Since that day I have been digging graves and burying the living dead. But the living dead are numerous and I am alone, having none to aid me. . . .

HONEYED POISON

IT WAS a beautiful morn of dizzying brilliance in North Lebanon when the people of the village of Tula gathered around the portico of the small church that stood in the midst of their dwellings. They were discussing busily the sudden and unexplained departure of Farris Rahal, who left behind his bride of but half a year.

Farris Rahal was the Sheik and leader of the village, and he had inherited this honourable status from his ancestors who had ruled over Tula for centuries. Although he was not quite twenty-seven years of age, he possessed an outstanding ability and sincerity that won the admiration, reverence, and respect of all the fellahin. When Farris married Susan, the people commented upon him, saying, "What a fortunate man is Farris Rahal! He has attained all that man can hope for in the bounty of life's happiness, and he is but a youth!"

That morning, when all of Tula arose from slumber and learned that the Sheik had gathered his gold, mounted his steed and left the village bidding

243

none farewell, curiosity and concern prevailed, and inquiries were many as to the cause that prompted him to desert his wife and his home, his lands and his vineyards.

By reason of tradition and geography, life in North Lebanon is highly sociable, and the people share their joys and sorrows, provoked by humble spirit and instinctive clannishness. Upon any occurrence, the entire populace of the village convenes to inquire upon the incident, offers all possible assistance, and returns to labour until fate again offers a congregant mission.

It was such a matter that drew the people of Tula from their work that day, and caused them to gather about the church of Mar Tula discussing the departure of their Sheik and exchanging views upon its singularity.

It was at this time that Father Estephan, head of the local church, arrived, and upon his drawn countenance one could read the unmistakable signs of deep suffering, the signs of a painfully wounded spirit. He contemplated the scene for a moment and then spoke. "Do not ask . . . do not ask any question of me! Before daybreak this day, Sheik Farris knocked upon the door of my house, and I saw him holding the rein of his horse, and from his face emanated grave sorrow and agonized grief. Upon my remark as to the strangeness of the hour, he replied, 'Father, I come to bid you farewell, for I am

sailing beyond the oceans and will never again return to this land.' And he handed to me a sealed
envelope, addressed to his dearest friend Nabih
Malik, asking me to deliver it. He mounted his steed
and sped off to the east, affording me no further opportunity to understand the purpose of his unusual
departure."

One of the villagers observed, "Undoubtedly the
missive will reveal to us the secret of his going, for
Nabih is his closest friend." Another added, "Have
you seen his bride, Father?" The priest replied, saying, "I visited her after the morning prayer and
found her standing at the window, staring with unseeing eyes at something invisible, appearing as one
who has lost all senses, and when I endeavoured to
ask concerning Farris she merely said, 'I do not
know! I do not know!' Then she wept like a child
who suddenly becomes an orphan."

As the father concluded talking, the group tight-
ened with fear at the startling report of a gunshot
coming from the east portion of the village, and it
was followed immediately by the bitter wailing of a
woman. The throng was in a dismayed trance of immobility for a moment, and then, men, women and
children, all ran toward the scene, and upon their
faces there was a dark mask of fear and evil omen.
As they reached the garden that surrounded the
Sheik's residence, they became witness to a most horrible drama, portrayed with death. Nabih Malik
was lying on the ground, a stream of blood issuing

THE TREASURED WRITINGS OF KAHLIL GIBRAN

from his breast, and by him stood Susan, wife of the
Sheik Farris Rahal, tearing her hair and shredding
her raiment and flailing her arms about and shrieking wildly, "Nabih . . . Nabih . . . why did you do
it!"

The onlookers were astounded, and it was as
though the unseen hands of fate had clutched with
icy fingers at their hearts. The priest found in the
dead Nabih's right hand the note he had delivered
that morning, and he placed it deftly into his robe
without notice by the milling multitude.

Nabih was carried to his miserable mother, who,
upon seeing the lifeless body of her only son, lost her
sanity in shock and soon joined him in Eternity.
Susan was led slowly into her home, wavering between faltering life and grasping death.

As Father Estephan reached his home, under bent
shoulders, he fastened the door, adjusted his reading
glasses, and in a quivering whisper commenced reading to himself the message he had taken from the
hand of the departed Nabih.

"My Dearest Friend Nabih,

"I must leave this village of my fathers, for my
continued presence is casting misery upon you and
upon my wife and upon myself. You are noble in
spirit, and scorn the betrayal of friend or neighbour,
and although I know that Susan is innocent and
virtuous, I know also that the true love which unites
your heart and her heart is beyond your power and

beyond my hopes. I cannot struggle longer against the mighty will of God, as I cannot halt the strong flow of the great Kadeesha River.

"You have been my sincere friend, Nabih, since we played as children in the fields; and before God, believe me, you remain my friend, I beg you to ponder with good thoughts upon me in the future as you did in the past. Tell Susan that I love her and that I wronged her by taking her in empty marriage. Tell her that my heart bled in burning pain each time I turned from restless sleep in the silence of the night and observed her kneeling before the shrine of Jesus, weeping and beating upon her bosom in anguish.

"There is no punishment so severe as that suffered by the woman who finds herself imprisoned between a man she loves and another man who loves her. Susan suffered through a constant and painful conflict, but performed sorrowfully and honourably and silently her duties as a wife. She tried, but could not choke her honest love for you.

"I am leaving for distant lands and will never again return, for I can no longer act as barrier to a genuine and eternal love, embraced by the enfolded arms of God; and may God, in his inscrutable wisdom, protect and bless both of you.

FARRIS"

Father Estephan folded the letter, returned it to his pocket, and sat by the window that opened upon the distant valley. He sailed long and deep in a great ocean of contemplation, and after wise and intense meditation, he stood suddenly, as if he had found between the plaited folds of his intricate thoughts a delicate and horrible secret, disguised with diabolical slyness, and wrapped with elaborate cunning! He cried out, "How sagacious you are, Farris! How massive, yet simple, is your crime! You sent to him honey blended with fatal poison, and enclosed death in a letter! And when Nabih pointed the weapon at his heart, it was your finger that discharged the missile, and it was your will that engulfed his will. . . . How clever you are, Farris!"

He returned quivering to his chair, shaking his head and combing his beard with his fingers, and upon his lips appeared a smile whose meaning was more terrible than the tragedy itself. He opened his prayer book and commenced reading and pondering, and at intervals he raised his head to hear the wailing and lamentation of the women, coming from the heart of the village of Tula, close by the Holy Cedars of Lebanon.

BOOK ELEVEN

SPIRITS REBELLIOUS

MADAME ROSE HANIE

Miserable is the man
who loves a woman and takes her for a wife, pouring at her feet the sweat of his skin and the blood
of his body and the life of his heart, and placing in
her hands the fruit of his toil and the revenue of his
diligence; for when he slowly wakes up, he finds
that the heart, which he endeavoured to buy, is given
freely and in sincerity to another man for the enjoyment of its hidden secrets and deepest love. Miserable is the woman who arises from the inattentive-
ness and restlessness of youth and finds herself in the
home of a man showering her with his glittering
gold and precious gifts and according her all the
honors and grace of lavish entertainment but unable
to satisfy her soul with the heavenly wine which God
pours from the eyes of a man into the heart of a
woman.

I knew Rashid Bey Namaan since I was a young-
ster; he was a Lebanese, born and reared in the City
of Beyrouth. Being a member of an old and rich

family which preserved the tradition and glory of his ancestry, Rashid was fond of citing incidents that dealt mainly with the nobility of his forefathers. In his routine life he followed their beliefs and customs which, at that time, prevailed in the Middle East.

Rashid Bey Namaan was generous and good-hearted, but like many of the Syrians, looked only at the superficial things instead of reality. He never hearkened to the dictates of his heart, but busied himself in obeying the voices of his environment. He amused himself with shimmering objects that blinded his eyes and heart to life's secrets; his soul was diverted away from an understanding of the law of nature, and to a temporary self-gratification. He was one of those men who hastened to confess their love or disgust to the people, then regretted their impulsiveness when it was too late for recall. And then shame and ridicule befell them, instead of pardon or sanction.

These are the characteristics that prompted Rashid Bey Namaan to marry Rose Hanie far before her soul embraced his soul in the shadow of the true love that makes union a paradise.

After a few years of absence, I returned to the City of Beyrouth. As I went to visit Rashid Bey Namaan, I found him pale and thin. On his face one could see the spectre of bitter disappointment; his sorrowful eyes bespoke his crushed heart and melancholy soul. I was curious to find the cause for his miserable plight; however, I did not hesitate to ask for explanation and said, "What became of you, Rashid? Where is the radiant smile and the happy countenance that accompanied you since childhood? Has death taken away from you a dear friend? Or have the black nights stolen from you the gold you have amassed during the white days? In the name of friendship, tell me what is causing this sadness of heart and weakness of body?"

He looked at me ruefully, as if I had revived to him some secluded images of beautiful days. With a distressed and faltering voice he responded, "When a person loses a friend, he consoles himself with the many other friends about him, and if he loses his gold, he meditates for a while and casts misfortune from his mind, especially when he finds himself healthy and still laden with ambition. But when a man loses the ease of his heart, where can he find comfort, and with what can he replace it? What mind can master it? When Death strikes close by, you will suffer. But when the day and night pass, you will feel the smooth touch of the soft fingers of Life; then you will smile and rejoice.

"Destiny comes suddenly, bringing concern; she stares at you with horrible eyes and clutches you at the throat with sharp fingers and hurls you to the ground and tramples upon you with ironclad feet; then she laughs and walks away, but later regrets her actions and asks you through good fortune to forgive her. She stretches forth her silky hand and lifts you high and sings to you the Song of Hope and causes you to lose your cares. She creates in you a new zest for confidence and ambition. If your lot in life is a beautiful bird that you love dearly, you gladly feed to him the seeds of your inner self, and make your heart his cage and your soul his nest. But while you are affectionately admiring him and looking upon him with the eyes of love, he escapes from your hands and flies very high; then he descends and enters into another cage and never comes back to you. What can you do? Where can you find patience and condolence? How can you revive your hopes and dreams? What power can still your turbulent heart?"

Having uttered these words with a choking voice and suffering spirit, Rashid Bey Namaan stood shaking like a reed between the north and south wind. He extended his hands as if to grasp something with his bent fingers and destroy it. His wrinkled face was livid, his eyes grew larger as he stared a few moments, and it seemed to him as if he saw a demon appearing from nonexistence to take him away; then he fixed his eyes on mine and his appearance suddenly changed; his anger was converted into keen suffering and distress, and he cried out saying, "It is the woman whom I rescued from between the deathly paws of poverty; I opened my coffers to her and made her envied by all women for the beautiful raiment and precious gems and magnificent carriages drawn by spirited horses; the woman whom my heart has loved and at whose feet I poured my affection; the woman, to whom I was a true friend, sincere companion and a faithful husband; the woman who betrayed me and departed me for another man to share with him destitution and partake his evil bread, kneaded with shame and mixed with disgrace. The woman I loved; the beautiful bird whom I fed, and to whom I made my heart a cage, and my soul a nest, has escaped from my hands and entered into another cage; that pure angel, who resided in the paradise of my affection and love, now appears to me as a horrible demon, descended into the darkness to suffer for her sin and cause me to suffer on earth for her crime."

He hid his face with his hands as if wanting to protect himself from himself, and became silent for a moment. Then he sighed and said, "This is all I can tell you; please do not ask anything further. Do not make a crying voice of my calamity, but let it rather be mute misfortune; perhaps it will grow in silence and deaden me away so that I may rest at last with peace."

I rose with tears in my eyes and mercy in my heart, and silently bade him goodbye; my words had no power to console his wounded heart, and my knowledge had no torch to illuminate his gloomy self.

PART TWO

A few days thereafter I met Madame Rose Hanie for the first time, in a poor hovel, surrounded by

flowers and trees. She had heard of me through
Rashid Bey Namaan, the man whose heart she had
crushed and stamped upon and left under the terrible hoofs of Life. As I looked at her beautiful
bright eyes, and heard her sincere voice, I said to
myself, "Can this be the sordid woman? Can this
clear face hide an ugly soul and a criminal heart? Is
this the unfaithful wife? Is this the woman of whom
I have spoken evil and imagined as a serpent disguised in the form of a beautiful bird?" Then I whispered again to myself saying, "Is it this beautiful
face that made Rashid Bey Namaan miserable?
Haven't we heard that obvious beauty is the cause of
many hidden distresses and deep suffering? Is not the
beautiful moon, that inspires the poets, the same
moon that angers the silence of the sea with a terrible roar?"

As we seated ourselves, Madame Hanie seemed to
have heard and read my thoughts and wanted not
to prolong my doubts. She leaned her beautiful head
upon her hands and with a voice sweeter than the
sound of the lyre, she said, "I have never met you,
but I heard the echoes of your thoughts and dreams
from the mouths of the people, and they convinced
me that you are merciful and have understanding
for the oppressed woman—the woman whose heart's
secrets you have discovered and whose affections you
have known. Allow me to reveal to you the full contents of my heart so you may know that Rose Hanie
never was an unfaithful woman.

"I was scarcely eighteen years of age when fate led me to Rashid Bey Namaan, who was then forty years old. He fell in love with me, according to what the people say, and took me for a wife and put me in his magnificent home, placing at my disposal servants and maids and dressing me with expensive clothes and precious gems. He exhibited me as a strange rarity at the homes of his friends and family; he smiled with triumph when he saw his contemporaries looking upon me with surprise and admiration; he lifted his chin high with pride when he heard the ladies speak of me with praise and affection. But never could he hear the whispers, 'Is this the wife of Rashid Bey Namaan, or his adopted daughter?' And another one commenting, 'If he had married at the proper age, his first born would have been older than Rose Hanie.'

"All that happened before my life had awakened from the deep swoon of youth, and before God inflamed my heart with the torch of love, and before the growth of the seeds of my affections. Yes, all this transpired during the time when I believed that real happiness came through beautiful clothes and magnificent mansions. When I woke up from the slumber of childhood, I felt the flames of sacred fire burning in my heart, and a spiritual hunger gnawing at my soul, making it suffer. When I opened my eyes, I found my wings moving to the right and left, trying to ascend into the spacious firmament of love, but shivering and dropping under the gusts of the shackles of laws that bound my body to a man before I knew the true meaning of that law. I felt all these things and knew that a woman's happiness does not come through man's glory and honour, nor through his generosity and affection, but through love that unites both of their hearts and affections, making them one member of life's body and one word upon the lips of God. When Truth showed herself to me, I found myself imprisoned by law in the mansion of Rashid Bey Nemaan, like a thief stealing his bread and hiding in the dark and friendly corners of the night. I knew that every hour spent with him was a terrible lie written upon my forehead with letters of fire before heaven and earth. I could not give him my love and affection in reward for his generosity and sincerity. I tried in vain to love him, but love is a power that makes our hearts, yet our hearts cannot make that power. I prayed and prayed in the silence of the night before God to create in the depths of my heart a spiritual attachment that would carry me closer to the man who had been chosen for me as a companion through life.

"My prayers were not granted, because Love descends upon our souls by the will of God and not by the demand or the plea of the individual. Thus I remained for two years in the home of that man, envying the birds of the field their freedom while my friends envied me my painful chains of gold. I was like a woman who is torn from her only child; like a lamenting heart, existing without attachment;

like an innocent victim of the severity of human law.
I was close to death from spiritual thirst and hunger.

"One dark day, as I looked behind the heavy skies,
I saw a gentle light pouring from the eyes of a man
who was walking forlornly on the path of life; I
closed my eyes to that light and said to myself, 'Oh,
my soul, darkness of the grave is thy lot, do not be
greedy for the light.' Then I heard a beautiful
melody from heaven that revived my wounded heart
with its .purity, but I closed my ears and said, 'Oh,
my soul, the cry of the abyss is thy lot, do not be
greedy for heavenly songs.' I closed my eyes again so
I could not see, and shut my ears so I could not hear,
but my closed eyes still saw that gentle light, and my
ears still heard that divine sound. I was frightened
for the first time and felt like the beggar who found
a precious jewel near the Emir's palace and could
not pick it up on account of fear, or leave it because
of poverty. I cried—a cry of a thirsty soul who sees
a brook surrounded by wild beasts, and falls upon
the ground waiting and watching fearfully."

Then she turned her eyes away from me as if she
remembered the past that made her ashamed to face
me, but she continued, "Those people who go back
to eternity before they taste the sweetness of real
life are unable to understand the meaning of a
woman's suffering. Especially when she devotes her
soul to a man she loves by the will of God, and her
body to another whom she caresses by the enforce-

ment of earthly law. It is a tragedy written with the woman's blood and tears which the man reads with ridicule because he cannot understand it; yet, if he does understand, his laughter will turn into scorn and blasphemy that act like fire upon her heart. It is a drama enacted by the black nights upon the stage of a woman's soul, whose body is tied up into a man, known to her as husband, ere she perceives God's meaning of marriage. She finds her soul hovering about the man whom she adores by all agencies of pure and true love and beauty. It is a terrible agony that began with the existence of weakness in a woman and the commencement of strength in a man. It will not end unless the days of slavery and superiority of the strong over the weak are abolished. It is a horrible war between the corrupt law of humanity and the sacred affections and holy purpose of the heart. In such a battlefield I was lying yesterday, but I gathered the remnants of my strength, and unchained my irons of cowardice, and untied my wings from the swaddles of weakness and arose into the spacious sky of love and freedom.

"Today I am one with the man I love, he and I sprang out as one torch from the hand of God before the beginning of the world. There is no power under the sun that can take my happiness from me, because it emanated from two embraced spirits, engulfed by understanding, radiated by Love, and protected by heaven."

She looked at me as if she wanted to penetrate

my heart with her eyes in order to discover the impression of her words upon me, and to hear the echo of her voice from within me; but I remained silent and she continued. Her voice was full of bitterness of memory and sweetness of sincerity and freedom when she said, "The people will tell you that Rose Hanie is an heretic and unfaithful woman who followed her desires by leaving the man who elated her into him and made her the elegance of his home. They will tell you that she is an adulteress and prostitute who destroyed with her filthy hands the wreath of a sacred marriage and replaced it with a besmirched union woven of the thorns of hell. She took off the garment of virtue and put on the cloak of sin and disgrace. They will tell you more than that, because the ghosts of their fathers are still living in their bodies. They are like the deserted caves of the mountains that echo voices whose meanings are not understood. They neither understand the law of God, nor comprehend the true intent of veritable religion, nor distinguish between a sinner and an innocent. They look only at the surface of objects without knowing their secrets. They pass their verdicts with ignorance, and judge with blindness, making the criminal and the innocent, the good and the bad, equal. Woe to those who prosecute and judge the people. . . .

"In God's eyes I was unfaithful and an adulteress only while at the home of Rashid Bey Namaan, because he made me his wife according to the customs and traditions and by the force of haste, before heaven had made him mine in conformity with the spiritual law of Love and Affection. I was a sinner in the eyes of God and myself when I ate his bread and offered him my body in reward for his generosity. Now I am pure and clean because the law of Love has freed me and made me honourable and faithful. I ceased selling my body for shelter and my days for clothes. Yes, I was an adulteress and a criminal when the people viewed me as the most honourable and faithful wife; today I am pure and noble in spirit, but in their opinion I am polluted, for they judge the soul by the outcome of the body and measure the spirit by the standard of matter."

Then she looked through the window and pointed out with her right hand toward the city as if she had seen the ghost of corruption and the shadow of shame among its magnificent buildings. She said pityingly, "Look at those majestic mansions and sublime palaces where hypocrisy resides; in those edifices and between their beautifully decorated walls resides Treason beside Putridity; under the ceiling painted with melted gold lives Falsehood beside Pretension. Notice those gorgeous homes that represent happiness, glory and domination; they are naught but caverns of misery and distress. They are plastered graves in which Treason of the weak woman hides behind her kohled eyes and crimsoned lips; in their corners selfishness exists, and the animality of man through his gold and silver rules supreme.

"If those high and impregnable buildings scented the odor of hatred, deceit and corruption, they would have cracked and fallen. The poor villager looks upon those residences with tearful eyes, but when he finds that the hearts of the occupants are empty of that pure love that exists in the heart of his wife and fills its domain, he will smile and go back to his fields contented."

And then she took hold of my hand and led me to the side of the window and said, "Come, I will show you the unveiled secrets of those people whose path I refused to follow. Look at that palace with giant columns. In it lives a rich man who inherited his gold from his father. After having led a life of filth and putrefaction, he married a woman about whom he knew nothing except that her father was one of the Sultan's dignitaries. As soon as the wedding trip was over he became disgusted and commenced associations with women who sell their bodies for pieces of silver. His wife was left alone in that palace like an empty bottle left by a drunkard. She cried and suffered for the first time; then she realized that her tears were more precious than her degenerate husband. Now she is busying herself in the love and devotion of a young man upon whom she showers her joyous hours, and into whose heart she pours her sincere love and affection.

"Let me take you now to that gorgeous home surrounded by beautiful gardens. It is the home of a man who comes from a noble family which ruled the country for many generations, but whose standards, wealth, and prestige have declined due to their indulgence in mad spending and slothfulness. A few years ago this man married an ugly but rich woman. After he acquired her fortune, he ignored her completely and commenced devoting himself to an attractive young woman. His wife today is devoting her time to curling her hair, painting her lips and perfuming her body. She wears the most expensive clothes and hopes that some young man will smile and come to visit her, but it is all in vain, for she cannot succeed except in receiving a smile from her ugly self in the mirror.

"Observe that big manor, encircled with marble statuary; it is the home of a beautiful woman who possesses strange character. When her first husband died, she inherited all his money and estates; then she selected a man with a weak mind and feeble body and became his wife to protect herself from the evil tongues, and to use him as a shield for her abominations. She is now among her admirers like a bee that sucks the sweetest and most delicious flowers.

"That beautiful home next to it was built by the greatest architect in the province; it belongs to a greedy and substantial man who devotes all of his time to amassing gold and grinding the faces of the poor. He has a wife of supernatural beauty, bodily and spiritually, but she is like the rest, a victim of early marriage. Her father committed a crime by giving her away to a man before she attained understanding age, placing on her neck the heavy yoke of corrupt marriage. She is thin and pale now, and cannot find an outlet for her imprisoned affection. She is sinking slowly and craving for death to free her from the mesh of slavery and deliver her from a man who spends his life gathering gold and cursing the hour he married a barren woman who could not bring him a child to carry on his name and inherit his money.

"In that home among those orchards lives an ideal poet; he married an ignorant woman who ridicules his works because she cannot understand them, and laughs at his conduct because she cannot adjust herself to his sublime way of life. That poet found freedom from despair in his love for a married woman who appreciates his intelligence and inspires him by kindling in his heart the torch of affections, and revealing to him the most beautiful and eternal sayings by means of her charm and beauty."

Silence prevailed for a few moments, and Madame Hanie seated herself on a sofa by the window as if her soul were tired of roaming those quarters. Then she slowly continued, "These are the residences in which I refused to live; these are the graves in which I, too, was spiritually buried. Those people from whom I have freed myself are the ones who become attracted by the body and repelled by the spirit, and who know naught of Love and Beauty. The only mediator between them and God is God's pity for their ignorance of the law of God. I cannot judge, for I was one of them, but I sympathize with all my heart. I do not hate them, but I hate their surrender to weakness and falsehood. I have said all these things to show you the reality of people from whom I have escaped against their will. I was trying to explain to you the life of persons who speak every evil against me because I have lost their friendship and finally gained my own. I emerged from their dark dungeon and directed my eyes towards the light where sincerity, truth and justice prevail. They have exiled me now from their society and I am pleased, because humanity does not exile except the one whose noble spirit rebels against despotism and oppression. He who does not prefer exile to slavery is not free by any measure of freedom, truth and duty.

"Yesterday I was like a tray containing all kinds of palatable food, and Rashid Bey Namaan never approached me unless he felt a need for that food; yet both of our souls remained far apart from us like two humble, dignified servants. I have tried to reconcile myself to what people call misfortune, but my spirit refused to spend all its life kneeling with me before a horrible idol erected by the dark ages and called LAW. I kept my chains until I heard Love calling me and saw my spirit preparing to embark. Then I broke them and walked out from Rashid Bey Namaan's home like a bird freed from his iron cage and leaving behind me all the gems, clothes and servants. I came to live with my beloved, for I knew that what I was doing was honest. Heaven does not want me to weep and suffer. Many times at night I prayed for dawn to come and when dawn came, I prayed for the day to be over. God does not want me to lead a miserable life, for He placed in the depths of my heart a desire for happiness; His glory rests in the happiness of my heart.

"This is my story and this my protest before heaven and earth; this is what I sing and repeat while the people are closing their ears for fear of hearing me and leading their spirits into rebellion that would crumble the foundation of their quavering society.

"This is the rough pathway I have carved until I reached the mountain peak of my happiness. Now if death comes to take me away, I will be more than willing to offer myself before the Supreme Throne of Heaven without fear or shame. I am ready for the day of judgment and my heart is white as the snow. I have obeyed the will of God in everything I have done and followed the call of my heart while listening to the angelic voice of heaven. This is my drama which the people of Beyrouth call 'A curse upon the lips of life,' and 'An ailment in the body of society.' But one day love will arouse their hearts like the sun rays that bring forth the flowers even from contaminated earth. One day the wayfarers will stop by my grave and greet the earth that enfolds my body and say, 'Here lies Rose Hanie who freed herself from the slavery of decayed human laws in order to comply with God's law of pure love. She turned her face toward the sun so she would not see the shadow of her body amongst the skulls and thorns.' "

The door was opened and a man entered. His eyes were shining with magic rays and upon his lips appeared a wholesome smile. Madame Hanie rose, took the young man's arm and introduced him to me, then gave him my name with flattering words. I knew that he was the one for whose sake she denied the whole world and violated all earthly laws and customs.

As we sat down, silence controlled. Each one of us was engrossed in deep thought. One minute worthy of silence and respect had passed when I looked at the couple sitting side by side. I saw something I had never seen before, and realized instantly the meaning of Madame Hanie's story. I comprehended the secret of her protest against the society which persecutes those who rebel against confining laws and customs before determining the cause for the rebellion. I saw one heavenly spirit before me, composed of two beautiful and united persons, in the midst of which stood the god of Love stretching his wings over them to protect them from evil tongues. I found a complete understanding emanating from two smiling faces, illuminated by sincerity and surrounded by virtue. For the first time in my life I found the phantom of happiness standing between a man and a woman, cursed by religion and opposed by the law. I rose and bade them goodbye and left that poor hovel which Affection had erected as an altar to Love and Understanding. I walked past the buildings which Madame Hanie pointed out to me. As I reached the end of these quarters I remembered Rashid Bey Namaan and meditated his miserable plight and said to myself, "He is oppressed; will heaven ever listen to him if he complains about Madame Hanie? Had that woman done wrong when she left him and followed the freedom of her heart? Or did he commit a crime by subduing her body in marriage before subduing her heart in love? Which of the two is the oppressed and which is the oppressor? Who is the criminal and who is the innocent?"

Then I resumed talking to myself after a few moments of deep thinking. "Many times deception had tempted woman to leave her husband and follow wealth, because her love for riches and beautiful raiment blinds her and leads her into shame. Was Madame Hanie deceitful when she left her rich husband's palace for a poor man's hut? Many times ignorance kills a woman's honour and revives her passion; she grows tired and leaves her husband, prompted by her desires, and follows a man to whom she lowers herself. Was Madame Hanie an ignorant woman following her physical desires when she declared publicly her independence and joined her beloved young man? She could have satisfied herself secretly while at her husband's home, for many men were willing to be the slaves of her beauty and martyrs of her love. Madame Hanie was a miserable woman. She sought only happiness, found it, and embraced it. This is the very truth which society disrespects." Then I whispered through the ether and inquired of myself, "Is it permissible for a woman to buy her happiness with her husband's misery?" And my soul added, "Is it lawful for a man to enslave his wife's affection when he realizes he will never possess it?"

I continued walking and Madame Hanie's voice was still sounding in my ears when I reached the extreme end of the city. The sun was disappearing and silence ruled the fields and prairies while the birds commenced singing their evening prayers. I stood there meditating, and then I sighed and said, "Before the throne of Freedom, the trees rejoice with the frolicsome breeze and enjoy the rays of the sun and the beams of the moon. Through the ears of Freedom these birds whisper and around Freedom they flutter to the music of the brooks. Throughout the sky of Freedom these flowers breathe their fragrance and before Freedom's eyes they smile when dawn comes.

"Everything on earth lives according to the law of nature, and from that law emerges the glory and joy of liberty; but man is denied this fortune, because he set for the God-given soul a limited and earthly law of his own. He made for himself strict rules. Man built a narrow and painful prison in which he secluded his affections and desires. He dug out a deep grave in which he buried his heart and its purpose. If an individual, through the dictates of his soul, declares his withdrawal from society and violates the law, his fellowmen will say he is a rebel worthy of exile, or an infamous creature worthy only of execution. Will man remain a slave of self-confinement until the end of the world? Or will he be freed by the passing of time and live in the Spirit for the Spirit? Will man insist upon staring downward and backward at the earth? Or will he turn his eyes toward the sun so he will not see the shadow of his body amongst the skulls and thorns?"

THE CRY OF THE GRAVES

PART ONE

Tʜᴇ Eᴍɪʀ walked into the court room and took the central chair while at his right and left sat the wise men of the country. The guards, armed with swords and spears, stood in attention, and the people who came to witness the trial rose and bowed ceremoniously to the Emir whose eyes emanated a power that revealed horror to their spirits and fear to their hearts. As the court came to order and the hour of judgment approached, the Emir raised his hand and shouted saying, "Bring forth the criminals singly and tell me what crimes they have committed." The prison door opened like the mouth of a ferocious yawning beast. In the obscure corners of the dungeon one could hear the echo of shackles rattling in unison with the moaning and lamentations of the prisoners. The spectators were eager to see the prey of Death emerging from the depths of that inferno. A few moments later, two soldiers came out leading a young man with his arms pinioned behind his back. His stern

272

face bespoke nobility of spirit and strength of the heart. He was halted in the middle of the court room and the soldiers marched a few steps to the rear. The Emir stared at him steadily and said, "What crime has this man, who is proudly and triumphantly standing before me, committed?" One of the courtmen responded, "He is a murderer; yesterday he slew one of the Emir's officers who was on an important mission in the surrounding villages; he was still grasping the bloody sword when he was arrested." The Emir retorted with anger, "Return the man to the dark prison and tie him with heavy chains, and at dawn cut off his head with his own sword and throw his body in the woods so that the beasts may eat the flesh, and the air may carry its remindful odor into the noses of his family and friends." The youth was returned to prison while the people looked upon him with sorrowful eyes, for he was a young man in the spring of life.

The soldiers returned back again from the prison leading a young woman of natural and frail beauty. She looked pale and upon her face appeared the signs of oppression and disappointment. Her eyes were soaked with tears and her head was bent under the burden of grief. After eyeing her thoroughly, the Emir exclaimed, "And this emaciated woman, who is standing before me like the shadow beside a corpse, what has she done?" One of the soldiers answered him, saying, "She is an adulteress; last night her husband discovered her in the arms of another.

273

After her lover escaped, her husband turned her over to the law." The Emir looked at her while she raised her face without expression, and he ordered, "Take her back to the dark room and stretch her upon a bed of thorns so she may remember the resting place which she polluted with her fault; give her vinegar mixed with gall to drink so she may remember the taste of those sweet kisses. At dawn drag her naked body outside the city and stone her. Let the wolves enjoy the tender meat of her body and the worms pierce her bones." As she walked back to the dark cell, the people looked upon her with sympathy and surprise. They were astonished with the Emir's justice and grieved over her fate. The soldiers reappeared, bringing with them a sad man with shaking knees and trembling like a tender sapling before the north wind. He looked powerless, sickly and frightened, and he was miserable and poor. The Emir stared at him loathfully and inquired, "And this filthy man, who is like dead amongst the living; what has he done?" One of the guards returned, "He is a thief who broke into the monastery and stole the sacred vases which the priests found under his garment when they arrested him."

As a hungry eagle who looks at a bird with broken wings, the Emir looked at him and said, "Take him back to the jail and chain him, and at dawn drag him into a lofty tree and hang him between heaven and earth so his sinful hands may perish and the members of his body may be turned into particles and scattered by the wind." As the thief stumbled back into the depths of the prison, the people commenced whispering one to another saying, "How dare such a weak and heretic man steal the sacred vases of the monastery?"

At this time the court adjourned and the Emir walked out accompanied by all his wise men, guarded by the soldiers, while the audience scattered and the place became empty except of the moaning and wailing of the prisoners. All this happened while I was standing there like a mirror before passing ghosts. I was meditating the laws, made by man for man, contemplating what the people call "justice," and engrossing myself with deep thoughts of the secrets of life. I tried to understand the meaning of the universe. I was dumbfounded in finding myself lost like a horizon that disappears beyond the cloud. As I left the place I said to myself, "The vegetable feeds upon the elements of the earth, the sheep eats the vegetable, the wolf preys upon the sheep, and the bull kills the wolf while the lion devours the bull; yet Death claims the lion. Is there any power that will overcome Death and make these brutalities an eternal justice? Is there a force that can convert all the ugly things into beautiful objects? Is there any might that can clutch with its hands all the elements of life and embrace them with joy as the sea joyfully engulfs all the brooks into its depths? Is there any power that can arrest the murdered and the murderer, the adulteress and the adulterer, the robber and the robbed, and bring them to a court loftier and more supreme than the court of the Emir?"

PART TWO

The next day I left the city for the fields where silence reveals to the soul that which the spirit desires, and where the pure sky kills the germs of despair, nursed in the city by the narrow streets and obscured places. When I reached the valley, I saw a flock of crows and vultures soaring and descending, filling the sky with cawing, whistling and rustling of the wings. As I proceeded I saw before me a corpse of a man hanged high in a tree, the body of a dead naked woman in the midst of a heap of stones, and a carcass of a youth with his head cut off and soaked with blood mixed with earth. It was a horrible sight that blinded my eyes with a thick, dark veil of sorrows. I looked in every direction and saw naught except the spectre of Death standing by those ghastly remains. Nothing could be heard except the wailing of non-existence, mingled with the cawing of crows hovering about the victims of human laws. Three human beings, who yesterday were in the lap of Life, today fell as victims to Death because they broke the rules of human society. When a man kills another man, the people say he is a murderer, but when the Emir kills him, the Emir is just. When a man robs a monastery, they say he is a thief, but when the Emir robs him of his life, the Emir is honourable. When a woman betrays her husband, they say she is an adulteress, but when the Emir makes her walk naked in the streets and stones her later, the Emir is noble. Shedding of blood is forbidden, but who made it lawful for the Emir? Stealing one's money is a crime, but taking away one's life is a noble act. Betrayal of a husband may be an ugly deed, but stoning of living souls is a beautiful sight. Shall we meet evil with evil and say this is the Law? Shall we fight corruption with greater corruption and say this is the Rule? Shall we conquer crimes with more crimes and say this is Justice? Had not the Emir killed an enemy in his past life? Had he not robbed his weak subjects of money and property? Had he not committed adultery? Was he infallible when he killed the murderer and hanged the thief and stoned the adulteress? Who are those who hanged the thief in the tree? Are they angels descended from heaven, or men looting and usurping? Who cut off the murderer's head? Are they divine prophets, or soldiers shedding blood wherever they go? Who stoned that adulteress? Were they virtuous hermits who came from their monasteries, or humans who loved to commit atrocities with glee, under the protection of ignorant Law? What is Law? Who saw it coming with the sun from the depths of heaven? What human saw the heart of God and found its will or purpose? In what century did the angels walk among the people and preach to them, saying, "Forbid the weak from enjoying life, and kill the outlaws with the sharp edge of the sword, and step upon the sinners with iron feet?"

As my mind suffered in this fashion, I heard a rustling of feet in the grass close by. I took heed and say a young woman coming from behind the trees; she looked carefully in every direction before she approached the three carcasses that were there. As she glanced, she saw the youth's head that was cut off. She cried fearfully, knelt, and embraced it with her trembling arms; then she commenced shedding tears and touching the blood-matted, curly hair with her soft fingers, crying in a voice that came from the remnants of a shattered heart. She could bear the sight no longer. She dragged the body to a ditch and placed the head gently between the shoulders, covered the entire body with earth, and upon the grave she planted the sword with which the head of the young man had been cut off.

As she started to leave, I walked toward her. She trembled when she saw me, and her eyes were heavy with tears. She sighed and said, "Turn me over to the Emir if you wish. It is better for me to die and follow the one who saved my life from the grip of disgrace than to leave his corpse as food for the ferocious beasts." Then I responded, "Fear me not, poor girl, I have lamented the young man before you did. But tell me, how did he save you from the grip of disgrace?" She replied with a choking and fainting voice, "One of the Emir's officers came to our farm to collect the tax; when he saw me, he looked upon me as a wolf looks upon a lamb. He imposed on my father a heavy tax that even a rich man could not pay. He arrested me as a token to take to the Emir in ransom for the gold which my father was unable to give. I begged him to spare me, but he took no heed, for he had no mercy. Then I cried for help, and this young man, who is dead now, came to my help and saved me from a living death. The officer attempted to kill him, but this man took an old sword that was hanging on the wall of our home and stabbed him. He did not run away like a criminal, but stood by the dead officer until the law came and took him into custody." Having uttered these words which would make any human heart bleed with sorrow, she turned her face and walked away.

In a few moments I saw a youth coming and hiding his face with a cloak. As he approached the corpse of the adulteress, he took off the garment and placed it upon her naked body. Then he drew a dagger from under the cloak and dug a pit in which he placed the dead girl with tenderness and care, and covered her with earth upon which he poured his tears. When he finished his task, he plucked some flowers and placed them reverently upon the grave. As he started to leave, I halted him saying, "What kin are you to this adulteress? And what prompted you to endanger your life by coming here to protect her naked body from the ferocious beasts?" When he stared at me, his sorrowful eyes bespoke his misery, and he said, "I am the unfortunate man for whose love she was stoned; I loved her and she loved me since childhood; we grew together; Love, whom

we served and revered, was the lord of our hearts.
Love joined both of us and embraced our souls. One
day I absented myself from the city, and upon my
return I discovered that her father obliged her to
marry a man she did not love. My life became a perpetual struggle, and all my days were converted into
one long and dark night. I tried to be at peace with
my heart, but my heart would not be still. Finally I
went to see her secretly and my sole purpose was to
have a glimpse of her beautiful eyes and hear the
sound of her serene voice. When I reached her house
I found her lonely, lamenting her unfortunate self.
I sat by her; silence was our important conversation
and virtue our companion. One hour of understanding quiet passed, when her husband entered. I cau-
tioned him to contain himself but he dragged her
with both hands into the street and cried out saying, "Come, come and see the adulteress and her
lover!" All the neighbours rushed about and later
the law came and took her to the Emir, but I was
not touched by the soldiers. The ignorant Law and
sodden customs punished the woman for her father's
fault and pardoned the man."

Having thus spoken, the man turned toward the
city while I remained pondering the corpse of the
thief hanging in that lofty tree and moving slightly
every time the wind shook the branches, waiting for
someone to bring him down and stretch him upon
the bosom of the earth beside the Defender of
Honour and Martyr of Love. An hour later, a frail

and wretched woman appeared, crying. She stood before the hanged man and prayer reverently. Then she struggled up into the tree and gnawed with her teeth on the linen rope until it broke and the dead fell on the ground like a huge wet cloth; whereupon she came down, dug a grave, and buried the thief by the side of the other two victims. After covering him with earth, she took two pieces of wood and fashioned a cross and placed it over the head. When she turned her face to the city and started to depart, I stopped her saying, "What incited you to come and bury this thief?" She looked at me miserably and said, "He is my faithful husband and merciful companion; he is the father of my children—five young ones starving to death; the oldest is eight years of age, and the youngest is still nursing. My husband was not a thief, but a farmer working in the monastery's land, making our living on what little food the priests and monks gave him when he returned home at eventide. He had been farming for them since he was young, and when he became weak, they dismissed him, advising him to go back home and send his children to take his place as soon as they grew older. He begged them in the name of Jesus and the angels of heaven to let him stay, but they took no heed to his plea. They had no mercy on him nor on his starving children who were helplessly crying for food. He went to the city seeking employment, but in vain, for the rich did not employ except the strong and the healthy. Then he sat on the dusty street stretching his hand toward all who passed, begging and repeating the sad song of his defeat in life, while suffering from hunger and humiliation, but the people refused to help him, saying that lazy people did not deserve alms. One night, hunger gnawed painfully at our children, especially the youngest, who tried hopelessly to nurse on my dry breast. My husband's expression changed and he left the house under the cover of night. He entered the monastery's bin and carried out a bushel of wheat. As he emerged, the monks woke up from their slumber and arrested him after beating him mercilessly. At dawn they brought him to the Emir and complained that he came to the monastery to steal the golden vases of the altar. He was placed in prison and hanged the second day. He was trying to fill the stomachs of his little hungry one with the wheat he had raised by his own labour, but the Emir killed him and used his flesh as food to fill the stomachs of the birds and the beasts." Having spoken in this manner, she left me alone in a sorrowful plight and departed.

I stood there before the graves like a speaker suffering wordlessness while trying to recite a eulogy. I was speechless, but my falling tears substituted for my words and spoke for my soul. My spirit rebelled when I attempted to meditate a while, because the soul is like a flower that folds its petals when dark comes, and breathes not its fragrance into the phan-

toms of the night. I felt as if the earth that enfolded
the victims of oppression in that lonely place were
filling my ears with sorrowful tunes of suffering
souls, and inspiring me to talk. I resorted to silence,
but if the people understood what silence reveals to
them, they would have been as close to God as the
flowers of the valleys. If the flames of my sighing soul
had touched the trees, they would have moved from
their places and marched like a strong army to fight
the Emir with their branches and tear down the
monastery upon the heads of those priests and
monks. I stood there watching, and felt that the
sweet feeling of mercy and the bitterness of sorrow
were pouring from my heart upon the newly dug
graves—a grave of a young man who sacrificed his life
in defending a weak maiden, whose life and honour
he had saved from between the paws and teeth of a
savage human; a youth whose head was cut off in reward for his bravery; and his sword was planted
upon his grave by the one he saved, as a symbol of
heroism before the face of the sun that shines upon
an empire laden with stupidity and corruption. A
grave of a young woman whose heart was inflamed
with love before her body was taken by greed,
usurped by lust, and stoned by tyranny. . . . She
kept her faith until death; her lover placed flowers
upon her grave to speak through their withering
hours of those souls whom Love had selected and
blessed among a people blinded by earthly substance
and muted by ignorance. A grave of a miserable

man, weakened by hard labour in the monastery's land, who asked for bread to feed his hungry little ones, and was refused. He resorted to begging, but the people took no heed. When his soul led him to restore a small part of the crop which he had raised and gathered, he was arrested and beaten to death. His poor widow erected a cross upon his head as a witness in the silence of the night before the stars of heaven to testify against those priests who converted the kind teaching of Christ into sharp swords by which they cut the people's necks and tore the bodies of the weak.

The sun disappeared behind the horizon as if tiring of the world's troubles and loathing the people's submission. At that moment the evening began to weave a delicate veil from the sinews of silence and spread it upon Nature's body. I stretched my hand toward the graves, pointing at their symbols, lifted my eyes toward heaven and cried out, "Oh, Bravery, this is your sword, buried now in the earth! Oh, Love, these are your flowers, scorched by fire! Oh, Lord Jesus, this is Thy Cross, submerged in the obscurity of the night!"

KHALIL THE HERETIC

PART ONE

SHEIK ABBAS was looked upon as a prince by the people of a solitary village in North Lebanon. His mansion stood in the midst of those poor villagers' huts like a healthy giant amidst sickly dwarfs. He lived amid luxury while they pursued an existence of penury. They obeyed him and bowed reverently before him as he spoke to them. It seemed as though the power of mind had appointed him its official interpreter and spokesman. His anger would make them tremble and scatter like autumn leaves before a strong wind. If he were to slap one's face, it would be heresy on the individual's part to move or lift his head or make any attempt to discover why the blow had come. If he smiled at a man, the villagers would consider the person thus honoured as the most fortunate. The people's fear and surrender to Sheik Abbas were not due to weakness; however, their poverty and need of him had brought about this state of continual humiliation. Even the huts they lived in and the fields they cultivated were owned by Sheik Abbas who had inherited them from his ancestors.

The farming of the land and the sowing of the seeds and the gathering of wheat were all done under the supervision of the Sheik who, in reward for their toil, compensated them with a small portion of the crop which barely kept them from falling as victims of gnawing starvation.

Often many of them were in need of bread before the crop was reaped, and they came to Sheik Abbas and asked him with pouring tears to advance them a few piastres or a bushel of wheat, and the Sheik gladly granted their request for he knew that they would pay their debts doubly when harvest time came. Thus those people remained obligated all their lives, left a legacy of debts to their children and were submissive to their master whose anger they had always feared and whose friendship and good will they had constantly but unsuccessfully endeavoured to win.

PART TWO

Winter came and brought heavy snow and strong winds; the valleys and the fields became empty of all things except leafless trees which stood as spectres of death above the lifeless plains.

Having stored the products of the land in the Sheik's bins and filled his vases with the wine of the vineyards, the villagers retreated to their huts to spend a portion of their lives idling by the fireside and commemorating the glory of the past ages and relating to one another the tales of weary days and long nights.

The old year had just breathed its last into the grey sky. The night had arrived during which the New Year would be crowned and placed upon the throne of the Universe. The snow began to fall heavily and the whistling winds were racing from the lofty mountains down to the abyss and blowing the snow into heaps to be stored away in the valleys.

The trees were shaking under the heavy storms and the fields and knolls were covered with a white floor upon which Death was writing vague lines and effacing them. The mists stood as partitions between the scattered villages by the sides of the valleys. The lights that flickered through the windows of those wretched huts disappeared behind the thick veil of Nature's wrath.

Fear penetrated the fellahin's hearts and the animals stood by their mangers in the sheds, while the dogs were hiding in the corners. One could hear the voices of the screaming winds and thundering of the storms resounding from the depths of the valleys. It seemed as if Nature were enraged by the passing of the old year and trying to wrest revenge from those peaceful souls by fighting with weapons of cold and frost.

That night under the raging sky, a young man was attempting to walk the winding trail that connected Deir Kizhaya * with Sheik Abbas' village. The youth's limbs were numbed with cold, while pain and hunger usurped him of his strength. The black raiment he wore was bleached with the falling snow, as if he were shrouded in death before the hour of his death had come. He was struggling against the wind. His progress was difficult, and he took but a few steps forward with each effort. He called for help and then stood silent, shivering in the cold night. He had slim hope, withering between great despair and deep sorrow. He was like a bird with a broken wing, who fell in a stream whose whirlpools carried him down to the depths.

The young man continued walking and falling until his blood stopped circulating and he collapsed. He uttered a terrible sound . . . the voice of a soul who encountered the hollow face of Death . . . a voice of dying youth, weakened by man and trapped by nature . . . a voice of the love of existence in the space of nothingness.

PART THREE

On the north side of that village, in the midst of the wind-torn fields, stood the solitary home of a woman named Rachel, and her daughter Miriam who had not then attained the age of eighteen. Rachel was the

* One of the richest and most famous convents in Lebanon. Kizhaya is a Syriac word meaning "Paradise of Life." (*Editor's note.*)

widow of Samaan Ramy, who was found slain six years earlier, but the law of man did not find the murderer.

Like the rest of the Lebanese widows, Rachel sustained life through long, hard work. During the harvest season, she would look for ears of corn left behind by others in the field, and in Autumn she gathered the remnants of some forgotten fruits in the gardens. In Winter she spun wool and made raiment for which she received a few piastres or a bushel of grain. Miriam, her daughter, was a beautiful girl who shared with her mother the burden of toil.

That bitter night the two women were sitting by the fireplace whose warmth was weakened by the frost and whose firebrands were buried beneath the ashes. By their side was a flickering lamp that sent its yellow, dimmed rays into the heart of darkness like prayer that sends phantoms of hope into the hearts of the sorrowful.

Midnight had come and they were listening to the wailing winds outside. Every now and then Miriam would get up, open the small transom and look toward the obscured sky, and then she would return to her chair worried and frightened by the raging elements. Suddenly Miriam started, as if she had awakened from a swoon of deep slumber. She looked anxiously toward her mother and said, "Did you hear that, Mother? Did you hear a voice calling for help?" The mother listened a moment and said,

"I hear nothing except the crying wind, my daughter." Then Miriam exclaimed, "I heard a voice deeper than the thundering heaven and more sorrowful than the wailing of the tempest."

Having uttered these words, she stood up and opened the door and listened for a moment. Then she said, "I hear it again, Mother!" Rachel hurried toward the frail door and after a moment's hesitation she said, "And I hear it, too. Let us go and see."

She wrapped herself with a long robe, opened the door and walked out cautiously, while Miriam stood at the door, the wind blowing her long hair.

Having forced her way a short distance through the snow, Rachel stopped and shouted out, "Who is calling . . . where are you?" There was no answer; then she repeated the same words again and again, but she heard naught except thunder. Then she courageously advanced forward, looking in every direction. She had walked for some time, when she found some deep footprints upon the snow; she followed them fearfully and in a few moments found a human body lying before her on the snow, like a patch on a white dress. As she approached him and leaned his head over her knees, she felt his pulse that bespoke his slowing heart beats and his slim chance in life. She turned her face toward the hut and called, "Come, Miriam, come and help me, I have found him!" Miriam rushed out and followed her mother's footprints, while shivering with cold and trembling with fear. As she reached the place and saw the youth lying motionless, she cried with an aching voice. The mother put her hands under his armpits, calmed Miriam and said, "Fear not, for he is still living; hold the lower edge of his cloak and let us carry him home."

Confronted with the strong wind and heavy snow, the two women carried the youth and started toward the hut. As they reached the little haven, they laid him down by the fireplace. Rachel commenced rubbing his numbed hands and Miriam drying his hair with the end of her dress. The youth began to move after a few minutes. His eyelids quivered and he took a deep sigh—a sigh that brought the hope of his safety into the hearts of the merciful women. They removed his shoes and took off his black robe. Miriam looked at her mother and said, "Observe his raiment, Mother; these clothes are worn by the monks." After feeding the fire with a bundle of dry sticks, Rachel looked at her daughter with perplexity and said, "The monks do not leave their convent on such a terrible night." And Miriam inquired, "But he has no hair on his face; the monks wear beards." The mother gazed at him with eyes full of mercy and maternal love; then she turned to her daughter and said, "It makes no difference whether he is a monk or a criminal; dry his feet well, my daughter." Rachel opened a closet, took from it a jar of wine and poured some in an earthenware bowl. Miriam held his head while the mother gave him some of it to stimulate his heart. As he sipped the wine he opened his eyes for the first time and gave his rescuers a sorrowful look mingled with tears of gratitude—the look of a human who felt the smooth touch of life after having been gripped in the sharp claws of death—a look of great hope after hope had died. Then he bent his head, and his lips trembled when he uttered the words, "May God bless both of you." Rachel placed her hand upon his shoulder and said, "Be calm, brother. Do not tire yourself with talking until you gain strength." And Miriam added, "Rest your head on this pillow, brother, and we will place you closer to the fire." Rachel refilled the bowl with wine and gave it to him. She looked at her daughter and said, "Hang his robe by the fire so it will dry." Having executed her mother's command, she returned and commenced looking at him mercifully, as if she wanted to help him by pouring into his heart all the warmth of her soul. Rachel brought two loaves of bread with some preserves and dry fruits; she sat by him and began to feed him small morsels, as a mother feeds her little child. At this time he felt stronger and sat up on the hearth mat while the red flames of fire reflected upon his sad face. His eyes brightened and he shook his head slowly, saying, "Mercy and cruelty are both wrestling in the human heart like the mad elements in the sky of this terrible night, but mercy shall overcome cruelty because it is divine, and the terror alone, of this night, shall pass away when daylight comes." Silence prevailed for a minute and then he added with a whispering voice, "A human hand drove me into desperation and a human hand rescued me; how severe man is, and how merciful man is!" And Rachel inquired, "How ventured you, brother, to leave the convent on such a terrible night, when even the beasts do not venture forth?"

The youth shut his eyes as if he wanted to restore his tears back into the depths of his heart, whence they came, and he said, "The animals have their caves, and the birds of the sky their nests, but the son of man has no place to rest his head." Rachel retorted, "That is what Jesus said about himself." And the young man resumed, "This is the answer for every man who wants to follow the Spirit and the Truth in this age of falsehood, hypocrisy and corruption."

After a few moments of contemplation, Rachel said, "But there are many comfortable rooms in the convent, and the coffers are full of gold, and all kinds of provisions. The sheds of the convent are stocked with fat calves and sheep; what made you leave such haven in this deathly night?" The youth sighed deeply and said, "I left that place because I hated it." And Rachel rejoined, "A monk in a convent is like a soldier in the battlefield who is required to obey the orders of his leader regardless of their nature. I heard that a man could not become a monk unless he did away with his will, his thoughts, his desires, and all that pertains to the mind. But a good head priest does not ask his monks to do unreasonable things. How could the head priest of Deir Kizhaya ask you to give up your life to the storms and snow?" And he remarked, "In the opinion of the head priest, a man cannot become a monk unless he is blind and ignorant, senseless and dumb. I left the convent because I am a sensible man who can see, feel, and hear."

Miriam and Rachel stared at him as if they had found in his face a hidden secret; after a moment of meditation the mother said, "Will a man who sees and hears go out on a night that blinds the eyes and deafens the ears?" And the youth stated quietly, "I was expelled from the convent." "Expelled!" exclaimed Rachel; and Miriam repeated the same word in unison with her mother.

He lifted his head, regretting his words, for he was afraid lest their love and sympathy be converted into hatred and disrespect; but when he looked at them and found the rays of mercy still emanating from their eyes, and their bodies vibrating with anxiety to learn further, his voice choked and he continued, "Yes, I was expelled from the convent because I could not dig my grave with my own hands, and my heart grew weary of lying and pilfering. I was expelled from the convent because my soul refused to enjoy the bounty of a people who surrendered themselves to ignorance. I was driven away because I could not find rest in the comfortable rooms, built with the money of the poor fellahin. My stomach could not hold bread baked with the tears of orphans. My lips could not utter prayers sold for gold and food by the heads to the simple and faithful people. I was expelled from the convent like a filthy leper because I was repeating to the monks the rules that qualified them to their present position."

Silence prevailed while Rachel and Miriam were contemplating his words and gazing at him, when they asked, "Are your father and mother living?" And he responded, "I have no father or mother nor a place that is my home." Rachel drew a deep sigh and Miriam turned her face toward the wall to hide her merciful and loving tears.

As a withering flower is brought back to life by dew drops that dawn pours into its begging petals, so the youth's anxious heart was enlivened by his benefactors' affection and kindness. He looked at them as a soldier looks upon his liberators who rescue him from the grip of the enemy, and he resumed, "I lost my parents before I reached the age of seven. The village priest took me to Deir Kizhaya and left me at the disposal of the monks who were happy to take me in and put me in charge of the cows and sheep, which I led each day to the pasture. When I attained the age of fifteen, they put on me this black robe and led me into the altar whereupon the head priest addressed me saying, "Swear by the name of God and all saints, and make a vow to live a virtuous life of poverty and obedience." I repeated the words before I realized their significance or comprehended his own interpretation of poverty, virtue and obedience.

"My name was Khalil, and since that time the monks addressed me as Brother Mobaarak,* but they never did treat me as a brother. They ate the most palatable foods and drank the finest wine, while I lived on dry vegetables and water, mixed with tears. They slumbered in soft beds while I slept on a stone slab in a dark and cold room by the shed. Oftentimes I asked myself, 'When will I become a monk and share with those fortunate priests their bounty? When will my heart stop craving for the food they eat and the wine they drink? When will I cease to tremble with fear before my superiors?' But all my hopes were in vain, for I was kept in the same state; and in addition to caring for the cattle, I was obliged to move heavy stones on my shoulders and to dig pits and ditches. I sustained life on a few morsels of bread given to me in reward for my toil. I knew of no other place to which I might go, and the clergymen at the convent had caused me to abhor everything they were doing. They had poisoned my mind until I commenced to think that the whole world was an ocean of sorrows and miseries and that the convent was the only port of salvation. But when I discovered the source of their food and gold, I was happy that I did not share it."

* Coincidentally, Mobaarak was the name of the Right Reverend Maronite Archbishop who officiated at Kahlil Gibran's last rites. (*Editor's note.*)

Khalil straightened himself and looked about with wonder, as if he had found something beautiful standing before him in that wretched hut. Rachel and Miriam remained silent and he proceeded, "God, who took my father and exiled me as an orphan to the convent, did not want me to spend all my life walking blindly toward a dangerous jungle; nor did He wish me to be a miserable slave for the rest of my life. God opened my eyes and ears and showed me the bright light and made me hear Truth when Truth was talking."

Rachel thought aloud, "Is there any light, other than the sun, that shines over all the people? Are human beings capable of understanding the Truth?" Khalil returned, "The true light is that which emanates from within man, and reveals the secrets of the heart to the soul, making it happy and contented with life. Truth is like the stars; it does not appear except from behind obscurity of the night. Truth is like all beautiful things in the world; it does not disclose its desirability except to those who first feel the influence of falsehood. Truth is a deep kindness that teaches us to be content in our everyday life and share with the people the same happiness."

Rachel rejoined, "Many are those who live according to their goodness, and many are those who believe that compassion to others is the shadow of the law of God to man; but still, they do not rejoice in life, for they remain miserable until death." Khalil replied, "Vain are the beliefs and teachings that make man miserable, and false is the goodness that leads him into sorrow and despair, for it is man's purpose to be happy on this earth and lead the way to felicity and preach its gospel wherever he goes. He who does not see the kingdom of heaven in this life will never see it in the coming life. We came not into this life by exile, but we came as innocent creatures of God, to learn how to worship the holy and eternal spirit and seek the hidden secrets within ourselves from the beauty of life. This is the truth which I have learned from the teachings of the Nazarene. This is the light that came from within me and showed me the dark corners of the convent that threatened my life. This is the deep secret which the beautiful valleys and fields revealed to me when I was hungry, sitting lonely and weeping under the shadow of the trees.

"This is the religion as the convent should impart it; as God wished it; as Jesus taught it. One day, as my soul became intoxicated with the heavenly intoxication of Truth's beauty, I stood bravely before the monks who were gathering in the garden, and criticized their wrong deeds saying, 'Why do you spend your days here and enjoy the bounty of the poor, whose bread you eat was made with the sweat of their bodies and the tears of their hearts? Why are you living in the shadow of parasitism, segregating yourselves from the people who are in need of knowledge? Why are you depriving the country of your help? Jesus has sent you as lambs amongst the wolves; what has made you as wolves amongst the lambs? Why are you fleeing from mankind and from God who created you? If you are better than the people who walk in the procession of life, you should go to them and better their lives; but if you think they are better than you, you should desire to learn from them. How do you take an oath and vow to live in poverty, then forget what you have said and live in luxury? How do you swear an obedience to God and then revolt against all that religion means? How do you adopt virtue as your rule when your hearts are full of lusts? You pretend that you are killing your bodies, but in fact you are killing your souls. You feign to abhor the earthly things, but your hearts are swollen with greed. You have the people believe in you as religious teachers; truly speaking you are like busy cattle who divert themselves from knowledge by grazing in a green and beautiful pasture. Let us restore to the neeay the vast land of the convent and give back to them the silver and gold we took from them. Let us disperse from our aloofness and serve the weak who made us strong, and cleanse the country in which we live. Let us teach this miserable nation to smile and rejoice with heaven's bounty and glory of life and freedom.

" 'The people's tears are more beautiful and God-joined than the ease and tranquillity to which you have accustomed yourselves in this place. The sympathy that touches the neighbour's heart is more

supreme than the hidden virtue in the unseen corners of the convent. A word of compassion to the
weak criminal or prostitute is nobler than the long
prayer which we repeat emptily every day in the
temple.' "

At this time Khalil took a deep breath. Then he
lifted his eyes toward Rachel and Miriam saying,
"I was saying all of these things to the monks and
they were listening with an air of perplexity, as if
they could not believe that a young man would dare
stand before them and utter such bold words. When
I finished, one of the monks approached and angrily
said to me, 'How dare you talk in such fashion in
our presence?' And another one came laughing and
added, 'Did you learn all this from the cows and pigs
you tended in the fields?' And a third one stood up
and threatened me saying, 'You shall be punished,
heretic!' Then they dispersed as though running
away from a leper. Some of them complained to the
head priest who summoned me before him at eventide. The monks took delight in anticipation of my
suffering, and there was glee on their faces when I
was ordered to be scourged and put into prison for
forty days and nights. They led me into the dark cell
where I spent the time lying in that grave without
seeing the light. I could not tell the end of the night
from the beginning of the day, and could feel nothing but crawling insects and the earth under me. I
could hear naught save the tramping of their feet
when my morsel of bread and dish of water mixed

with vinegar were brought to me at great intervals.

"When I came out of the prison I was weak and frail, and the monks believed that they had cured me of thinking, and that they had killed my soul's desire. They thought that hunger and thirst had choked the kindness which God placed in my heart. In my forty days of solitude I endeavoured to find a method by which I could help these monks to see the light and hear the true song of life, but all of my ponderings were in vain, for the thick veil which the long ages had woven around their eyes could not be torn away in a short time; and the mortar with which ignorance had cemented their ears was hardened and could not be removed by the touch of soft fingers."

Silence prevailed for a moment, and then Miriam looked at her mother as if asking permission to speak. She said, "You must have talked to the monks again, if they selected this terrible night in which to banish you from the convent. They should learn to be kind even to their enemies."

Khalil returned, "This evening, as the thunder storms and warring elements raged in the sky, I withdrew myself from the monks who were crouching about the fire, telling tales and humourous stories. When they saw me alone they commenced to place their wit at my expense. I was reading my Gospel and contemplating the beautiful sayings of Jesus that made me forget for the time the enraged nature and belligerent elements of the sky, when they approached me with a new spirit of ridicule.

I ignored them by occupying myself and looking through the window, but they became furious because my silence dried the laughter of their hearts and the taunting of their lips. One of them said, 'What are you reading, GreatReformer?' In response to his inquiry, I opened my book and read aloud the following passage, 'But when he saw many of the Pharisees and Saducees come to his baptism, he said unto them, "O generation of vipers, who hath warned you to flee from the wrath to come? Bring forth therefore fruits for repentance; And think not to say within yourselves, 'We have Abraham to our father;'" 'for I say unto you, that God is able of these stones to raise children unto Abraham. And now also the axe is laid unto the root of the trees; therefore every tree which bringeth not forth good fruit is hewn down, and cast into the fire.'

"As I read to them these words of John the Baptist, the monks became silent as if an invisible hand strangled their spirits, but they took false courage and commenced laughing. One of them said, 'We have read these words many times, and we are not in need of a cow grazier to repeat them to us.'

"I protested, 'If you had read these words and comprehended their meaning, these poor villagers would not have frozen or starved to death.' When I said this, one of the monks slapped my face as if I had spoken evil of the priests; another kicked me and a third took the book from me and a fourth one called the head priest who hurried to the scene

302

shaking with anger. He cried out, 'Arrest this rebel and drag him from this sacred place, and let the storm's fury teach him obedience. Take him away and let nature do unto him the will of God, and then wash your hands of the poisonous germs of heresy infesting his raiment. If he should return pleading for forgiveness, do not open the door for him, for the viper will not become a dove if placed in a cage, nor will the briar bear figs if planted in the vineyards.'

"In accordance with the command, I was dragged out by the laughing monks. Before they locked the door behind me, I heard one saying, 'Yesterday you were king of cows and pigs, and today you are de-throned, Oh Great Reformer; go now and be the king of wolves and teach them how to live in their lairs.' "

Khalil sighed deeply, then turned his face and looked toward the flaming fire. With a sweet and loving voice, and with a pained countenance he said, "Thus was I expelled from the convent, and thus did the monks deliver me over to the hands of Death. I fought through the night blindly; the heavy wind was tearing my robe and the piling snow was trapping my feet and pulling me down until I fell, crying desperately for help. I felt that no one heard me except Death, but a power which is all knowledge and mercy had heard my cry. That power did not want me to die before I had learned what is left of life's secrets. That power sent you

303

both to me to save my life from the depth of the abyss and non-existence."

Rachel and Miriam felt as if their spirits understood the mystery of his soul, and they became his partners in feeling and understanding. Notwithstanding her will, Rachel stretched forth and gently touched his hand while tears coursed down from her eyes, and she said, "He who has been chosen by heaven as a defender of Truth will not perish by heaven's own storms and snow." And Miriam added, "The storms and snow may kill the flowers, but cannot deaden the seeds, for the snow keeps them warm from the killing frost."

Khalil's face brightened upon hearing those words of encouragement, and he said, "If you do not look upon me as a rebel and an heretic as the monks did, the persecution which I have sustained in the convent is the symbol of an oppressed nation that has not yet attained knowledge; and this night in which I was on the verge of death is like a revolution that precedes full justice. And from a sensitive woman's heart springs the happiness of mankind, and from the kindness of her noble spirit comes mankind's affection."

He closed his eyes and leaned down on the pillow; the two women did not bother him with further conversation for they knew that the weariness caused by long exposure had allured and captured his eyes. Khalil slept like a lost child who had finally found safety in his mother's arms.

Rachel and her daughter slowly walked to their bed and sat there watching him as if they had found in his trouble-torn face an attraction bringing their souls and hearts closer to him. And the mother whispered, saying, "There is a strange power in his closed eyes that speaks in silence and stimulates the soul's desires."

And Miriam rejoined, "His hands, Mother, are like those of Christ in the Church." The mother replied, "His face possesses at the same time a woman's tenderness and a man's boldness."

And the wings of slumber carried the women's spirits into the world of dream, and the fire went down and turned into ashes, while the light of the oil lamp dimmed gradually and disappeared. The fierce tempest continued its roar, and the obscured sky spread layers of snow, and the strong wind scattered them to the right and left.

PART FOUR

Five days passed, and the sky was still heavy with snow, burying the mountains and prairies relentlessly. Khalil made three attempts to resume his journey toward the plains, but Rachel restrained him each time, saying, "Do not give up your life to the blind elements, brother; remain here, for the bread that suffices two will also feed three, and the fire will still be burning after your departure as it was before your arrival. We are poor, brother, but like the rest of the people, we live our lives before the face of the sun and mankind, and God gives us our daily bread."

And Miriam was begging him with her kind glances, and pleading with her deep sighs, for since he entered the hut she felt the presence of a divine power in her soul sending forth life and light into her heart and awakening new affection in the Holy of Holies of her spirit. For the first time she experienced the feeling which made her heart like a white rose that sips the dew drops from the dawn and breathes its fragrance into the endless firmament.

There is no affection purer and more soothing to the spirit than the one hidden in the heart of a maiden who awakens suddenly and fills her own spirit with heavenly music that makes her days like poets' dreams and her nights prophetic. There is no secret in the mystery of life stronger and more beautiful than that attachment which converts the silence of a virgin's spirit into a perpetual awareness that makes a person forget the past, for it kindles fiercely in the heart the sweet and overwhelming hope of the coming future.

The Lebanese woman distinguishes herself from the woman of other nations by her simplicity. The manner in which she is trained restricts her progress educationally, and stands as a hindrance to her future. Yet for this reason, she finds herself inquiring of herself as to the inclination and mystery of her heart. The Lebanese young woman is like a spring that comes out from the heart of the earth and follows its course through winding depressions, but since it cannot find an outlet to the sea, it turns into a calm lake that reflects upon its growing surface the glittering stars and the shining moon. Khalil felt the vibration of Miriam's heart twining steadily about his soul, and he knew that the divine torch that illuminated his heart had also touched her heart. He rejoiced for the first time, like a parched brook greeting the rain, but he blamed himself for his haste, believing that this spiritual understanding would pass like a cloud when he departed from that village. He often spoke to himself saying, "What is this mystery that plays so great a part in our lives? What is this Law that drives us into a rough road and stops us just before we reach the face of the sun where we might rejoice? What is this power that elevates our spirits until we reach the mountain top, smiling and glorying, then suddenly we are cast to the depths of the valley, weeping and suffering? What is this life that embraces us like a lover one day, and fights us like an enemy the second day? Was I not persecuted yesterday? Did I not survive hunger and thirst and suffering and mockery for the sake of the Truth which heaven had awakened in my heart? Did I not tell the monks that happiness through Truth is the will and the purpose of God in man? Then what is this fear? And why do I close my eyes to the light that emanates from that young woman's eyes? I am expelled and she is poor, but is it on bread only that man can

307

live? Are we not, between famine and plenty, like trees between winter and summer? But what would Rachel say if she knew that my heart and her daughter's heart came to an understanding in silence, and approached close to each other and neared the circle of the Supreme Light? What would she say if she discovered that the young man whose life she saved longed to gaze upon her daughter? What would the simple villagers say if they knew that a young man, reared in the convent, came to their village by necessity and expulsion, and desired to live near a beautiful maiden? Will they listen to me if I tell them that he who leaves the convent to live amongst them is like a bird that flies from the bruising walls of the cage to the light of freedom? What will Sheik Abbas say if he hears my story? What will the priest of the village do if he learns of the cause of my expulsion?"

Khalil was talking to himself in this fashion while sitting by the fireplace, meditating the flames, symbol of his love; and Miriam was stealing a glance now and then at his face and reading his dreams through his eyes, and hearing the echo of his thoughts, and feeling the touch of his love, even though no word was uttered.

One night, as he stood by the small transom that faced the valleys where the trees and rocks were shrouded with white coverings, Miriam came and stood by him, looking at the sky. As their eyes turned and met, he drew a deep sigh and shut his

eyes as if his soul were sailing in the spacious sky
looking for a word. He found no word necessary,
for the silence spoke for them. Miriam ventured,
"Where will you go when the snow meets the stream
and the paths are dry?" His eyes opened, looking
beyond the horizon, and he explained, "I shall follow the path to wherever my destiny and my mission for Truth shall take me." Miriam sighed sadly
and offered, "Why will you not remain here and
live close to us? Is it that you are obliged to go
elsewhere?" He was moved by her kindness and
sweet words, but protested, "The villagers here will
not accept an expelled monk as their neighbour,
and will not permit him to breathe the air they
breathe because they believe that the enemy of the
convent is an infidel, cursed by God and His saints."
Miriam resorted to silence, for the Truth that
pained her prevented further talk. Then Khalil
turned aside and explained, "Miriam, these villagers
are taught by those in authority to hate everyone
who thinks freely; they are trained to remain afar
from those whose minds soar aloft; God does not
like to be worshipped by an ignorant man who
imitates someone else; if I remained in this village
and asked the people to worship as they please, they
would say that I am an infidel disobeying the authority that was given to the priest by God. If I
asked them to listen and hear the voices of their
hearts and do according to the will of the spirit
within, they would say that I am an evil man who

wants them to do away with the clergy that God placed between heaven and earth." Khalil looked straight into Miriam's eyes, and with a voice that bespoke the sound of silver strings said, "But, Miriam, there is a magic power in this village that possesses me and engulfs my soul; a power so divine that it causes me to forget my pain. In this village I met Death to his very face, and in this place my soul embraced God's spirit. In this village there is a beautiful flower grown over the lifeless grass; its beauty attracts my heart and its fragrance fills its domain. Shall I leave this important flower and go out preaching the ideas that caused my expulsion from the convent, or shall I remain by the side of that flower and dig a grave and bury my thoughts. and truths among its neighbouring thorns? What shall I do, Miriam?" Upon hearing these words, she shivered like a lily before the frolicsome breeze of the dawn. Her heart glowed through her eyes when she faltered, "We are both in the hands of a mysterious and merciful power. Let it do its will."

At that moment the two hearts joined and thereafter both spirits were one burning torch illuminating their lives.

PART FIVE

Since the beginning of the creation and up to our present time, certain clans, rich by inheritance, in co-operation with the clergy, had appointed themselves the administrators of the people. It is an old, gaping wound in the heart of society that cannot be removed except by intense removal of ignorance.

The man who acquires his wealth by inheritance builds his mansion with the weak poor's money. The clergyman erects his temple upon the graves and bones of the devoted worshippers. The prince grasps the fellah's arms while the priest empties his pocket; the ruler looks upon the sons of the fields with frowning face, and the bishop consoles them with his smile, and between the frown of the tiger and the smile of the wolf the flock is perished; the ruler claims himself as king of the law, and the priest as the representative of God, and between these two, the bodies are destroyed and the souls wither into nothing.

In Lebanon, that mountain rich in sunlight and poor in knowledge, the noble and the priest joined hands to exploit the farmer who ploughed the land and reaped the crop in order to protect himself from the sword of the ruler and the curse of the priest. The rich man in Lebanon stood proudly by his palace and shouted at the multitudes saying, "The Sultan had appointed me as your lord." And the priest stands before the altar saying, "God has delegated me as an executive of your souls." But the Lebanese resorted to silence, for the dead could not talk.

Sheik Abbas had friendship in his heart for the clergymen, because they were his allies in choking the people's knowledge and reviving the spirit of stern obedience among his workers.

That evening, when Khalil and Miriam were approaching the throne of Love, and Rachel was looking upon them with the eyes of affection, Father Elias informed Sheik Abbas that the head priest had expelled a rebellious young man from the convent and that he had taken refuge at the house of Rachel, the widow of Samaan Ramy. And the priest was not satisfied with the little information he gave the Sheik, but commented, "The demon they chased out of the convent cannot become an angel in this village, and the fig tree which is hewn and cast into the fire, does not bear fruit while burning. If we wish to clean this village of the filth of this beast, we must drive him away as the monks did." And the Sheik inquired, "Are you certain that the young man will be a bad influence upon our people? Is it not better for us to keep him and make him a worker in our vineyards? We are in need of strong men."

The priest's face showed his disagreement. Combing his beard with his fingers, he said shrewdly, "If he were fit to work, he would not have been expelled from the convent. A student who works in the convent, and who happened to spend last night at my house, informed me that this young man had violated the rules of the head priest by preaching danger-ridden ideas among the monks, and he quoted him as saying, 'Restore the fields and the vineyards and the silver of the convent to the poor and scatter it in all directions; and help the people who are in need of knowledge; by thus doing, you will please your Father in Heaven.' "

On hearing these words, Sheik Abbas leaped to his feet, and like a tiger making ready to strike the victim, he walked to the door and called to the servants, ordering them to report immediately. Three men entered, and the Sheik commanded, "In the house of Rachel, the widow of Samaan Ramy, there is a young man wearing a monk's raiment. Tie him and bring him here. If that woman objects to his arrest, drag her out by her braided hair over the snow and bring her with him, for he who helps evil is evil himself." The men bowed obediently and hurried to Rachel's home while the priest and the Sheik discussed the type of punishment to be awarded to Khalil and Rachel.

PART SIX

The day was over and the night had come spreading its shadow over those wretched huts, heavily laden with snow. The stars finally appeared in the sky, like hopes in the coming eternity after the suffering of death's agony. The doors and windows were closed and the lamps were lighted. The fellahin sat by the fireside warming their bodies. Rachel, Miriam and Khalil were seated at a rough wooden table eating their evening meal when there was a knock at the door and three men entered. Rachel and Miriam were frightened, but Khalil remained calm, as if he awaited the coming of those men. One of the Sheik's servants walked toward Khalil, laid his hand upon his shoulder and asked, "Are you the one who was expelled from the convent?" And Khalil responded, "Yes, I am the one, what do you want?" The man replied, "We are ordered to arrest you and take you with us to Sheik Abbas' home, and if you object we shall drag you out like a butchered sheep over the snow."

Rachel turned pale as she exclaimed, "What crime has he committed, and why do you want to tie him and drag him out?" The two women pleaded with tearful voices, saying, "He is one individual in the hands of three and it is cowardly of you to make him suffer." The men became enraged and shouted, "Is there any woman in this village who opposes the Sheik's order?" And he drew forth a rope and started to tie Khalil's hands. Khalil lifted his head proudly, and a sorrowful smile appeared on his lips when he said, "I feel sorry for you men, because you are a strong and blind instrument in the hands of a man who oppresses the weak with the strength of your arms. You are slaves of ignorance. Yesterday I was a man like you, but tomorrow you shall be free in mind as I am now. Between us there is a deep precipice that chokes my calling voice and hides my reality from you, and you cannot hear or see. Here I am, tie my hands and do as you please." The three men were moved by his talk and it seemed that his voice had awakened in them a new spirit, but the

voice of Sheik Abbas still rang in their minds, warning them to complete the mission. They bound his
hands and led him out silently with a heavy conscience. Rachel and Miriam followed them to the
Sheik's home, like the daughters of Jerusalem who
followed Christ to Mount Calvary.

PART SEVEN

Regardless of its import, news travels swiftly among
the fellahin in the small villages, because their absence from the realm of society makes them anxious
and busy in discussing the happenings of their limited environs. In winter, when the fields are slumbering under the quilts of snow, and when human
life is taking refuge and warming itself by the fireside, the villagers become most inclined to learn of
current news in order to occupy themselves.

It was not long after Khalil was arrested, when
the story spread like a contagious disease amongst
the villagers. They left their huts and hurried like
an army from every direction into the home of
Sheik Abbas. When Khalil's feet stepped into the
Sheik's home, the residence was crowded with men,
women and children who were endeavouring for a
glance at the infidel who was expelled from the
convent. They were also anxious to see Rachel and
her daughter, who had helped Khalil in spreading
the hellish disease of heresy in the pure sky of their
village.

The Sheik took the seat of judgment and beside

him sat Father Elias, while the throng was gazing at the pinioned youth who stood bravely before them. Rachel and Miriam were standing behind Khalil and trembling with fear. But what could fear do to the heart of a woman who found Truth and followed him? What could the scorn of the crowd do to the soul of a maiden who had been awakened by Love? Sheik Abbas looked at the young man, and with a thundering voice he interrogated him saying, "What is your name, man?" "Khalil is my name," answered the youth. The Sheik returned, "Who are your father and mother and relatives, and where were you born?" Khalil turned toward the fellahin, who looked upon him with hateful eyes, and said, "The oppressed poor are my clan and my relatives, and this vast country is my birthplace."

Sheik Abbas, with an air of ridicule, said, "Those people whom you claim as kin demand that you be punished, and the country you assert as your birthplace objects to your being a member of its people." Khalil replied, "The ignorant nations arrest their good men and turn them into their despots; and a country, ruled by a tyrant, persecutes those who try to free the people from the yoke of slavery. But will a good son leave his mother if she is ill? Will a merciful man deny his brother who is miserable? Those poor men who arrested me and brought me here today are the same ones who surrendered their lives to you yesterday. And this vast earth that disapproves my existence is the one that does not yawn and swallow the greedy despots."

The Sheik uttered a loud laugh, as if wanting to depress the young man's spirit and prevent him from influencing the audience. He turned to Khalil and said impressively, "You cattle grazier, do you think that we will show more mercy than did the monks, who expelled you from the convent? Do you think that we feel pity for a dangerous agitator?" Khalil responded, "It is true that I was a cattle grazier, but I am glad that I was not a butcher. I led my herds to the rich pastures and never grazed them on arid land. I led my animals to pure springs and kept them from contaminated marshes. At eventide I brought them safely to their shed and never left them in the valleys as prey for the wolves. Thus I have treated the animals; and if you had pursued my course and treated human beings as I treated my flock, these poor people would not live in wretched huts and suffer the pangs of poverty, while you are living like Nero in this gorgeous mansion."

The Sheik's forehead glittered with drops of perspiration, and his smirk turned into anger, but he tried to show only calm by pretending that he did not heed Khalil's talk, and he expostulated, pointing at Khalil with his finger, "You are a heretic, and we shall not listen to your ridiculous talk; we summoned you to be tried as a criminal, and you realize that you are in the presence of the Lord of this village who is empowered to represent his Excellency

Emir Ameen Shebab. You are standing before Father
Elias, the representative of the Holy Church whose
teachings you have opposed. Now, defend yourself,
or kneel down before these people and we will
pardon you and make you a cattle grazier, as you
were in the convent." Khalil calmly returned, "A
criminal is not to be tried by another criminal, as
an atheist will not defend himself before sinners."
And Khalil looked at the audience and spoke to
them saying, "My brethren, the man whom you
call the Lord of your fields, and to whom you have
yielded thus long, has brought me to be tried before
you in this edifice which he built upon the graves of
your forefathers. And the man who became a pastor
of your church through your faith, has come to
judge me and help you to humiliate me and increase
my sufferings. You have hurried to this place from
every direction to see me suffer and hear me plead
for mercy. You have left your huts in order to witness your pinioned son and brother. You have come
to see the prey trembling between the paws of a
ferocious beast. You came here tonight to view an
infidel standing before the judges. I am the criminal
and I am the heretic who has been expelled from
the convent. The tempest brought me into your
village. Listen to my protest, and do not be merciful, but be just, for mercy is bestowed upon the
guilty criminal, while justice is all that an innocent
man requires.

"I select you now as my jury, because the will of

318

the people is the will of God. Awaken your hearts and listen carefully and then prosecute me according to the dictates of your conscience. You have been told that I am an infidel, but you have not been informed of what crime or sin I have committed. You have seen me tied like a thief, but you have not yet heard about my offenses, for wrongdoings are not revealed in this court, while punishment comes out like thunder. My crime, dear fellowmen, is my understanding of your plight, for I felt the weight of the irons which have been placed upon your necks. My sin is my heartfelt sorrows for your women; it is my sympathy for your children who suck life from your breast mixed with the shadow of death. I am one of you, and my forefathers lived in these valleys and died under the same yoke which is bending your heads now. I believe in God who listens to the call of your suffering souls, and I believe in the Book that makes all of us brothers before the face of heaven. I believe in the teachings that make us all equal, and that render us unpinioned upon this earth, the stepping place of the careful feet of God.

"As I was grazing my cows at the convent, and contemplating the sorrowful condition you tolerate, I heard a desperate cry coming from your miserable homes—a cry of oppressd souls—a cry of broken hearts which are locked in your bodies as slaves to the lord of these fields. As I looked, I found me in the convent and you in the fields, and I saw you as a flock of lambs following a wolf to the lair; and as I stopped in the middle of the road to aid the lambs, I cried for help and the wolf snapped me with his sharp teeth.

"I have sustained imprisonment, thirst, and hunger for the sake of Truth that hurts only the body. I have undergone suffering beyond endurance because I turned your sad sighs into a crying voice that rang and echoed in every corner of the convent. I never felt fear, and my heart never tired, for your painful cry was injecting a new strength into me every day, and my heart was healthy. You may ask yourself now saying, 'When did we ever cry for help, and who dares open his lips?' But I say unto you; your souls are crying every day, and pleading for help every night, but you cannot hear them, for the dying man cannot hear his own heart rattling, while those who are standing by his bedside can surely hear. The slaughtered bird, in spite of his will, dances painfully and unknowingly, but those who witness the dance know what caused it. In what hour of the day do you sigh painfully? Is it in the morning, when love of existence cries at you and tears the veil of slumber off your eyes and leads you like slaves into the fields? Is it at noon, when you wish to sit under a tree to protect yourself from the burning sun? Or at eventide, when you return home hungry, wishing for sustaining food instead of a meagre morsel and impure water? Or at night when fatigue throws you upon your rough bed, and as

soon as slumber closes your eyes, you sit up with
open eyes, fearing that the Sheik's voice is ringing
in your ears?

"In what season of the year do you not lament
yourselves? Is it in Spring, when nature puts on her
beautiful dress and you go to meet her with tattered raiment? Or in Summer, when you harvest
the wheat and gather the sheaves of corn and fill the
shelves of your master with the crop, and when the
reckoning comes you receive naught but hay and
tare? Is it in Autumn, when you pick the fruits and
carry the grapes into the wine-press, and in reward
for your toil you receive a jar of vinegar and a
bushel of acorns? Or in Winter, when you are confined to your huts laden with snow, do you sit by
the fire and tremble when the enraged sky urges
you to escape from your weak minds?

"This is the life of the poor; this is the perpetual
cry I hear. This is what makes my spirit revolt
against the oppressors and despise their conduct.
When I asked the monks to have mercy upon you,
they thought that I was an atheist, and expulsion
was my lot. Today I came here to share this miserable life with you, and to mix my tears with yours.
Here I am now, in the grip of your worst enemy.
Do you realize that this land you are working like
slaves was taken from your fathers when the law was
written on the sharp edge of the sword? The monks
deceived your ancestors and took all their fields and
vineyards when the religious rules were written on

the lips of the priests. Which man or woman is not influenced by the lord of the fields to do according to the will of the priests? God said, 'With the sweat of thy brow, thou shall eat thy bread.' But Sheik Abbas is eating his bread baked in the years of your lives and drinking his wine mixed with your tears. Did God distinguish this man from the rest of you while in his mother's womb? Or is it your sin that made you his property? Jesus said, 'Gratis you have taken and gratis you shall give. . . . Do not possess gold, nor silver, neither copper.' Then what teachings allow the clergymen to sell their prayers for pieces of gold and silver? In the silence of the night you pray saying, 'Give us today our daily bread.' God has given you this land from which to draw your daily bread, but what authority has He given the monks to take this land and this bread away from you?

"You curse Judas because he sold his Master for a few pieces of silver, but you bless those who sell Him every day. Judas repented and hanged himself for his wrongdoing, but these priests walk proudly, dressed with beautiful robes, resplendent with shining crosses hanging over their chests. You teach your children to love Christ and at the same time you instruct them to obey those who oppose His teachings and violate His law.

"The apostles of Christ were stoned to death in order to revive in you the Holy Spirit, but the monks and the priests are killing that spirit in you

322

so they may live on your pitiful bounty. What persuades you to live such a life in this universe, full of misery and oppression? What prompts you to kneel before that horrible idol which has been erected upon the bones of your fathers? What treasure are you reserving for your posterity?

"Your souls are in the grip of the priests, and your bodies are in the closing jaws of the rulers. What thing in life can you point at and say 'this is mine!' My fellowmen, do you know the priest you fear? He is a traitor who uses the Gospel as a threat to ransom your money . . . a hypocrite wearing a cross and using it as a sword to cut your veins . . . a wolf disguised in lambskin . . . a glutton who respects the tables more than the altars . . . a gold-hungry creature who follows the Denar to the farthest land . . . a cheat pilfering from widows and orphans. He is a queer being, with an eagle's beak, a tiger's clutches, a hyena's teeth and a viper's clothes. Take the Book away from him and tear his raiment off and pluck his beard and do whatever you wish unto him; then place in his hand one Denar, and he will forgive you smilingly.

"Slap his face and spit on him and step on his neck; then invite him to sit at your board. He will immediately forget and untie his belt and gladly fill his stomach with your food.

"Curse him and ridicule him; then send him a jar of wine or a basket of fruit. He will forgive you your sins. When he sees a woman, he turns his face, saying, 'Go from me, Oh, daughter of Babylon.' Then he whispers to himself saying, 'Marriage is better than coveting.' He sees the young men and women walking in the procession of Love, and he lifts his eyes toward heaven and says, 'Vanity of vanities, all is vanity.' And in his solitude he talks to himself saying, 'May the laws and traditions that deny me the joys of life, be abolished.'

"He preaches to the people saying, 'Judge not, lest ye be judged.' But he judges all those who abhor his deeds and sends them to hell before Death separates them from this life.

"When he talks he lifts his head toward heaven, but at the same time, his thoughts are crawling like snakes through your pockets.

"He addresses you as beloved children, but his heart is empty of paternal love, and his lips never smile at a child, nor does he carry an infant between his arms.

"He tells you, while shaking his head, 'Let us keep away from earthly things, for life passes like a cloud.' But if you look thoroughly at him, you will find that he is gripping on to life, lamenting the passing of yesterday, condemning the speed of today, and waiting fearfully for tomorrow.

"He asks you for charity when he has plenty to give; if you grant his request, he will bless you publicly, and if you refuse him, he will curse you secretly.

"In the temple he asks you to help the needy, and

about his house the needy are begging for bread, but he cannot see or hear.

"He sells his prayers, and he who does not buy is an infidel, excommunicated from Paradise.

"This is the creature of whom you are afraid. This is the monk who sucks your blood. This is the priest who makes the sign of the Cross with the right hand, and clutches your throat with the left hand.

"This is the pastor whom you appoint as your servant, but he appoints himself as your master.

"This is the shadow that embraces your souls from birth until death.

"This is the man who came to judge me tonight because my spirit revolted against the enemies of Jesus the Nazarene Who loved all and called us brothers, and Who died on the Cross for us."

Khalil felt that there was understanding in the villagers' hearts; his voice brightened and he resumed his discourse saying, "Brethren, you know that Sheik Abbas has been appointed as Master of this village by Emir Shehab, the Sultan's representative and Governor of the Province, but I ask you if anyone has seen that power appoint the Sultan as the god of this country. That Power, my fellowmen, cannot be seen, nor can you hear it talk, but you can feel its existence in the depths of your hearts. It is that Power which you worship and pray for every day saying, 'Our Father which art in heaven.' Yes, your Father Who is in heaven is the one Who appoints kings and princes, for He is powerful and above all. But do you think that your Father, Who loved you and showed you the right path through His prophets, desires for you to be oppressed? Do you believe that God, Who brings forth the rain from heaven, and the wheat from the hidden seeds in the heart of the earth, desires for you to be hungry in order that but one man will enjoy His bounty? Do you believe that the Eternal Spirit Who reveals to you the wife's love, the children's pity and the neighbor's mercy, would have upon you a tyrant to enslave you through your life? Do you believe that the Eternal Law that made life beautiful, would send you a man to deny you of that happiness and lead you into the dark dungeon of painful Death? Do you believe that your physical strength, provided you by nature, belongs beyond your body to the rich?

"You cannot believe in all these things, because if you do you will be denying the justice of God who made us all equal, and the light of Truth that shines upon all peoples of the earth. What makes you struggle against yourselves, heart against body, and help those who enslave you while God has created you free on this earth?

"Are you doing yourselves justice when you lift your eyes towards Almighty God and call him Father, and then turn around, bow your heads before a man, and call him Master?

"Are you contented, as sons of God, with being slaves of man? Did not Christ call you brethren?

Yet Sheik Abbas calls you servants. Did not Jesus make you free in Truth and Spirit? Yet the Emir made you slaves of shame and corruption. Did not Christ exalt you to heaven? Then why are you descending to hell? Did He not enlighten your hearts? Then why are you hiding your souls in darkness? God has placed a glowing torch in your hearts that glows in knowledge and beauty, and seeks the secrets of the days and nights; it is a sin to extinguish that torch and bury it in ashes. God has created your spirits with wings to fly in the spacious firmament of Love and Freedom; it is pitiful that you cut your wings with your own hands and suffer your spirits to crawl like insects upon the earth."

Sheik Abbas observed in dismay the attentiveness of the villagers, and attempted to interrupt, but Khalil, inspired, continued, "God has sown in your hearts the seeds of Happiness; it is a crime that you dig those seeds out and throw them wilfully on the rocks so the wind will scatter them and the birds will pick them. God has given you children to rear, to teach them the truth and fill their hearts with the most precious things of existence. He wants you to bequeath upon them the joy of Life and the bounty of Life; why are they now strangers to their place of birth and cold creatures before the face of the Sun? A father who makes his son a slave is the father who gives his child a stone when he asks for bread. Have you not seen the birds of the sky training their young ones to fly? Why, then, do you teach your children to drag the shackles of slavery? Have you not seen the flowers of the valleys deposit their seeds in the sun-heated earth? Then why do you commit your children to the cold darkness?"

Silence prevailed for a moment, and it seemed as if Khalil's mind were crowded with pain. But now with a low and compelling voice he continued, "The words which I utter tonight are the same expressions that caused my expulsion from the convent. If the lord of your fields and the pastor of your church were to prey upon me and kill me tonight, I will die happy and in peace because I have fulfilled my mission and revealed to you the Truth which demons consider a crime. I have now completed the will of Almighty God."

There had been a magic message in Khalil's voice that forced the villagers' interest. The women were moved by the sweetness of his words and looked upon him as a messenger of peace, and their eyes were rich with tears.

Sheik Abbas and Father Elias were shaking with anger. As Khalil finished, he walked a few steps and stopped near Rachel and Miriam. Silence dominated the courtroom, and it seemed as if Khalil's spirit hovered in that vast hall and diverted the souls of the multitude from fearing Sheik Abbas and Father Elias, who sat trembling in annoyance and guilt.

The Sheik stood suddenly and his face was pale. He looked toward the men who were standing about him as he said, "What has become of you, dogs? Have your hearts been poisoned? Has your blood stopped running and weakened you so that you cannot leap upon this criminal and cut him to pieces? What awful thing has he done to you?" Having finished reprimanding the men, he raised a sword and started toward the fettered youth, whereupon a strong villager walked to him, gripped his hand and said, "Lay down your weapon, Master, for he who draws the sword to kill, shall, by the sword, be killed!"

The Sheik trembled visibly and the sword fell from his hand. He addressed the man saying, "Will a weak servant oppose his Master and benefactor?" And the man responded, "The faithful servant does not share his Master in the committing of crimes; this young man has spoken naught but the truth." Another man stepped forward and assured, "This man is innocent and is worthy of honour and respect." And a woman raised her voice saying, "He did not swear at God or curse any saint; why do you call him heretic?" And Rachel asked, "What is his crime?" The Sheik shouted, "You are rebellious, you miserable widow; have you forgotten the fate of your husband who turned rebel six years ago?" Upon hearing these impulsive words, Rachel shivered with painful anger, for she had found the murderer of her husband. She choked her tears and looked upon the throng and cried out, "Here is the criminal you have been trying for six years to find; you hear him now confessing his guilt. He is the killer who has been hiding his crime. Look at him and read his face; study him well and observe his fright; he shivers like the last leaf on winter's tree. God has shown you that the Master whom you have always feared is a murderous criminal. He caused me to be a widow amongst these women, and my daughter an orphan amidst these children." Rachel's utterance fell like thunder upon the Sheik's head, and the uproar of men and exaltation of women fell like firebrands upon him.

The priest assisted the Sheik to his seat. Then he called the servants and ordered them saying, "Arrest this woman who has falsely accused your Master of killing her husband; drag her and this young man into a dark prison, and any who oppose you will be criminals, excommunicated as he was from the Holy Church." The servants gave no heed to his command, but remained motionless staring at Khalil who was still bound with rope. Rachel stood at his right and Miriam at his left like a pair of wings ready to soar aloft into the spacious sky of Freedom.

His beard shaking with anger, Father Elias said, "Are you denying your Master for the sake of an infidel criminal and a shameless adulteress?" And the oldest one of the servants answered him saying, "We have served Sheik Abbas long for bread and shelter, but we have never been his slaves." Having thus spoken, the servant took off his cloak and turban and threw them before the Sheik and added, "I shall no longer require this raiment, nor do I wish

my soul to suffer in the narrow house of a criminal."
And all the servants did likewise and joined the
crowd whose faces radiated with joy, symbol of
Freedom and Truth. Father Elias finally saw that
his authority had declined, and he left the place
cursing the hour that brought Khalil to the village.
A strong man strode to Khalil and untied his hands,
looked at Sheik Abbas who fell like a corpse upon
his seat, and boldly addressed him saying, "This
fettered youth, whom you have brought here tonight to be tried as a criminal, has lifted our depressed spirits and enlightened our hearts with
Truth and Knowledge. And this poor widow whom
Father Elias referred to as a false accuser has revealed to us the crime you committed six years past.
We came here tonight to witness the trial of an innocent youth and a noble soul. Now, heaven has
opened our eyes and has shown us your atrocity; we
shall leave you and ignore you and allow heaven to
do its will."

Many voices were raised in that hall, and one
could hear a certain man saying, "Let us leave this
ill-famed residence for our homes." And another
one remarking, "Let us follow this young man to
Rachel's home and listen to his wise sayings and
consoling wisdom." And a third one saying, "Let
us seek his advice, for he knows our needs." And a
fourth one calling out, "If we are seeking justice,
let us complain to the Emir and tell him of Abbas'
crime." And many were saying, "Let us petition the

Emir to appoint Khalil as our Master and ruler, and tell the Bishop that Father Elias was a partner in these crimes." While the voices were rising and falling upon the Sheik's ears like sharp arrows, Khalil lifted his hands and calmed the villagers saying, "My brethren, do not seek haste, but rather listen and meditate. I ask you, in the name of my love and friendship for you, not to go to the Emir, for you will not find justice. Remember that a ferocious beast does not snap another one like him, neither should you go to the Bishop, for he knows well that the house cloven amid itself shall be ruined. Do not ask the Emir to appoint me as the Sheik in this village, for the faithful servant does not like to be an aid to the evil Master. If I deserve your kindness and love, let me live amongst you and share with you the happiness and sorrows of Life. Let me join hands and work with you at home and in the fields, for if I could not make myself one of you, I would be a hypocrite who does not live according to his sermon. And now, as the axe is laid unto the root of the tree, let us leave Sheik Abbas alone in the courtroom of his conscience and before the Supreme Court of God whose sun shines upon the innocent and the criminal."

Having thus spoken, he left the place, and the multitude followed him as if there were a divine power in him that attracted their hearts. The Sheik remained alone with the terrible silence, like a destroyed tower, suffering his defeat quietly like a surrendering commander. When the multitude reached the church yard and the moon was just showing from behind the cloud, Khalil looked at them with the eyes of love like a good shepherd watching over his herd. He was moved with sympathy upon those villagers who symbolized an oppressed nation; and he stood like a prophet who saw all the nations of the East walking in those valleys and dragging empty souls and heavy hearts.

He raised both hands toward heaven and said, "From the bottom of these depths we call thee, Oh, Liberty. Give heed to us! From behind the darkness we raise our hands to thee, Oh, Liberty. Look upon us! Upon the snow, we worship before thee, Oh, Liberty. Have mercy on us! Before thy great throne we stand, hanging on our bodies the blood-stained garments of our forefathers, covering our heads with the dust of the graves mixed with their remains, carrying the swords that stabbed their hearts, lifting the spears that pierced their bodies, dragging the chains that slowed their feet, uttering the cry that wounded their throats, lamenting and repeating the song of our failure that echoed throughout the prison, and repeating the prayers that came from the depths of our fathers' hearts. Listen to us, Oh Liberty, and hear us. From the Nile to the Euphrates comes the wailing of the suffering souls, in unison with the cry of the abyss; and from the end of the East to the mountains of Lebanon, hands are stretched to you, trembling with the presence of

Death. From the shores of the sea to the end of the desert, tear-flooded eyes look beseechingly toward you. Come, Oh Liberty, and save us.

"In the wretched huts standing in the shadow of poverty and oppression, they beat at their bosoms, soliciting thy mercy; watch us, Oh Liberty, and have mercy on us. In the pathways and in the houses miserable youth calls thee; in the churches and the mosques, the forgotten Book turns to thee; in the courts and in the palaces the neglected Law appeals to thee. Have mercy on us, Oh Liberty, and save us. In our narrow streets the merchant sells his days in order to make tribute to the exploiting thieves of the West, and none would give him advice. In the barren fields the fellah tills the soil and sows the seeds of his heart and nourishes them with his tears, but he reaps naught except thorns, and none would teach him the true path. In our arid plains the Bedouin roams barefoot and hungry, but none would have mercy on him; speak, Oh Liberty, and teach us! Our sick lambs are grazing upon the grassless prairie, our calves are gnawing on the roots of the trees, and our horses are feeding on dry plants. Come, Oh Liberty, and help us. We have been living in darkness since the beginning, and like prisoners they take us from one prison to another, while time ridicules our plight. When will dawn come? Until when shall we bear the scorn of the ages? Many a stone have we been dragging, and many a yoke has been placed upon our necks. Until when shall we bear this human outrage? The Egyptian slavery, the Babylonian exile, the tyranny of Persia, the despotism of the Romans, and the greed of Europe . . . all these things we have suffered. Where are we going now, and when shall we reach the sublime end of the rough roadway? From the clutches of Pharaoh to the paws of Nebuchadnezzar, to the iron hands of Alexander, to the swords of Herod, to the talons of Nero, and the sharp teeth of Demon . . . into whose hands are we now to fall, and when will Death come and take us, so we may rest at last?

"With the strength of our arms we lifted the columns of the temple, and upon our backs we carried the mortar to build the great walls and the impregnable pyramids for the sake of glory. Until when shall we continue building such magnificent palaces and living in wretched huts? Until when shall we continue filling the bins of the rich with provisions, while sustaining weak life on dry morsels? Until when shall we continue weaving silk and wool for our lords and masters while we wear naught except tattered swaddles?

"Through their wickedness we were divided amongst ourselves; and the better to keep their thrones and be at ease, they armed the Druze to fight the Arab, and stirred up the Shiite to attack the Sunnite, and encouraged the Kurdish to butcher the Bedouin, and cheered the Mohammedan to dispute with the Christian. Until when shall a brother continue killing his own brother upon his mother's bosom? Until when shall the Cross be kept apart from the Crescent * before the eyes of God? Oh Liberty, hear us, and speak in behalf of but one individual, for a great fire is started with a small spark. Oh Liberty, awaken but one heart with the rustling of thy wings, for from one cloud alone comes the lightning which illuminates the pits of the valleys and the tops of the mountains. Disperse with thy power these black clouds and descend like thunder and destroy the thrones that were built upon the bones and skulls of our ancestors."

"Hear us, Oh Liberty;
Bring mercy, Oh Daughter of Athens;
Rescue us, Oh Sister of Rome;
Advise us, Oh Companion of Moses;
Help us, Oh Beloved of Mohammed;
Teach us, Oh Bride of Jesus;
Strengthen our hearts so we may live,
Or harden our enemies so we may perish
And live in peace eternally."

As Khalil was pouring forth his sentiment before heaven, the villagers were gazing at him in reverence, and their love was springing forth in unison with the song of his voice until they felt that he became part of their hearts. After a short silence,

* The crescent is the emblem of the Mohammedan flag, flown over Syria during the Turkish rule. (*Editor's note.*)

Khalil brought his eyes upon the multitude and quietly said, "Night has brought us to the house of Sheik Abbas in order to realize the daylight; oppression has arrested us before the cold Space, so we may understand one another and gather like chicks under the wings of the Eternal Spirit. Now let us go to our homes and sleep until we meet again tomorrow."

Having thus spoken, he walked away, following Rachel and Miriam to their poor hovel. The throng departed and each went to his home, contemplating what he had seen and heard that memorable night. They felt that a burning torch of a new spirit had scoured their inner selves and led them into the right path. In an hour all the lamps were extinguished and Silence engulfed the whole village while Slumber carried the fellahin's souls into the world of strong dreams; but Sheik Abbas found no sleep all night, as he watched the phantoms of darkness and the horrible ghosts of his crimes in procession.

PART EIGHT

Two months had already passed and Khalil was still preaching and pouring his sentiments in the villagers' hearts, reminding them of their usurped rights and showing them the greed and oppression of the rulers and the monks. They listened to him with care, for he was a source of pleasure; his words fell upon their hearts like rain upon thirsty land.

In their solitude, they repeated Khalil's sayings as they did their daily prayers. Father Elias commenced fawning upon them to regain their friendship; he became docile since the villagers found out that he was the Sheik's ally in crime, and the fellahin ignored him.

Sheik Abbas had a nervous suffering, and walked through his mansion like a caged tiger. He issued commands to his servants, but no one answered except the echo of his voice inside the marble walls. He shouted at his men, but no one came to his aid except his poor wife who suffered the pang of his cruelty as much as the villagers did. When Lent came and Heaven announced the coming of Spring, the days of the Sheik expired with the passing of Winter. He died after a long agony, and his soul was carried away on the carpet of his deeds to stand naked and shivering before that high Throne whose existence we feel, but cannot see. The fellahin heard various tales about the manner of Sheik Abbas' death; some of them related that the Sheik died insane, while others insisted that disappointment and despair drove him to death by his own hand. But the women who went to offer their sympathies to his wife reported that he died from fear, because the ghost of Samaan Ramy hunted him and drove him every midnight out to the place where Rachel's husband was found slain six years before.

The month of Nisan proclaimed to the villagers the love secrets of Khalil and Miriam. They rejoiced the good tidings which assured them that Khalil would thereby remain in their village. As the news reached all the inhabitants of the huts, they congratulated one another upon Khalil's becoming their beloved neighbour.

When harvest time came, the fellahin went to the fields and gathered the sheaves of corn and bundles of wheat to the threshing floor. Sheik Abbas was not there to take the crop and have it carried to his bins. Each fellah harvested his own crop; the villagers' huts where filled with wheat and corn; their vessels were replenished with good wine and oil. Khalil shared with them their toils and happiness; he helped them in gathering the crop, pressing the grapes and picking the fruits. He never distinguished himself from any one of them except by his excess of love and ambition. Since that year and up to our present time, each fellah in that village commenced to reap with joy the crop which he sowed with toil and labour. The land which the fellahin tilled and the vineyards they cultivated became their own property.

Now, half a century has passed since this incident, and the Lebanese have awakened.

On his way to the Holy Cedars of Lebanon, a traveller's attention is caught by the beauty of that village, standing like a bride at the side of the valley. The wretched huts are now comfortable and happy homes surrounded by fertile fields and blooming orchards. If you ask any one of the resi-

dents about Sheik Abbas' history, he will answer
you, pointing with his finger to a heap of demolished
stones and destroyed walls saying, "This is the
Sheik's palace, and this is the history of his life."
And if you inquire about Khalil, he will raise his
hand toward heaven saying, "There resides our beloved Khalil, whose life's history was written by
God with glittering letters upon the pages of our
hearts, and they cannot be effaced by the ages."

BOOK TWELVE

BOOK TWELVE

THE BROKEN WINGS

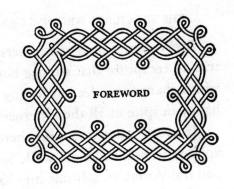

WAS EIGHTEEN years of age when love opened my eyes with its magic rays and touched my spirit for the first time with its fiery fingers, and Selma Karamy was the first woman who awakened my spirit with her beauty and led me into the garden of high affection, where days pass like dreams and nights like weddings.

Selma Karamy was the one who taught me to worship beauty by the example of her own beauty and revealed to me the secret of love by her affection; she was the one who first sang to me the poetry of real life.

Every young man remembers his first love and tries to recapture that strange hour, the memory of which changes his deepest feeling and makes him so happy in spite of all the bitterness of its mystery.

In every young man's life there is a "Selma" who appears to him suddenly while in the spring of life and transforms his solitude into happy moments and fills the silence of his nights with music.

I was deeply engrossed in thought and contemplation and seeking to understand the meaning of nature and the revelation of books and scriptures when I heard LOVE whispered into my ears through Selma's lips. My life was a coma, empty like that of Adam's in Paradise, when I saw Selma standing before me like a column of light. She was the Eve of my heart who filled it with secrets and wonders and made me understand the meaning of life.

The first Eve led Adam out of Paradise by her own will, while Selma made me enter willingly into the paradise of pure love and virtue by her sweetness and love; but what happened to the first man also happened to me, and the fiery sword which chased Adam out of Paradise was like the one which frightened me by its glittering edge and forced me away from the paradise of my love without having disobeyed any order or tasted the fruit of the forbidden tree.

Today, after many years have passed, I have nothing left out of that beautiful dream except painful memories flapping like invisible wings around me, filling the depths of my heart with sorrow, and bringing tears to my eyes; and my beloved, beautiful Selma, is dead and nothing is left to commemorate her except my broken heart and a tomb surrounded by cypress trees. That tomb and this heart are all that is left to bear witness of Selma.

The silence that guards the tomb does not reveal God's secret in the obscurity of the coffin, and the rustling of the branches whose roots suck the body's elements do not tell the mysteries of the grave, but the agonized sighs of my heart announce to the living the drama which love, beauty, and death have performed.

Oh, friends of my youth who are scattered in the city of Beirut, when you pass by that cemetery near the pine forest, enter it silently and walk slowly so the tramping of your feet will not disturb the slumber of the dead, and stop humbly by Selma's tomb and greet the earth that encloses her corpse and mention my name with a deep sigh and say to yourself, "Here, all the hopes of Gibran, who is living as a prisoner of love beyond the seas, were buried. On this spot he lost his happiness, drained his tears, and forgot his smile."

By that tomb grows Gibran's sorrow together with the cypress trees, and above the tomb his spirit flickers every night commemorating Selma, joining the branches of the trees in sorrowful wailing, mourning and lamenting the going of Selma, who, yesterday, was a beautiful tune on the lips of life and today is a silent secret in the bosom of the earth.

> *Oh, comrades of my youth! I appeal to you in the names of those virgins whom your hearts have loved, to lay a wreath of flowers on the forsaken tomb of my beloved, for the flowers you lay on Selma's tomb are like falling drops of dew from the eyes of dawn on the leaves of a withering rose.*

SILENT SORROW

Y NEIGHBORS,
you remember the dawn of youth with pleasure and
regret its passing; but I remember it like a prisoner
who recalls the bars and shackles of his jail. You
speak of those years between infancy and youth as a
golden era free from confinement and cares, but I
call those years an era of silent sorrow which dropped
as a seed into my heart and grew with it and could
find no outlet to the world of knowledge and wisdom
until love came and opened the heart's doors and
lighted its corners. Love provided me with a tongue

347

and tears. You people remember the gardens and orchids and the meeting places and street corners that witnessed your games and heard your innocent whispering; and I remember, too, the beautiful spot in North Lebanon. Every time I close my eyes I see those valleys full of magic and dignity and those mountains covered with glory and greatness trying to reach the sky. Every time I shut my ears to the clamor of the city I hear the murmur of the rivulets and the rustling of the branches. All those beauties which I speak of now and which I long to see, as a child longs for his mother's breast, wounded my spirit, imprisoned in the darkness of youth, as a falcon suffers in its cage when it sees a flock of birds flying freely in the spacious sky. Those valleys and hills fired my imagination, but bitter thoughts wove round my heart a net of hopelessness.

Every time I went to the fields I returned disappointed, without understanding the cause of my disappointment. Every time I looked at the gray sky I felt my heart contract. Every time I heard the singing of the birds and babbling of the spring I suffered without understanding the reason for my suffering. It is said that unsophistication makes a man empty and that emptiness makes him carefree. It may be true among those who were born dead and who exist like frozen corpses; but the sensitive boy who feels much and knows little is the most unfortunate creature under the sun, because he is torn by two forces. The first force elevates him and shows him the beauty of existence through a cloud of dreams; the second ties him down to the earth and fills his eyes with dust and overpowers him with fears and darkness.

Solitude has soft, silky hands, but with strong fingers it grasps the heart and makes it ache with sorrow. Solitude is the ally of sorrow as well as a companion of spiritual exaltation.

The boy's soul undergoing the buffeting of sorrow is like a white lily just unfolding. It trembles before the breeze and opens its heart to daybreak and folds its leaves back when the shadow of night comes. If that boy does not have diversion or friends or companions in his games, his life will be like a narrow prison in which he sees nothing but spiderwebs and hears nothing but the crawling of insects.

That sorrow which obsessed me during my youth was not caused by lack of amusement, because I could have had it; neither from lack of friends, because I could have found them. That sorrow was caused by an inward ailment which made me love solitude. It killed in me the inclination for games and amusement. It removed from my shoulders the wings of youth and made me like a pond of water between mountains which reflects in its calm surface the shadows of ghosts and the colors of clouds and trees, but cannot find an outlet by which to pass singing to the sea.

Thus was my life before I attained the age of eighteen. That year is like a mountain peak in my life, for it awakened knowledge in me and made me understand the vicissitudes of mankind. In that year I was reborn and unless a person is born again his life will remain like a blank sheet in the book of existence. In that year, I saw the angels of Heaven looking at me through the eyes of a beautiful woman. I also saw the devils of hell raging in the heart of an evil man. He who does not see the angels and devils in the beauty and malice of life will be far removed from knowledge, and his spirit will be empty of affection.

THE HAND OF DESTINY

N THE SPRING OF that wonderful year, I was in Beirut. The gardens were full of Nisan flowers and the earth was carpeted with green grass, all like a secret of earth revealed to Heaven. The orange trees and apple trees, looking like houris or brides sent by nature to inspire poets and excite the imagination, were wearing white garments of perfumed blossoms.

Spring is beautiful everywhere, but it is most beautiful in Lebanon. It is a spirit that roams round the earth but hovers over Lebanon, conversing with kings and prophets, singing with the rivers the songs of Solomon, and repeating with the Holy Cedars of Lebanon the memory of ancient glory. Beirut, free from the mud of winter and the dust of summer, is like a bride in the spring, or like a mermaid sitting by the side of a brook drying her smooth skin in the rays of the sun.

One day, in the month of Nisan, I went to visit a friend whose home was at some distance from the glamorous city. As we were conversing, a dignified man of about sixty-five entered the house. As I rose to greet him, my friend introduced him to me as Farris Effandi Karamy and then gave him my name with flattering words. The old man looked at me a moment, touching his forehead with the ends of his fingers as if he were trying to regain his memory. Then he smilingly approached me, saying, "You are the son of a very dear friend of mine, and I am happy to see that friend in your person."

Much affected by his words, I was attracted to him like a bird whose instinct leads him to his nest before the coming of the tempest. As we sat down, he told us about his friendship with my father, recalling the time which they spent together. An old man likes to return in memory to the days of his youth like a stranger who longs to go back to his own country. He delights to tell stories of the past like a poet who takes pleasure in reciting his best poem. He lives spiritually in the past because the present passes swiftly, and the future seems to him an approach to the oblivion of the grave. An hour full of old memories passed like the shadows of the trees over the grass. When Farris Effandi started to leave, he put his left hand on my shoulder and shook my right hand, saying, "I have not seen your father for twenty years. I hope you will take his place in frequent visits to my house." I promised gratefully to do my duty toward a dear friend of my father.

When the old man left the house, I asked my friend to tell me more about him. He said, "I do not know any other man in Beirut whose wealth has made him kind and whose kindness has made him wealthy. He is one of the few who come to this world and leave it without harming any one, but people of that kind are usually miserable and oppressed because they are not clever enough to save themselves from the crookedness of others. Farris Effandi has one daughter whose character is similar to his and whose beauty and gracefulness are beyond description, and she will also be miserable because her father's wealth is placing her already at the edge of a horrible precipice."

As he uttered these words, I noticed that his face clouded. Then he continued, "Farris Effandi is a good old man with a noble heart, but he lacks will power. People lead him like a blind man. His daughter obeys him in spite of her pride and intelligence, and this is the secret which lurks in the life of father and daughter. This secret was discovered by an evil man who is a bishop and whose wickedness hides in the shadow of his Gospel. He makes the people believe that he is kind and noble. He is the head of religion in this land of the religious. The people obey and worship him. He leads them like a flock of lambs to the slaughter house. This bishop has a nephew who is full of hatefulness and corruption. The day will come sooner or later when he will place his nephew on his right and Farris Effandi's daughter on his left, and, holding with his evil hand the wreath of matrimony over their heads, will tie a pure virgin to a filthy degenerate, placing the heart of the day in the bosom of night.

"That is all I can tell you about Farris Effandi and his daughter, so do not ask me any more questions."

Saying this, he turned his head toward the window as if he were trying to solve the problems of human existence by concentrating on the beauty of the universe.

As I left the house, I told my friend that I was going to visit Farris Effandi in a few days for the purpose of fulfilling my promise and for the sake of the friendship which had joined him and my father. He stared at me for a moment, and I noticed a change in his expression as if my few simple words had revealed to him a new idea. Then he looked straight through my eyes in a strange manner, a look of love, mercy, and fear—the look of a prophet who foresees what no one else can divine. Then his lips trembled a little, but he said nothing when I started toward the door. That strange look followed me, the meaning of which I could not understand until I grew up in the world of experience, where hearts understand each other intuitively and where spirits are mature with knowledge.

Entrance to the Shrine

N A FEW DAYS,
loneliness overcame me; and I tired of the grim faces
of books; I hired a carriage and started for the house
of Farris Effandi. As I reached the pine woods where
people went for picnics, the driver took a private
way, shaded with willow trees on each side. Passing
through, we could see the beauty of the green grass,
the grapevines, and the many colored flowers of
Nisan just blossoming.

In a few minutes the carriage stopped before a
solitary house in the midst of a beautiful garden. The

scent of roses, gardenia, and jasmine filled the air. As I dismounted and entered the spacious garden, I saw Farris Effandi coming to meet me. He ushered me into his house with a hearty welcome and sat by me, like a happy father when he sees his son, showering me with questions on my life, future and education. I answered him, my voice full of ambition and zeal; for I heard ringing in my ears the hymn of glory, and I was sailing the calm sea of hopeful dreams. Just then a beautiful young woman, dressed in a gorgeous white silk gown, appeared from behind the velvet curtains of the door and walked toward me. Farris Effandi and I rose from our seats.

"This is my daughter Selma," said the old man. Then he introduced me to her, saying, "Fate has brought back to me a dear old friend of mine in the person of his son." Selma stared at me a moment as if doubting that a visitor could have entered their house. Her hand, when I touched it, was like a white lily, and a strange pang pierced my heart.

We all sat silent as if Selma had brought into the room with her a heavenly spirit worthy of mute respect. As she felt the silence she smiled at me and said, "Many a time my father has repeated to me the stories of his youth and of the old days he and your father spent together. If your father spoke to you in the same way, then this meeting is not the first one between us."

The old man was delighted to hear his daughter talking in such a manner and said, "Selma is very sentimental. She sees everything through the eyes of the spirit." Then he resumed his conversation with care and tact as if he had found in me a magic charm which took him on the wings of memory to the days of the past.

As I considered him, dreaming of my own later years, he looked upon me, as a lofty old tree that has withstood storms and sunshine throws its shadow upon a small sapling which shakes before the breeze of dawn.

But Selma was silent. Occasionally, she looked first at me and then at her father as if reading the first and last chapters of life's drama. The day passed fast in that garden, and I could see through the window the ghostly yellow kiss of sunset on the mountains of Lebanon. Farris Effandi continued to recount his experiences and I listened entranced and responded with such enthusiasm that his sorrow was changed to happiness.

Selma sat by the window, looking on with sorrowful eyes and not speaking, although beauty has its own heavenly language, loftier than the voices of tongues and lips. It is a timeless language, common to all humanity, a calm lake that attracts the singing rivulets to its depth and makes them silent.

Only our spirits can understand beauty, or live and grow with it. It puzzles our minds; we are unable to describe it in words; it is a sensation that our eyes cannot see, derived from both the one who observes and the one who is looked upon. Real beauty is a ray which emanates from the holy of holies of the spirit, and illuminates the body, as life comes from the depths of the earth and gives color and scent to a flower.

Real beauty lies in the spiritual accord that is called love which can exist between a man and a woman.

Did my spirit and Selma's reach out to each other that day when we met, and did that yearning make me see her as the most beautiful woman under the sun? Or was I intoxicated with the wine of youth which made me fancy that which never existed?

Did my youth blind my natural eyes and make me imagine the brightness of her eyes, the sweetness of her mouth, and the grace of her figure? Or was it that her brightness, sweetness, and grace opened my eyes and showed me the happiness and sorrow of love?

It is hard to answer these questions, but I say truly that in that hour I felt an emotion that I had never felt before, a new affection resting calmly in my heart, like the spirit hovering over the waters at the creation of the world, and from that affection was born my happiness and my sorrow. Thus ended the hour of my first meeting with Selma, and thus the will of Heaven freed me from the bondage of youth and solitude and let me walk in the procession of love.

Love is the only freedom in the world because it so elevates the spirit that the laws of humanity and the phenomena of nature do not alter its course.

As I rose from my seat to depart, Farris Effandi came close to me and said soberly, "Now my son, since you know your way to this house, you should come often and feel that you are coming to your father's house. Consider me as a father and Selma as a sister." Saying this, he turned to Selma as if to ask confirmation of his statement. She nodded her head positively and then looked at me as one who has found an old acquaintance.

Those words uttered by Farris Effandi Karamy placed me side by side with his daughter at the altar of love. Those words were a heavenly song which started with exaltation and ended with sorrow; they raised our spirits to the realm of light and searing flame; they were the cup from which we drank happiness and bitterness.

I left the house. The old man accompanied me to the edge of the garden, while my heart throbbed like the trembling lips of a thirsty man.

4

THE WHITE TORCH

HE MONTH OF NISAN had nearly passed. I continued to visit the home of Farris Effendi and to meet Selma in that beautiful garden, gazing upon her beauty, marveling at her intelligence, and hearing the stillness of sorrow. I felt an invisible hand drawing me to her.

Every visit gave me a new meaning to her beauty and a new insight into her sweet spirit, until she became a book whose pages I could understand and whose praises I could sing, but which I could never finish reading. A woman whom Providence has provided with beauty of spirit and body is a truth, at the same time both open and secret, which we can understand only by love, and touch only by virtue; and when we attempt to describe such a woman she disappears like a vapor.

Selma Karamy had bodily and spiritual beauty, but how can I describe her to one who never knew her? Can a dead man remember the singing of a nightingale and the fragrance of a rose and the sigh of a brook? Can a prisoner who is heavily loaded with shackles follow the breeze of the dawn? Is not silence more painful than death? Does pride prevent me from describing Selma in plain words since I cannot draw her truthfully with luminous colors? A hungry man in a desert will not refuse to eat dry bread if Heaven does not shower him with manna and quails.

In her white silk dress, Selma was slender as a ray of moonlight coming through the window. She walked gracefully and rhythmically. Her voice was low and sweet; words fell from her lips like drops of dew falling from the petals of flowers when they are disturbed by the wind.

But Selma's face! No words can describe its expression, reflecting first great internal suffering, then heavenly exaltation.

The beauty of Selma's face was not classic; it

was like a dream of revelation which cannot be measured or bound or copied by the brush of a painter, or the chisel of a sculptor. Selma's beauty was not in her golden hair, but in the virtue and purity which surrounded it; not in her large eyes, but in the light which emanated from them; not in her red lips, but in the sweetness of her words; not in her ivory neck, but in its slight bow to the front. Nor was it in her perfect figure, but in the nobility of her spirit, burning like a white torch between earth and sky. Her beauty was like a gift of poetry. But poets are unhappy people, for, no matter how high their spirits reach, they will still be enclosed in an envelope of tears.

Selma was deeply thoughtful rather than talkative, and her silence was a kind of music that carried one to a world of dreams and made him listen to the throbbing of his heart, and see the ghosts of his thoughts and feelings standing before him, looking him in the eyes.

She wore a cloak of deep sorrow through her life, which increased her strange beauty and dignity, as a tree in blossom is more lovely when seen through the mist of dawn.

Sorrow linked her spirit and mine, as if each saw in the other's face what the heart was feeling and heard the echo of a hidden voice. God had made two bodies in one, and separation could be nothing but agony.

The sorrowful spirit finds rest when united with a similar one. They join affectionately, as a stranger is cheered when he sees another stranger in a strange land. Hearts that are united through the medium of sorrow will not be separated by the glory of happiness. Love that is cleansed by tears will remain eternally pure and beautiful.

5

THE TEMPEST

NE DAY FARRIS
Effandi invited me to dinner at his home. I accepted,
my spirit hungry for the divine bread which Heaven
placed in the hands of Selma, the spiritual bread
which makes our hearts hungrier the more we eat of
it. It was this bread which Kais, the Arabian poet,
Dante, and Sappho tasted and which set their hearts
afire; the bread which the Goddess prepares with the
sweetness of kisses and the bitterness of tears.

As I reached the home of Farris Effandi, I saw
Selma sitting on a bench in the garden resting her

head against a tree and looking like a bride in her white silk dress, or like a sentinel guarding that place.

Silently and reverently I approached and sat by her. I could not talk; so I resorted to silence, the only language of the heart, but I felt that Selma was listening to my wordless call and watching the ghost of my soul in my eyes.

In a few minutes the old man came out and greeted me as usual. When he stretched his hand toward me, I felt as if he were blessing the secrets that united me and his daughter. Then he said, "Dinner is ready, my children; let us eat." We rose and followed him, and Selma's eyes brightened; for a new sentiment had been added to her love by her father's calling us his children.

We sat at the table enjoying the food and sipping the old wine, but our souls were living in a world far away. We were dreaming of the future and its hardships.

Three persons were separated in thoughts, but united in love; three innocent people with much feeling but little knowledge; a drama was being performed by an old man who loved his daughter and cared for her happiness, a young woman of twenty looking into the future with anxiety, and a young man, dreaming and worrying, who had tasted neither

the wine of life nor its vinegar, and trying to reach
the height of love and knowledge but unable to lift
himself up. We three sitting in twilight were eating
and drinking in that solitary home, guarded by
Heaven's eyes, but at the bottoms of our glasses were
hidden bitterness and anguish.

As we finished eating, one of the maids announced the presence of a man at the door who
wished to see Farris Effandi. "Who is he?" asked the
old man. "The Bishop's messenger," said the maid.
There was a moment of silence during which Farris
Effandi stared at his daughter like a prophet who
gazes at Heaven to divine its secret. Then he said to
the maid, "Let the man in."

As the maid left, a man, dressed in oriental uni-
form and with a big mustache curled at the ends,
entered and greeted the old man, saying, "His Grace,
the Bishop, has sent me for you with his private carriage; he wishes to discuss important business with
you." The old man's face clouded and his smile disappeared. After a moment of deep thought he came
close to me and said in a friendly voice, "I hope to
find you here when I come back, for Selma will enjoy
your company in this solitary place."

Saying this, he turned to Selma and, smiling,
asked her if she agreed. She nodded her head, but
her cheeks became red, and with a voice sweeter than

the music of a lyre she said, "I will do my best, Father, to make our guest happy."

Selma watched the carriage that had taken her father and the Bishop's messenger until it disappeared. Then she came and sat opposite me on a divan covered with green silk. She looked like a lily bent to the carpet of green grass by the breeze of dawn. It was the will of Heaven that I should be with Selma alone, at night, in her beautiful home surrounded by trees, where silence, love, beauty, and virtue dwelt together.

We were both silent, each waiting for the other to speak, but speech is not the only means of understanding between two souls. It is not the syllables that come from the lips and tongues that bring hearts together.

There is something greater and purer than what the mouth utters. Silence illuminates our souls, whispers to our hearts, and brings them together. Silence separates us from ourselves, makes us sail the firmament of spirit, and brings us closer to Heaven; it makes us feel that bodies are no more than prisons and that this world is only a place of exile.

Selma looked at me and her eyes revealed the secret of her heart. Then she quietly said, "Let us go to the garden and sit under the trees and watch the moon come up behind the mountains." Obediently I rose from my seat, but I hesitated.

"Don't you think we had better stay here until the moon has risen and illuminates the garden?" And I continued, "The darkness hides the trees and flowers. We can see nothing."

Then she said, "If darkness hides the trees and flowers from our eyes, it will not hide love from our hearts."

Uttering these words in a strange tone, she turned her eyes and looked through the window. I remained silent, pondering her words, weighing the true meaning of each syllable. Then she looked at me as if she regretted what she had said and tried to take away those words from my ears by the magic of her eyes. But those eyes, instead of making me forget what she had said, repeated through the depths of my heart more clearly and effectively the sweet words which had already become graven in my memory for eternity.

Every beauty and greatness in this world is created by a single thought or emotion inside a man. Every thing we see today, made by past generations, was, before its appearance, a thought in the mind of a man or an impulse in the heart of a woman. The revolutions that shed so much blood and turned men's minds toward liberty were the idea of one man who lived in the midst of thousands of men. The devastating wars which destroyed empires were a thought that existed in the mind of an individual. The supreme teachings that changed the course of humanity were the ideas of a man whose genius separated him from his environment. A single thought built the Pyramids, founded the glory of Islam, and caused the burning of the library at Alexandria.

One thought will come to you at night which will elevate you to glory or lead you to the asylum. One look from a woman's eye makes you the happiest man in the world. One word from a man's lips will make you rich or poor.

That word which Selma uttered that night arrested me between my past and future, as a boat which is anchored in the midst of the ocean. That word awakened me from the slumber of youth and solitude and set me on the stage where life and death play their parts.

The scent of flowers mingled with the breeze as we came into the garden and sat silently on a bench near a jasmine tree, listening to the breathing of sleeping nature, while in the blue sky the eyes of heaven witnessed our drama.

The moon came out from behind Mount Sunnin

and shone over the coast, hills, and mountains; and we could see the villages fringing the valley like apparitions which have suddenly been conjured from nothing. We could see the beauty of all Lebanon under the silver rays of the moon.

Poets of the West think of Lebanon as a legendary place, forgotten since the passing of David and Solomon and the Prophets, as the Garden of Eden became lost after the fall of Adam and Eve. To those Western Poets, the word "Lebanon" is a poetical expression associated with a mountain whose sides are drenched with the incense of the Holy Cedars. It reminds them of the temples of copper and marble standing stern and impregnable and of a herd of deer feeding in the valleys. That night I saw Lebanon dream-like with the eyes of a poet.

Thus, the appearance of things changes according to the emotions, and thus we see magic and beauty in them, while the magic and beauty are really in ourselves.

As the rays of the moon shone on the face, neck, and arms of Selma, she looked like a statue of ivory sculptured by the fingers of some worshiper of Ishtar, goddess of beauty and love. As she looked at me, she said, "Why are you silent? Why do you not tell me something about your past?" As I gazed at her, my muteness vanished, and I opened my lips and said, "Did you not hear what I said when we came to this orchard? The spirit that hears the whispering of flowers and the singing of silence can also hear the shrieking of my soul and the clamor of my heart."

She covered her face with her hands and said in a trembling voice, "Yes, I heard you—I heard a voice coming from the bosom of night and a clamor raging in the heart of the day."

Forgetting my past, my very existence—everything but Selma—I answered her, saying, "And I heard you, too, Selma. I heard exhilarating music pulsing in the air and causing the whole universe to tremble."

Upon hearing these words, she closed her eyes and on her lips I saw a smile of pleasure mingled with sadness. She whispered softly, "Now I know that there is something higher than heaven and deeper than the ocean and stranger than life and death and time. I know now what I did not know before."

At that moment Selma became dearer than a friend and closer than a sister and more beloved than a sweetheart. She became a supreme thought, a beautiful dream, an overpowering emotion living in my spirit.

It is wrong to think that love comes from long

companionship and persevering courtship. Love is the offspring of spiritual affinity and unless that affinity is created in a moment, it will not be created in years or even generations.

Then Selma raised her head and gazed at the horizon where Mount Sunnin meets the sky, and said, "Yesterday you were like a brother to me, with whom I lived and by whom I sat calmly under my father's care. Now, I feel the presence of something stranger and sweeter than brotherly affection, an unfamiliar commingling of love and fear that fills my heart with sorrow and happiness."

I responded, "This emotion which we fear and which shakes us when it passes through our hearts is the law of nature that guides the moon around the earth and the sun around God."

She put her hand on my head and wove her fingers through my hair. Her face brightened and tears came out of her eyes like drops of dew on the leaves of a lily, and she said, "Who would believe our story—who would believe that in this hour we have surmounted the obstacles of doubt? Who would believe that the month of Nisan which brought us together for the first time, is the month that halted us in the Holy of Holies of life?"

Her hand was still on my head as she spoke, and

I would not have preferred a royal crown or a wreath of glory to that beautiful smooth hand whose fingers were twined in my hair.

Then I answered her: "People will not believe our story because they do not know that love is the only flower that grows and blossoms without the aid of seasons, but was it Nisan that brought us together for the first time, and is it this hour that has arrested us in the Holy of Holies of life? Is it not the hand of God that brought our souls close together before birth and made us prisoners of each other for all the days and nights? Man's life does not commence. in the womb and never ends in the grave; and this firmament, full of moonlight and stars, is not deserted by loving souls and intuitive spirits."

As she drew her hand away from my head, I felt a kind of electrical vibration at the roots of my hair mingled with the night breeze. Like a devoted worshiper who receives his blessing by kissing the altar in a shrine, I took Selma's hand, placed my burning lips on it, and gave it a long kiss, the memory of which melts my heart and awakens by its sweetness all the virtue of my spirit.

An hour passed, every minute of which was a year of love. The silence of the night, moonlight, flowers, and trees made us forget all reality except love, when suddenly we heard the galloping of horses and rattling of carriage wheels. Awakened from our pleasant swoon and plunged from the world of dreams into the world of perplexity and misery, we found that the old man had returned from his mission. We rose and walked through the orchard to meet him.

When the carriage reached the entrance of the garden, Farris Effandi dismounted and slowly walked towards us, bending forward slightly as if he were carrying a heavy load. He approached Selma and placed both of his hands on her shoulders and stared at her. Tears coursed down his wrinkled cheeks and his lips trembled with sorrowful smile. In a choking voice, he said, "My beloved Selma, very soon you will be taken away from the arms of your father to the arms of another man. Very soon fate will carry you from this lonely home to the world's spacious court, and this garden will miss the pressure of your footsteps, and your father will become a stranger to you. All is done; may God bless you."

Hearing these words, Selma's face clouded and her eyes froze as if she felt a premonition of death. Then she screamed, like a bird shot down, suffering, and trembling, and in a choked voice said, "What do you say? What do you mean? Where are you sending me?"

Then she looked at him searchingly, trying to discover his secret. In a moment she said, "I understand.

I understand everything. The Bishop has demanded me from you and has prepared a cage for this bird with broken wings. Is this your will, Father?"

His answer was a deep sigh. Tenderly he led Selma into the house while I remained standing in the garden, waves of perplexity beating upon me like a tempest upon autumn leaves. Then I followed them into the living room, and to avoid embarrassment, shook the old man's hand, looked at Selma, my beautiful star, and left the house.

As I reached the end of the garden I heard the old man calling me and turned to meet him. Apologetically he took my hand and said, "Forgive me, my son. I have ruined your evening with the shedding of tears, but please come to see me when my house is deserted and I am lonely and desperate. Youth, my dear son, does not combine with senility, as morning does not meet the night; but you will come to me and call to my memory the youthful days which I spent with your father, and you will tell me the news of life which does not count me as among its sons any longer. Will you not visit me when Selma leaves and I am left here in loneliness?"

While he said these sorrowful words and I silently shook his hand, I felt the warm tears falling from his eyes upon my hand. Trembling with sorrow and filial affection, I felt as if my heart were choked with grief. When I raised my head and he saw the tears in my eyes, he bent toward me and touched my forehead with his lips. "Good-bye, son, Good-bye."

An old man's tear is more potent than that of a young man because it is the residuum of life in his weakening body. A young man's tear is like a drop of dew on the leaf of a rose, while that of an old man is like a yellow leaf which falls with the wind at the approach of winter.

As I left the house of Farris Effandi Karamy, Selma's voice still rang in my ears, her beauty followed me like a wraith, and her father's tears dried slowly on my hand.

My departure was like Adam's exodus from Paradise, but the Eve of my heart was not with me to make the whole world an Eden. That night, in which I had been born again, I felt that I saw death's face for the first time.

Thus the sun enlivens and kills the fields with its heat.

6

THE LAKE OF FIRE

EVERYTHING THAT
a man does secretly in the darkness of night will be
clearly revealed in daylight. Words uttered in privacy will become unexpectedly common conversation. Deeds which we hide today in the corners of
our lodgings will be shouted on every street tomorrow.

Thus the ghosts of darkness revealed the purpose
of Bishop Bulos Galib's meeting with Farris Effandi
Karamy, and his conversation was repeated all over
the neighborhood until it reached my ears.

The discussion that took place between Bishop Bulos Galib and Farris Effandi that night was not over the problems of the poor or the widows and orphans. The main purpose for sending after Farris Effandi and bringing him in the Bishop's private carriage was the betrothal of Selma to the Bishop's nephew, Mansour Bey Galib.

Selma was the only child of the wealthy Farris Effandi, and the Bishop's choice fell on Selma, not on account of her beauty and noble spirit, but on account of her father's money which would guarantee Mansour Bey a good and prosperous fortune and make him an important man.

The heads of religion in the East are not satisfied with their own munificence, but they must strive to make all members of their families superiors and oppressors. The glory of a prince goes to his eldest son by inheritance, but the exaltation of a religious head is contagious among his brothers and nephews. Thus the Christian bishop and the Moslem imam and the Brahman priest become like sea reptiles who clutch their prey with many tentacles and suck their blood with numerous mouths.

When the Bishop demanded Selma's hand for his nephew, the only answer that he received from her father was deep silence and falling tears, for he hated to lose his only child. Any man's soul trembles when he is separated from his only daughter whom he has reared to young womanhood.

The sorrow of parents at the marriage of a daughter is equal to their happiness at the marriage of a son, because a son brings to the family a new member, while a daughter, upon her marriage, is lost to them.

Farris Effandi perforce granted the Bishop's request, obeying his will unwillingly, because Farris Effandi knew the Bishop's nephew very well, knew that he was dangerous, full of hate, wickedness, and corruption.

In Lebanon, no Christian could oppose his bishop and remain in good standing. No man could disobey his religious head and keep his reputation. The eye could not resist a spear without being pierced, and the hand could not grasp a sword without being cut off.

Suppose that Farris Effandi had resisted the Bishop and refused his wish; then Selma's reputation would have been ruined and her name would have been blemished by the dirt of lips and tongues. In the opinion of the fox, high bunches of grapes that can't be reached are sour.

Thus destiny seized Selma and led her like a humiliated slave in the procession of miserable oriental woman, and thus fell that noble spirit into the trap after having flown freely on the white wings of love in a sky full of moonlight scented with the odor of flowers.

In some countries, the parent's wealth is a source of misery for the children. The wide strong box which the father and mother together have used for the safety of their wealth becomes a narrow, dark prison for the souls of their heirs. The Almighty Dinar* which the people worship becomes a demon which punishes the spirit and deadens the heart. Selma Karamy was one of those who were victims of their parents' wealth and bridegrooms' cupidity. Had it not been for her father's wealth, Selma would still be living happily.

A week had passed. The love of Selma was my sole entertainer, singing songs of happiness for me at night and waking me at dawn to reveal the meaning of life and the secrets of nature. It is a heavenly love that is free from jealousy, rich and never harmful to the spirit. It is a deep affinity that bathes the soul in contentment; a deep hunger for affection which, when satisfied, fills the soul with bounty; a tenderness that creates hope without agitating the soul, changing earth to paradise and life to a sweet and beautiful dream. In the morning, when I walked in the fields, I saw the token of Eternity in the awakening of

* Kind of money used in the Near East.

382

nature, and when I sat by the seashore I heard the waves singing the song of Eternity. And when I walked in the streets I saw the beauty of life and the splendor of humanity in the appearance of passers-by and movements of workers.

Those days passed like ghosts and disappeared like clouds, and soon nothing was left for me but sorrowful memories. The eyes with which I used to look at the beauty of spring and the awakening of nature, could see nothing but the fury of the tempest and the misery of winter. The ears with which I formerly heard with delight the song of the waves, could hear only the howling of the wind and the wrath of the sea against the precipice. The soul which had observed happily the tireless vigor of mankind and the glory of the universe, was tortured by the knowledge of disappointment and failure. Nothing was more beautiful than those days of love, and nothing was more bitter than those horrible nights of sorrow.

When I could no longer resist the impulse, I went, on the weekend, once more to Selma's home—the shrine which Beauty had erected and which Love had blessed, in which the spirit could worship and the heart kneel humbly and pray. When I entered the garden I felt a power pulling me away from this world and placing me in a sphere supernaturally free from struggle and hardship. Like a mystic who receives a revelation of Heaven, I saw myself amid the trees and flowers, and as I approached the entrance of the house I beheld Selma sitting on the bench in the shadow of a jasmine tree where we both had sat the week before, on that night which Providence had chosen for the beginning of my happiness and sorrow.

She neither moved nor spoke as I approached her. She seemed to have known intuitively that I was coming, and when I sat by her she gazed at me for a moment and sighed deeply, then turned her head and looked at the sky. And, after a moment full of magic silence, she turned back toward me and tremblingly took my hand and said in a faint voice, "Look at me, my friend; study my face and read in it that which you want to know and which I can not recite. Look at me, my beloved . . . look at me, my brother."

I gazed at her intently and saw that those eyes, which a few days ago were smiling like lips and moving like the wings of a nightingale, were already sunken and glazed with sorrow and pain. Her face, that had resembled the unfolding, sunkissed leaves of a lily, had faded and become colorless. Her sweet lips were like two withering roses that autumn has left on their stems. Her neck, that had been a column of ivory, was bent forward as if it no longer could support the burden of grief in her head.

All these changes I saw in Selma's face, but to me they were like a passing cloud that covered the face of the moon and makes it more beautiful. A look which reveals inward stress adds more beauty to the face, no matter how much tragedy and pain it bespeaks; but the face which, in silence, does not announce hidden mysteries is not beautiful, regardless of the symmetry of its features. The cup does not entice our lips unless the wine's color is seen through the transparent crystal.

Selma, on that evening, was like a cup full of heavenly wine concocted of the bitterness and sweetness of life. Unaware, she symbolized the oriental woman who never leaves her parents' home until she puts upon her neck the heavy yoke of her husband, who never leaves her loving mother's arms until she must live as a slave, enduring the harshness of her husband's mother.

I continued to look at Selma and listen to her depressed spirit and suffer with her until I felt that time had ceased and the universe had faded from existence. I could see only her two large eyes staring fixedly at me and could feel only her cold, trembling hand holding mine.

I woke from my swoon hearing Selma saying

quietly, "Come, my beloved, let us discuss the horrible future before it comes. My father has just left the house to see the man who is going to be my companion until death. My father, whom God chose for the purpose of my existence, will meet the man whom the world has selected to be my master for the rest of my life. In the heart of this city, the old man who accompanied me during my youth will meet the young man who will be my companion for the coming years. Tonight the two families will set the marriage date. What a strange and impressive hour! Last week at this time, under this jasmine tree, Love embraced my soul for the first time, while Destiny was writing the first word of my life's story at the Bishop's mansion. Now, while my father and my suitor are planning the day of marriage, I see your spirit quivering around me as a thirsty bird flickers above a spring of water guarded by a hungry serpent. Oh, how great this night is! And how deep is its mystery!"

Hearing these words, I felt that the dark ghost of complete despondency was seizing our love to choke it in its infancy, and I answered her, "That bird will remain flickering over that spring until thirst destroys him or falls into the grasp of a serpent and becomes its prey."

She responded, "No, my beloved, this nightingale should remain alive and sing until dark comes, until spring passes, until the end of the world, and keep on singing eternally. His voice should not be silenced, because he brings life to my heart, his wings should not be broken, because their motion removes the cloud from my heart."

Then I whispered, "Selma, my beloved, thirst will exhaust him; and fear will kill him."

She replied immediately with trembling lips, "The thirst of soul is sweeter than the wine of material things, and the fear of spirit is dearer than the security of the body. But listen, my beloved, listen carefully, I am standing today at the door of·a new life which I know nothing about. I am like a blind man who feels his way so that he will not fall. My father's wealth has placed me in the slave market, and this man has bought me. I neither know nor love him, but I shall learn to love him, and I shall obey him, serve him, and make him happy. I shall give him all that a weak woman can give a strong man.

"But you, my beloved, are still in the prime of life. You can walk freely upon life's spacious path, carpeted with flowers. You are free to traverse the world, making of your heart a torch to light your way. You can think, talk, and act freely; you can write your name on the face of life because you are a man; you can live as a master because your father's wealth will not place you in the slave market to be bought and sold; you can marry the woman of your choice and, before she lives in your home, you can let her reside in your heart and can exchange confidences without hindrance."

Silence prevailed for a moment, and Selma continued, "But, is it now that Life will tear us apart so that you may attain the glory of a man and I the duty of a woman? Is it for this that the valley swallows the song of the nightingale in its depths, and the wind scatters the petals of the rose, and the feet tread upon the wine cup? Were all those nights we spent in the moonlight by the jasmine tree, where our souls united, in vain? Did we fly swiftly toward the stars until our wings tired, and are we descending now into the abyss? Or was Love asleep when he came to us, and did he, when he woke, become angry and decide to punish us? Or did our spirits turn the night's breeze into a wind that tore us to pieces and blew us like dust to the depth of the valley? We disobeyed no commandment, nor did we taste of forbidden fruit, so what is making us leave this paradise? We never conspired or practised mutiny, then why are we descending to hell? No, no, the moments which united us are greater than centuries, and the light that illuminated our spirits is stronger than the dark; and if the tempest separates us on this rough ocean, the waves will unite us on the calm shore; and if this life kills us, death will unite us. A woman's heart will not change with time or season; even if it dies eternally, it will never perish. A woman's heart is like a field turned into a battleground; after the trees are uprooted and the grass is burned and the rocks are reddened with blood and the earth is planted with bones and skulls, it is calm and silent as if nothing has happened; for the spring and autumn come at their intervals and resume their work.

"And now, my beloved, what shall we do? How shall we part and when shall we meet? Shall we consider love a strange visitor who came in the evening and left us in the morning? Or shall we suppose this affection a dream that came in our sleep and departed when we awoke?

"Shall we consider this week an hour of intoxication to be replaced by soberness? Raise your head and let me look at you, my beloved; open your lips and let me hear your voice. Speak to me! Will you remember me after this tempest has sunk the ship of our love? Will you hear the whispering of my wings in the silence of the night? Will you hear my spirit fluttering over you? Will you listen to my sighs? Will you see my shadow approach with the shadows of dusk and disappear with the flush of dawn? Tell me, my beloved, what will you be after having been

magic ray to my eyes, sweet song to my ears, and
wings to my soul? What will you be?"

Hearing these words, my heart melted, and I
answered her, "I will be as you want me to be, my
beloved."

Then she said, "I want you to love me as a poet
loves his sorrowful thoughts. I want you to remember
me as a traveler remembers a calm pool in which his
image was reflected as he drank its water. I want you
to remember me as a mother remembers her child
that died before it saw the light, and I want you to
remember me as a merciful king remembers a prisoner who died before his pardon reached him. I want
you to be my companion, and I want you to visit my
father and console him in his solitude because I shall
be leaving him soon and shall be a stranger to him."

I answered her, saying, "I will do all you have
said and will make my soul an envelope for your
soul, and my heart a residence for your beauty and
my breast a grave for your sorrows. I shall love you,
Selma, as the prairies love the spring, and I shall
live in you the life of a flower under the sun's rays.
I shall sing your name as the valley sings the echo of
the bells of the village churches; I shall listen to the
language of your soul as the shore listens to the story
of the waves. I shall remember you as a stranger remembers his beloved country, and as a hungry man

remembers a banquet, and as a dethroned king remembers the days of his glory, and as a prisoner remembers the hours of ease and freedom. I shall remember you as a sower remembers the bundles of wheat on his threshing floor, and as a shepherd remembers the green prairies and sweet brooks."

Selma listened to my words with palpitating heart, and said, "Tomorrow the truth will become ghostly and the awakening will be like a dream. Will a lover be satisfied embracing a ghost, or will a thirsty man quench his thirst from the spring of a dream?"

I answered her, "Tomorrow, destiny will put you in the midst of a peaceful family, but it will send me into the world of struggle and warfare. You will be in the home of a person whom chance has made most fortunate through your beauty and virtue, while I shall be living a life of suffering and fear. You will enter the gate of life, while I shall enter the gate of death. You will be received hospitably, while I shall exist in solitude, but I shall erect a statue of love and worship it in the valley of death. Love will be my sole comforter, and I shall drink love like wine and wear it like a garment. At dawn, Love will wake me from slumber and take me to the distant field, and at noon will lead me to the shadows of trees, where I will find shelter with the birds from the heat of the sun. In the evening, it will cause me to pause before sunset to hear nature's farewell song to the light of day and will show me ghostly clouds sailing in the sky. At night, Love will embrace me, and I shall sleep, dreaming of the heavenly world where the spirits of lovers and poets abide. In the Spring I shall walk side by side with love among violets and jasmines and drink the remaining drops of winter in the lily cups. In Summer we shall make the bundles of hay our pillows and the grass our bed, and the blue sky will cover us as we gaze at the stars and moon.

"In Autumn, Love and I will go to the vineyard and sit by the wine press and watch the grapevines being denuded of their golden ornaments, and the migrating flocks of birds will wing over us. In Winter we shall sit by the fireside reciting stories of long ago and chronicles of far countries. During my youth, Love will be my teacher; in middle age, my help; and in old age, my delight. Love, my beloved Selma, will stay with me to the end of my life, and after death the hand of God will unite us again."

All these words came from the depths of my heart like flames of fire which leap raging from the hearth and then disappear in the ashes. Selma was weeping as if her eyes were lips answering me with tears.

Those whom love has not given wings cannot fly behind the cloud of appearances to see the magic

world in which Selma's spirit and mine existed together in that sorrowfully happy hour. Those whom
Love has not chosen as followers do not hear when
Love calls. This story is not for them. Even if they
should comprehend these pages, they would not be
able to grasp the shadowy meanings which are not
clothed in words and do not reside on paper, but
what human being is he who has never sipped the
wine from the cup of love, and what spirit is it that
has never stood reverently before that lighted altar in
the temple whose pavement is the hearts of men and
women and whose ceiling is the secret canopy of
dreams? What flower is that on whose leaves the
dawn has never poured a drop of dew; what streamlet is that which lost its course without going to the
sea?

Selma raised her face toward the sky and gazed at
the heavenly stars which studded the firmament. She
stretched out her hands; her eyes widened, and her
lips trembled. On her pale face, I could see the signs
of sorrow, oppression, hopelessness, and pain. Then
she cried, "Oh, Lord, what has a woman done that
hath offended Thee? What sin has she committed to
deserve such a punishment? For what crime has she
been awarded everlasting castigation? Oh, Lord,
Thou art strong, and I am weak. Why hast Thou
made me suffer pain? Thou art great and almighty,

while I am nothing but a tiny creature crawling before Thy throne. Why hast Thou crushed me with Thy foot? Thou art a raging tempest, and I am like dust; why, my Lord, hast Thou flung me upon the cold earth? Thou art powerful, and I am helpless; why art Thou fighting me? Thou art considerate, and I am prudent; why art Thou destroying me? Thou hast created woman with love, and why, with love, dost Thou ruin her? With Thy right hand dost Thou lift her, and with Thy left hand dost Thou strike her into the abyss, and she knows not why. In her mouth Thou blowest the breath of life, and in her heart Thou sowest the seeds of death. Thou dost show her the path of happiness, but Thou leadest her in the road of misery; in her mouth Thou dost place a song of happiness, but then Thou dost close her lips with sorrow and dost fetter her tongue with agony. With Thy mysterious fingers dost Thou dress her wounds, and with Thine hands Thou drawest the dread of pain round her pleasures. In her bed Thou hidest pleasure and peace, but beside it Thou dost erect obstacles and fear. Thou dost excite her affection through Thy will, and from her affection does shame emanate. By Thy will Thou showest her the beauty of creation, but her love for beauty becomes a terrible famine. Thou dost make her drink life in the cup of death, and death in the cup of life.

Thou purifiest her with tears, and in tears her life streams away. Oh, Lord, Thou hast opened my eyes with love, and with love Thou hast blinded me. Thou hast kissed me with Thy lips and struck me with Thy strong hand. Thou hast planted in my heart a white rose, but around the rose a barrier of thorns. Thou hast tied my present with the spirit of a young man whom I love, but my life with the body of an unknown man. So help me, my Lord, to be strong in this deadly struggle and assist me to be truthful and virtuous until death. Thy will be done, Oh, Lord God."

Silence continued. Selma looked down, pale and frail; her arms dropped, and her head bowed and it seemed to me as if a tempest had broken a branch from a tree and cast it down to dry and perish.

I took her cold hand and kissed it, but when I attempted to console her, it was I who needed consolation more than she did. I kept silent, thinking of our plight and listening to my heartbeats. Neither of us said more.

Extreme torture is mute, and so we sat silent, petrified, like columns of marble buried under the sand of an earthquake. Neither wished to listen to the other because our heart-threads had become weak and even breathing would have broken them.

It was midnight, and we could see the crescent

moon rising from behind Mt. Sunnin, and it looked, in the midst of the stars, like the face of a corpse, in a coffin surrounded by the dim lights of candles. And Lebanon looked like an old man whose back was bent with age and whose eyes were a haven for insomnia, watching the dark and waiting for dawn, like a king sitting on the ashes of his throne in the debris of his palace.

The mountains, trees, and rivers change their appearance with the vicissitudes of times and seasons, as a man changes with his experiences and emotions. The lofty poplar that resembles a bride in the daytime, will look like a column of smoke in the evening; the huge rock that stands impregnable at noon, will appear to be a miserable pauper at night, with earth for his bed and the sky for his cover; and the rivulet that we see glittering in the morning and hear singing the hymn of Eternity, will, in the evening, turn to a stream of tears wailing like a mother bereft of her child, and Lebanon, that had looked dignified a week before, when the moon was full and our spirits were happy, looked sorrowful and lonesome that night.

We stood up and bade each other farewell, but love and despair stood between us like two ghosts, one stretching his wings with his fingers over our throats, one weeping and the other laughing hideously.

As I took Selma's hand and put it to my lips, she came close to me and placed a kiss on my forehead, then dropped on the wooden bench. She shut her eyes and whispered softly, "Oh, Lord God, have mercy on me and mend my broken wings!"

As I left Selma in the garden, I felt as if my senses were covered with a thick veil, like a lake whose surface is concealed by fog.

The beauty of trees, the moonlight, the deep silence, everything about me looked ugly and horrible. The true light that had showed me the beauty and wonder of the universe was converted to a great flame of fire that seared my heart; and the Eternal music I used to hear became a clamor, more frightening than the roar of a lion.

I reached my room, and like a wounded bird shot down by a hunter, I fell on my bed, repeating the words of Selma: "Oh, Lord God, have mercy on me and mend my broken wings!"

BEFORE THE THRONE OF DEATH

ARRIAGE IN
these days is a mockery whose management is in the
hands of young men and parents. In most countries
the young men win while the parents lose. The
woman is looked upon as a commodity, purchased
and delivered from one house to another. In time her
beauty fades and she becomes like an old piece of
furniture left in a dark corner.

Modern civilization has made woman a little
wiser, but it has increased her suffering because of
man's covetousness. The woman of yesterday was a

happy wife, but the woman of today is a miserable mistress. In the past she walked blindly in the light, but now she walks open-eyed in the dark. She was beautiful in her ignorance, virtuous in her simplicity, and strong in her weakness. Today she has become ugly in her ingenuity, superficial and heartless in her knowledge. Will the day ever come when beauty and knowledge, ingenuity and virtue, and weakness of body and strength of spirit will be united in a woman?

I am one of those who believe that spiritual progress is a rule of human life, but the approach to perfection is slow and painful. If a woman elevates herself in one respect and is retarded in another, it is because the rough trail that leads to the mountain peak is not free of ambushes of thieves and lairs of wolves.

This strange generation exists between sleeping and waking. It holds in its hands the soil of the past and the seeds of the future. However, we find in every city a woman who symbolizes the future.

In the city of Beirut, Selma Karamy was the symbol of the future Oriental woman, but, like many who live ahead of their time, she became the victim of the present; and like a flower snatched from its stem and carried away by the current of a river, she walked in the miserable procession of the defeated.

Mansour Bey Galib and Selma were married, and lived together in a beautiful house at Ras Beyrouth, where all the wealthy dignitaries resided. Farris Effandi Karamy was left in his solitary home in the midst of his garden and orchards like a lonely shepherd amid his flock.

The days and merry nights of the wedding passed, but the honeymoon left memories of times of bitter sorrow, as wars leave skulls and dead bones on the battlefield. The dignity of an Oriental wedding inspires the hearts of young men and women, but its termination may drop them like millstones to the bottom of the sea. Their exhilaration is like footprints on sand which remain only till they are washed away by the waves.

Spring departed, and so did summer and autumn, but my love for Selma increased day by day until it became a kind of mute worship, the feeling that an orphan has toward the soul of his mother in Heaven. My yearning was converted to blind sorrow that could see nothing but itself, and the passion that drew tears from my eyes was replaced by perplexity that sucked the blood from my heart, and my sighs of affection became a constant prayer for the happiness of Selma and her husband and peace for her father.

My hopes and prayers were in vain, because

Selma's misery was an internal malady that nothing but death could cure.

Mansour Bey was a man to whom all the luxuries of life came easily; but, in spite of that, he was dissatisfied and rapacious. After marrying Selma, he neglected her father in his loneliness and prayed for his death so that he could inherit what was left of the old man's wealth.

Mansour Bey's character was similar to his uncle's; the only difference between the two was that the Bishop got everything he wanted secretly, under the protection of his ecclesiastical robe and the golden cross which he wore on his chest, while his nephew did everything publicly. The Bishop went to church in the morning and spent the rest of the day pilfering from the widows, orphans, and simple-minded people. But Mansour Bey spent his days in pursuit of sexual satisfaction. On Sunday, Bishop Bulos Galib preached his Gospel; but during weekdays he never practiced what he preached, occupying himself with the political intrigues of the locality. And, by means of his uncle's prestige and influence, Mansour Bey made it his business to secure political plums for those who could offer a sufficient bribe.

Bishop Bulos was a thief who hid himself under the cover of night, while his nephew, Mansour Bey, was a swindler who walked proudly in daylight.

However, the people of Oriental nations place trust in such as they—wolves and butchers who ruin their country through covetousness and crush their neighbors with an iron hand.

Why do I occupy these pages with words about the betrayers of poor nations instead of reserving all the space for the story of a miserable woman with a broken heart? Why do I shed tears for oppressed peoples rather than keep all my tears for the memory of a weak woman whose life was snatched by the teeth of death?

But my dear readers, don't you think that such a woman is like a nation that is oppressed by priests and rulers? Don't you believe that thwarted love which leads a woman to the grave is like the despair which pervades the people of the earth? A woman is to a nation as light is to a lamp. Will not the light be dim if the oil in the lamp is low?

Autumn passed, and the wind blew the yellow leaves from the trees, making way for winter, which came howling and crying. I was still in the City of Beirut without a companion save my dreams, which would lift my spirit to the sky and then bury it deep in the bosom of the earth.

The sorrowful spirit finds relaxation in solitude. It abhors people, as a wounded deer deserts the herd and lives in a cave until it is healed or dead.

One day I heard that Farris Effandi was ill. I left my solitary abode and walked to his home, taking a new route, a lonely path between olive trees, avoiding the main road with its rattling carriage wheels.

Arriving at the old man's house, I entered and found Farris Effandi lying on his bed, weak and pale. His eyes were sunken and looked like two deep, dark valleys haunted by the ghosts of pain. The smile which had always enlivened his face was choked with pain and agony; and the bones of his gentle hands looked like naked branches trembling before the tempest. As I approached him and inquired as to his health, he turned his pale face toward me, and on his trembling lips appeared a smile, and he said in a weak voice, "Go—go, my son, to the other room and comfort Selma and bring her to sit by the side of my bed."

I entered the adjacent room and found Selma lying on a divan, covering her head with her arms and burying her face in a pillow so that her father would not hear her weeping. Approaching slowly, I pronounced her name in a voice that seemed more like sighing than whispering. She moved fearfully, as if she had been interrupted in a terrible dream, and sat up, looking at me with glazed eyes, doubting whether I was a ghost or a living being. After a deep silence which took us back on the wings of memory to that hour when we were intoxicated with the wine of love, Selma wiped away her tears and said, "See how time has changed us! See how time has changed the course of our lives and left us in these ruins. In this place spring united us in a bond of love, and in this place has brought us together before the throne of death. How beautiful was spring, and how terrible is this winter!"

Speaking thus, she covered her face again with her hands as if she were shielding her eyes from the spectre of the past standing before her. I put my hand on her head and said, "Come, Selma, come and let us be as strong towers before the tempest. Let us stand like brave soldiers before the enemy and face his weapons. If we are killed, we shall die as martyrs; and if we win, we shall live as heroes. Braving obstacles and hardships is nobler than retreat to tranquility. The butterfly that hovers around the lamp until it dies is more admirable than the mole that lives in a dark tunnel. Come, Selma, let us walk this rough path firmly, with our eyes toward the sun so that we may not see the skulls and serpents among the rocks and thorns. If fear should stop us in the middle of the road, we would hear only ridicule from the voices of the night, but if we reach the mountain peak bravely we shall join the heavenly spirits in songs of triumph and joy. Cheer up, Selma, wipe away your tears and remove the sorrow from your face. Rise, and let us sit by the bed of your father, because his life depends on your life, and your smile is his only cure."

Kindly and affectionately she looked at me and said, "Are you asking me to have patience, while you are in need of it yourself? Will a hungry man give his bread to another hungry man? Or will a sick man give medicine to another which he himself needs badly?"

She rose, her head bent slightly forward, and we walked to the old man's room and sat by the side of his bed. Selma forced a smile and pretended to be patient, and her father tried to make her believe that he was feeling better and getting stronger; but both father and daughter were aware of each other's sorrow and heard the unvoiced sighs. They were like two equal forces, wearing each other away silently. The father's heart was melting because of his daughter's plight. They were two pure souls, one departing and the other agonized with grief, embracing in love and death; and I was between the two with my own troubled heart. We were three people, gathered and crushed by the hands of destiny; an old man like a dwelling ruined by flood, a young woman whose symbol was a lily beheaded by the sharp edge of a sickle, and a young man who was a weak sapling, bent by a snowfall; and all of us were toys in the hands of fate.

Farris Effandi moved slowly and stretched his weak hand toward Selma, and in a loving and tender voice said, "Hold my hand, my beloved." Selma held his hand; then he said, "I have lived long enough, and I have enjoyed the fruits of life's seasons. I have experienced all its phases with equanimity. I lost your mother when you were three years of age, and she left you as a precious treasure in my lap. I watched you grow, and your face reproduced your mother's features as stars reflected in a calm pool of water. Your character, intelligence, and beauty are your mother's, even your manner of speaking and gestures. You have been my only consolation in this life because you were the image of your mother in every deed and word. Now, I grow old, and my only resting place is between the soft wings of death. Be comforted, my beloved daughter, because I have lived long enough to see you as a woman. Be happy because I shall live in you after my death. My departure today would be no different from my going tomorrow or the day after, for our days are perishing like the leaves of autumn. The hour of my death approaches rapidly, and my soul is desirous of being united with your mother's."

As he uttered these words sweetly and lovingly,

his face was radiant. Then he put his hand under his pillow and pulled out a small picture in a gold frame. With his eyes on the little photograph, he said, "Come, Selma, come and see your mother in this picture."

Selma wiped away her tears, and after gazing long at the picture, she kissed it repeatedly and cried, "Oh, my beloved mother! Oh, mother!" Then she placed her trembling lips on the picture as if she wished to pour her soul into that image.

The most beautiful word on the lips of mankind is the word "Mother," and the most beautiful call is the call of "My mother." It is a word full of hope and love, a sweet and kind word coming from the depths of the heart. The mother is every thing—she is our consolation in sorrow, our hope in misery, and our strength in weakness. She is the source of love, mercy, sympathy, and forgiveness. He who loses his mother loses a pure soul who blesses and guards him constantly.

Every thing in nature bespeaks the mother. The sun is the mother of earth and gives it its nourishment of heat; it never leaves the universe at night until it has put the earth to sleep to the song of the sea and the hymn of birds and brooks. And this earth is the mother of trees and flowers. It produces them, nurses them, and weans them. The trees and flowers become kind mothers of their great fruits and seeds. And the mother, the prototype of all existence, is the eternal spirit, full of beauty and love.

Selma Karamy never knew her mother because she had died when Selma was an infant, but Selma wept when she saw the picture and cried, "Oh, mother!" The word mother is hidden in our hearts, and it comes upon our lips in hours of sorrow and happiness as the perfume comes from the heart of the rose and mingles with clear and cloudy air.

Selma stared at her mother's picture, kissing it repeatedly, until she collapsed by her father's bed.

The old man placed both hands on her head and said, "I have shown you, my dear child, a picture of your mother on paper. Now listen to me and I shall let you hear her words."

She lifted her head like a little bird in the nest that hears its mother's wing, and looked at him attentively.

Farris Effandi opened his mouth and said, "Your mother was nursing you when she lost her father; she cried and wept at his going, but she was wise and patient. She sat by me in this room as soon as the funeral was over and held my hand and said, 'Farris, my father is dead now and you are my only consolation in this world. The heart's affections are divided like the branches of the cedar tree; if the tree loses one strong branch, it will suffer but it does not die. It will pour all its vitality into the next branch so that it will grow and fill the empty place.' This is what your mother told me when her father died, and you should say the same thing when death takes my body to its resting place and my soul to God's care."

Selma answered him with falling tears and broken heart, "When Mother lost her father, you took his place; but who is going to take yours when you are gone? She was left in the care of a loving and truthful husband; she found consolation in her little daughter, and who will be my consolation when you pass away? You have been my father and mother and the companion of my youth."

Saying these words, she turned and looked at me, and, holding the side of my garment, said, "This is the only friend I shall have after you are gone, but how can he console me when he is suffering also? How can a broken heart find consolation in a disappointed soul? A sorrowful woman cannot be comforted by her neighbor's sorrow, nor can a bird fly with broken wings. He is the friend of my soul, but I have already placed a heavy burden of sorrow upon him and dimmed his eyes with my tears till he can see nothing but darkness. He is a brother whom I dearly love, but he is like all brothers who share my sorrow and help me shed tears which increase my bitterness and burn my heart."

Selma's words stabbed my heart, and I felt that I could bear no more. The old man listened to her with depressed spirit, trembling like the light of a lamp before the wind. Then he stretched out his hand and said, "Let me go peacefully, my child. I have broken the bars of this cage; let me fly and do not stop me, for your mother is calling me. The sky is clear and the sea is calm and the boat is ready to sail; do not delay its voyage. Let my body rest with those who are resting; let my dream end and my soul awaken with the dawn; let your soul embrace mine and give me the kiss of hope; let no drops of sorrow or bitterness fall upon my body lest the flowers and grass refuse their nourishment. Do not shed tears of misery upon my hand, for they may grow thorns upon my grave. Do not draw lines of agony upon my forehead, for the wind may pass and read them and refuse to carry the dust of my bones to the green prairies . . . I loved you, my child, while I lived, and I shall love you when I am dead, and my soul shall always watch over you and protect you."

Then Farris Effandi looked at me with his eyes half closed and said, "My son, be a real brother to Selma as your father was to me. Be her help and friend in need, and do not let her mourn, because mourning for the dead is a mistake. Repeat to her pleasant tales and sing for her the songs of life so that she may forget her sorrows. Remember me to your father; ask him to tell you the stories of our youth and tell him that I loved him in the person of his son in the last hour of my life."

Silence prevailed, and I could see the pallor of death on the old man's face. Then he rolled his eyes and looked at us and whispered, "Don't call the physician, for he might extend my sentence in this prison by his medicine. The days of slavery are gone, and my soul seeks the freedom of the skies. And do not call the priest to my bedside, because his incantations would not save me if I were a sinner, nor would it rush me to Heaven if I were innocent. The will of humanity cannot change the will of God, as an astrologer cannot change the course of the stars. But after my death let the doctors and priest do what they please, for my ship will continue sailing until it reaches its destination."

At midnight Farris Effandi opened his tired eyes for the last time and focused them on Selma, who was kneeling by his bedside. He tried to speak, but could not, for death had already choked his voice; but he finally managed to say, "The night has passed

... Oh, Selma ... Oh ... Oh, Selma ..." Then he bent his head, his face turned white, and I could see a smile on his lips as he breathed his last.

Selma felt her father's hand. It was cold. Then she raised her head and looked at his face. It was covered with the veil of death. Selma was so choked that she could not shed tears, nor sigh, nor even move. For a moment she stared at him with fixed eyes like those of a statue; then she bent down until her forehead touched the floor, and said, "Oh, Lord, have mercy and mend our broken wings."

Farris Effandi Karamy died; his soul was embraced by Eternity, and his body was returned to the earth. Mansour Bey Galib got possession of his wealth, and Selma became a prisoner for life—a life of grief and misery.

I was lost in sorrow and reverie. Days and nights preyed upon me as the eagle ravages its victim. Many a time I tried to forget my misfortune by occupying myself with books and scriptures of past generations, but it was like extinguishing fire with oil, for I could see nothing in the procession of the past but tragedy and could hear nothing but weeping and wailing. The Book of Job was more fascinating to me than the Psalms and I preferred the Elegies of Jeremiah to the Song of Solomon. *Hamlet* was closer to my heart than all other dramas of western writers. Thus despair weakens our sight and closes our ears. We can see nothing but spectres of doom, and can hear only the beating of our agitated hearts.

BETWEEN CHRIST AND ISHTAR

N THE MIDST OF
the gardens and hills which connect the city of Beirut
with Lebanon there is a small temple, very ancient,
dug out of white rock, surrounded by olive, almond,
and willow trees. Although this temple is a half mile
from the main highway, at the time of my story very
few people interested in relics and ancient ruins had
visited it. It was one of many interesting places hidden and forgotten in Lebanon. Due to its seclusion,
it had become a haven for worshipers and a shrine for
lonely lovers.

As one enters this temple he sees on the wall at
the east side an old Phoenician picture, carved in the

rock, depicting Ishtar, goddess of love and beauty, sitting on her throne, surrounded by seven nude virgins standing in different poses. The first one carries a torch; the second, a guitar; the third, a censer; the fourth, a jug of wine; the fifth, a branch of roses; the sixth, a wreath of laurel; the seventh, a bow and arrow; and all of them look at Ishtar reverently.

On the second wall there is another picture, more modern than the first one, symbolizing Christ nailed to the cross, and at His side stand His sorrowful mother and Mary Magdalene and two other women weeping. This Byzantine picture shows that it was carved in the fifteenth or sixteenth century.*

On the west side wall there are two round transits through which the sun's rays enter the temple and strike the pictures and make them look as if they were painted with gold water color. In the middle of the temple there is a square marble with old paintings on its sides, some of which can hardly be seen under the petrified lumps of blood which show that the ancient people offered sacrifices on this rock and poured perfume, wine, and oil upon it.

There is nothing else in that little temple except deep silence, revealing to the living the secrets of the

* It is known by the students of relics that most of the Christian churches in the East were temples for the old Phoenician and Greek gods. In Damascus, Antioch and Constantinople, there are many edifices, the walls of which echoed heathen hymns; these places were converted into churches and then into mosques.

goddess and speaking wordlessly of past generations and the evolution of religions. Such a sight carries the poet to a world far away from the one in which he dwells and convinces the philosopher that men were born religious; they felt a need for that which they could not see and drew symbols, the meaning of which divulged their hidden secrets and their desires in life and death.

In that unknown temple, I met Selma once every month and spent the hours with her, looking at those strange pictures, thinking of the crucified Christ and pondering upon the young Phoenician men and women who lived, loved and worshipped beauty in the person of Ishtar by burning incense before her statue and pouring perfume on her shrine, people for whom nothing is left to speak except the name, repeated by the march of time before the face of Eternity.

It is hard to write down in words the memories of those hours when I met Selma—those heavenly hours, filled with pain, happiness, sorrow, hope, and misery.

We met secretly in the old temple, remembering the old days, discussing our present, fearing our future, and gradually bringing out the hidden secrets in the depths of our hearts and complaining to each other of our misery and suffering, trying to console ourselves with imaginary hopes and sorrowful dreams. Every now and then we would become calm and wipe our tears and start smiling, forgetting everything except Love; we embraced each other until our hearts melted; then Selma would print a pure kiss on my forehead and fill my heart with ecstasy; I would return the kiss as she bent her ivory neck while her cheeks became gently red like the first ray of dawn on the forehead of hills. We silently looked at the distant horizon where the clouds were colored with the orange ray of sunset.

Our conversation was not limited to love; every now and then we drifted on to current topics and exchanged ideas. During the course of conversation Selma spoke of woman's place in society, the imprint that the past generation had left on her character, the relationship between husband and wife, and the spiritual diseases and corruption which threatened married life. I remember her saying: "The poets and writers are trying to understand the reality of woman, but up to this day they have not understood the hidden secrets of her heart, because they look upon her from behind the sexual veil and see nothing but externals; they look upon her through a magnifying glass of hatefulness and find nothing except weakness and submission."

On another occasion she said, pointing to the

carved pictures on the walls of the temple, "In the heart of this rock there are two symbols depicting the essence of a woman's desires and revealing the hidden secrets of her soul, moving between love and sorrow—between affection and sacrifice, between Ishtar sitting on the throne and Mary standing by the cross. The man buys glory and reputation, but the woman pays the price."

No one knew about our secret meetings except God and the flock of birds which flew over the temple. Selma used to come in her carriage to a place named Pasha Park and from there she walked to the temple, where she found me anxiously waiting for her.

We feared not the observer's eyes, neither did our consciences bother us; the spirit which is purified by fire and washed by tears is higher than what the people call shame and disgrace; it is free from the laws of slavery and old customs against the affections of the human heart. That spirit can proudly stand unashamed before the throne of God.

Human society has yielded for seventy centuries to corrupted laws until it cannot understand the meaning of the superior and eternal laws. A man's eyes have become accustomed to the dim light of candles and cannot see the sunlight. Spiritual disease is inherited from one generation to another until it has become a part of the people, who look upon it, not as a disease, but as a natural gift, showered by God upon Adam. If those people found someone free from the germs of this disease, they would think of him with shame and disgrace.

Those who think evil of Selma Karamy because she left her husband's home and met me in the temple are the diseased and weak-minded kind who look upon the healthy and sound as rebels. They are like insects crawling in the dark for fear of being stepped upon by the passers-by.

The oppressed prisoner, who can break away from his jail and does not do so, is a coward. Selma, an innocent and oppressed prisoner, was unable to free herself from slavery. Was she to blame because she looked through the jail window upon the green fields and spacious sky? Will the people count her as being untruthful to her husband because she came from his home to sit by me between Christ and Ishtar? Let the people say what they please; Selma had passed the marshes which submerge other spirits and had landed in a world that could not be reached by the howling of wolves and rattling of snakes. People may say what they want about me, for the spirit who has seen the spectre of death cannot be scared by the faces of thieves; the soldier who has seen the swords glittering over his head and streams of blood under his feet does not care about rocks thrown at him by the children on the streets.

THE SACRIFICE

ONE DAY IN THE LATE part of June, as the people left the city for the mountain to avoid the heat of summer, I went as usual to the temple to meet Selma, carrying with me a little book of Andalusian poems. As I reached the temple I sat there waiting for Selma, glancing at intervals at the pages of my book, reciting those verses which filled my heart with ecstasy and brought to my soul the memory of the kings, poets, and knights who bade farewell to Granada, and left, with tears in their eyes and sorrow in their hearts, their palaces, institutions and hopes behind. In an hour I saw Selma walking in the midst of the gardens and approaching the temple, leaning on her parasol as if she were carrying all the worries of the world upon her shoulders. As she entered the temple and sat by me, I noticed some sort of change in her eyes and I was anxious to inquire about it.

Selma felt what was going on in my mind, and she put her hand on my head and said, "Come close to me, come my beloved, come and let me quench my thirst, for the hour of separation has come."

I asked her, "Did your husband find out about our meetings here?" She responded, "My husband does not care about me, neither does he know how I spend my time, for he is busy with those poor girls whom poverty has driven into the houses of ill fame; those girls who sell their bodies for bread, kneaded with blood and tears."

I inquired, "What prevents you from coming to this temple and sitting by me reverently before God? Is your soul requesting our separation?"

She answered with tears in her eyes, "No, my beloved, my spirit did not ask for separation, for you are a part of me. My eyes never get tired of looking at you, for you are their light; but if destiny ruled that I should walk the rough path of life loaded with shackles, would I be satisfied if your fate should be like mine?" Then she added, "I cannot say everything, because the tongue is mute with pain and cannot talk; the lips are sealed with misery and cannot move; all I can say to you is that I am afraid you may fall in the same trap I fell in."

Then I asked, "What do you mean, Selma, and of whom are you afraid?" She covered her face with her hands and said, "The Bishop has already found out that once a month I have been leaving the grave which he buried me in."

I inquired, "Did the Bishop find out about our meetings here?" She answered, "If he did, you would not see me here sitting by you; but he is getting suspicious and he informed all his servants and guards to watch me closely. I am feeling that the house I live in and the path I walk on are all eyes watching me, and fingers pointing at me, and ears listening to the whisper of my thoughts."

She was silent for a while, and then she added, with tears pouring down her cheeks, "I am not afraid of the Bishop, for wetness does not scare the drowned, but I am afraid you might fall into the trap and become his prey; you are still young and free as the sunlight. I am not frightened of fate which has shot all its arrows in my breast, but I am afraid the serpent might bite your feet and detain you from climbing the mountain peak where the future awaits you with its pleasure and glory."

I said, "He who has not been bitten by the serpents of light and snapped at by the wolves of darkness will always be deceived by the days and nights. But listen, Selma, listen carefully; is separation the only means of avoiding people's evils and meanness? Has the path of love and freedom been closed and is nothing left except submission to the will of the slaves of death?"

She responded, "Nothing is left save separation and bidding each other farewell."

With rebellious spirit I took her hand and said excitedly, "We have yielded to the people's will for a long time; since the time we met until this hour we have been led by the blind and have worshipped with them before their idols. Since the time I met you we have been in the hands of the Bishop like two balls which he has thrown around as he pleased. Are we going to submit to his will until death takes us away? Did God give us the breath of life to place it under death's feet? Did He give us liberty to make it a shadow for slavery? He who extinguishes his spirit's fire with his own hands is an infidel in the eyes of Heaven, for Heaven set the fire that burns in our spirits. He who does not rebel against oppression is doing himself injustice. I love you, Selma, and you love me, too; and Love is a precious treasure, it is God's gift to sensitive and great spirits. Shall we throw this treasure away and let the pigs scatter it and trample on it? This world is full of wonder and beauty. Why are we living in this narrow tunnel which the Bishop and his assistants have dug out for us? Life is full of happiness and freedom; why don't we take this heavy yoke off our shoulders and break the chains tied to our feet, and walk freely toward peace? Get up and let us leave this small temple for God's great temple. Let us leave this country and all its slavery and ignorance for another country far away and unreached by the hands of the thieves. Let us go to the coast under the cover of night and catch a boat that will take us across the oceans, where we can find a new life full of happiness and understanding. Do not hesitate, Selma, for these minutes are more precious to us than the crowns of kings and more sublime than the thrones of angels. Let us follow the column of light that leads us from this arid desert into the green fields where flowers and aromatic plants grow."

She shook her head and gazed at something invisible on the ceiling of the temple; a sorrowful smile appeared on her lips; then she said, "No, no my beloved. Heaven placed in my hand a cup, full of vinegar and gall; I forced myself to drink it in order to know the full bitterness at the bottom until nothing was left save a few drops, which I shall drink patiently. I am not worthy of a new life of love and peace; I am not strong enough for life's pleasure and sweetness, because a bird with broken wings cannot fly in the spacious sky. The eyes that are accustomed to the dim light of a candle are not strong enough to stare at the sun. Do not talk to me of happiness; its memory makes me suffer. Mention not peace to me; its shadow frightens me; but look at me and I will show you the holy torch which Heaven has lighted in the ashes of my heart —you know that I love you as a mother loves her only child, and Love only taught me to protect you even from myself. It is Love, purified with fire, that stops me from following you to the farthest land. Love kills my desires so that you may live freely and virtuously. Limited love asks for possession of the beloved, but the unlimited asks only for itself. Love that comes between the naiveté and awakening of youth satisfies itself with possessing, and grows with embraces. But Love which is born in the firmament's lap and has descended with the night's secrets is not contented with anything but Eternity and immortality; it does not stand reverently before anything except deity.

"When I knew that the Bishop wanted to stop me from leaving his nephew's house and to take my only pleasure away from me, I stood before the window of my room and looked toward the sea, thinking of the vast countries beyond it and the real freedom and personal independence which can be found there. I felt that I was living close to you, surrounded by the shadow of your spirit, submerged in the ocean of your affection. But all these thoughts which illuminate a woman's heart and make her rebel against old customs and live in the shadow of freedom and justice, made me believe that I am weak and that our love is limited and feeble, unable to stand before the sun's face. I cried like a king whose kingdom and treasures have been usurped, but immediately I saw your face through my tears and your eyes gazing at me and I remembered what you said to me once (*Come, Selma, come and let us be strong towers before the tempest. Let us stand like brave soldiers before the enemy and face his weapons. If we are killed, we shall die as martyrs; and if we win, we shall live as heroes. Braving obstacles and hardships is nobler than retreat to tranquility.*) These words, my beloved, you uttered when the wings of death were hovering around my father's bed; I remembered them yesterday when the wings of despair were hovering above my head. I strengthened myself and felt, while in the darkness of my prison, some sort of precious freedom easing our difficulties and diminishing our sorrows. I found out that our love was as deep as the ocean and as high as the stars and as spacious as the sky. I came here to see you, and in my weak spirit there is a new strength, and this strength. is the ability to sacrifice a great thing in order to obtain a greater one; it is the sacrifice of my happiness so that you may remain virtuous and honorable in the eyes of the people and be far away from their treachery and persecution . . .

"In the past, when I came to this place I felt as if heavy chains were pulling down on me, but today I came here with a new determination that laughs at the shackles and shortens the way. I used to come to this temple like a scared phantom, but today I came like a brave woman who feels the urgency of sacrifice and knows the value of suffering, a woman who likes to protect the one she loves from the ignorant people and from her hungry spirit. I used to sit by you like a trembling shadow, but today I came here to show you my true self before Ishtar and Christ.

"I am a tree, grown in the shade, and today I stretched my branches to tremble for a while in the daylight. I came here to tell you good-bye, my beloved, and it is my hope that our farewell will be great and awful like our love. Let our farewell be like fire that bends the gold and makes it more resplendent."

Selma did not allow me to speak or protest, but she looked at me, her eyes glittering, her face retaining its dignity, seeming like an angel worthy of silence and respect. Then she flung herself upon me, something which she had never done before, and put her smooth arms around me and printed a long, deep, fiery kiss on my lips.

As the sun went down, withdrawing its rays from those gardens and orchards, Selma moved to the middle of the temple and gazed long at its walls and corners as if she wanted to pour the light of her eyes on its pictures and symbols. Then she walked forward and reverently knelt before the picture of Christ and kissed His feet, and she whispered, "Oh, Christ, I have chosen Thy Cross and deserted Ishtar's world of pleasure and happiness; I have worn the wreath of thorns and discarded the wreath of laurel and washed myself with blood and tears instead of perfume and scent; I have drunk vinegar and gall from a cup which was meant for wine and nectar; accept me, my Lord, among Thy followers and lead me toward Galilee with those who have chosen Thee, contented with their sufferings and delighted with their sorrows."

Then she rose and looked at me and said, "Now I shall return happily to my dark cave, where horrible ghosts reside. Do not sympathize with me, my beloved, and do not feel sorry for me, because the soul that sees the shadow of God once will never be frightened, thereafter, of the ghosts of devils. And the eye that looks on Heaven once will not be closed by the pains of the world."

Uttering these words, Selma left the place of worship; and I remained there lost in a deep sea of thoughts, absorbed in the world of revelation where God sits on the throne and the angels write down the acts of human beings, and the souls recite the tragedy of life, and the brides of Heaven sing the hymns of love, sorrow and immortality.

Night had already come when I awakened from my swoon and found myself bewildered in the midst of the gardens, repeating the echo of every word uttered by Selma and remembering her silence, her actions, her movements, her expressions and the touch of her hands, until I realized the meaning of farewell and the pain of lonesomeness. I was depressed and heart-broken. It was my first discovery of the fact that men, even if they are born free, will remain slaves of strict laws enacted by their forefathers; and that the firmament, which we imagine as unchanging, is the yielding of today to the will of tomorrow and submission of yesterday to the will of today—Many a time, since that night, I have thought of the spiritual law which made Selma prefer death to life, and many a time I have made a comparison between nobility of sacrifice and happiness of rebellion to find out which one is nobler and more beautiful; but until now I have distilled only one truth out of the whole matter, and this truth is *sincerity,* which makes all our deeds beautiful and honorable. And this *sincerity* was in Selma Karamy.

THE RESCUER

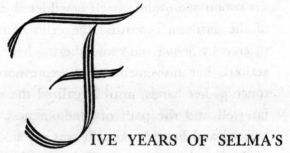IVE YEARS OF SELMA'S
marriage passed without bringing children to
strengthen the ties of spiritual relation between her
and her husband and bind their repugnant souls
together.

A barren woman is looked upon with disdain
everywhere because of most men's desire to perpetuate themselves through posterity.

The substantial man considers his childless wife
as an enemy; he detests her and deserts her and
wishes her death. Mansour Bey Galib was that kind

of man; materially, he was like earth, and hard like steel and greedy like a grave. His desire of having a child to carry on his name and reputation made him hate Selma in spite of her beauty and sweetness.

A tree grown in a cave does not bear fruit; and Selma, who lived in the shade of life, did not bear children. . . .

The nightingale does not make his nest in a cage lest slavery be the lot of its chicks. . . . Selma was a prisoner of misery and it was Heaven's will that she would not have another prisoner to share her life. The flowers of the field are the children of sun's affection and nature's love; and the children of men are the flowers of love and compassion. . . .

The spirit of love and compassion never dominated Selma's beautiful home at Ras Beyrouth; nevertheless, she knelt down on her knees every night before Heaven and asked God for a child in whom she would find comfort and consolation. . . . She prayed successively until Heaven answered her prayers. . . .

The tree of the cave blossomed to bear fruit at last. The nightingale in the cage commenced making its nest with the feathers of its wings.

Selma stretched her chained arms toward Heaven to receive God's precious gift and nothing in the

THE TREASURED WRITINGS OF KAHLIL GIBRAN

world could have made her happier than becoming
a potential mother. . . .

She waited anxiously, counting the days and looking forward to the time when Heaven's sweetest
melody, the voice of her child, should ring in her
ears. . . .

She commenced to see the dawn of a brighter
future through her tears. . . .

It was in the month of Nisan when Selma was
stretched on the bed of pain and labor, where life
and death were wrestling. The doctor and the midwife were ready to deliver to the world a new guest.
Late at night Selma started her successive cry . . . a
cry of life's partition from life . . . a cry of continu-
ance in the firmament of nothingness . . . a cry of a
weak force before the stillness of great forces . . . the
cry of poor Selma who was lying down in despair
under the feet of life and death.

At dawn Selma gave birth to a baby boy. When
she opened her eyes she saw smiling faces all over the
room, then she looked again and saw life and death
still wrestling by her bed. She closed her eyes and
cried, saying for the first time, "Oh, my son." The
midwife wrapped the infant with silk swaddles and
placed him by his mother, but the doctor kept looking at Selma and sorrowfully shaking his head.

The voices of joy woke the neighbors, who rushed into the house to felicitate the father upon the birth of his heir, but the doctor still gazed at Selma and her infant and shook his head. . . .

The servants hurried to spread the good news to Mansour Bey, but the doctor stared at Selma and her child with a disappointed look on his face.

As the sun came out, Selma took the infant to her breast; he opened his eyes for the first time and looked at his mother; then he quivered and closed them for the last time. The doctor took the child from Selma's arms, and on his cheeks fell tears; then he whispered to himself, "He is a departing guest."

The child passed away while the neighbors were celebrating with the father in the big hall at the house and drinking to the health of the heir; and Selma looked at the doctor, and pleaded, "Give me my child and let me embrace him."

Though the child was dead, the sounds of the drinking cups increased in the hall. . . .

He was born at dawn and died at sunrise. . . .

He was born like a thought and died like a sigh and disappeared like a shadow.

He did not live to console and comfort his mother.

His life began at the end of the night and ended at the beginning of the day, like a drop of dew poured by the eyes of the dark and dried by the touch of the light.

A pearl brought by the tide to the coast and returned by the ebb into the depth of the sea. . . .

A lily that has just blossomed from the bud of life and is mashed under the feet of death.

A dear guest whose appearance illuminated Selma's heart and whose departure killed her soul.

This is the life of men, the life of nations, the life of suns, moons and stars.

And Selma focused her eyes upon the doctor and cried, "Give me my child and let me embrace him; give me my child and let me nurse him."

Then the doctor bent his head. His voice choked and he said, "Your child is dead, Madame, be patient."

Upon hearing the doctor's announcement, Selma uttered a terrible cry. Then she was quiet for a moment and smiled happily. Her face brightened as if she had discovered something, and quietly she said, "Give me my child; bring him close to me and let me see him dead."

The doctor carried the dead child to Selma and placed him between her arms. She embraced him, then turned her face toward the wall and addressed the dead infant saying, "You have come to take me

away, my child; you have come to show me the way
that leads to the coast. Here I am, my child; lead me
and let us leave this dark cave."

And in a minute the sun's ray penetrated the window curtains and fell upon two calm bodies lying on
a bed, guarded by the profound dignity of silence and
shaded by the wings of death. The doctor left the
room with tears in his eyes, and as he reached the big
hall the celebration was converted into a funeral, but
Mansour Bey Galib never uttered a word or shed a
tear. He remained standing motionless like a statue,
holding a drinking cup with his right hand.

. . . . .

The second day Selma was shrouded with her
white wedding dress and laid in a coffin; the child's
shroud was his swaddle; his coffin was his mother's
arms; his grave was her calm breast. Two corpses
were carried in one coffin, and I walked reverently
with the crowd accompanying Selma and her infant
to their resting place.

Arriving at the cemetery, Bishop Galib commenced chanting while the other priests prayed, and
on their gloomy faces appeared a veil of ignorance
and emptiness.

As the coffin went down, one of the bystanders
whispered, "This is the first time in my life I have

seen two corpses in one coffin." Another one said, "It seems as if the child had come to rescue his mother from her pitiless husband."

A third one said, "Look at Mansour Bey: he is gazing at the sky as if his eyes were made of glass. He does not look like he has lost his wife and child in one day." A fourth one added, "His uncle, the Bishop, will marry him again tomorrow to a wealthier and stronger woman."

The Bishop and the priests kept on singing and chanting until the grave digger was through filling the ditch. Then, the people, individually, approached the Bishop and his nephew and offered their respects to them with sweet words of sympathy, but I stood lonely aside without a soul to console me, as if Selma and her child meant nothing to me.

The farewell-bidders left the cemetery; the grave digger stood by the new grave holding a shovel with his hand.

As I approached him, I inquired, "Do you remember where Farris Effandi Karamy was buried?"

He looked at me for a moment, then pointed at Selma's grave and said, "Right here; I placed his daughter upon him and upon his daughter's breast rests her child, and upon all I put the earth back with this shovel."

Then I said, "In this ditch you have also buried my heart."

As the grave digger disappeared behind the poplar trees, I could not resist any more; I dropped down on Selma's grave and wept.